JEFFERSON ON RACE

Jefferson on Race

A READER

Edited by Annette Gordon-Reed

PRINCETON UNIVERSITY PRESS
PRINCETON AND OXFORD

Published by Princeton University Press
41 William Street, Princeton, New Jersey 08540
99 Banbury Road, Oxford OX2 6JX

press.princeton.edu

GPSR Authorized Representative: Easy Access System Europe - Mustamäe tee 50,
10621 Tallinn, Estonia, gpsr.requests@easproject.com

ISBN 9780691122069
ISBN (epub) 9780691289014
ISBN (PDF) 9780691274997

Library of Congress Control Number: 2025947008

British Library Cataloging-in-Publication Data is available

Editorial: David McBride and Alena Chekanov
Production Editorial: Mark Bellis
Production: Erin Suydam
Publicity: James Schneider
Copyeditor: Norman Ware
Jacket Credit: Leandro PP / Shutterstock

This book has been composed in Miller

Printed in the United States of America

10 9 8 7 6 5 4 3 2 1

CONTENTS

THEORIES

ACTIONS AND INTERACTIONS

PREFACE

THIS IS A BOOK about Thomas Jefferson and race, using his writings over his very long and eventful life to try to understand his views on a subject that has bedeviled the country he helped to found before it was even in existence. This book will also, necessarily, contain a few documents written by Jefferson's friends, family, and acquaintances describing his actions and views on various subjects. Jefferson was an intensely private individual who was not given to frequently expressing his real emotions on paper. He did not keep a diary, viewing letters as the most important window into his thoughts. Diaries can be misleading, but there is no doubt that letters, which Jefferson took great pains to write, allowed him to present himself in just the way he wanted. Letters from his grandchildren describing in detail events that Jefferson mentioned only in a perfunctory fashion reveal much about the man that he preferred to keep secret.

Slavery in North America was racially based; therefore, documents related to slavery will inevitably play a major role in this work—and not just Jefferson's formal pronouncements about the subjects of race and slavery. In addition to his letters, I include notations about his plantation as well as financial and legal records. Because the cliché "actions speak louder than words" reveals an important truth—particularly when dealing with one not given to speaking openly about important aspects of his life—I will also consider Jefferson's actions and what reasonable inferences can be drawn from them. Racial attitudes are reflected not only in what people have to say on the topic. Often, people *say* things to influence how others view them, to create a particular image of themselves. Even in Jefferson's time, expressing rank prejudice was frowned upon. On the other hand, what people actually do can tell a different story than the words they utter. So, drawing reasonable inferences from Jefferson's overt actions must be a part of this inquiry. Jefferson wrote a lot, and he was an inveterate record keeper. Not everything he said, or did, that was related to race can be included in this volume and there may be documents others feel should have been included. Nevertheless, I have cast a wide enough net to gather as much information as needed to be instructive.

The first thing to keep in mind is that we live in an era in which Blacks and Whites, despite the end of de jure segregation, tend to live in different neighborhoods, go to different churches and schools, and socialize within racial categories. Jefferson's world was quite different. African American people were part of his life on a daily basis, in the most intimate circumstances, from the beginning of his life to the end. This is because he was born into a slave society, and Black people worked in his family's fields and household. A Black woman was almost certainly his earliest nursemaid, as having an enslaved woman care for the children of the household was the practice in upper-class slaveholding families. There is reason to believe that an enslaved woman was young Thomas's wet nurse, because evidence indicates that his mother, Jane Randolph Jefferson, did not breastfeed her children. Later, when his wife, Martha, had difficulty nursing their first child, the "good breast of milk" from the enslaved Ursula Granger allowed the child to thrive. As an elderly man, Jefferson recalled that his earliest memory was of being handed up on a pillow to an enslaved person on horseback before their family made a journey from their home at Shadwell, Virginia, to Tuckahoe, where they would live for several years during his early childhood. Enslaved people were his primary attendants during his final days and may have been the last people he saw before he died.

While most of the material reproduced here will address Jefferson's attitudes toward Black people, he had much to say about Indigenous people as well. By the time of his birth in 1743, their numbers had been greatly reduced in the area in which the Jeffersons lived, but Native Americans were still present. Members of local groups had dealings with his father, Peter, and some stayed at the Jefferson home when they traveled from their home territories to Williamsburg to conduct business. Young Thomas had contact with them on those occasions. His most profound dealings with Native Americans came when he was in various government offices, particularly when he was president of the United States. He had to make decisions about them—how the government would deal with them and under what circumstances White settlers would move to the West after taking by force, treaty, or sale Native American land.

Although we know that some Native Americans were enslaved in North America, it was by far people of African descent who suffered under that condition. In the largest forced migration in history, millions of Africans were transported from the African continent to the Americas, although smaller numbers came to what would become the United States than to other destinations in the hemisphere. It was African-based chattel slavery that occupied Jefferson's thinking on race, and the "African" part was of enormous importance to him. This book will show through his writings just how the nature of Jefferson's thinking about race grew out of his experiences with Black people in slavery, his participation in the American Revolution, his time in Paris, and his hopes and dreams for the American republic, which he helped to create.

No prominent member of the founding generation engaged more directly, and some would argue more disastrously, with the subject of race than Thomas Jefferson. The man who wrote what has come to be called the American creed, the Declaration of Independence, proclaiming the "self-evident" truth "that all men are created equal," enslaved hundreds of people of African descent over the course of his life, even as he wrote extremely critical words about the institution and believed himself to be antislavery. How could this be? How could these contrasting sentiments exist so strongly in one person?

Importantly, these questions are not just the product of our present time, reflecting modern-day concerns and beliefs about equality—beliefs, ironically enough, that have their genesis in the words Jefferson wrote in the Declaration. Equality has been a central value in American life because the foundational document cited as helping to create the country made it so. People asked these questions during Jefferson's lifetime, though it was most often political opponents seeking to use whatever tools were available to thwart the ascent of the most successful politician of his age. Jefferson raised questions himself, poignantly, when writing to Jean Nicolas Démeunier in June 1786:

> What a stupendous, what an incomprehensible machine is man! Who can endure toil, famine, stripes [whippings], imprisonment or death itself in vindication of his own liberty, and the next moment be deaf to all those motives whose power supported him thro' his trial, and inflict

> on his fellow men a bondage, one hour of which is fraught with more misery than ages of that which he rose in rebellion to oppose. But we must await with patience the workings of an overruling providence, and hope that that is preparing the deliverance of these our suffering brethren. When the measure of their tears shall be full, when their groans shall have involved heaven itself in darkness, doubtless a god of justice will awaken to their distress, and by diffusing light and liberality among their oppressors, or at length by his exterminating thunder, manifest his attention to the things of this world, and that they are not left to the guidance of a blind fatality.

Jefferson was in Paris at the time of his missive to Démeunier expressing his disappointment about the failure of a measure in the Virginia legislature to create a plan for the emancipation of those enslaved in Virginia.

As we shall see in this volume, slavery was a subject that had concerned Jefferson from the time of his youth when he was a subject of the British Empire. Now, he was writing as the minister to France from the newly constituted United States of America. The matter looked different from this vantage point. Once he and the American colonists decided that there was no path toward reconciliation with the Mother Country, and that they were going to make a break with Great Britain, Jefferson saw that there was an opportunity for a new beginning, not only for the new country but for his home state of Virginia.

There were aspects of his home territory that he thought backward and deleterious to the state's future. He eagerly participated in the process of drafting new laws and a new constitution for Virginia in the 1770s. In keeping with his Enlightenment-based philosophy, he felt it imperative that the new state reform its property laws to do away with feudal implements like primogeniture and entail. He also pushed for the disestablishment of the Anglican Church with the goal of bringing about the complete separation of church and state, which he believed was necessary in a republican form of government. The third area that required reform was, of course, slavery.

Jefferson recalled participating in an effort to establish a plan of emancipation when he was a young member of the House of Burgesses, the Virginia colony's legislative body. The measure, which he had pressed with a kinsman, was summarily shot down. One gets the impression from his writings, some of which will be presented in this volume, that the vehemence of this rejection convinced him that there could be no legislative solution to the problem of slavery anytime in the foreseeable future. Throughout the years, until well into his old age, Jefferson made references to the "prejudices" of his fellow Virginians against Black people. Strangely enough, he sometimes wrote in a way that suggested that their prejudice against Black people was greater than his, if indeed he had any.

Though Jefferson never used the exact phrase "necessary evil" to describe slavery, his writings do suggest strongly that there was a countervailing concern that had to be considered when discussing how to deal with the question of slavery and emancipation. That countervailing concern was the interests and desires of White people, particularly Virginians and other Whites from slaveholding societies—the prejudices described above. No matter how awful slavery may have been as a moral question, no matter how much it held Southern society back, White people's hostility to the idea of abolishing slavery was always to be given deference. The best that one could hope for, in Jefferson's oft-repeated formulation, was making efforts to change their attitudes over time. Naturally, this meant that the interests of the enslaved, the objects of the oppression he so perfectly described, had to come second to the interests of their White oppressors.

In fact, one can see in the Démeunier letter the basic Jeffersonian position over the years on slavery—recognition of the wrongness of slavery, condemnation of it in the strongest terms, an expressed exasperation with people's acceptance of and support for the institution, followed by a call for patience about the goal of eradicating slavery. We will see all of this in a number of the documents reproduced in this volume.

It is that last turn—putting the brakes on a swift and decisive end to slavery—that has frustrated so many modern-day observers of Jefferson. His insistence that the problem could only be solved after the passage of time, even a long period of time, makes his commitment to ending slavery suspect. It is hard to exaggerate how much this notion of taking time to solve problems was in keeping with Jefferson's adherence to Enlightenment philosophy. He saw the world through the concept of science. As time went by, new cures for diseases, new inventions, and new ideas would come to the fore and make life better.

But even with this way of thinking, it is important to ask why a society should ever acquiesce in doing a grave moral wrong, particularly one that Jefferson himself identified as ultimately corrosive to that society. As he did when he participated as a revolutionary in the rebellion against Great Britain, at considerable risk to himself and his family, why would he be unwilling to spend social and political capital to rid Virginia of a practice that he identified as morally reprehensible and a drag on the future success of his home state?

The peopling of North America—with Indigenous groups already in place—had unfolded under the auspices of the British Empire, creating a multiracial society that quickly developed a fixed racial hierarchy with enslaved Africans at the bottom. This was all done under a system of monarchy, with Americans as subjects of the British Crown. Then, they broke away from that empire under circumstances in which slavery existed in all thirteen colonies, though it was much more entrenched in the Southern colonies, including Jefferson's Virginia. Mobilization for the conflict that became the American Revolution upset the social order in numerous ways, but more significantly for the questions raised in this volume, in regard to people of African descent. War created the opportunity for Blacks, enslaved and free, to challenge their status. Even before Lord Dunmore's famous Proclamation in November 1775 offering freedom to men enslaved by the American patriots if they joined the British Army, enslaved men and women started to leave plantations and follow the British. After the Proclamation, even more left to join the British Army. There were also some, including free Blacks in the North, who joined the patriot forces. These actions created a different way for Blacks to view themselves, and a different way for Whites to view them.

Jefferson muses about this in perhaps his most often cited letters about slavery, written to the young, idealistic Edward Coles in 1814. Coles, who wanted to enlist Jefferson in a concerted public effort to end slavery, wrote to Jefferson announcing his plan to leave Virginia with his slaves and free them once he was resettled in Illinois. He speaks frankly about how the revolution had changed Virginians' (and of course he meant his own) views about African Americans and what their presence meant for the new nation. Jefferson thought that slavery would do damage to the new republican society that he championed. At the same time, there was the question of what was to become of Black people after emancipation. Could they become a part of the "the People" as he conceived of the notion? He explained in the only book he wrote and published, *Notes on the State of Virginia*, that he did not believe they could become part of "the People." The history between the two groups would not allow them to come together. Whites would never give up their prejudices, and Blacks would never forgive Whites for what they had done. Most importantly, Blacks and Whites could not form legitimate families with one another because of the strictures, which he supported but did not live by, against interracial sex. Jefferson feared Black people, particularly Black men, whom he saw as potential soldiers who would fight to maintain their place in the United States. The revolution created a republican society. How could that society function with what amounted to a captive nation, that is to say, Black people, in its midst?

Jefferson on race is, in many ways, a frustrating matter. He was without doubt an extraordinary human, but he was just that: a human being. As we consider his twists and turns, his dead-on assessments and obfuscations, we can see ourselves, the way we sometime have intellectual beliefs that we cannot bring ourselves to live by because it would cause us too much personal and, sometimes, emotional discomfort. Slavery is in many ways distinct from the other moral issues with which we grapple. But his world, thankfully gone, was more familiar to him than it is to us. And though we would definitely get a different view of things from the people whom he enslaved, the focus of this inquiry is Jefferson and, in part, our desire to want him to be better on this subject than he was. It appears that many of us are convinced that he could have been better on the subject. That may be more on us than on him, however.

Still, it is particularly fascinating and instructive to see Jefferson grapple with the issues of race and slavery. He spent so much time thinking seriously about the future of the United States, visualizing what it would become—its culture, its religion, its politics—that he could not sidestep the elephant in the room. Jefferson the visionary saw things that others did not, or saw but decided not to comment upon. Europeans had forced millions of African people from their homeland onto the American continent to live as slaves, a gross injustice that, as we shall see, he recognized as a young man, well before he entered public life. He also called this injustice out, first in 1774 in his *Summary View of the Rights of British America*, the pamphlet that first brought him to attention outside of Virginia. He did so again more famously in his first draft of the Declaration of Independence in words that were excised by members of the Continental Congress, who feared offending the Southern delegates. Given the uses that have been made of his words in the preamble to the Declaration of Independence, it is maddening to think of what could have been made of his characterization of Africans as "people" who had their "sacred right to liberty" taken away.

Again, we should ask how a person who could write that passage, along with other trenchant criticisms of slavery, then fail to carry the ball forward in the newly constituted United States. The only plausible explanation is that Jefferson's attitude about the institution of slavery as it was practiced in the Americas, that is to say racially based slavery, was shaped by his attitude toward Black people. And we may also say that his attitude toward Black people shaped his view of slavery. The sense of urgency about ending a form of oppression practiced exclusively against Black people was simply not in Jefferson. Nor could he think that the interests of Black people in escaping from that oppression should ever override the thoughts and feelings of his White neighbors. They could not be asked to give anything up on behalf of Black people. It was one thing to champion the rights of White men and women in his *Summary View of the Rights of British America* and to risk execution by writing and signing the Declaration of Independence and participating in an armed revolt against king and country. The freedom and self-determination of White colonists demanded this type of action, this type of sacrifice. The freedom and self-determination of people of African descent did not.

This is not in any way to make excuses for him, but one wonders if Jefferson, the most astute and successful politician of his time, was reading the room in ways that we cannot, or do not want to. In our desire to take the notion of contingency seriously—and, perhaps, because of our tendency to imagine the people of that era as more open to persuasion on the questions of slavery and race than they actually were—we may too quickly dismiss Jefferson's assessment of how unready his fellow Virginians, and other White Southerners, were to give up their way of life and how hostile they were to the Black people in their midst.

Historians disdain the idea of inevitability or the suggestion that things had to happen in a particular way. But, in fact, realistic boundaries can be placed on the possibilities in any given era. To say that anything was possible in Jefferson's time speaks to our desires and hopes for our own time. There is little reason to believe that Virginians in the late eighteenth and early nineteenth centuries could have been persuaded out of the institution of slavery. As dispiriting as it may be, we have to at least consider that Jefferson's judgment on this point was correct. It is very likely that, had he decided to press the case of emancipation to the extent that we wish he had, he would not be the subject of this book because he would not have had the political career that he made for himself. He could not have maintained the important base of support that helped propel him forward from the forefront of Virginia politics to the forefront of national politics. We have such high expectations of members of the founding generation that it is sometimes easy to forget that they were human beings working in a particular context. Being clear eyed about their strengths and weaknesses demands being equally clear eyed about the strengths and weakness of the members of society with whom they had to deal.

There is also the somewhat neglected issue of demographics and the role it played in attitudes about slavery and emancipation. It should come as no surprise that South Carolina, the state with the largest population of Black people—with a 3 to 1 ratio of Black to White by the time of the Civil War—should have been the most vociferous about maintaining slavery. As a colony, South Carolina was the most belligerent in its defense of the institution, and its delegates to the Constitutional Convention in Philadelphia almost walked away from the deliberations when they thought that Northern states were pressing for a system of government that might one day threaten the existence of slavery. And then, of course, South Carolina was the first state to leave the Union in 1860 after the election of Abraham Lincoln, whom they were convinced would move against slavery. Certainly the economy of the colony, and then the state, was economically dependent upon it, but the question of maintaining social control over a Black majority population was central to the matter as well. After the end of legalized slavery, which put Blacks under the control of Whites with no need for any questions, what mechanisms would take the place of the laws of slavery? Jefferson's Virginia had a population that was around 40 percent Black during his lifetime, and that was large enough to cause concern among Whites; and as we will see from some of his correspondence, it concerned Jefferson.

Although we understand what it took to end slavery in the United States—the near dissolution of the American Union and a destructive war in which hundreds of thousands perished—there seems to be no thought of what this might say about Jefferson's attitude in an earlier time. The story of the struggle over slavery at the Constitutional Convention in Philadelphia is often told, usually to highlight the fragility of the Union at its inception and to foreshadow the breakdown to come in the mid-nineteenth century when the country came apart over the very issue that had nearly prevented the Union's formation. There is every reason to believe that the strong feelings that Southerners had about the institution remained during the years after the compromise and before the cataclysm of war. The move from Philadelphia in 1787 to the Missouri Crisis of 1819–1820 was, in historical terms, the blink of an eye—thirty-three years. Scholars like Adam Rothman have shown that this three-decade period was not actually a period of quiescence on the issue of slavery. As the historian John Larsen has shown, issues like federal internal improvements that implicated the powers of the federal government were treated as stalking horses for the issue of slavery. Southerners remained wary of the federal government, which they thought might attempt to launch an attack on an institution that Northern states, since the end of the revolution, had been moving toward eradicating, albeit mostly with gradual emancipation schemes. Jefferson saw the possible death of the Union in all of this. That is an important point to keep in mind, because what obsessed Jefferson more than anything was the country he helped to create. Everything else was secondary to that. When we understand that our legitimate concerns about the history of slavery and race did not engage him in the same way, it is possible to see his actions and inaction differently.

Looming over all of this, of course, is Jefferson's relationship with the Hemings family, the mixed-race enslaved people who came into his life when he married Martha Wayles Skelton. Martha Jefferson shared a father, John Wayles, with six members of the Hemings family. They were all brought to Monticello in the early 1770s upon Wayles's death. The family was treated differently than other enslaved people, and it appears that Jefferson viewed himself as an enslaver through the prism of his relationship with them. The men were allowed to travel relatively freely, take jobs, and keep the money they earned. He spent money having clothes made for them, gave them spending money, and for periods of time paid them full wages for their work. The only people he freed were members of the Hemings family.

Most importantly of all, Jefferson carried on a thirty-eight-year connection to Sally Hemings that produced seven children, four who lived to adulthood: Beverley, Harriet, Madison, and Eston Hemings. On the surface, his documents betray no special connection to them. But, if you look carefully, over time, it is clear that they were different. He placed the three boys under the tutelage of his best artisan, their uncle John Hemmings, with whom Jefferson spent a good deal of time at Monticello and his Bedford country retreat, Poplar Forest. The daughter, Harriet, learned to spin and weave. None of them worked as servants, and all four were freed upon their adulthood. A *Farm Book* listing notes that the two eldest, Beverley and Harriet, "ran away" in 1822 when they were actually allowed to leave. Harriet was put on a stagecoach with money, most likely to join her brother, who had left a few months earlier. The two disappeared into the White world. The two youngest, Madison and Eston, were freed formally in Jefferson's will. Madison Hemings's recollections appear at the end of this volume, along with the reminiscences of three other people who were enslaved at Monticello. The lack of information about Jefferson's hidden family was planned, and that is tragic.

This book is divided into three sections: "Self-Image," which presents documents that show how Jefferson saw himself on the questions of Black people, Native people, and slavery; "Theories," which gives examples of how Jefferson wrote about those topics for both public and private consumption; and finally "Actions and Interactions," which presents evidence of things that Jefferson did regarding slavery and race and what his dealings with individual Black and Native people tell us about his thoughts and feelings. These are not totally clean categories. They sometimes bleed into one another, and in the process of arranging this book I have moved material from one section to another. Jefferson's self-image often informed his theories and actions. His overt actions can sometimes be a product of his self-image. And, of course, one can see him doing things that are in complete contravention of what his self-image and theories suggest he would or should do. Nevertheless, I think the broad categories work and allow us to focus and at least get a handle on this very complicated man.

Self-Image

Introduction

THOMAS JEFFERSON SAW HIMSELF as, and desperately wanted to be seen as, a progressive—a man of the future always on the lookout for the new improvements that science and the education of the general population would inevitably bring. During his famous late-in-life correspondence with John Adams, he wrote that he "like[d] the dreams of the future better than the history of the past." In that same letter, he predicted that the United States would take the lead in standing guard against the "return of bigotry and barbarism," because "Old Europe" would still be under the influence of Old World structures and beliefs. Although he wrote those words as an elderly man, the evidence indicates that he held this view about an inevitably progressive future from his youth.

The times in which Jefferson lived sparked and nurtured his ideas about the nature of progress. He was enormously influenced by the Enlightenment philosophy of the eighteenth century, which promoted reason and the scientific approach to life as the guiding principles for humankind. Driving this point home, Jefferson said that he considered "Sir Francis Bacon, Sir Isaac Newton and Sir John Locke" his "trinity of the three greatest men the world has ever produced." All three, of course, are considered giants of Enlightenment thinking. This way of viewing the world meant questioning cherished notions that were in opposition to reason—including casting a suspicious eye toward religion, being willing to sew doubt about the wisdom of set hierarchies, and being willing to upset established orders. Throughout his life, Jefferson exhibited a healthy skepticism about religion and hierarchy, and he was willing to upset established orders.

The Enlightenment also emphasized the value of liberty and equality. This was a challenging concept in a world dominated by monarchy and established churches, institutions that worked together to maintain a type of stability and order in given societies. Jefferson was born into a world in which monarchy and an established church were facts of life. There would be no reason for him to doubt the rightness of the government under which he lived, or the religious practices of his family and his neighbors. The British had, with the Glorious Revolution of 1688, changed the nature of their monarchy by strengthening the power of Parliament and lessening the power of the king. This was done, in part, as move against despotic rule and to support greater liberty and justice. It was, in that broad sense, in keeping with the Enlightenment.

While the British were forming their ideas about liberty for those who lived in the British Isles and in their colonies, they were also taking steps to establish African chattel slavery in North America and the West Indies. In the decade before Jefferson was born, the Virginia colony had reached its high point of importation of Africans. Thus, slavery existed in a world where British people had developed a heightened awareness of the idea of liberty and were professed enemies of despotism. The historian Edmund S. Morgan sought to explain this "paradox" in his magisterial work *American Slavery, American Freedom: The Ordeal of Colonial Virginia.* The existence of slavery, he said, supported the "liberty" that White Virginians enjoyed. How so? The existence of a Black permanent underclass tamped down on the class conflict and competition that would normally have existed among White colonials. Poor Whites would always count themselves as possessing British liberty because they could never occupy the status of enslaved Blacks. Rather than being resentful of their economic and social "betters," they would tend to see themselves as in solidarity with them.

Jefferson was an interesting case. Virginia, the land of his birth, was the very site of the paradox that Morgan described in *American Slavery, American Freedom.* The social, economic, and legal system worked to the great benefit of his prominent family. It would have been a simple matter for him to have accepted the terms of this social arrangement without question and gone about his life. But he did not. And the evidence indicates that his critique of this arrangement started early on, well before the American Revolution opened up a broader discussion about the nature of freedom and slavery. The scholar Douglas Wilson put it this way:

> How did a man who was born into a slave holding society, whose family and admired friends owned slaves, who inherited a fortune that was dependent on slaves and slave labor, decide at an early age that slavery was morally wrong and forcefully declare that it ought to be abolished?

One of the great losses to American history is the destruction of early Jefferson documents in the fire that took place at his boyhood home in 1775. It destroyed what could have been revealing documents from Jefferson's early years. So, we will likely never know the precise moment that young Thomas decided that slavery was a problem. Nor can we discern a contemporaneous view of his attitude toward Black people in his statements about individual Blacks he encountered during this period of his life. The basic outlines of his early beginnings really give no hint of the genesis of his views about the slavery of African American people.

Jefferson was born on April 13 (O.S. April 2), 1743, at his family's plantation in Goochland (now Albemarle) County, Virginia. His father, Peter Jefferson, was a surveyor and a planter, something of a self-made man who rose to prominence in his community. Jefferson's mother, Jane, was a member the more well-known and numerous Randolph family, which had a long history in Virginia. Although the house in which Jefferson grew up with his numerous siblings was nowhere as large as the house he would build at Monticello, archaeological evidence and written records of the family reveal that the Jeffersons lived the life of upper-class people. They ordered cloth and shoes from England and had the family's clothes made by tailors.

Although Peter Jefferson's education had been "quite neglected," Thomas Jefferson noted that his father worked hard at self-improvement and created a library that sparked young Thomas's interest in reading and education. Peter Jefferson, who died in 1757 when Thomas was fourteen years old, made sure that his son had a first-rate early education through tutors and boarding school. The earliest correspondence we have from Thomas Jefferson is a letter to one of his guardians requesting that he be able to attend the College of William and Mary. It was written the same years his father died.

It was at William and Mary that we find a hint of Jefferson's adherence to Enlightenment views. He studied under William Small, who taught mathematics, science, and philosophy. The Scottish Small was a devotee of the Enlightenment, and Jefferson viewed him as an important figure to his development. In his autobiography, Jefferson praised Small's "enlarged & liberal mind" and viewed Small as an important mentor.

Small introduced Jefferson to a man who would play an even greater role in his life, George Wythe, a noted lawyer, judge, and signer of the Declaration of Independence. Jefferson studied law under Wythe for five years. In addition to being a supporter of Enlightenment philosophy, Wythe was antislavery, even though he enslaved people until the last decade of his life. Jefferson considered Wythe like a father. Perhaps his dear friend and mentor's position as a critic of slavery while holding slaves helped Jefferson accommodate himself to this way of being. It is hard to imagine that these two people, who were so close to one another, did not discuss the issue of slavery. As we will see later in this volume, the matter hit home to the pair in the most personal and poignant way.

The documents in this section show Jefferson, in both his private life and public life, attempting to live his vision of himself as an enlightened individual, starting as a young man, presenting his views—explicitly and implicitly—on the subjects of slavery and race. Perhaps his earliest notation that relates to the subjects is a stanza of a poem written by William Shenstone that Jefferson copied into his memorandum book when he was in his twenties, which he titled "Inscription for an African Slave." It appeared along with an inscription for his favorite sister Jane's gravestone. The Shenstone stanza is part of poem that tells the story of an African torn from his homeland and brought across the sea to do unpaid labor for other people and be treated as an item of property. It is not known whether the passage in the poem was for an individual enslaved person at Monticello or whether it was to serve as a general statement for the burial ground as a whole. But this was before Jefferson the public man, who would become aware of his contemporary image to the world at large and be concerned about the ways in which posterity might view his legacy.

Perhaps the most famous documents in this section are Jefferson's correspondence with Benjamin Banneker, an African American astronomer and almanac writer. Banneker wrote to Jefferson in 1791, sending him a copy of his almanac and requesting his aid in dealing with the issue of slavery and improving the status of Black people. Banneker noted that Jefferson had a reputation as one who would be amenable to his entreaty. Jefferson responded quickly, thanking Banneker for the almanac and saying that he had forwarded it to the Marquis de Condorcet. Jefferson's cordial response, signing off as "Your most obedt. Humble Servant," drew derision from enemies, who suggested that he had demeaned himself with the respectful valediction and that he was gullible in believing that Banneker had done the work for the almanac on his own. This last charge got to Jefferson, and, as we will see in the last section of this book, "Actions and Interactions," he attempted to backtrack by suggesting that Banneker had received help in preparing his almanac. Perhaps because he was so sure of his position, and because it reinforced his view of himself as a fair-minded individual, Jefferson never had a problem extending small courtesies to people of color, using honorifics like Mr. or Mrs. and the valediction in the Banneker letter. Members of his cohort took these types of things more seriously than he.

Although there is no written record of his involvement, Jefferson insisted over the course of his life that he was partly responsible for having introduced early legislation in the House of Burgesses to strike blows against slavery. Given his record otherwise, there is no reason to doubt him on this point. But even more important for our consideration is the fact that Jefferson *wanted* to be associated with antislavery efforts. He could easily have emphasized other achievements or, like most of his cohort, not associated himself with the question at all. He could have achieved everything he did without it. This indicates that he knew the institution was a problem and would be seen as a problem for succeeding generations. He wanted people in his time, and later generations, to see him as having been on the right side of that issue.

And then there is the Jefferson who periodically latched onto quixotic methods to attack slavery or at least to make it more palatable. Letters and notations in his *Farm Book* and *Memorandum Book* show his enthusiasm for sugar from maple trees, seeing this as a way to potentially destroy West Indian slavery, on which the Caribbean sugarcane industry was so dependent. He substituted sugar from maple trees for cane sugar at his residences and made an unsuccessful attempt to grow maple at Monticello. He especially liked the idea because it would unite morality with self-interest. The horrors of the cane field could be avoided *and* the United States, at least those regions that had the climate for it, might be able to produce a salable crop. And then there was the plan to grow olive trees on the Mountain, to provide less strenuous work for enslaved women. These types of actions are akin to methods individual citizens in modern times employ to combat huge systemic problems that would actually require deep sacrifices that the concerned citizens would be reluctant to endure.

In letters to family and friends, in notations in the memorandum notes that he made daily, in writings that ended up in the public sphere, in gestures toward individual people of color, enslaved and free, we see Jefferson attempting to live out his own beliefs about his character. This mixture of private and public gives a window into Jefferson's view of himself. The record ranges from the time he had no reason to think that he would become a figure remembered in history to the time he was an elder statesman certain that he would be remembered. *How* he was remembered mattered a great deal to him. Jefferson wanted to make sure that his legacy on this matter signaled that he was the progressive person that he so wanted to be.

Notes

1. Jefferson to John Adams, August 1, 1816, *Papers of Thomas Jefferson* (*PTJ*) (Retirement Series) 10:285.

2. Jefferson to John Trumbull, February 15, 1789, *PJT* 14:561.

3. Douglas L. Wilson, "Thomas Jefferson and the Character Issue," *Atlantic Monthly*, November 1992, 57–74.

4. Thomas Jefferson, *Autobiography*, Yale Avalon Project Online.

5. Jefferson, *Autobiography*.

6. Annette Gordon-Reed, *The Hemingses of Monticello: An American Family* (New York: W. W. Norton, 2008), 381, 716n11.

Documents

Inscription for an African Slave

Shores there are, bless'd shores for us remain,
And favor'd isles with golden fruitage crown'd
Where tufted flow'rets paint the verdant plain,
Where ev'ry breeze shall med'cine ev'ry wound.
There the stern tyrant that embitters life,
Shall vainly suppliant, spread his asking hand;
There shall we view the billow's raging strife,
Aid the kind breast, and waft his boat to land.

Summary View of the Rights of British America *(1774)*

That we next proceed to consider the conduct of his majesty, as holding the executive powers of the laws of these states, and mark out his deviations from the line of duty: By the constitution of Great Britain, as well as of the several American states, his majesty possesses the power of refusing to pass into a law any bill which has already passed the other two branches of legislature. His majesty, however, and his ancestors, conscious of the impropriety of opposing their single opinion to the united wisdom of two houses of parliament, while their proceedings were unbiassed by interested principles, for several ages past have modestly declined the exercise of this power in that part of his empire called Great Britain. But by change of circumstances, other principles than those of justice simply have obtained an influence on their determinations; the addition of new states to the British empire has produced an addition of new, and sometimes opposite interests. It is now, therefore, the great office of his majesty, to resume the exercise of his negative power, and to prevent the passage of laws by any one legislature of the empire, which might bear injuriously on the rights and interests of another. Yet this will not excuse the wanton exercise of this power which we have seen his majesty practise on the laws of the American legislatures. For the most trifling reasons, and sometimes for no conceivable reason at all, his majesty has rejected laws of the most salutary tendency. The abolition of domestic slavery is the great object of desire in those colonies, where it was unhappily introduced in their infant state. But previous to the enfranchisement of the slaves we have, it is necessary to exclude all further importations from Africa; yet our repeated attempts to effect this by prohibitions, and by imposing duties which might amount to a prohibition, have been hitherto defeated by his majesty's negative: Thus preferring the immediate advantages of a few African corsairs to the lasting interests of the American states, and to the rights of human nature, deeply wounded by this infamous practice. Nay, the single interposition of an interested individual against a law was scarcely ever known to fail of success, though in the opposite scale were placed the interests of a whole country. That this is so shameful an abuse of a power trusted with his majesty for other purposes, as if not reformed, would call for some legal restrictions.

Language Congress Excised from TJ's Draft of the Declaration of Independence, 1776

. . . he has waged cruel war against human nature itself, violating it's most sacred rights of life & liberty in the persons of a distant people who never offended him, captivating & carrying them into slavery in another hemisphere, or to incur miserable death in their transportation thither. This piratical warfare, the opprobrium of *infidel* powers, is the warfare of the CHRISTIAN king of Great Britain. Determined to keep open a market where MEN should be bought

& sold, he has prostituted his negative for suppressing every legislative attempt to prohibit or to restrain this execrable commerce: and that this assemblage of horrors might want no fact of distinguished die, he is now exciting those very people to rise in arms among us, and to purchase that liberty of which *he* has deprived them, by murdering the people upon whom *he* also obtruded them; thus paying off former crimes committed against the *liberties* of one people, with crimes which he urges them to commit against the *lives* of another.

The Declaration of Independence as Adopted by Congress

IN CONGRESS, JULY 4, 1776

The Unanimous Declaration of the Thirteen United States of America,

When in the Course of human events, it becomes necessary for one people to dissolve the political bands which have connected them with another, and to assume among the powers of the earth, the separate and equal station to which the Laws of Nature and of Nature's God entitle them, a decent respect to the opinions of mankind requires that they should declare the causes which impel them to the separation. We hold these truths to be self-evident, that all men are created equal, that they are endowed by their Creator with certain unalienable Rights, that among these are Life, Liberty and the pursuit of Happiness. . . . He has excited domestic insurrections amongst us, and has endeavoured to bring on the inhabitants of our frontiers, the merciless Indian Savages, whose known rule of warfare, is an undistinguished destruction of all ages, sexes and conditions . . .

Bill to Prevent the Importation of Slaves, &c.

[16 June 1777]

To prevent more effectually the practice of holding persons in Slavery and importing them into this State Be it enacted by the General Assembly that all persons who shall be hereafter imported into this

Commonwealth by Sea or Land whether they were bond or free in their native Country upon their taking the oath of Fidelity to this Commonwealth shall from thenceforth become free and absolutely exempted from all Slavery or Bondage to which they had be subjected in any other State or Country whatsoever. That it shall and may be lawful for any person by Deed duly executed in the presence of two or more Witnesses and acknowledged or proved and recorded in the General Court or Court of the County where he or she resides within eight Months from the making thereof or by their last Will and Testament in writing fully and absolutely to manumit and set at Liberty any Slave or Slaves to which they are entitled, But no Slave absconding from the owner who resides in any of the thirteen united States of America, or any other state in amity with them, and coming into this commonwealth, or coming with the owner to dwell here, or attending him as a Servant, or falling to any Inhabitant of this Commonwealth by Marriage Will or Inheritance and not brought to be sold, shall not become free, And if any Slave manumitted shall, within years thereafter, become chargeable to a Parish, the former owner, or his Executors or Administrators shall be compelled to reimburse the expenses of his or her maintenance, And so much of the Act of general Assembly made in the year of our Lord one thousand seven hundred and fifty three intitled "an act for the better government of Servants and Slaves" as is contrary to this act, is hereby declared to be repealed.

Speech to Jean Baptiste Ducoigne

Charlottesville,
[ca. 1] June, 1781.

Brother John Baptist de Coigne

I am very much pleased with the visit you have made us, and particularly that it has happened when the wise men from all parts of our country were assembled together in council, and had an opportunity of hearing the friendly discourse you held to me. We are all sensible of your friendship, and of the services you have rendered, and I now, for my countrymen, return you thanks, and, most particularly, for your assistance to the garrison which was besieged by the hostile Indians. I hope it will please the Great Being above to continue you long in life, in health and in friendship to us; and that your son will afterwards succeed you in wisdom, in good disposition, and in power over your people. I consider the name you have given as particularly honorable to me, but I value it the more as it proves your attachment to my country. We, like you, are Americans, born in the same land, and having the same interests. I have carefully attended to the figures represented on the skins, and to their explanation, and shall always keep them hanging on the walls in remembrance of you and your nation. I have joined with you sincerely in smoking the pipe of peace; it is a good old custom handed down by your ancestors, and as such I respect and join in it with reverence. I hope we shall long continue to smoke in friendship together. You find us, brother, engaged in war with a powerful nation. Our forefathers were Englishmen, inhabitants of a little island beyond the great water, and, being distressed for land, they came and settled here. As long as we were young and weak, the English whom we had left behind, made us carry all our wealth to their country, to enrich them; and, not satisfied with this, they at length began to say we were their slaves, and should do whatever they ordered us. We were now grown up and felt ourselves strong; we knew we were free as they were, that we came here of our own accord and not at their biddance, and were determined to be free as long as we should exist. For this reason they made war on us. They have now waged that war six years, and have not yet won more land from us than will serve to bury the warriors they have lost. Your old father, the King of France, has joined us in the war and done many good things for us. We are bound forever to love him, and wish you to love him, brother, because he is a good and true friend to us. The Spaniards have also joined us, and other powerful nations are now entering into the war to punish the robberies and violences the English have committed on them. The English stand alone, without a friend to support them, hated by all mankind because they are proud and unjust. This quarrel, when it first began, was a family quarrel between us and the English, who were then our brothers. We, therefore, did not wish you to engage in it at all. We are strong enough of ourselves without wasting your blood in fighting our battles. The English, knowing this, have been always suing to the Indians to help them fight. We do not wish you to take up the hatchet. We love and esteem you. We wish you to multiply and be strong. The English, on the other hand, wish to set you and us to cutting one another's throats, that when we are dead they may take all our land. It is better for you not to join in this quarrel, unless the English have killed any of your warriors or done you any other injury. If they have, you have a right to go to war with them, and revenge the injury, and we have none to restrain you. Any free nation has a right to punish those who have done them an injury. I say the same, brother, as to the Indians who treat you ill. While I advise you, like an affectionate friend, to avoid unnecessary war, I do not assume the right of restraining you from punishing your enemies. If the English have injured you, as they have injured the French and Spaniards, do like them and join us in the war. General Clarke will receive you and show you the way to their towns. But if they have not injured you, it is better for you to lie still and be quiet. This is the advice which has been always given by the great council of the Americans. We must give the same, because we are but one of thirteen nations, who have agreed to act and speak together. These nations keep a council of wise men always sitting together, and each of us separately follow their advice. They have the care of all the people and the lands between the Ohio and Mississippi, and will see that no wrong be committed on them. The French settled at Kaskaskias, St. Vincennes, and the Cohos, are subject to that council, and they will punish them if they do you any injury. If you will make known to me any just cause of complaint against them, I will represent it to the great council at Philadelphia, and have justice done you.

Our good friend, your father, the King of France, does not lay any claim to them. Their misconduct should not be imputed to him. He gave them up to the English the last war, and we have taken them from the English. The Americans alone have a right to maintain justice in all the lands on this side the Mississippi,—on the other side the Spaniards rule. You complain, brother, of the want of goods for the use of your people. We know that your wants are great, notwithstanding we have done everything in our power to supply them, and have often grieved for you. The path from hence to Kaskaskias is long and dangerous; goods cannot be carried to you in that way. New Orleans has been the only place from which we could get goods for you. We have bought a great deal there; but I am afraid not so much of them have come to you as we intended.

Some of them have been sold of necessity to buy provisions for our posts. Some have been embezzled by our own drunken and roguish people. Some have been taken by the Indians and many by the English.

The Spaniards, having now taken all the English posts on the Mississippi, have opened that channel free for our commerce, and we are in hopes of getting goods for you from them. I will not boast to you, brother, as the English do, nor promise more than we shall be able to fulfil. I will tell you honestly, what indeed your own good sense will tell you, that a nation at war cannot buy so many goods as when in peace. We do not make so many things to send over the great waters to buy goods, as we made and shall make again in time of peace. When we buy those goods, the English take many of them, as they are coming to us over the great water. What we get in safe, are to be divided among many, because we have a great many soldiers, whom we must clothe. The remainder we send to our brothers the Indians, and in going, a great deal of it is stolen or lost. These are the plain reasons why you cannot get so much from us in war as in peace. But peace is not far off. The English cannot hold out long, because all the world is against them. When that takes place, brother, there will not be an Englishman left on this side the great water. What will those foolish nations then do, who have made us their enemies, sided with the English, and laughed at you for not being as wicked as themselves? They are clothed for a day, and will be naked forever after; while you, who have submitted to short inconvenience, will be well supplied through the rest of your lives. Their friends will be gone and their enemies left behind; but your friends will be here, and will make you strong against all your enemies. For the present you shall have a share of what little goods we can get. We will order some immediately up the Mississippi for you and for us. If they be little, you will submit to suffer a little as your brothers do for a short time. And when we shall have beaten our enemies and forced them to make peace, we will share more plentifully. General Clarke will furnish you with ammunition to serve till we can get some from New Orleans. I must recommend to you particular attention to him. He is our great, good, and trusty warrior; and we have put everything under his care beyond the

Alleghanies. He will advise you in all difficulties, and redress your wrongs. Do what he tells you, and you will be sure to do right. You ask us to send schoolmasters to educate your son and the sons of your people. We desire above all things, brother, to instruct you in whatever we know ourselves. We wish to learn you all our arts and to make you wise and wealthy. As soon as there is peace we shall be able to send you the best of school-masters; but while the war is raging, I am afraid it will not be practicable. It shall be done, however, before your son is of an age to receive instruction.

This, brother, is what I had to say to you. Repeat it from me to all your people, and to our friends, the Kickapous, Piorias, Piankeshaws and Wyattanons. I will give you a commission to show them how much we esteem you. Hold fast the chain of friendship which binds us together, keep it bright as the sun, and let them, you and us, live together in perpetual love.

TJ to Jean Nicolas Démeunier

[26 June 1786]

. . . M. de Meusnier, where he mentions that the slave-law has been passed in Virginia, without the clause of emancipation, is pleased to mention that neither Mr. Wythe nor Mr. Jefferson were present to make the proposition they had meditated; from which people, who do not give themselves the trouble to reflect or enquire, might conclude hastily that their absence was the cause why the proposition was not made; and of course that there were not in the assembly persons of virtue and firmness enough to propose the clause for emancipation. This supposition would not be true. There were persons there who wanted neither the virtue to propose, nor talents to enforce the proposition had they seen that the disposition of the legislature was ripe for it. These worthy characters would feel themselves wounded, degraded, and discouraged by this idea. Mr. Jefferson would therefore be obliged to M. de Meusnier to mention it in some such manner as this. "Of the two commissioners who had concerted the amendatory clause for the gradual emancipation of slaves Mr. Wythe could not be present as being a member of the judiciary department, and Mr. Jefferson was absent on the legation to France. But there wanted not in that assembly men of virtue enough to propose, and talents to vindicate this clause. But they saw that the moment of doing it with success was not yet arrived, and that an unsuccessful effort, as too often happens, would only rivet still closer the chains of bondage, and retard the moment of delivery to this oppressed description of men. What a stupendous, what an incomprehensible machine is man! Who can endure toil, famine, stripes, imprisonment or death itself in vindication of his own liberty, and the next moment be deaf to all those motives whose power supported him thro' his trial, and inflict on his fellow men a bondage, one hour of which is fraught with more misery than ages of that which he rose in rebellion to oppose. But we must await with patience the workings of an overruling providence, and hope that that is preparing the deliverance of these our suffering brethren. When the measure of their tears shall be full, when their groans shall have involved heaven itself in darkness, doubtless a god of justice will awaken to their distress, and by diffusing light and liberality among their oppressors, or at length by his exterminating thunder, manifest his attention to the things of this world, and that they are not left to the guidance of a blind fatality.

Payment of Wages to James and Sally Hemings in Paris

Jan. 1. Paid assistants on breakg. axle tree on road to Versailles 3ᵺ.

	Wages		etrennes		
	ᵺ		ᵺ		ᵺ
Paid Petit	72	+	24	=	96
Espagnol	60	+	12	=	72
l'Ardennois	60	+	12	=	72
Boileau	50	+	12	=	62
Nomeni	50	+	12	=	62
James	24	+	12	=	36
Sally	24	+	12	=	36
Garçon de cuisine	15	+	12	=	27
Mr. Short's servant		+	12	=	12
Mr. Trumbul's servts.		+	12	=	12
	355	+	132		487

2. Pd. Court fees, to servts. of Introductors & secretary 72ᵺ.

3. Petit's accts. from Nov. 25. to Dec. 29.

TJ to Nicholas Lewis

Dear Sir, Paris July 29. 1787.

... The torment of mind I endure till the moment shall arrive when I shall not owe a shilling on earth is such really as to render life of little value. I cannot decide to sell my lands. I have sold too much of them already, and they are the only sure provision for my children. Nor would I willingly sell the slaves as long as there remains any prospect of paying my debts with their labour. In this I am governed solely by views to their happiness which will render it worth their while to use extraordinary cautions for some time to enable me to put them ultimately on an easier footing, which I will do the moment they have paid the debts due from the estate, two thirds of which have been contracted by purchasing them. I am therefore strengthened in the idea of renting out my whole estate; not to any one person, but in different parts to different persons, as experience proves that it is only small concerns that are gainful, and it would be my interest that the tenants should make a reasonable gain. The lease I made to Garth and Moseley would be a good model. I do not recollect whether in that there was reserved a right of distraining on the lands for the whole rent. If not, such a clause would be essential, especially in the present relaxed state of the laws. I know there was in that no provision against paper money. This is still more essential. The best way of stating the rent would be in ounces of silver. The rent in that lease, tho expressed in current money, was meant to be 11.£ sterling a titheable. When we consider the rise in the price of tobacco, it should balance any difference for the worse which may have taken place in the lands in Albemarle, so as to entitle us there to equal terms. In Cumberland, Goochland, Bedford, where the lands are better, perhaps better terms might be expected. Calculating this on the number of working slaves, it holds up to us a clear revenue capable of working off the debts in a reasonable time. Think of it, my dear Sir, and if you do not find it disadvantageous be so good as to try to execute it, by leases of 3, 4, or 5 years: not more, because no dependance can be reposed in our laws continuing the same for any length of time. Indeed 3. years might be the most eligible term. The mill should be separated from the lease, finished, and rented by itself. All the lands reserved to my own use in Garth and Mousley's lease should still be reserved, and the privileges of that lease in general. House negroes still to be hired separately. The old and infirm, who could not be hired, or whom it would be a pity to hire, could perhaps be employed in raising cotton, or some other easy culture on lands to be reserved; George still to be reserved to take care of my orchards, grasses &c. The lands in Albemarle should be relieved by drawing off a good number of the labourers to Bedford, where a better hire might be expected and more lands be opened there. I feel all the weight of the objection that we cannot guard the negroes perfectly against ill usage. But in a question between hiring and selling them (one of which is necessary) the hiring will be temporary only, and will end in their happiness; whereas if we sell them, they will be subject to equal ill usage, without a prospect of change. It is for their good therefore ultimately, and it appears to promise a relief to me within such a term as I would be willing to wait for. I do not mention the rate of hire with a view to tie you up to that, but merely to shew that hiring presents a hopeful prospect. I should rely entirely on your judgment for that, for the choice of kind and hopeful tenants, and for every other circumstance . . .

TJ to William Drayton

Sir Paris July 30. 1787.

The fig and the mulberry are so well known in America, that nothing need be said of them. Their culture too is by women and children, and therefore earnestly to be desired in countries where there are slaves. In these, the women and children are often employed in labours disproportioned to their sex and age. By presenting to the master objects of culture, easier and equally beneficial, all temptation to misemploy them would be removed, and the lot of this tender part of our species be much softened. By varying too the articles of culture, we multiply the chances for making something, and disarm the seasons in a proportionable degree of their calamitous effects.

The Olive is a tree the least known in America, and yet the most worthy of being known. Of all the gifts of heaven to man, it is next to the most precious, if it be not the most precious. Perhaps it may claim a preference even to bread; because there is such an infinitude of vegetables which it renders a proper and comfortable nourishment. In passing the Alps at the Col de Tende, where they are mere masses of rock, wherever there happens to be a little soil, there are a number of olive trees, and a village supported by them. Take away these trees, and the same ground in corn would not support a single family. A pound of oil which can be bought for 3d. or 4d. sterling is equivalent to many pounds of flesh by the quantity of vegetables it will prepare and render fit and comfortable food. Without this tree the county of Provence and territory of Genoa would not support one half, perhaps not one third, their present inhabitants. The nature of the soil is of little consequence, if it be dry. The trees are planted from 15. to 20. f. apart, and, when tolerably good, will yeild 15. or 20. ℔. of oil yearly, one with another. There are trees which yeild much more. They begin to render good crops at 20. years old, and last till killed by cold, which happens at some time or other even in their best positions in France. But they put out again from their roots. In Italy I am told they have trees 200 years old. They afford an easy but constant employment thro' the year, and require so little nourishment that, if the soil be fit for any other production, it may be cultivated among the olive trees, without injuring them. The Northern limits of this tree are the mountains of the Cevennes from about the meridian of Carcassonne to the Rhone, and from thence the Alps and Appennines as far as Genoa, I know, and how much farther I am not informed. The shelter of these mountains may be considered as equivalent to a degree and a half of latitude at least; because Westward of the commencement of the Cevennes there are no olive trees in 43½° or even 43.° of latitude; whereas we find them *now* on the Rhone at Pierrelatte in 44½° and *formerly* they were at Tains, above the mouth of the Isere in 45.° sheltered by the near approach of the Cevennes and Alps, which only leave there a passage for the Rhone. Whether such a shelter exists, or not, in the states of South Carolina and Georgia, I know not. But this we may say, either that it exists, or that it is not necessary there: because we know that they produce the orange in open air; and wherever the Orange will stand at all, experience shews that the Olive will stand well; being a hardier tree. Notwithstanding the great quantities of oil made in France, they have not enough for their own consumption, and therefore import from other countries. This is an article, the consumption of which will always keep pace with it's production. Raise it; and it begets it's own demand. Little is carried to America because Europe has it not to spare. We therefore have not learnt the use of it. But cover the Southern states with it, and every man will become a consumer of oil, within whose reach it can be brought in point of price. If the memory of those persons is held in great respect in South Carolina who introduced there the culture of rice, a plant which sows life and death with almost equal hand, what obligations would be due to him who should introduce the Olive tree, and set the example of it's culture! Were the owner of slaves to view it only as the means of bettering their condition, how much would he better that by planting one of those trees for every slave he possessed! Having been myself an eyewitness to the blessings which this tree sheds on the poor, I never had my wishes so kindled for the introduction of any article of new culture into our own country. South Carolina and Georgia appear to me to be the states wherein it's success, in favorable positions at least, could not be doubted, and I flattered myself it would come within the views of the society for agriculture to begin the experiments which are to prove it's practicability. Carcassonne is the place from which the plants may be most certainly and cheaply obtained. They can be sent from thence by water to Bordeaux, where they may be embarked on vessels bound for Charleston. There is too little intercourse between Charleston and Marseilles to propose this as the port of exportation. I offer my service to the society for the obtaining and forwarding any number of plants which may be desired. Th: Jefferson

TJ to Francis Eppes

Dear Sir, Paris July 30. 1787.

Your favor of May 23. 1786. was not received till May 3. 1787. Those of 1786. Oct. 23, 1787. Mar. 30. Apr. 14. and May 2. have duly come to hand. I wrote you on the 14th. of Dec. 1786. and again the 26. of May 1787. The latter was merely to announce a batch of wine sent you by Capt. Gregory from Bordeaux while I was there. It is now so long since I have had occasion to think on subjects of law that I am not able, with any degree of confidence, to answer your questions on the execution against Mr. Cary's estate. I suppose that the execution directed to the Coroner bound the whole property of Mr. Cary from the moment of it's date. If the slaves taken under the erroneous execution were afterwards sold under the good one, the proceeds of that sale will be secure to us, and any question about the property of the slaves, under pretence they were passed away by the deed of trust, will be a question between the purchaser and trustees and will not affect us. If the good execution could not be satisfied from those particular slaves, yet it could lay hold of all his other slaves and personal property. But were we reduced to seek our remedy against those identical slaves only which were taken under the erroneous execution, I think that they would be subject to the good execution: because the deeds of trust were palpably made to defraud us of a just debt, and are therefore made void by the statute 13. of Elizabeth except against bona fide purchasers for valuable consideration, and having no notice of the fraudulent object of the deed. Even a deed of trust, if not within this description, is not saved out of the condemnation of the statute. With respect to Colo. T. M. Randolph's securityship for this debt, I suppose it to be a very certain fact, tho' I cannot charge myself with the recollection of having seen the bill endorsed by him. 1. I was charged by Mr. Wayles with the having the bill of exchange executed for him at Varina by Mr. Cary, and to be endorsed by Colo. TMR. They did not come to Varina as expected and therefore it was not done then. 2. I am almost certain, I think quite certain, Mr. Wayles told me afterwards he had got the bill so drawn and endorsed. 3. I am also certain that this endorsement has been frequently the subject of conversation between Colo. TMR and myself, that he always spoke of himself as security and often wished we would press for the money. Colo. TMR is too honest a man to question this fact, and would not put you to the trouble of a Bill of Discovery. 4. How it happens that two copies of the bill are without endorsement is unaccountable to me, nor do I know any thing of the third. I delivered every paper of that kind to Frank Harris. Should it be necessary to have recourse against the security, should he declare himself not bound, it may be proper to try whether a copy of the bill and protest cannot be obtained from the notary's office in England.

Mr. Wayles's letters about that date should be examined. Doubtless there is one to whatever friend he inclosed the bill in order to obtain the protest. Probably the answer of his friend re-inclosing the bill and protest will explain it. I should wish that this money, when recovered, should be applied in the first place to pay the debt due to Cary of London because we have always assured him it should be so, and should it not, he will justly accuse us of a gross violation of faith. From the conversation I had with him in London he knows that we will not pay interest from Apr. 19. 1775. to April. 19. 1783. I paid him that interest on a small debt of mine, but took care to explain to him explicitly, that it was on account of the peculiar confidence he had reposed in me, having sent me the articles after the commencement of our national quarrel.

Jones has never sent me a copy of his account current. All I know of it is from memory. I think the balance on the account rendered us after Mr. Wayles's debt was about 9000? sterling. I think after the date of that account there were in his hands about 300 hhds. of tobacco made the year preceding Mr. Wayles's death and the year of his death, that is 1772 and 1773, or perhaps 1773 and 1774. And moreover 120 hhds. or thereabouts shipped by us separately the first year after the division. Stating this tobacco only at the ordinary price and deducting it from the 9000?, and stopping the interest at Apr. 19. 1775. and not recommencing it till Apr. 19. 1783. the debt should not be so very formidable. On the information I received from Mr. Lewis in his letter of Mar. 14. 1786. that the bonds due and the crops to the end of 1785. would pay all my debts except that to my sister Nancy, and those to Jones and McCaul, I made propositions to them for commencing the paiment of their debts. The conditions were 1. To pay to Jones two thirds of the profits of my estate and to McCaul one third annually; or if they should prefer it, 400? sterl. to the former and 200? sterl. to the latter annually. [2.] To pay no interest between Apr. 19. 1775. and Apr. 19. 1783. 3. That the crop of 1787. should begin the paiment. 4. That their accounts, notwithstanding these paiments, should be open to settlement and rectification. McCaul has acceded, and the matter is so far settled with him. To Jones I added two other articles, viz. that the paiment into the treasury should not affect him at all, and that in proportion as I should proceed paying my third of the just balance, I should be discharged from the remaining two thirds. This last article I thought we should all wish to make with him, that, the estate being now divided the debt should also be divided and our families be left clear of all responsibility but for themselves. Jones answered that he could not decide till he should hear from his agent in Virginia. He neither approved nor disapproved the conditions, except that of the release as to the two thirds, saying he apprehended if he released any part of the estate it would release the whole; but he said he would answer me finally when he should hear from his agent. I rather believe he will accept my conditions. But I am quite thrown off the hinges by your information that notwithstanding the state of things from Mr. Lewis in March 1786. that all would be paid, you had found on an estimate in Sep. 1786. there would yet be a balance of 1200? to pay. When I consider the quantity of tobacco to be counted on, the charges to come out of that, it appears evident that the debts can not be paid in this way. I am decided against selling my lands. They are the only sure provision for my children, and I have sold too much of them already. I am also unwilling to sell negroes, if the debts can be paid without. This unwillingness is for their sake, not my own; because my debts once cleared off, I shall try some plan of making their situation happier, determined to content myself with a small portion of their labour. I think it better for them therefore to be submitted to harder conditions for a while in order that they may afterwards be put into a better situation. I hired my estate in Albemarle once for 11.? sterl. for every titheable hand. Tobacco is since risen, and the lands of Goochland, Cumberland, and Bedford are more profitable. I may hope therefore a good rent may be obtained for the whole estate, letting it out in small parcels to different tenants known to be kind and careful in their natures. I propose my former lease to Garth and Mousley as the model, reserving all the advantages and privileges reserved in that, as also the lands reserved in that to my own use; inserting a clause for distraining on the lands for the whole hire, which I believe was not in that, and which, so far as concerned the hire of the slaves, would not result from the general provisions of the law, unless expressly provided for;

guarding also against paper money by stating the rent in ounces of silver, restraining the leases to three years, or at any rate not more than five; retaining rigorously the clauses which had for their object the good treatment of my slaves, particularly that which denied a diminution of rent on the death of a slave; otherwise it would be their interest to kill all the old and infirm by hard usage. Supposing there are about 90 titheable slaves, a reasonable rent on them, my lands and stocks, the tenants paying every tax and charge of every kind, will make a nett annual sum which may clear off the debts within such a term of years as I should be willing to wait for. It will substitute certain calculation for incertainty, and relieve my friends from the perplexity of my affairs added to their own. The only objection is the difficulty of guarding my negroes against ill usage. I put it in all it's force, and I shall go through the operation, as a man does that of being cut for the stone, with a view to relief. I have therefore written to Mr. Lewis to pray him to put my affairs on this footing immediately, in which I know your goodness will aid him. It is taking one great trouble in the lump, to be relieved from it in the detail. It may be lessened too by each undertaking the part to which he is convenient. When this arrangement shall be taken, I shall feel like a person on shore, escaped from shipwreck. But this cannot be in time for the first year's paiment to McCaul, in which I would on no account fail. I hope resources may be found to effect that. I am to thank you for the Magnolia seeds which came by the way of London. I have heard nothing yet of the Cedar berries which should have come to Havre in a ship of Ross McConnico & Ritson. There are some seeds arrived for me at Bordeaux but I have no information what they are, nor from whence. Perhaps they are the cedar berries. Thanks for all the trouble you have taken and take for me are next to nothing. A sensibility of it is deeply engraven in my heart. I write to Mrs. Eppes, to Jack, and to Mr. Skipwith, making them the channel of my good wishes to the families. I have only to add therefore assurances to yourself of the sincere esteem with which I am Dear Sir your affectionate friend & servant,

Th: Jefferson

TJ to Edward Bancroft

Dear Sir Paris Jan. 26. 1788.

I have deferred answering your letter on the subject of slaves, because you permitted me to do it till a moment of leisure, and that moment rarely comes, and because too, I could not answer you with such a degree of certainty as to merit any notice. I do not recollect the conversation at Vincennes to which you allude, but can repeat still on the same ground, on which I must have done then, that as far as I can judge from the experiments which have been made, to give liberty to, or rather, to abandon persons whose habits have been formed in slavery is like abandoning children. Many quakers in Virginia seated their slaves on their lands as tenants. They were distant from me, and therefore I cannot be particular in the details, because I never had very particular information. I cannot say whether they were to pay a rent in money, or a share of the produce: but I remember that the landlord was obliged to plan their crops for them, to direct all their operations during every season and according to the weather, but, what is more afflicting, he was obliged to watch them daily and almost constantly to make them work, and even to whip them. A man's moral sense must be unusually strong, if slavery does not make him a thief. He who is permitted by law to have no property of his own, can with difficulty conceive that property is founded in any thing but force. These slaves chose to steal from their neighbors rather than work. They became public nuisances, and in most instances were reduced to slavery again. But I will beg of you to make no use of this imperfect information (unless in common conversation). I shall go to America in the Spring and return in the fall. During my stay in Virginia I shall be in the neighborhood where many of these trials were made. I will inform myself very particularly of them, and communicate the information to you. Besides these, there is an instance since I came away of a young man (Mr. Mayo) who died and gave freedom to all his slaves, about 200. This is about 4. years ago. I shall know how they have turned out. Notwithstanding the discouraging result of these experiments, I am decided on my final return to America to try this one. I shall endeavor to import as many Germans as I have grown slaves. I will settle them and my slaves, on farms of 50. acres each, intermingled, and place all on the footing of the Metayers [Medietarii] of Europe. Their children shall be brought up, as others are, in habits of property and foresight, and I have no doubt but that they will be good citizens. Some of their fathers will be so: others I suppose will need government. With these, all that can be done is to oblige them to labour as the labouring poor of Europe do, and to apply to their comfortable subsistence the produce of their labour, retaining such a moderate portion of it as may be a just equivalent for the use of the lands they labour and the stocks and other necessary advances. Th: Jefferson

TJ to Brissot de Warville

Sir

Paris Feb. 11. 1788.

I am very sensible of the honour you propose to me of becoming a member of the society for the abolition of the slave trade. You know that nobody wishes more ardently to see an abolition not only of the trade but of the condition of slavery: and certainly nobody will be more willing to encounter every sacrifice for that object. But the influence and information of the friends to this proposition in France will be far above the need of my association. I am here as a public servant; and those whom I serve having never yet been able to give their voice against this practice, it is decent for me to avoid too public a demonstration of my wishes to see it abolished. Without serving the cause here, it might render me less able to serve it beyond the water. I trust you will be sensible of the prudence of those motives therefore which govern my conduct on this occasion, and be assured of my wishes for the success of your undertaking and the sentiments of esteem and respect with which I have the honour to be Sir your most obedt. humble servt.,

Th: Jefferson

P.S. I send you the journals of Congress of 1787.

TJ to Benjamin Vaughan

Dear Sir New York June 27. 1790.

Your favor of March 27. came duly to hand on the 12th.inst. . . . Though large countries within our Union are covered with the Sugar maple as heavily as can be concieved, and that this tree yeilds a sugar equal to the best from the cane, yeilds it in great quantity, with no other labor than what the women and girls can bestow, who attend to the drawing off and boiling the liquor, and the trees when skilfully tapped will last a great number of years, yet the ease with which we had formerly got cane sugar, had prevented our attending to this resource. Late difficulties in the sugar trade have excited attention to our sugar trees, and it seems fully believed by judicious persons, that we can not only supply our own demand, but make for exportation. I will send you a sample of it if I can find a conveyance without passing it through the expensive one of the post. What a blessing to substitute a sugar which requires only the labour of children, for that which it is said renders the slavery of the blacks necessary . . . I am with sentiments of sincere esteem Dear Sir your sincere friend & servt.,

Th: Jefferson

TJ to Martha Jefferson Randolph

New York Aug. 8. 1790.

Congress being certainly to rise the day after tomorrow, I can now, my dear Patsy, be more certain of the time at which I can be at Monticello, and which I think will be from the 8th. to the 15th. of September: more likely to be sooner than later. I shall leave this about a fortnight hence, but must stay some days to have arrangements taken for my future residence in Philadelphia. I hope to be able to pass a month at least with you at Monticello. I am in hopes Mr. Randolph will take dear Poll in his pocket. Tell him I have sent him the model of the mould-board by Mr. David Randolph who left this place yesterday. I must trouble you to give notice to Martin to be at Monticello by the 1st. of September that he may have things prepared. If you know any thing of Bob, I should be glad of the same notice to him, tho' I suppose him to be in the neighborhood of Fredericksbg. and in that case I will have him notified thro' Mr. Fitzhugh. I have written to Mr. Brown for some necessaries to be sent to Monticello, and to send on some chairs which will go hence to the care of Mr. D. Randolph at the Hundred, to be forwarded to Mr. Brown at Richmond. If Mr. Randolph can give a little attention to the forwarding these articles we shall be the more comfortable. Present me to him and Maria affectionately, and continue to love me as I do you, my dear. Most sincerely,

Th: Jefferson

Calculating the Cost of Maple Sugar for Daily Use at Monticello

March 18, 1791

*On trial it takes 11. dwt. Troy of double refd. maple sugar to a dish of coffee or 1 ℔ Avoirdupoise to 26.5 dishes, so that at 20 cents pr. ℔ it is 8 mills per dish. An ounce of coffee @ 20. cents pr. ℔ is 12.5 mills so that sugar & coffee of a dish is worth 2 cents.

Benjamin Banneker to TJ

Maryland. Baltimore County.
Near Ellicotts Lower Mills August 19th: 1791

Sir

I am fully sensible of the greatness of that freedom which I take with you on the present occasion; a liberty which Seemed to me scarcely allowable, when I reflected on that distinguished, and dignifyed station in which you Stand; and the almost general prejudice and prepossession which is so prevailent in the world against those of my complexion.

I suppose it is a truth too well attested to you, to need a proof here, that we are a race of Beings who have long laboured under the abuse and censure of the world, that we have long been looked upon with an eye of contempt, and that we have long been considered rather as brutish than human, and Scarcely capable of mental endowments.

Sir I hope I may Safely admit, in consequence of that report which hath reached me, that you are a man far less inflexible in Sentiments of this nature, than many others, that you are measurably friendly and well disposed toward us, and that you are willing and ready to Lend your aid and assistance to our relief from those many distresses and numerous calamities to which we are reduced.

Now Sir if this is founded in truth, I apprehend you will readily embrace every opportunity to eradicate that train of absurd and false ideas and oppinions which so generally prevails with respect to us, and that your Sentiments are concurrent with mine, which are that one universal Father hath given being to us all, and that he hath not only made us all of one flesh, but that he hath also without partiality afforded us all the Same Sensations, and endued us all with the same faculties, and that however variable we may be in Society or religion, however diversifyed in Situation or colour, we are all of the Same Family, and Stand in the Same relation to him.

Sir, if these are Sentiments of which you are fully persuaded, I hope you cannot but acknowledge, that it is the indispensible duty of those who maintain for themselves the rights of human nature, and who profess the obligations of Christianity, to extend their power and influence to the relief of every part of the human race, from whatever burthen or oppression they may unjustly labour under, and this I apprehend a full conviction of the truth and obligation of these principles should lead all to.

Sir, I have long been convinced, that if your love for your Selves, and for those inesteemable laws which preserve to you the rights of human nature, was founded on Sincerity, you could not but be Solicitous, that every Individual of whatsoever rank or distinction, might with you equally enjoy the blessings thereof, neither could you rest Satisfyed, short of the most active diffusion of your exertions, in order to their promotion from any State of degradation, to which the unjustifyable cruelty and barbarism of men may have reduced them.

Sir I freely and Chearfully acknowledge, that I am of the African race, and in that colour which is natural to them of the deepest dye,* and it is under a Sense of the most profound gratitude to the Supreme Ruler of the universe, that I now confess to you, that I am not under that State of tyrannical thraldom, and inhuman captivity, to which too many of my brethren are doomed; but that I have abundantly tasted of the fruition of those blessings which proceed from that free and unequalled liberty with which you are favoured and which I hope you will willingly allow you have received from the immediate hand of that Being, from whom proceedeth every good and perfect gift.

Sir, Suffer me to recall to your mind that time in which the Arms and tyranny of the British Crown were exerted with every powerful effort in order to reduce you to a State of Servitude, look back I intreat you on the variety of dangers to which you were exposed, reflect on that time in which every human aid appeared unavailable, and in which even hope and fortitude wore the aspect of inability to the Conflict, and you cannot but be led to a Serious and grateful Sense of your miraculous and providential preservation; you cannot but acknowledge, that the present freedom and tranquility which you enjoy you have mercifully received, and that it is the peculiar blessing of Heaven.

This Sir, was a time in which you clearly saw into the injustice of a State of Slavery, and in which you had just apprehensions of the horrors of its condition, it was now Sir, that your abhorrence thereof was so excited, that you publickly held forth this true and invaluable doctrine, which is worthy to be recorded and remember'd in all Succeeding ages. "We hold these truths to be Self evident, that all men are created equal, and that they are endowed by their creator with certain unalienable rights, that among these are life, liberty, and the pursuit of happyness."

Here Sir, was a time in which your tender feelings for your selves had engaged you thus to declare, you were then impressed with proper ideas of the great valuation of liberty, and the free possession of those blessings to which you were entitled by nature; but Sir how pitiable is it to reflect, that altho you were so fully convinced of the benevolence of the Father of mankind, and of his equal and impartial distribution of those rights and privileges which he had conferred upon them, that you should at the Same time counteract his mercies, in detaining by fraud and violence so numerous a part of my brethren under groaning captivity and cruel oppression, that you should at the Same time be found guilty of that most criminal act, which you professedly detested in others, with respect to yourselves.

Sir, I suppose that your knowledge of the situation of my brethren is too extensive to need a recital here; neither shall I presume to prescribe methods by which they may be relieved; otherwise than by recommending to you and all others, to wean yourselves from these narrow prejudices which you have imbibed with respect to them, and as Job proposed to his friends "Put your Souls in their Souls stead," thus shall your hearts be enlarged with kindness and benevolence toward them, and thus shall you need neither the direction of myself or others in what manner to proceed herein.

And now, Sir, altho my Sympathy and affection for my brethren hath caused my enlargement thus far, I ardently hope that your candour and generosity will plead with you in my behalf, when I make known to you, that it was not originally my design; but that having taken up my pen in order to direct to you as a present, a copy of an Almanack which I have calculated for the Succeeding year, I was unexpectedly and unavoidably led thereto.

This calculation, Sir, is the production of my arduous Study in this my advanced Stage of life; for having long had unbounded desires to become acquainted with the Secrets of nature, I have had to gratify my curiosity herein thro my own assiduous application to Astronomical Study, in which I need not to recount to you the many difficulties and disadvantages which I have had to encounter.

And altho I had almost declined to make my calculation for the ensuing year, in consequence of that time which I had allotted therefor being taking up at the Federal Territory by the request of Mr. Andrew Ellicott, yet finding myself under Several engagements to printers of this state to whom I had communicated my design, on my return to my place of residence, I industriously apply'd myself thereto, which I hope I have accomplished with correctness and accuracy, a copy of which I have taken the liberty to direct to you, and which I humbly request you will favourably receive, and you may have the opportunity of perusing it after its publication, yet I chose to send it to you in manuscript previous thereto, that thereby you might not only have an earlier inspection, but that you might also view it in my own hand writing.—And now Sir, I shall conclude and Subscribe my Self with the most profound respect your most Obedient humble Servant, Benjamin Banneker

NB any communication to me may be had by a direction to Mr. Elias Ellicott merchant in Baltimore Town.

B B

As an Essay of my calculation is put into the hand of Mr. Cruckshank of Philadelphia, for publication I would wish that you might neither have this Almanack copy published nor give any printer an opportunity thereof, as it might tend to disappoint Mr. Joseph Cruckshank in his sale. B B

*My Father was brought here a S[lav]e from Africa.

TJ to Benjamin Banneker

Sir, Philadelphia Aug. 30. 1791.

I thank you sincerely for your letter of the 19th. instant and for the Almanac it contained. No body wishes more than I do to see such proofs as you exhibit, that nature has given to our black brethren, talents equal to those of the other colours of men, and that the appearance of a want of them is owing merely to the degraded condition of their existence both in Africa and America. I can add with truth that no body wishes more ardently to see a good system commenced for raising the condition both of their body and mind to what it ought to be, as fast as the imbecility of their present existence, and other circumstances which cannot be neglected, will admit.—I have taken the liberty of sending your almanac to Monsieur de Condorcet, Secretary of the Academy of sciences at Paris, and member of the Philanthropic society because I considered it as a document to which your whole colour had a right for their justification against the doubts which have been entertained of them. I am with great esteem, Sir Your most obedt. humble servt.,

Th: Jefferson

TJ to Condorcet

Dear Sir Philadelphia Aug. 30. 1791.

I am happy to be able to inform you that we have now in the United States a negro, the son of a black man born in Africa, and of a black woman born in the United States, who is a very respectable Mathematician. I procured him to be employed under one of our chief directors in laying out the new federal city on the Patowmac, and in the intervals of his leisure, while on that work, he made an Almanac for the next year, which he sent me in his own handwriting, and which I inclose to you. I have seen very elegant solutions of Geometrical problems by him. Add to this that he is a very worthy and respectable member of society. He is a free man. I shall be delighted to see these instances of moral eminence so multiplied as to prove that the want of talents observed in them is merely the effect of their degraded condition, and not proceeding from any difference in the structure of the parts on which intellect depends.

I am looking ardently to the completion of the glorious work in which your country is engaged. I view the general condition of Europe as hanging on the success or failure of France. Having set such an example of philosophical arrangement within, I hope it will be extended without your limits also, to your dependants and to your friends in every part of the earth.—Present my affectionate respects to Madame de Condorcet, and accept yourself assurance of the sentiments of esteem & attachment with which I have the honour to be Dear Sir Your most obedt & most humble servt,

Th: Jefferson

Invoice from William Prince

Flushing Novr. 8th 1791,
Bot. of Wm. Prince—

The following trees—

No.	1	60	Sugar Maple trees	at	1/	3- 0-0
	2	6	Cranberry trees		2/	0-12-0
	3	3	Balsam Poplar		1/6	0- 4-6
	4	6	Venetian Sumach		1/6	0- 9-0
	5	8	Burré Pears		1/6	0-12-0

6	4	Brignole Plumbs		0- 6-0
7	4	Red Roman Nectarine	1/6	0- 6-0
8	4	Large early Apricot		
9	4	Brussels do.		
10	4	Roman do.	40 trees at 1/6	3- 0-0
11	4	Yellow Roman Nectarine		
12	4	Green Nutmeg Peach		
13	4	Yellow October Clingne.		
14	12	Esopus Spitzenburgh apple		
15	4	Large early harvest apple		
16	2	Moss rose	3/1	0- 6-0
17	2	Rosa mundi	2/	0- 4-0
18	2	Monthly rose	2/	0- 4-0
19	2	Large Provence rose	1/6	0- 3-0
20	2	Musk rose	2/	0- 4-0

Purchase of 50 lbs of Maple Sugar, November 29, 1791

Nov. 25. Note the residue of my salary for the last quarter, being 800.D. is lodged in the bank.

Pd. for pr. of slippers 4/4.

27. Received from the bank by Francis Seche 100.D.

Pd. to Mr. Remsen to be by him transmitted to Mr. Bruce at N. York 70. Doll. on account of rent.

29. Pd. for visiting cards 1/6.

Pd. Pennington for 50. ℔ maple sugar refd. @ 1/8 £4-3-4.

Pd. Francis for washing 13/9.

Pd. do. for wages &c. 4½ D.

TJ to Lafayette

Philadelphia June 16. 1792.

Behold you then, my dear friend, at the head of a great army, establishing the liberties of your country against a foreign enemy. May heaven favor your cause, and make you the channel thro' which it may pour it's favors. While you are exterminating the monster aristocracy, and pulling out the teeth and fangs of it's associate monarchy, a contrary tendency is discovered in some here. A sect has shewn itself among us, who declare they espoused our new constitution, not as a good and sufficient thing itself, but only as a step to an English constitution, the only thing good and sufficient in itself, in their eye. It is happy for us that these are preachers without followers, and that our people are firm and constant in their republican purity. You will wonder to be told that it is from the Eastward chiefly that these champions for a king, lords and commons come. They get some important associates from New York, and are puffed off by a tribe of Agioteurs which have been hatched in a bed of corruption made up after the model of their beloved England. Too many of these stock jobbers and king-jobbers have come into our legislature, or rather too many of our legislature have become stock jobbers and king-jobbers. However the voice of the people is beginning to make itself heard, and will probably cleanse their seats at the ensuing election.—The machinations of our old enemies are such as to keep us still at bay with our Indian neighbors.—What are you doing for your colonies? They will be lost if not more effectually succoured. Indeed no future efforts you can make will ever be able to reduce the blacks. All that can be done in my opinion will be to compound with them as has been done formerly in Jamaica. We have been less zealous in aiding them, lest your government should feel any jealousy on our account. But in truth we as sincerely wish their restoration, and their connection with you, as you do yourselves. We are satisfied that neither your justice nor their distresses will ever again permit their being forced to seek at dear and distant markets those first necessaries of life which they may have at cheaper markets placed by nature at their door, and formed by her for their support:—What is become of Mde. de Tessy and Mde. de Tott? I have not heard of them since they went to Switzerland. I think they would have done better to have come and reposed under the Poplars of Virginia. Pour into their bosoms the warmest effusions of my friendship and tell them they will be warm and constant unto death. Accept of them also for Mde. de la Fayette and your dear children—but I am forgetting that you are in the feilds of war and they I hope in those of peace. Adieu my dear friend! God bless you all. Your's affectionately Th: Jefferson

TJ to Bolling Clark

Sir Monticello Sep. 21. 1792.

The following are the slaves which I have concluded to sell from Bedford, to wit.

Sam. Dilcey (daughter of Bess) born in 1769. Ambrose born in 1785. Hanah born in 1789. And Dinah born in 1791. Forming one family.

York and Jame boy sons of old Will and Judy. The purchasers will have [to] be willing to receive the two old people for nothing, should they chuse to go with their sons. This as they please.

Judy (Abbey's daughter) and Amy.

Frank, Lunda's. Will, the one which has no wife in the estate. These being only 11. in number are not sufficient to make a sale by themselves, and indeed I do not (while in public life) like to have my name annexed in the public papers to the sale of property. On consultation with Mr. Winston and Mr. Clay, we conclude it will be best to carry them to some other sale of slaves in that part of the country to be sold. Sam's family to be sold in one lot, the credit to be one year for half, and 2 years for the other half, with interest from the date. But if paid at the day of paiment the interest to be given up. For ready money allow 5. per cent discount. If the purchaser is substantial, take one substantial security with him in each bond. If he is not substantial himself require two good securities in each bond, to be bound *jointly and severally*. I have joined Mr. Winston and Mr. Clay in the power of attorney now inclosed to you, as their experience in business will render their advice and assistance useful.

You were observing when here that the sale of Peter had deprived you of your shoemaker but Jam[e?] Hubbard is a much better shoemaker than Peter: he always assisted in making the shoes here, and can certainly make those for the Bedford plantation. I mentioned to you my wish that you would tend hemp and cotton the next year sufficient to clothe the negroes. I think it will require 1000 hills of cotton for every working hand, and 2 or 3 acres of hemp for the whole. Mr. Clay tells me his negroes collect a good deal of white clover seed every year for sale, and could collect a great deal if desired. I wish you to get from them as much as they will get, and to sow it on your wheat about the last snow that falls in the spring. I cannot too earnestly recommend to you the substituting the culture of wheat instead of corn to as great a degree as the situation of the plantation will admit. Also to sort your tobacco for the London market as well as you can, and by all means to quicken it down to Richmond. Mr. Brown has expressed a desire to have one third of it stemmed: but this I leave altogether to your own discretion. I send you herewith some blank bonds for the sale of the negroes. When the sale is over, send the bonds by any safe conveyance to Mr. Randolph at this place keeping, for fear of accident, an exact list of them, naming the obligors, sum, day of paiment, and for which negroes they were given. I am Sir your humble servt Th: Jefferson

Enclosure: Power of Attorney for Sale of Slaves

[21 Sep. 1792]

I Thomas Jefferson of Albemarle in Virginia do hereby constitute Edmund Winston and Charles Clay esquires and Bowling Clarke my attornies for the special purpose of selling, and conveying the following slaves to wit, Sam, Dilcey, Ambrose, Hanah and Dinah of one family, York Jameboy, Judy, Amy, Will and Frank, and taking paiment or obligations of paiment for the same: and I hereby ratify and confirm whatever acts relative to the premises shall be done by them, or any two of them, in like manner as if done by myself. In witness whereof I have hereto set my hand and seal this twenty first day of September 1792. Witness

P. DeRieux

Th: Jefferson

TJ to Martha Jefferson Randolph

My Dear Martha Philadelphia Dec. 13. 1792.

By capt. Swaile, who sailed yesterday for Richmond I sent addressed to Mr. Randolph to the care of Mr. Brown a box containing the following articles for your three house maids.

2. peices of linen. 52. yards
9. pair cotton stockings (3 of them small)
13. yds. cotton in three patterns
36. yards Calimanco.
9. yards muslin.

Bob is to have a share of the linen. I had promised to send him a new suit of clothes. Instead of this I send a suit of superfine ratteen of my own, which I have scarcely ever worn. I forgot to get stockings for him: therefore must desire you to have him furnished with them from Colo. Bell's on my account.—In the same box you will find 4. pair tongs and shovels which I observed the house to be in want of. I hope our dear Anne is got well and that all of you continue so. Maria is well. She begun a letter to you Sunday was sennight: but it is not finished. My affections to Mr. Randolph and your friends. Adieu, my dear, yours with all love

Th: Jefferson

TJ to Angelica Schuyler Church

Germantown Nov. 27. 1793.

. . . In the mean time I am going to Virginia. I have at length been able to fix that to the beginning of the new year. I am then to be liberated from the hated occupations of politics, and to sink into the bosom of my family, my farm and my books. I have my house to build, my feilds to form, and to watch for the happiness of those who labor for mine. I have one daughter married to a man of science, sense, virtue, and competence; in whom indeed I have nothing more to wish. They live with me. If the other shall be as fortunate in due process of time, I shall imagine myself as blessed as the most blessed of the patriarchs. Nothing could then withdraw my thoughts a moment from home, but the recollection of my friends abroad. I often put the question Whether yourself and Kitty will ever come to see your friends at Monticello? But it is my affection, and not my experience of things, which has leave to answer. And I am determined to believe the answer; because, in that belief, I find I sleep sounder and wake more cheerful. En attendant, god bless you; accept the homage of my sincere & constant affection.

Th: Jefferson

TJ to Martha Jefferson Randolph

My Dear Martha Philadelphia Dec. 1. 1793.

This place being entirely clear of all infection, the members of Congress are coming into it without fear. The President moved in yesterday, as did I also. I have got comfortably lodged at the corner of 7th. and Market street.—Dr. Waters is returned; not well, but better. Still always Hectic. He and Mrs. Waters are just gone to housekeeping for the first time. Mrs. Trist is also returned to town and means to take a small house and 3. or 4. boarders. Mr. Randolph, the Atty. Genl. having removed to German town during the fever, proposes not to return again to live in the city. Mrs. Washington is not yet returned.—So much for small news. As to great, we can only perceive in general that the French are triumphing in every quarter. They suffered a check as is said by the D. of Brunswick, losing about 2000. men, but this is nothing to their numerous victories. The account of the recapture of Toulon comes so many ways that we think it may now be believed.—St. Domingo has expelled all it's whites, has given freedom to all it's blacks, has established a regular government of the blacks and coloured people, and seems now to have taken it's ultimate form, and that to which all of the West India islands must come. The English have possession of two ports in the island, but acting professedly as the patrons of the whites, there is no danger of their gaining ground.—Freneau's and Fenno's papers are both put down for ever. My best affection to Mr. Randolph, Maria and friends. Kisses to the little ones. Adieu affectionately Th: J.

Robert Pleasants to TJ

Respected Friend Richmond 6 mo. 1. 1796

Concieving the Instruction of black Children to be a duty we owe to that much degraded part of our fellow Creatures, and probably would tend to the spiritual and temporal advantage of that unhappy race, as well as to the Community at large, in fitting them for freedom, which at this enlightened day is generally acknowledged to be their right, I have much desired to see some sutable steps taken to promote such work; And believing thee to be a real friend to the cause of liberty, and endowed with ability and influence in regulating and promoting sutable plans for such a purpose, I take the liberty by my Friend Richard Dobs of sending thee a rough Essay for thy consideration, with a request, that should thou approve the subject, thou wilt please to make such alterations or amendments as may appear to thee more likely to answer the desired purpose, and to give it such other incouragement as thou may think right—I hope thou will excuse the freedom I have now taken, and believe me to be with sincere respect & Esteem Thy Friend

Robert Pleasants

TJ to Robert Pleasants

[27 Aug. 1796]

. . . the establishment of the plan of emancipation if it should precede I am not prepared to decide. If it should precede, I would refer to your consideration whether the plan you propose is adequate to the object. I apprehend that private liberalities will never be equal but to local and partial effects. I venture therefore to suggest what alone can, in my opinion, accomplish the general object. Among the laws proposed in what was called the Revised code printed in 1784. was a bill entitled "for the more general diffusion of knowledge." This bill was much approved, [and] was taken from [the] bundle and printed for public consideration when it was first reported. I believe that it would now be [as] generally approved, and needs only to be brought into view again to be adopted. This might be effected by petitions from the several counties to the assembly to take that bill into consideration. Very small alterations would make it embrace the object of your paper, it's effect would be general, and the means for carrying it on would be certain and permanent. Permit me therefore to suggest to you the substitution of that as a more general and certain means of providing for the instruction of the slaves, and more desireable as they would in the course of it be mixed with those of free condition. Whether, for their happiness, it should extend beyond those destined to be free, is questionable. Ignorance and despotism seem made for each other. I am, with perfect esteem Dear Sir Your friend & servt

Th: Jefferson

TJ to St. George Tucker

Dear Sir Monticello Aug. 28. 97.

I have to acknolege the receipt of your two favors of the 2d. and 22d. inst. and to thank you for the pamphlet covered by the former. You know my subscription to it's doctrines, and as to the mode of emancipation, I am satisfied that that must be a matter of compromise between the passions the prejudices, and the real difficulties which will each have their weight in that operation. Perhaps the first chapter of this history, which has begun in St. Domingo, and the next succeeding ones which will recount how all the whites were driven from all the other islands, may prepare our minds for a peaceable accommodation between justice, policy and necessity, and furnish an answer to the difficult question Whither shall the coloured emigrants go? And the sooner we put some plan under way, the greater hope there is that it may be permitted to proceed peaceably to it's ultimate effect. But if something is not done, and soon done, we shall be the murderers of our own children. The "Murmura, venturos nautis prodentia ventos" has already reached us; the revolutionary storm now sweeping the globe will be upon us, and happy if we make timely provision to give it an easy passage over our land. From the present state of things in Europe and America the day which begins our combustion must be near at hand, and only a single spark is wanting to make that day tomorrow. If we had begun sooner, we might probably have been allowed a lengthier operation to clear ourselves, but every day's delay lessens the time we may take for emancipation. Some people derive hope from the aid of the confederated states. But this is a delusion. There is but one state in the Union which will aid us sincerely if an insurrection begins; and that one may perhaps have it's own fire to quench at the same time.

The facts stated in yours of the 22d. were not identically known to me, but others like them were. From the general government no interference need be expected. Even the merchant and navigator, the immediate sufferers, are prevented by various motives from wishing to be redressed. I see nothing but a state procedure which can vindicate us from the insult. It is in the power of any single magistrate, or of the attorney for the Commonwealth to lay hold of the commanding officer whenever he comes ashore for the breach of the peace, and to proceed against him by indictment. This is so plain an operation that no power can prevent it's being carried through with effect, but the want of will in the officers of the state. I think that the matter of finances, which has set the people of Europe to thinking, is now advanced to that point with us, that the next step, and it is an unavoidable one, a land tax, will awaken our constituents, and call for inspection into past proceedings.—I am with great esteem Dear Sir Your friend & servt

Th: Jefferson

Statement of Nailery Profits

Statement of annual disbursements and receipts on account of the Nailery.

1794.			D	D
May. 31.	To paid Caleb Lownes for 1. ton of nail rod		106.67	
		transportation	12.33	119.00
July. 1.	To do.	1. ton & transportn		119.00
Sep. 30.	To coal @ 2d. per bushel & 666. bushels for every ton is 18.50 per ton. for 2. Ton			37.
	To 3. pr. ct. on £49.2.11. to George			4.85
1795.				
Feb. 28.	To Lownes for nail rod 3. tons @ 105.33 =		316	
		transportn @ 16.D.	48	364.
July 1.	To Lownes nailrod	2. ton @ 105.	210	
		transprtn @ 16.D.	32	242.67
Sep. 30.	To coal for 5. ton of rod @ 18.50.			92.50
	To George & Isaac this year.			32.65
	Profit from beginning to this day			593.41
				1605.08

Date	Account	Item	Rate	Amount	£ s d		Total
1794. May 21 – Sep. 30	By amount of sale of nails during this period £49.2.11 =					163.82	
Oct. 1 1795 – Sep. 30	By amount of sale of nails during this period £432.7.7 =					1441.26	1605.08
Oct.	To Lownes for	nail rod 3. ton	@ 112. =	336.			
		transportation	@ 16.	48			384.
Nov.	To Gamble for	nailrod 1. ton	@ 133.				
		transportn	@ 8.33				141.33
1796. Apr.	To Gamble for	nailrod ½ ton	@	80.			
		transportn		4.16			84.16
May 13	To Howell for	nailrod 3 ton	@ 122.67=	368.			
		hoops ½ ton	@ 144.62=	72.31			
		transportn	@ 16.	56.			496.31
Sep. 24.	To Howell for	nailrod 3. ton	@ 138.67=	416			
		transportn	@ 16. =	48.			464.
30.	To coal for 11. ton of rod @ 18.50						203.50
	To George 2. p.c. on 2127.33.						42.54
	To Fleming & Mc.lanachan on their sales of this year				£ s d 111— 2—1	5. per cent	18.52
	To T. Carr	do.			48— 8—4		8.06
	To S. Clarke	do.			254—18—4		42.50
	transportn to Staunton						42.50
	Profit from Oct. 1. 95. to Sep. 30. 96.						199.91
							2127.33

TJ to John Henry

Dear Sir Philadelphia Dec. 31. 1797.

Mr. Tazewell has communicated to me the enquiries you have been so kind as to make relative to a passage in the Notes on Virginia, which has lately excited some newspaper publications. I feel with great sensibility the interest you take in this business and with pleasure go into explanations with one whose objects I know to be truth and justice alone. Had Mr. Martin thought proper to suggest to me that doubts might be entertained of the transaction respecting Logan, as stated in the Notes on Virginia, and to enquire on what grounds that statement was founded, I should have felt myself obliged by the enquiry, have informed him candidly of the grounds, and cordially have co-operated in every means of investigating the fact, and correcting whatsoever in it should be found to have been erroneous. But he chose to step at once into the newspapers, and in his publications there, and the letters he wrote to me, adopted a style which forbade the respect of an answer. Sensible however that no act of his could absolve me from the justice due to others, as soon as I found that the story of Logan could be doubted, I determined to enquire into it as accurately as the testimony remaining after a lapse of twenty odd years would permit, and that the result should be made known either in the first new edition which should be printed of the Notes on Virginia, or by publishing an Appendix. I thought that so far as that work had contributed to impeach the memory of Cresap, by handing on an erroneous charge, it was proper it should be made the vehicle of retribution. Not that I was at all the author of the injury. I had only concurred with thousands and thousands of others in believing a transaction on authority which merited respect. For the story of Logan is only repeated in the Notes on Virginia precisely as it had been current more than a dozen years before they were published. When Ld. Dunmore returned from the expedition against the Indians in 1774. he and his officers brought the speech of Logan, and related the circumstances of it. These were so affecting, and the speech itself so fine a morsel of eloquence that it became the theme of every conversation, in Williamsburg particularly, and generally indeed wheresoever any of the officers resided or resorted. I learned it in Williamsburg; I believe at Lord Dunmore's; and I find in my pocket book of that year (1774.) an entry of the narrative as taken from the mouth of some person whose name however is not noted, nor recollected, precisely in the words stated in the Notes on Virginia. The speech was published in the Virginia gazette of that time: (I have it myself in the volume of gazettes of that year:) and though it was the translation made by the common Interpreter, and in a style by no means elegant, yet it was so admired, that it flew thro' all the public papers of the continent, and thro' the magazines and other periodical publications of Great Britain; and those who were boys at that day will now attest that the speech of Logan used to be given them as a school-exercise for repetition. It was not till about 13. or 14. years after the newspaper publications that the Notes on Virginia were published In America. Combating in these the contumelious theory of certain European writers, whose celebrity gave currency and weight to their opinions, that our country from the combined effects of soil and climate, degenerated animal nature, in the general, and particularly the moral faculties of man, I considered the speech of Logan as an apt proof of the contrary, and used it as such: and I copied verbatim the narrative I had taken down in 1774. and the speech as it had been given us in a better translation by Ld. Dunmore. I knew nothing of the Cresaps, and could not possibly have a motive to do them an injury with design. I repeated what thousands had done before, on as good authority as we have for most of the facts we learn through life, and such as to this moment I have seen no reason to doubt. That any body questioned it, was never suspected by me till I saw the letter of Mr. Martin in the Baltimore paper. I endeavored then to recollect who among my cotemporaries, of the same circle of society, and consequently of the same recollections, might still be alive. Three and twenty years of death and dispersion had left very few. I remembered however that General Gibson was still living and knew that he had been the translater of the speech. I wrote to him immediately. He, in answer, declares to me that he was the very person sent by Ld. Dunmore to the Indian town, that after he had delivered his message there, Logan took him out to a neighboring wood, sat down with him, and rehearsing with tears the catastrophe of his family, gave him that speech for Ld. Dunmore; that he carried it to Ld. Dunmore, translated it for him, has turned to it in the Encyclopedia, as taken from the Notes on Virginia, and finds that it was his translation I had used, with only two or three verbal variations of no importance. These I suppose had arisen in the course of successive copies. I cite General Gibson's letter by memory, not having it with me; but I am sure I cite it substantially right. It establishes unquestionably that the speech of Logan is genuine: and that being established, it is Logan himself who is author of all the important facts. "Colo. Cresap, says he, in cold blood and unprovoked, murdered all the relations of Logan, not sparing even my women and children. There runs not a drop of my blood in the veins of any living creature." The person, and the fact, in all it's material circumstances, are here given by Logan himself. Genl. Gibson indeed says that the title was mistaken: that Cresap was a Captain, and not a Colonel. This was Logan's mistake. He also observes that it was on a water of the Kanhaway, and not on the Kanhaway itself that his family was killed. This is an error which has crept into the traditionary account: but surely of little moment in the moral view of the subject. The material question is Was Logan's family murdered, and by whom? That it was murdered, has not I believe been denied. That it was by one of the Cresaps, Logan affirms. This is a question which concerns the memories of Logan and Cresap; to the issue of which I am as indifferent as if I had never heard the name of either. I have begun and shall continue to enquire into the evidence, additional to Logan's, on which the fact was founded. Little indeed can now be heard of, and that little dispersed and distant. If it shall appear on enquiry that Logan has been wrong in charging Cresap with the murder of his family, I will do justice to the memory of Cresap, as far as I have contributed to the injury by believing and repeating what others had believed and repeated before me. If on the other hand, I find that Logan was right in his charge, I will vindicate as far as my suffrage may go, the truth of a Chief, whose talents and misfortunes have attached to him the respect and commiseration of the world.

I have gone, my dear Sir, into this lengthy detail to satisfy a mind, in the candour and rectitude of which I have the highest confidence. So far as you may incline to use the communication for rectifying the judgments of those who are willing to see things truly as they are, you are free to use it. But I pray that no confidence which you may repose in any one may induce you to let it go out of your hands so as to get into a newspaper. Against a contest in that field I am entirely decided. I feel extraordinary gratification indeed in addressing this letter to you, with whom shades of difference in political sentiment have not prevented the interchange of good opinion, nor cut off the friendly offices of society and good correspondence. This political tolerance is the more valued by me who consider social harmony as the first of human felicities, and the happiest moments those which are given to the effusions of the heart. Accept them sincerely, I pray you from one who has the honor to be, with sentiments of high respect and attachment Dear Sir Your most obedient & most humble servt

Th: Jefferson

William Short to TJ

Dear Sir Paris Feb. 27. 1798

. . . It is probable you will have followed in your mind the progress of the Philanthropic establishment at Sierra Leona—If you have not read, I recommend to you a work published two or three years ago in London by a Swede of the name of Wadstrom entitled an Essay on Colonization &c. & on Sierra Leona & Bulama—It gives very encouraging hopes with respect to the perfectibility of the black race—It is more than probable that the establishment at S.L. will degenerate from its first principles & become in time an establishment merely commercial, shackled by the mother country & by the succeeding proprietors in England, with exclusions monopolies &c. &c.—but in the mean time it has done & will have done infinite good, by turning the researches of Philanthropes & of Philosophers, towards the black inhabitants of Africa—Several travellers have lately explored their country beyond what has been hitherto done—& it is even affirmed that one of them has discovered a city larger than London—we are expecting the publication of his work with impatience—Abating a great deal for exageration, still it leaves enough to suppose a state of civilization far advanced—What has been already seen & authentically established by late travellers leaves no doubt of their susceptibility of all the arts of civilization & gives sanguine hopes that our posterity at least will see improved, populous & extensive nations of the black color, formed into powerful societies who will par in every respect with whites under the same circumstances—

This will insure the restoration of the rights of citizenship of those blacks who inhabit the U.S. if it be not sooner done, as it may be expected, by the gradual & beneficial operation of our own laws—& will tend to remove the aversion (wch. it is so natural shd. exist, even among the least subjected to prejudice, with those who have been [bore & bred] among blacks all of them in the state of degradation inseparable from the most mitigated degree of slavery) to the mixture of the two colors—If this be an evil, is it not the least that can take place under present circumstances? It is certainly less than keeping 700,000 people & their descendants in perpetual slavery even if it were possible—Is it not less also than having that number of free people living in the same country & separated from the rest of the community by a marked & impassable line?—Is it not less even than the expopulation of the U.S. of so great a number of their inhabitants by any possible means? The revocation of the edict of Nantes, or what may perhaps be considered as still more in point, the expulsion of the Moors from Spain during the last century, shews us how deep such wounds go & how difficult, if not impossible, to cicatrize them. It will be said that the expulsed in these cases were the most industrious artisans & manufacturers of the country—many of them undoubtedly were—but the blacks with us are the tillers of the land & I can never believe that for any people (unquestionably for us it cannot be) the loss of their manufacturers is a greater evil than that of their agriculturers—

As to the evils to be apprehended from the mixture of the two colors (& I know that the most enlightened & virtuous minds do apprehend such) the subject is certainly worthy of serious attention—Facts are certainly wanting to guide us—It is impossible yet to know, notwithstanding the long systems drawn from short experiments, what influence the climate alone will produce on the black color—If I do not mistake the blacks in our country several generations removed from their imported ancestors are sensibly less dark than the Africans themselves—some part of this may be imputed perhaps to a mixture of the whites in their production, but a part also to the climate—Suppose a black family transplanted to Sweden, may we not presume, for as yet there is no possibility of the fact, that in a sufficient number of succeeding generations, the color would disappear from the meer effect of the climate—If the climate has this tendency by however gradual degrees, we may well suppose that in time the color of our inhabitants will revert to its present state, even if the blacks should be incorporated, as we may be assured that this incorporation will take place by slow & very slow degrees, owing to the real preference that the whites will give to their own color & the deep rooted prejudices against the other—But even admitting that this mixture should change our hue & that all of our Southern inhabitants should advance to the middle ground between their present color & the black (& this is granting more than can be asked as there are every where more whites than blacks) still they would not be of a darker color than the inhabitants of some of the provinces of Spain—& I do not see that these provinces labour under any inconvenience greater than the rest of the Spaniards or that the Spaniards in general labour under any inconvenience with respect to the rest of Europe, merely on account of their color—Even in our own country there are some people darker, than the gradual mixture of the blacks can ever make us, & yet I do not know that they suffer from thence—I don't know if you ever saw, a Mrs. Randolph afterwards Mrs. Tucker,—There is no country that might not be content to have its women like her—There is no sentiment arising from the contemplation of beauty that they would not be capable of inspiring equally with those who can boast the perfect mixture of the rose & the lilly.

The next thing to be considered is, how is to be effected this great & momentous object, the transformation of 700,000 slaves into free citizens—& here I own a great many difficulties present themselves even to my contemplation & at this distance—how many more will be seen by a penetrating genius capable of diving into the bosom of futurity, & who examines the subject on the spot—The first desideratum is that such geniuses should turn their attention towards the examination of this subject, & certainly none can be more worthy to exercise the talents of the statesman, the philosopher, the philanthrope, in short all who have any regard to the interests of their country or the rights of humanity—but let them have always before their eyes this golden rule "ne soyez pas jaloux du tems"—the longer I live in the world the more I see the danger of ever losing sight of this polar star of every political mariner—the best measures on earth may become the most disastrous by this means—Let Hispaniola & what has taken place there within these last seven years be adverted to—I hope it will operate on our citizens, as well those who have the misfortune to have slaves as those who having not, might from an impatient indignation, be disposed to break at once their irons & turn them loose, without preparation for that state, on the society—they cannot fail to become beasts of prey if their numbers surpass at once the means of subsistence—To avoid all such risks (& there must come many instances in time where there will be such risks either from external or internal enemies) let the owners of slaves begin to prepare them as well as themselves for the gradual transmutation—let the legislatures of the different states adopt also some gentle operation (this I fear is more to be wished than expected from some of them)—let the enlightened & virtuous citizens, who toil for public instruction, turn the public mind towards this subject, & endeavour to demonstrate that the owners of slaves would gain in point of interest, by the change—for it is perhaps a melancholy consideration but it is not the less true, that the only way to bring men in general to desire an event is to shew that they have an interest in it—if they see their interest on one side & humanity on the other, never count on the majority for the last—see how ingenious they are to satisfy their own conscience & then to prove to others that their interest is not opposed to the general good—how many good Christians are there, who consider themselves the beloved of Christ & the invariable followers of his gospel, who with all his precepts in their mind go to Africa, wrest the mother from the infant—the husband from the wife—chain them to the whip & lash, they & their posterity for ever, nay hold this scourge in their own hand & inflict it with all the *gout* of their abominable appetites, & who do not doubt that they are violating the whole doctrine of the author of their religion—To what absurdities may not the human mind bring itself when this can be thought by them less offensive to God, than eating meat on a Friday?—

I wish the slave holders to be attacked by proofs that their interest would not suffer, because I think it the most certain way of converting them, & because I believe firmly that observation, & still more, experience, will shew this to be the case—As example will of course have more weight than precept, suppose some person of fortune & well known should attempt a plan somewhat like this—Let him ascertain what his slaves bring him of neat revenue, deduction made of taxes paid on them, food clothing &c. &c.—Let him if it be possible find a sufficient number of tenants (better if free blacks as being more convincing) & lease out a like quantity of land to them, & compare the neat rent wch. he may recieve—Or let him separate from among his slaves such as are most to be relied on for care & industry, & let him give them a certain portion of land on rent, & let him compare the neat revenue, produced by a like number of slaves—Let all the minute calculations of detail be entered into & published in the gazettes—Whatever may be the result of the first essays, time & repetition will I think infallibly shew the advantage of free, above forced, labor.

I have thought sometimes that one step wch. might be obtained towards an amelioration of the condition of our slaves, would be to assimilate them to the serfs of Europe, by attaching them to the glebe—the owners perhaps wd. not be averse to this, or at least many of them, & the slaves would thus gain an exemption from the cruel separations of father, mother, husband, wife, so often seen—& I believe also that this security of a permanent residence, would settle their minds towards improving any little lot of ground that might be given them to work for their own account, during the time allowed them—If the legislature should consider this change in the tenure of slaves as an attack on what is called property, let them, instead of a general law obliging this change, make one that shall authorize the holders of slaves to make this change & attach their own slaves to the glebe, so as to be binding on their heirs—Let them follow also the example of Spain & having each slave valued, oblige the owner to recieve that value, whenever the slave shall offer it—& further oblige them to yield to the slaves one day in the week more, or any other portion of their time, that the slaves shall have been able to purchase—It is easy to see that only the most industrious & most ripe for liberty will be emancipated in this way—Let humane societies be formed for the gradual emancipation & instruction of the blacks—let them recieve subscriptions & purchase such as appear most worthy, preferring always the females, because each individual thus manumitted stops one continual source of slavery—thus the purchasing all the female slaves at once, wch. would cost less than the same number of males, is purchasing in fact all future generations instead of one only—if any female purchased be unable to provide for her children, let them be provided for like other poor children—they can never be a charge to a young country like ours—they may be bound for a time sufficient to pay for the food of their infancy.—

Notwithstanding the immense length of this letter I should have a great deal more to say to you if I were not afraid of wearing out your patience—I therefore put to a stop to this subject for the present, & will detain you no longer . . .

W: Short

TJ to Thomas Mann Randolph

Th:J. to TMR Feb 4, 1800.

... By a letter recieved to-day also from mr Richardson I learn the death of Jupiter. he has fallen a victim to an imprudent perseverance in journeying. I was extremely against his coming to Fredsbg with me & had engaged Davy Bowles, but Jupiter was so much disturbed at this that I yielded. at the end of the second day's journey I saw how much he was worsted, & pressed him to wait at Hyde's a very excellent house till the horses should return, & I got the promise of a servant from thence. but he would not hear of it. at Fredericksburg again I engaged the tavernkeeper to take care of him till he should be quite well enough to proceed. and it seems that immediately on his arrival at home, he took another journey to my brother's where he died. I am sorry for him as well as sensible he leaves a void in my [domestic] administration which I cannot fill up.—I must get Martha or yourself to give orders for bottling the cyder in the proper season in March. there is nobody there but Ursula who unites trust & skill to do it. she may take any body she pleases to aid her. I am in hopes if any keys had been delivered to Jupiter that they have been taken care of. mr Richardson may perhaps be useful in seeing to the cyder. when I say that Ursula may have any body she pleases to help her, I mean to except John, who must have nothing to do with drink.—pray conclude with Kerr, & I will confirm what you do. my constant love to my dear Martha & the little ones, and affectionate attachment to yourself. Adieu.

TJ to Thomas Mann Randolph

Th:J. to TMR Washington Jan. 23. 1801.

... I forgot to ask the favor of you to speak to Lilly as to the treatment of the nailers. it would destroy their value in my estimation to degrade them in their own eyes by the whip. this therefore must not be resorted to but in extremities. as they will be again under my government, I would chuse they should retain the stimulus of character. after Lilly shall have compleated the clearing necessary for this year for mr Craven, I would have him go on with what will be wanting for him the next year, that being my most important object. the building of the negro houses should be done whenever mr Craven prefers it; as all the work is for him, he may arrange it. I will thank you to continue noting the day of the reciept of my letters, that I may know whether the postmaster corrects the mismanagement.—we continue as uncertain as ever as to the event of an election by the H. of R. some appearances are favorable. but they may be meant to throw us off our guard. mr Adams is entirely for their complying with the will of the people. Hamilton the same. the mercantile or paper interest also. still, the individuals who are to decide, will decide according to their own desires. the Jersey election damps them. so does the European intelligence. but their main body is still firm & compact.—my tenderest love to my dear Martha. I wrote to her the last week. kisses to all the little ones, and affectionate attachments to yourself. Adieu.

P.S. when I come home I shall lay off the canal, if Lilly's gang can undertake it. I had directed Lilly to make a dividing fence between Craven's fields at Monticello, & those I retain. the object was to give me the benefit of the latter for pasture. if I stay here, the yard will be pasture enough, and may spare, or at least delay this great & perishable work of the dividing fence. at least it may lie for further consideration.—I hope Lilly keeps the small nailers engaged so as to supply our customers in the neighborhood, so that we may not lose them during this interregnum. mr Higginbotham particularly & mr Kelly should be attended to.

Joseph Rapin to TJ

Editors' Translation

Washington this 3d of April at 4 in the afternoon

Since Your Excellency left, Edward has appeared at the house for only one half hour to eat his dinner. That was yesterday. Mr. McMunn, who came to see the house, told me that he had seen him at his house, complaining that you had given the preference to a Negro rather than to him to accompany you. I myself heard him murmuring that he would not wear similar clothing to what a Negro wears, while speaking of the livery. Captain Lewis can tell me your intention. On that subject you will remember that he is an early riser and that your office is all in order at six o'clock when you come downstairs. Captain Lewis has a young soldier for a servant, with whom he is very pleased. He will be very useful to me for washing the windows. I took down the curtains that need washing; five suites also need it. The plasterers who are going to work at Monticello will whitewash them at 5 dollars for each room.

TJ to Joseph Rapin

Sir Monticello Apr. 17. 1801.

I duly recieved your letter under cover of Capt. Lewis's. what you propose as to the arranging the apartments is very right. of Edward I know very little, as he has been but a short time in my service. it is yet to be seen therefore how far he may be fit for his present station. the negro whom he thinks so little of, is a most valuable servant. I propose to leave this place on the 25th. instant, and if health & weather permits, I shall be with you on the 28th. I shall have with me two gentlemen, travelling companions, who will possibly take beds with us. I would wish you therefore to have rooms & beds prepared for them. I hope I shall find Julien with you, and every thing ready mounted for the entertainment of company. accept assurances of my friendly attachment.

Th: Jefferson

TJ to Albert Gallatin

Th:J. to mr Gallatin Nov. 28. 1801.

Your own opinion & that of the Atty Genl. are sufficient authorities to me to approve of prosecuting in the case of the Schooner Sally. and I will candidly add that my judgment also concurs. the handcuffs & bolts are palpable testimonials of the intention of the voyage, & the concealment of them, & their omission in the statement of the cargo, strengthens the proof. the traffic too is so odious that no indulgences can be claimed.

Proclamation Offering a Reward for Murderers of a Cherokee Woman

BY THE PRESIDENT OF THE UNITED STATES OF AMERICA

A Proclamation:

Whereas information has been received that an atrocious murder was in the month of August last committed on an Indian Woman of the Cherokee Tribe in the peace and friendship of the United States, in the County of Knox in the State of Tenessee, aggravated also by the consideration that it was committed at a moment when a friendly meeting was about to be held by Commissioners of the United States with the Chiefs of the said Tribe of Indians, for the purpose of making certain arrangements favorable to the tranquility and advantage of the Frontier Settlers, as well as just and eligible to the Indians themselves; And Whereas the apprehension and punishment of the murderers and their accessaries will be an example due to justice and humanity, and every way salutary in its operation; I have therefore thought fit to issue this my proclamation hereby exhorting the citizens of the United States, and requiring all the Officers thereof, according to their respective stations, to use their utmost endeavors to apprehend and bring the principals and accessaries to the said murder to justice: and I do moreover offer a reward of one thousand dollars for each principal, and five hundred dollars for each accessary to the same before the fact, who shall be apprehended and brought to justice.

In Testimony whereof, I have caused the seal of the United States of America to be affixed to these Presents and signed the same with my hand,

Done at the City of Washington the thirtieth day of November in the year of our Lord one thousand eight hundred and one, and of the Independence of the United States of America the twenty sixth.

Th: Jefferson

TJ to White Hair and Others

My Children White hairs,
Chiefs & Warriors of the Osage nation July 12. 1804.

I recieve you with great pleasure at the seat of the govmt of the 17. United nations, and tender you a sincere welcome. I thank the Great Spirit who has inspired you with a desire to visit your new friends, & who has conducted you in safety to take us this day by the hand. the journey you have come is long, the weather has been warm & wet, & I fear you have suffered on the road, not withstanding our endeavors for your accomodation. but you have come through a land of friends, all of whom I hope have looked on you kindly, & been ready to give you every aid and comfort by the way.

You are as yet fatigued with your journey. but you are under the roof of your fathers and best friends, who will spare nothing for your refreshment and comfort. repose yourselves therefore, and recruit your health and strength, and when you are rested we will open the bottoms of our hearts more fully to one another. in the mean time we will be considering how we may best secure everlasting peace, friendship & commerce between the Osage nation, and the 17. United nations in whose name I speak to you, and take you by the hand. Th: Jefferson

TJ to John Jordan

Sir Washington Dec. 21. 05.

Being now endeavoring to purchase young & able negro men for my own works, it is exactly counter to these views to sell Brown to you as proposed in your letter. however, always willing to indulge connections seriously formed by those people where it can be done reasonably, I shall consent, however reluctantly to sell him to you. I should be glad to get such men equal to him in age, ability, & character, without any qualification to a trade, for 500. D. each, and think 100. D. in addition to this quite little enough for his trade. For 600. D. therefore, (if he desires it, & not else) I may agree to part with him, and to yield reasonable accomodation as to the times of paiment. some other work remains to be done at Monticello which could go in part. Accept my best wishes

Th: Jefferson

To a Delegation of Missouri River Tribes

My friends & children, Chiefs of the Osages, Missouris, Kansas, Ottos, Panis, Ayowas, & Sioux.

I take you by the hand of friendship and give you a hearty welcome to the seat of the govmt of the US. the journey which you have taken to visit your fathers on this side of our island is a long one, and your having undertaken it is a proof that you desired to become acquainted with us. I thank the great spirit that he has protected you through the journey and brought you safely to the residence of your friends, and I hope he will have you constantly in his safekeeping and restore you in good health to your nations and families.

My friends & children. We are descended from the old nations which live beyond the great water: but we & our forefathers have been so long here that we seem like you to have grown out of this land: we consider ourselves no longer as of the old nations beyond the great water, but as united in one family with our red brethren here. The French, the English, the Spaniards, have now agreed with us to retire from all the country which you & we hold between Canada & Mexico, and never more to return to it. and remember the words I now speak to you my children, they are never to return again. we are become as numerous as the leaves of the trees, and, tho' we do not boast, we do not fear any nation. we are now your fathers; and you shall not lose by the change. as soon as Spain had agreed to withdraw from all the waters of the Missouri & Missisipi, I felt the desire of becoming acquainted with all my red children beyond the Missipi, and of uniting them with us, as we have done those on this side of that river in the bonds of peace & friendship. I wished to learn what we could do to benefit them by furnishing them the necessaries they want in exchange for their furs & peltries. I therefore sent our beloved man Capt Lewis one of my own family, to go up the Missouri river, to get acquainted with all the

Indian nations in it's neighborhood, to take them by the hand, deliver my talks to them, and to inform us in what way we could be useful to them. some of you who are here have seen him & heard his words. you have taken him by the hand, and been friendly to him. my children I thank you for the services you rendered him, and for your attention to his words. when he returns he will tell us where we should establish factories to be convenient to you all, and what we must send to them. in establishing a trade with you, we desire to make no profit. we shall ask from you only what every thing costs us, and give you for your furs & pelts whatever we can get for them again. be assured you shall find your advantage in this change of your friends. it will take us some time to be in readiness to supply your wants, but in the mean while & till Capt. Lewis returns, the traders who have heretofore furnished you will continue to do so.

My friends & children

I have now an important advice to give you. I have already told you that you are all my children, and I wish you to live in peace [a] & friendship with one another as brethren of the same family ought to do. how much better is it for neighbors to help than to hurt one another, how much happier must it make them. if you will cease to make war on one another, if you will live in friendship with all mankind, you can employ all your time in providing food & clothing for yourselves and your families, your men will not be destroyed in war and your women & children will lie down to sleep in their cabins without fear of being surprised by their enemies & killed or carried away. your numbers will be increased, instead of diminishing, and you will live in plenty & in quiet. [b] my children, I have given this advice to all your red brethren on this side the Misipi, they are following it, they are increasing [c] in their numbers, are learning to clothe & provide for their families as we do, and you see the proofs of it in such of them as you happened to find here. my children, we are strong, we are numerous as the stars in the heavens, & we are all gun-men. yet we live in peace with all nations; and all nations esteem & honour us because we are peaceable & just. be you then, my children, peaceable & just also; take each other by the hand, and hold it fast. if ever bad men among your neighbors should do you wrong, and their nation refuse you justice, apply to the beloved man whom we shall place nearest to you; he will go to the offending nation, & endeavor to obtain right, & preserve peace. if ever bad men among yourselves injure your neighbors, be always ready to do justice. it is always honorable in those who have done wrong to acknolege & make amends for it; and it is the only way in which peace can be maintained among men. remember then my advice, my children, carry it home to your people, [d] and tell them that from the day that they have become all of the same family, from the day that we became father to them all, we wish as a true father should do, that we may all live together as one houshold, and that before they strike one another, they should come to their father and let him endeavor to make up the quarrel. My children. You are come from the other side of our great island, from where the sun sets to see your new friends at the sun rising. you have now arrived where the waters are constantly rising [e] & falling every day, but you are still distant from the sea. I very much desire that you should not stop here, but go on and see your brethren as far as the edge of the great water. I am persuaded you have so far seen that every man by the way has recieved you as his brothers, and has been ready to do you all the kindnesses in his power. you will see the same thing quite to the sea shore; and I wish you therefore to go and visit our great cities in that quarter, & to see how many friends & brothers you have here. [f] you will then have travelled a long line from West to East, and if you had time to go from North to South, from Canada to Florida, you would find it as long in that direction, & all the people as sincerely your friends. I wish you, my children to see all you can, [g] and to tell your people all you see; because I am sure the more they know of us, the more they will be our hearty friends. I invite you therefore to pay a visit to Baltimore, Philadelphia, New York, & the cities still beyond that if you should be willing to go further. we will provide carriages to convey you, & a person to go with you & to see that you want for nothing. by the time you come back, the snows will be melted on the mountains ice in the rivers broken up and you will be wishing to set out on your return home.

My children, I have long desired to see you: I have now opened my heart to you; let my words sink into your hearts & never be forgotten. if ever lying people or bad spirits should raise up any clouds between us, call to mind what I have said, & what you have seen yourselves. besure there is some lying spirits between us: let us come together as friends & explain to each other what is misrepresented or misunderstood. the clouds will fly away like the morning fog and the sun of friendship appear, & shine for ever bright & clear between us.

My children, it may happen that while you are here, occasion may arise to talk about many things which I do not now particularly mention. the Secretary at war will always be ready to talk with you: and you are to consider whatever he says as said by myself. he will also take care of you & see that you are furnished with all comforts here.

Th: Jefferson
Jan. 4: 1806

From a Delegation of Missouri River Tribes

[on or after 4 Jan. 1806]

Speech of the
Osages, Missouri, Otos, Panis, Cansas, Ayowois & Sioux Nations to the president of the U.S. & to the Secretary at War.—

My Grandfather
&
My father—

it is with an open heart that we recieve your hands, friendship streches ours in yours & unites them together

fathers

We feel entirely our happiness at this Day, since you tell us that we are wellcome in the Grand lodge of prosperity We percieve that we are numbered among your most Cherished Children.—

fathers

you observe that we have undertaken a very long journey in order to see our fathers & Brethren; it is most true: but fathers, we will tell you that we Did not look back for to measure the road, & our sight streching, to the rising sun, discovered every New day the pleasure Rising with him, as we were reflecting our daily approach, our hearts were overjoy'd, for we were soon to see our New good fathers who wish to pity us.

Fathers

there is a long While that we wish to be acquainted with our fathers & Brothers of the rising Sun & we hope that, when w'ill return back, where the sun sets, we will Dispell all the thick Clouds whose Darkness obscures the Light of the Day

Fathers

that Great Spirit who disposes of every thing, & fixes into our Bosom the ardent desire of seeing you, we thank him & we will thank him more when w'ill be at home amongst our Wives & children, for, then, our eyes Will be satisfied, our ears full with your words, & our hearts with joy. But, fathers, we have to thank our interpreters who advis'd us to strengten our hearts, & listen not to the sense of those men who wanted to prevent us from Coming to see you, alledging that we would be unwellcome & all of us should die. Our interpreters told us that our fathers were good & would pity us, that they wanted to be acquainted with their new red Children; & that we ought not to listen to the Crowing of Bad Birds

fathers

You do not Know yet your new red Children, & we see that you are as much worthy of pity as we are; flatterers Came Before you, made vast promises, but when far away, they Constitute themselves masters, decieve you & your Children Suffer.

fathers

Do pity your Children who wish to do Good & Behave well, if you lay it in their power, but, fathers trust them we Know: we Know them who love your new red Children who wish them to be happy, who hear your word, fill up our ears with it insinuate it in our hearts & spread it all over our fields; & fathers, that Spirit who took Care of us in Coming hither, here he is! he alone Can Carry your Words together with us, to our Warriors wives & Children & they all will Call you then their fathers

Fathers

We Believe that you wish to pity us & to prevent our wants by sending us supplies of goods, but look sharp & tell to your men to take not too much fur for a little of goods, should they act in that way we would not be better off than we are now with our actual traders

Fathers

We have Seen the belov'd Man, We shook hands with him & we heard the Words you put in his mouth. We wish him well, where he is, we have him in our hearts, & when he will return we believe that he will take Care of us prevent our wants & make us happy: he told us you wished us to Come to see you & our Brethren of the rising Sun: here we are: we are happy to see you & glad to hear the words of good fathers

Fathers

You tell us to be in peace & amity with Our Brethren: we wish to be so: Misunderstanding Sometimes Breaks peace & Amity, because we listen too much to those men who Live yet amongst us & who do not belong to your famely, but when we will have but your own Children with us, then it will be easy for you to maintain the peace of your red children & we will all acknowledge that we have good fathers

Fathers

Meditate What you say, you tell us that your children of this side of the mississipi hear your Word, you are Mistaken, since every day they Rise their tomahawks Over our heads, but we believe it to be Contrary to your orders & inclination, & that, before long, should they be deaf to your voice, you will chastise them

Fathers

though your forefathers were inhabiting the other side of the Big lake, we Consider you as ourselves, since, like us, you sprung out of our land, for the Same reason, we believe you Consider us to be your Children, that you pity us & wish to make us happy Should we follow your advices.—

Fathers

You Say that the french, English & Spanish nations have left the waters of the Missouri & Mississipi, We are all glad of it, & we believe that the day they will leave us the weather will be Clear, the paths Clean, & our ears will be no More affected With the disagreable Sounds of the bad Birds who wish us to relinquish the words of our Good fathers whose words we Keep in Our hearts—

Although fathers

Do not believe that the number of Our new Brethren would be able to frighten us, were we not inclined to acknowledge you for our fathers; but we wish to live like you & to be Men like you; we hope you will protect us from the wicked, you will punish them who wont hear your word, open their ears, & lead them in the good path.

Fathers

Since you wish to be acquainted with your new children of the other Side of the mississipi, you may Believe that they have the same desire, but if we Contempt your word as they do on this side of that River you will soon be Compell'd to Chastise the wicked, but, fathers, we shall not do as they do, for we wish to be numbered among your best Children, & we will try only to punish the wicked.

Fathers

You say that you are as numerous as the stars in the Skies, & as strong as numerous. so much the better, fathers, tho', if you are so, we will see you ere long punishing all the wicked Red skins that you'll find amongst us, & you may tell to your white Children on our lands, to follow your orders, & to do not as they please, for they do not Keep your word. Our Brothers who Came here before told us you had ordered good things to be done & sent to our villages, but we have seen nothing, & your waged Men think that truth will not reach your ears, but we are Conscious that we must speak the truth, truth must be spoken to the ears of our fathers, & our fathers must open their ears to truth to get in.

Fathers—

You tell us to Complain to the beloved Man, should any one Commit injury & decline Compensation, but you Know fathers that the beloved man is gone far away, that he Can not do the justice which you want him to do; while he is absent we do better to Complain to his fathers, & when he will arrive we will Complain to him, then he will have justice done to the injuried man & if he loves his fathers he will chastise the one who Broke the peace which our good fathers told us to make together & to maintain.

Fathers

We hear your Word, we will Carry it into our villages, & spread it all over our fields, we will tell to our warriors, wives & Children that, ever since you became the fathers of all the red skins, like good fathers, you wish us to live like Children of but one famely who have but one father, & that before we Should go at war we have to take the advice of our good fathers & then we shall know what these latter will tell us.

Fathers

Our hearts are good, though we are powerfull & strong, & we Know how to fight, we do not wish to fight but shut the mouth of your Children who Speak war, Stop the arm of those who rise the tomahawk over our heads & Crush those who Strike first, then we will Confess that we have good fathers who wish to make their red Children happy & peace maintained among them. for when we are at peace we hunt freely, our wives & Children Do not Stand in want, we smoke & sleep easy—

Fathers

We left the place where the Sun sets in order to see & hear you. fathers we see & hear you & we are happy, the skies are Clear where our fathers breathe & we wish it May be so where the sun Sets we wish our wives & children may be joy full when they think that we breathe where our fathers Breathe, for we are wellcome to Breathe with you, fathers.

fathers

pity your own new Children, they wish to follow your advice, tell them what you wish them to do, they will do any thing that you wish them to do, they do not Belong any more to themselves but they are your own property, dispose of them as you please—

Fathers

as you Spoke that we had brethren inhabiting the shores of the big Lake & that you offered us to visit them, we do wish to be acquainted with them, to shake hands with them & to tell them that we are their Brothers & if they are good Children we will tell them that we are so, for you Know fathers we acknoledge you for our fathers

Fathers

after shaking hands with all our new Brothers, being acquainted with them all, then we will tell to our warriors, our wives, our Children how many things we have Seen, they all will listen to Our sayings, they will gather around us, hear the words of their New fathers & Brethren, love them all & wonder at all things; yes fathers, we will speak the truth, you Know the truth must Come out of the mouth of a father—

Fathers

We hope the more we will See Our new Brethren the more we will love them for we hope they will wellcome us & receive us as their Brethren.

Fathers

We Wish to have this, your Warrior {major Rodger} for our leader in the journey that we will undertake to visit our Brethren: he will take good Care of us; for he does love us, he will hold the weather Clear, Clean & smooth the paths of his red Brethren. Our Brother {Captn Stoddert} is a good man, but he is not acquainted with his Brethren the red Skins, he can not take good Care of them for he is always Sick & leaves them to the Care of Careless people who are not acquainted with your new Children the red Skins.—

Fathers

You Say that, when we will Come back the ice will be broken, the Snow Melted & then we will return into our Villages:—yes, fathers, when we will see our Warriors, when we will see our Wives, when we will See our Children, our hearts will be overjoy'd, their hearts will be overjoyed they will hear the word you put in our mouth, we will Carry it to them Deeply engraved in our hearts. our Warriors will bury the tomahawk, the wicked will be good, when ever they will hear the word of their fathers & Know them to be good to all the red Skins.

Fathers

We will Keep your Word in our Bosom; the Stinking Cloud may Rise, it will melt away, when we will remember the Word of our fathers; the bad birds may fly over our heads, & Crow mischief, their flesh will be poor, their voice weak, they will hush & fly away when hearing the word of our fathers; we will be happy with your word, fathers, & never part with it.

Fathers

it is most true, there is some people amongst us, who wish us to be deaf to your word, they have a Smooth lying tongue but they Can't be your Children, because a Child allways says the word of his father, they are unhappy for we will not listen to them, your sun will give them light, & shine heretofore over all your Children.

Grand father {the president}

you told us to go Now & then to See our father the great chief of War {the secretary at war}, that he would Communicate your word to us, we have visited him & have been wellcome. we hope that he does, love your new Children Worthy of pity, & Consider us as Your white Children.

fathers

We give you again the hand of freindship.

Chiefe Osage	Sioux
Ta gui Sagai	Waske ygnes
Le vent	pettis plas
Cansasa	Panis
Va Kan chias	Ta chre Varres
Se Lhuis qui fonse	La loupe
Otos	Ayovoy
mit chi oquippa	Verri grand
Se Lhuis qui ren contre	Se Luis qui dailibai
Lourse blanc	

TJ to Henry Dearborn

Dear Sir Jan. 6. 1806.

Colo. Hawkins has put into my hands the papers respecting the claim of the Creek nation on behalf of Emantlau Thlucco, from whom two horses have been stolen, within the Indian limits, by Harries & Allen, citizens of the US. the former of whom has fled out of the US. leaving no property, & the other is insolvent. he communicated to me also the Attorney General's opinion on the case. this case being of importance as a precedent, I have considered it maturely under the law, the treaty, and the principles which prevail between independant nations: the Creeks being in law, as well as in fact, an independant nation.

The opinion of the Atty Genl. is unquestionable, considering the case as it relates to the offending individuals. the laws have reserved to all our citizens charged within our jurisdiction with any crime or misdemeanor, wheresoever committed, a right of being tried by a jury, before a court of competent authority, before they can be punished. whether prosecuted capitally or for the penalty of double value, the sentence of a court could alone subject them to either. accordingly the 15th. section of the act of Congress provides expressly how & where the offender may be tried, convicted & punished; & evidently confines it's views to the proceedings against the citizen solely.

But when death, flight, insolvency, or other accident puts the offender out of the way, it then becomes a question between nation & nation, between whom the municipal laws of evidence of either can have no bearing on the other. the same law therefore, in it's 4th. section, only declares that *if the offender be unable to pay* for the property he has taken from an Indian, the US. shall pay, without saying where the fact shall be tried, or on what evidence: and, in it's 14th. section, enacts that if an Indian shall take property within our limits, the superintendant being furnished *with the necessary documents & proofs*, shall demand satisfaction from the Indian nation, without specifying that these must be such documents & proofs as would be required by our municipal law, to which the Indian is not at all subject. the proofs then of course are to be such as are usually resorted to between nation & nation, that is to say, public documents, depositions, affidavits, certificates, letters, parol evidence, or even common report. all of these are freely adduced between nations, each of them is weighed, in the scales of reason & experience, & according to the aggregate impression they make on the common sense of mankind, they are estimated in determining the belief or disbelief of the fact. neither party thinks of calling the other to a trial of the fact in a court of it's own, where it would be both party & judge. the constitutional organs for foreign relations of the two nations compose jointly the competent tribunal.

The instruction therefore given originally by a former Executive to the Agent for Indian affairs, appears to have been well weighed, when it directs him to ascertain, *by the best evidence in his power*, the value of the property taken: and of course authorises him to recieve, as well the testimony of red men, given in what they deem the most solemn manner, as such other evidence as can be obtained, and may be of any weight in the common judgment of mankind towards producing a belief or disbelief of the fact in question. this is the only practical construction which can be given of the act of Congress, which never could be carried into execution in this part, if a strict conformity with our municipal laws were requisite; because such evidence as is required by our courts of justice between citizen & citizen, could never be had in the cases now under consideration. the law therefore wisely & justly avoids specifying the evidence, & leaves the fact to be settled agreeably to the usage of nations. here then the Creeks affirm that property has been taken from one of their nation, that this cannot be recovered in our courts of justice by the individual injured, because one offender is dead, the other fled, and no property of either existing; & the law says, *if the offender is unable*, paiment *shall be* made out of the Treasury of the US. the Superintendant therefore according to his instructions is to "ascertain the facts affirmed by the Creeks, *by the best evidence in his power*, and make report of the same & of the case to the department of war that justice may be done." I do not see any cause for changing the course of proceeding so established; but on the contrary I believe it to be right & lawful, & that it ought to be pursued in this instance.

Th: Jefferson
Jan. 5. 1806.

To a Delegation of the Sacs, Foxes, and Potawatomis

[6 Jan. 1806]

My Friends and Children, Chiefs of Foxes, Sacs and Pautewatamies—

We have long known each other by hearsay, our people have had some intercourse together, but this is the first time that our friends the Sacs and Foxes have visited us at the Seat of Government. I take you all by the hand of friendship, and give you a hearty welcome. I thank the Great Spirit who has inspired you with a desire to come and see us, and who has protected you through the journey and brought you safely to the residence of your friends;—and I hope he will have you constantly in his safe keeping and restore you in good health to your Nations & families.—

My Friends and Children, born in the same land, and approaching every day nearer and nearer one another as neighbours, we should live together as one family, in peace and friendship, doing to each other all the good we can. Our nation is numerous and strong; but we wish to be just to all: and particularly to be kind and useful to all our red children. We propose as fast as we can do it, to establish factories among them to supply them with the necessaries they want; and to receive their furs and peltries in exchange. We want no profit in this business: We shall ask from them only what everything costs us, and give for their furs & peltries whatever we can get for them again. I am persuaded that in doing this we can make your situation better than it is; and we have no other motive for doing it.—

My Friends and Children, I am endeavoring to persuade all the nations of red men to live in peace & friendship with one another as brethren of the same family ought to do.—How much better is it for neighbours to help than to hurt one another—How much happier must it make them. If you will cease to make war on one another, if you will live in friendship with all mankind, you can employ all your time in providing food and clothing for yourselves and your families, your men will not be destroyed in War, & your women & children will lie down to sleep in their cabins, without fear of being surprised by their enemies and killed or carried away.—Your numbers will be increased instead of diminishing, and you will live in plenty and in quiet.

Look at your brethren in the South—They have been for some time following my advice, they have left off Wars, they are increasing in their numbers, and learning to clothe and provide for their families as we do, and you see the proofs of it in such of them as you happened to find here:

My Children, we are strong, we are numerous as the Stars in the Heavens, and we are all gun men, yet we live in peace and friendship with all Nations and all nations esteem and honor us because we are peaceable and just. Be you then peaceable & just also, take each other by the hand and hold it fast. If ever bad men among your neighbours should do you wrong and their Nation refuse you justice, apply to the beloved man whom we shall place nearest to you; he will go to the offending Nation and endeavour to obtain right & preserve peace.—If ever bad men among yourselves injure your neighbours, be always ready to do justice. It is always honorable in those who have done wrong to acknowledge and make amends for it; and it is the only way in which peace can be maintained among men. Remember then my advice, my Children, carry it home to your people, and tell them that we wish as a true father should do, that we may all live together as one household, and that before they strike one another, they should come to their father and let him endeavour to make up the quarrel.

My Children, you have come a long journey to see us.—You have now reached to where the waters are constantly rising and falling every day, but you are still distant from the sea. I very much desire that you should not stop here, but go on and see your brethren as far as the edge of the great Water.—I am persuaded you have so far seen that every man by the way has received you as his brothers, and has been ready to do you all the kindnesses in his power.—You will see the same thing quite to the sea shore; And I wish you therefore to go and visit our Great Cities in that quarter, and see how many friends and brothers you have here.—I wish you to see all you can and to tell your people all you see; because I am sure the more they know of us, the more they will be our hearty friends.—I invite you therefore to pay a visit to Baltimore, Philadelphia, New York and the cities still beyond that if you should be willing to go further. We will provide carriages to convey you, and a person to go with you and to see that you want for nothing; by the time you come back the snows on the mountains will be melted, and the Ice in the rivers broken up, and you will be wishing to set out on your return home.—

My Children, I have long desired to see you. I have now opened my heart to you—let my words sink into your hearts and never be forgotten; If ever lying people or bad spirits should raise up clouds between us, call to mind what I have said, and what you have seen yourselves. Besure there are some lying spirits between us: let us come together as friends, and explain to each other what is misrepresented or misunderstood, the clouds will fly away like the morning Fog, & the Sun of friendship appear and shine forever bright & clear between us.—

My Childen, it may happen that while you are here, occasion may arise to talk about many things, which I do not now particularly mention. The Secretary at War will always be ready to talk with you & you are to consider whatever he says as said by myself—He will also take care of you & see that you are furnished with all comfort here.— January—

George Wythe: Will and Three Codicils

Contemplating that event, which one in the second year of his sixteenth lustrum may suppose to be fast approaching, at this time, the twentieth day of April in the third year of the nineteenth centurie since the Christian epoch, when such is my health of bodie that vivere amem, and yet, such my disposition of mind that, convinced of this truth, what supreme wisdom destinateth is best, obeam libens, i, George Wythe of the citie of Richmond, declare what is herein after written to be my testament, probablie the last: Appointing my friendlie neighbour William Duval executor, and desiring him to accept fifty pounds for his trouble in performing that office over a commission upon his disbursements and receipts inclusive, i devise to him the houses and ground in Richmond, which i bought of William Nelson, and my stock in the funds, in trust, with the rents of one and interest of the other to support my freed woman Lydia Brodnax, and my freed man Benjamin, and freed boy Michael Brown, during the lives of the two former, and after their deaths in trust to the use of the said Michael Brown; and all the other estate to which i am and shall at the time of my death be entitled i devise to George Wythe Sweney the grandson of my sister.

George Wythe SS

FIRST CODICIL (JANUARY 19, 1806)

I, who have here under written my name, this nineteenth day of January in the sixth year of the before mentioned centurie, revoke so much of the preceding devise to George Wythe Sweney as is inconsistent with what followeth. The residuarie estate devised to him is hereby charged with debts and demands. I give my books and small philosophical apparatus to Thomas Jefferson President of the United States of America: a legacie considered abstractlie; perhaps not deserving a place in his museum, but, estimated by my good will to him, the most valuable to him of anything which I have power to bestow. My stock in the funds before mentioned hath been changed into stock in the Bank of Virginia. I devise the latter to the same uses except as to Ben who is dead, as those to which the former was devoted. To the said Thomas Jefferson's patronage i recommend the freed boy Michael Brown in my Testament named, for whose maintenance, education or other benefit, as the said Thomas Jefferson shall direct, i will the said bank stock or the value thereof, if it be changed again to be disponed. And now

Good Lord most mercifull, let penitence
Sincere to me restore lost innocence;
In wrath my grievous sins remember not;
My secret faults out of thy record blot,
That after deaths sleep, when i shall awake
Of pure beatitude i may partake

George Wythe SS

ὃς
φιλος δ' ην ανθρωποισι;
Παντας γαρ φιλεεσκεν.

SECOND CODICIL (FEBRUARY 24, 1806)

I will that Michael Brown have no more than one half my Bank Stock, and George Wythe Sweney, have the other immediatelie.

I give to my friend Thomas Jefferson my silver cups and gold-headed cane, and to my friend William Duval my silver ladle and table and teaspoons. *If* Michael die before his full age, i give what is devised to him to George Wythe Sweney. I give to Lydia Brodnax my fuel: This is to be part of my will and as it were written of the parchment inclosed with my name in two places.

24 of February 1806.
G. Wythe SS

THIRD CODICIL (JUNE 1, 1806)

In the name of God Amen!

I, George Wythe, of the city of Richmond, having heretofore made my last will on the 20th day of April, in the third year of the nineteenth centurie since the Christian Epoch, and a codicil thereto on the 19th day of January in the sixth year of the aforesaid centurie and another codicil on the 24th day of February 1806—do ordain and constitute the following to be a third codicil to my said will;

hereby revoking the said will and codicils in all the devises and legacies in them or either of them contained, relating to, or in any manner concerning George Wythe Sweney, the grandson of my sister; but I confirm the said will and codicils in all other parts except as to the devise and bequest to Michael Brown, in the said will mentioned, who, I am told, died this morning, and therefore they are void. And I do hereby devise and bequeath all the estate which I have devised or bequeathed to the said George Wythe Sweney or for his use in the said will or codicils and all the interest and estate, which I have therein devised or bequeathed in trust for, or to the use of the said Michael Brown, to the brothers and sisters of the said George Wythe Sweney, the grand children of my said sister to be equally divided among them share and share alike. In testimony whereof I have hereunto subscribed my name and affixed my seal, this first day of June in the year 1806.

G. Wythe Seal
Signed, sealed, published
and declared by the said
George Wythe the testator,
as and for his last will and
testament in our presence;
and at his desire we have
hereunto subscribed our
names as witnesses in his
presence and in the
presence of each other.
Edm: Randolph
Wm. Price
Samuel Grenhow
Saml. McCraw

Will Proved (June 11, 1806)

Virginia, to wit:

At a General Court held at the Capitol in Richmond the eleventh day of June 1806.

This Will was this day produced in Court, and there being no subscribing witnesses thereto Edmund Randolph and Peter Tinsley Gent. were sworn, and deposed that they are well acquainted with the hand writing of the testator and verily believe the said Will and the two codicils thereto annexed,—bearing date one on the nineteenth day of January 1806, the other on the twenty fourth day of February 1806, and the name "George Wythe" to said Will, and each of said codicils subscribed, were wholly written by the testators own hand—and another codicil to said Will annexed was proved by the oaths of Edmund Randolph, William Price and Samuel McCraw witnesses thereto—Whereupon the said Will and codicils were ordered to be recorded. And on the motion of William Duval, the executor therein named, who made oath, and together with William Price, Register, his security entered into and acknowledged bond, in the penalty of five thousand dollars, conditioned as the law directs—Certificate was granted him for obtaining a probate of the said Will in due form.

Teste Wilson Allen. C: Civc:
A copy
Teste Wilson Allen. C: gl.

William DuVal to TJ

Worthy Sir, Richmond June 4th. 1806

Geo W. Sweeny who lived with Mr Wythe was committed to Goal on the 27th. of May last for forging Six Checks on the Bank of Virginia on the 25th of May Mr Wythe was taken with a Cholora Morbus on the 26th & 27 all the Rest of the Family were seized with the same violent disorder on the 27 We had no idea that Sweeny had poisoned the whole Family—On Sunday Morning June the first last Michael the Mulatto Boy Died—Yellow Arsenac was found in Sweeny's Room & many other strong Circumstances concured to in duce a beleive he had poisoned the whole Family—As a Magistrate I requested four eminent Physicians to open the body of the Boy—They did so, from the Inflamation on the Stomach & Bowels they said that it was the kind of Inflamation produced by Poison—Our Wathy Friend is still alive—he has suffered greatly. On What sunday Evening, he told me he never suffered more in his Life—that in the Morning he attended to his Official Duties, the Chancery Court being in Session, that he ate his Breakfast as usual, that about Nine O'Clock in the Morning he was attacked in the most violent Manner. & had rose from his Bed, Forty Times, to evacute the Feces—I had Doctrs. McClurg Currie & McCan to attend him—They pronounce his Death to be certain in a day or two—They say that his Constitution was remarkably Strong for a person of his Age—Thus by the hands of a Youth to whom he was kinder than a Father, is about to be taken from us the most virtuous and illustrious of our Citizens—one among the best of Men to whom even Death, cant terrify, or alarm.

I am Yr mo. Obt. Servt Wm. DuVal

William DuVal to TJ

Sir Richmond June 8th. 1806

Our venerable great and pious Friend departed His Life about half an Hour after Nine of the Clock this Morning. Doctrs. Foushee Carrie Grunhow McClurg & McCan opened his Chest & Bowels, there was considerable inflamation in the Stomach. It is strongly suspected that he & Michael Brown were poisoned with Yellow Arsenic by Geo W. Sweeny.—On Thursday he said I am murdered but mentioned no name—The day before Yesterday he said Let me die righteous—he during his severe complaint displayed uncommon patience & Fortitude—He called on the Lord Jesus Christ to have mercy on him—

The Governour & Council have desired that his Body shall be conveyed to the Capitol. Tomorrow at four O'Clock in the Afternoon his Funeral Oration will be pronounced by Mr Wm. Montford who lived with Mr Wythe formerly, and is a Member of our Council of State. When Mr Wythe's will shall be proven, I shall enclose you a Copy of the Will with the Codecils. I believe he enclosed to you a Copy of it.

I am, with great Respect Yr obt. Servt

Wm DuVal

TJ to William DuVal

Sir Washington June 14. 06.

Your letters of the 4th. and 8th. inst. have been duly recieved, the last announcing the death of the venerable mr Wythe, than whom a purer character has never lived. his advanced years had left us little hope of retaining him much longer, and had his end been brought on by the ordinary decays of time & nature, altho' always a subject of regret, it would not have been aggravated by the horror of his falling by the hand of a parricide. such an instance of depravity has been hitherto known to us only in the fables of the poets. I thank you for the attention you have been so kind as to shew in communicating to me the incidents of a case so interesting to my affections. he was my antient master, my earliest & best friend; and to him I am indebted for first impressions which have had the most salutary influence on the course of my life. I had reserved with fondness, for the day of my retirement, the hope of inducing him to pass much of his time with me. it would have been a great pleasure to recollect with him first opinions on the new state of things which arose soon after my acquaintance with him; to pass in review the long period which has elapsed since that time, and to see how far those opinions had been affected by experience & reflection, or confirmed and acted on with self-approbation. but this may yet be the enjoiment of another state of being. You seem to suppose mr Wythe had inclosed to me a copy of his will. but this was not the case. I hope he had time to alter it's dispositions as to him who has brought it prematurely into force. Accept my salutations & assurances of esteem & respect. Th: Jefferson

TJ to William DuVal

Dear Sir Washington June 19. 06.

I have this moment recieved by post the paper directed to me in the handwriting of my best & most revered departed friend, mr Wythe, & superscribed by yourself as found among his papers. it covers his will in his own handwriting, dated Apr. 20. 1803. with a codicil of Jan. 19. 1806. with a label indorsed "Testament of G. Wythe to be published when he shall cease to breathe, if not by him required before" and making yourself his executor. is this a duplicate, of which another copy is with you? or is it the sole original? if the latter, it shall be forwarded for publication & proof by the first safe conveyance, & in the mean time a copy shall be furnished you. he recommends in it to my patronage "the freed boy Michael Brown." is this the boy who is said to have died a few days before mr Wythe, or is he still living, & in this case will you be so good as to give me such information of him as may enable me to judge how I may best fulfill the wishes of my friend. Accept my friendly salutations & assurances of esteem & respect. Th: Jefferson

TJ to William DuVal

Dear Sir Washington June 22. 06.

Your's of the 19th. is recieved & anticipates the answers to mine of the same date, respecting the will of our deceased friend, and the freed boy Michael Brown. I sincerely regret the loss of the latter not only for the affliction it must have cost mr Wythe in his last moments, but also as it has deprived me of an object for attentions which would have gratified me unceasingly with the constant recollection and execution of the wishes of my friend. does there exist a portrait of mr Wythe? I fear not. if there be one I presume it must be with some member of the family of Majr. Taliaferro his father in law.

Mr. Jefferson of Richmond will recieve from you the bequests of my venerable friend, & take off of your hands the trouble & expence of packing Etc. I salute you with esteem & respect

Th: Jefferson

TJ to William DuVal

Dear Sir Washington July 17. 06.

Your favor of the 12th. was recieved yesterday. I infer from it's tenor that the seal, key, & perhaps the Watch itself of mr Wythe are to be disposed of. if so, I will take them with desire, either at the appraised prices stated by you, or any greater prices at which they shall be estimated by any persons of skill whom you may chuse to consult. mr [George] Jefferson, has I expect by this time funds of mine in hand, out of which he will pay for these articles on sight of this letter. I infer from a former letter that the portrait of mr Wythe was the property of Lydia Broadnax, or, if not, doubtless it would be desired by some of his relations. I ask only therefore to borrow it that I may get it copied by mr Peale & the original shall be safely returned. Accept my salutations and assurances of esteem & respect.

Th: Jefferson

William DuVal to TJ

Sir Richmond November 21st. 1806

I have a profile of the venerable George Wythe taken by Mr W. Bache in 1804 by an Instrument he calls by the name of his Patent Physiognotrace which profile much resembles that great and good Man, & Mr E Deane, I have written to, who is a man of some eminence as a Portrait Limner to take a Copy thereof,—Both of which I will leave with Mr George Jefferson, that you may take either of them— The profile you have, will shew his Appearance at that period of his Life, & the one I have, will exhibit a strong likeness a few Years before his untimely Death—

I was at the Sweet Springs when your Letter of the 17 July was recieved here—The portrait of Mr Wythe which you desired was inventoried and accounted for at the appraised value

If you prefered the Original Lyddia would be contented with a profile Copy—I know from what Mr Wythe often said, that you were dearer to him than any Relation he had—that his attachment arose from that impulse that unite great Minds, the sincere Love of Virtue—

May providence long preserve you to be a Blessing to our Country and an Example to all Nations

I am with sincere Respect Yr obedient Servt

William DuVal

TJ to William DuVal

Dear Sir — Washington Dec. 4. 06.

Your favor of Nov. 21. has been duly recieved and I thank you for the offer of the profile of mr Wythe, every trace of whom will be dear to me. if you will be so good as to desire mr [George] Jefferson to forward me either the original or the copy, as you please, it will be recieved with equal thankfulness. it should be rolled on a stick, & not folded. the original of the other profile, after taking a copy, I had packed in a box addressed to yourself that it might be returned to Lydia [Broadnax] with my thanks for the opportunity of copying it. in the same box I put 2. folio volumes of mr Wythe's accounts which had come by mistake with his books. the box I directed to be forwarded to you. Accept my friendly salutations & assurances of great respect. Th: Jefferson

Lydia Broadnax to TJ

Sir, — Richmond 9 April 1807.

I beg leave to trouble you with these lines, hoping you will lay such favorable constructions as the nature of my distressed situation shall appear & at present require.

You must know Sir, that since the death of my dear old Master (Judge Wythe) I have, already labored under many tedious difficulties, and what is more unfortunate my eyesight has almost failed me, I believe it is owing to the dreadful complaint the whole family was afflicted with at the decease of my poor Master—supposed to be the effect of poison.—It is true I have a tolerable & comfortable house to live in, but being almost intirely deprived of my eyesight, together with old age and infirmness of health I find it extremely difficult in procuring merely the daily necessaries of life—and without some assistance I am fearful I shall sink under the burden. This being my situation I am compelled to resort to this crisis from the old and intimate acquaintance, and Knowing your benevolence do now appeal to you for some charitable aid, which I have no doubt your generous hands will not refuse when considering my embarrassed circumstances—and be well assured that nothing but this, and this alone sires me with fortitude to make my supplications Known to you. If this should meet your approbation—and such charity as you shall think proper to bestow to me, you will please inclose in a letter directed to me by the Mail to [me] at this City—and the favor will ever be remembered by Your Obt. & humble Servant

Lydia Broadnax

TJ to George Jefferson

Dear Sir Monticello Apr. 18. 07.

I arrived here on the 11th. and found here your two favors of Mar. 24. & 31. & have since recieved that of the 14th. inst. I am satisfied with the sale of my tobo. & will thank you in your first letter for information of the weight as Griffin has failed to communicate it to me; as also whether he informed you of his proportion of it, and gave any directions about that. the thousand Dollars, first paiment, are to be paid to mr Tazewell according to former advice. I have recieved a letter from Lydia Broadnax, the freed woman of my deceased friend mr Wythe, stating that she is in considerable embarrasment for the daily necessaries of life, & asking some charity. I cannot from hence make any remittance, but will thank you to inform her that you are authorised to pay her 50. D. out of the monies you are to recieve for me. I must trouble you to send me by the stage which leaves Richmd. first after your reciept of this 4. gross of corks, as the cyder you are sending from mr Cocke cannot be bottled till I recieve them, and the season is nearly over for bottling—a keg of cranberries by the first boats would be very acceptable. I wonder much that my groceries &c which left Alexandria Mar. 27. had not arrived at Richmond at the date of your last. we are much in want of them. I salute you with cordial affection

Th: Jefferson

Sixth Annual Message to Congress

DECEMBER 2, 1806

To the Senate & House of Representatives of the United States of America in Congress Assembled.—

. . . We continue to receive proofs of the growing attachment of our Indian neighbors, & of their disposition to place all their interests under the patronage of the United States. These dispositions are inspired by their confidence in our justice, & in the sincere concern we feel for their welfare. And as long as we discharge these high & honorable functions with the integrity & good faith, which alone can entitle us to their continuance, we may expect to reap the just reward in their peace & friendship—

The expedition of Messrs. Lewis & Clarke, for exploring the river Missouri, & the best communication from that to the Pacific Ocean, has had all the success which could have been expected. They have traced the Missouri nearly to it's source, descended the Columbia to the Pacific Ocean, ascertained with accuracy the geography of that interesting communication across our continent, learnt the Character of the Country, of it's commerce & Inhabitants, & it is but justice to say that Messrs. Lewis & Clarke, and their brave Companions, have by this arduous service, deserved well of their Country.

The attempt to explore the Red river, under the direction of Mr. Freeman, though conducted with a zeal & prudence meriting entire approbation, has not been equally successful. After proceeding up it about six hundred miles, nearly as far as the French settlements had extended while the country was in their possession, our geographers were obliged to return without completing their work.

Very useful additions have also been made to our knowledge of the Missisipi, by Lieutt. Pike, who has ascended to it's source, and whose journal & map, giving the details of the journey, will shortly be ready for communication to both Houses of Congress. Those of Messrs. Lewis, Clarke, & Freeman will require further time to be digested & prepared. These important surveys, in addition to those before possessed, furnish materials for commencing an accurate map of the Missisipi & it's western waters. Some principal Rivers, however, remain still to be explored, towards which the Authorisation of Congress, by moderate Appropriations, will be requisite.

I congratulate you, fellow Citizens, on the approach of the period at which you may interpose your authority Constitutionally, to withdraw the citizens of the United States from all further participation in those violations of human rights, which have been so long continued on the unoffending Inhabitants of Africa, & which the morality, the reputation, & the best interests of our country have long been eager to proscribe. Although no law you may pass can take prohibitory effect till the first day of the year one thousand eight hundred & eight, yet the intervening period is not too long to prevent, by timely notice, expeditions which cannot be completed before that day.

TJ to Kitchao-Geboway

My son
Kitchao-geboway — Washington Feb. 27. 1808.

I have recieved the speech which you sent me through Genl. Gansevoort from Albany on the 13th. of this month, and now return you my answer. it would have given me great pleasure to have been able to converse with & understand you when you visited me at Washington; but the want of an interpreter rendered that impossible.

My son, tell your nation, the Chippeways, that I take them by the hand, and consider them as a part of the great family of the United States, which extends to the great lakes and the lake of the Woods, Northwardly, and from the rising to the setting sun; that the United States wish to live in peace with them, to consider them as a part of themselves, to establish a commerce with them, as advantageous to the Chippeways as they can make it, and in all cases to render them every service in our power. we shall never ask them to enter into our quarrels, nor to spill their blood in fighting our enemies. My son, in visiting this quarter of the United States, you have seen a part of our country, and some of our people from East to West. if you had travelled also from North to South, you would have seen it the same. you see that we are as numerous as the leaves of the trees, that we are strong enough to fight our own battles, & too strong to fear any enemy. when therefore we wish you to live in peace with all people, red and white, we wish it because it is for your good, and because it is our desire that your women & children shall live in safety not fearing the tomahawk of any enemy, that they may learn to raise food enough to support their families, and that your nation may multiply & be strong. if any white men advise you to go to war for them, it is a proof they are too weak to defend themselves, that they are in truth your enemies, wishing to sacrifice you to save themselves: and when they shall be driven away, my son, what is to become of the red men who may join in their battles. take the advice then of a father, and meddle not in the quarrels of the white people, should any war take place between them; but stay at home in peace, taking care of your wives & children. in that case, not a hair of your heads shall be touched. never will we do you an injury unprovoked, or disturb you in your towns or lands by any violence.

My son, I confirm every thing which your father, Governor Hull, said to you at Detroit on my part: and in all your difficulties and dangers, apply to him. & take his advice. if some of your principal chiefs will pay me a visit at Washington, I shall be very happy to recieve them, to smoke the pipe of friendship with them, to take them by the hands, and never to let go their friendship. they shall see that I want nothing from them but their good will, and to do them all the good in my power.

My son, the Secretary at War will comply with your request in giving you a chief's coat with epaulettes, & a stand of the colours of the United States, to plant in your town, to let all the world see that you are a part of the family of the United States.

My son, I wish you a pleasant journey, and a safe return to your family & friends. Th: Jefferson

TJ to Cherokee Nation

My Children,
Chiefs of the Upper Cherokees. May 4. 1808.

I am glad to see you at the seat of Government, to take you by the hand, and to assure you in person of the friendship of the U.S. towards all their red Children, & of their desires to extend, to them all, their protection & good Offices. the journey you have come is a long one, & the object expressed in our conference of the other day is important. I have listened to it with attention & given it the Consideration it deserves. You complain that you do not receive your just proportion of the Annuities we pay your Nation; that the Chiefs of the lower Town's take for them more than their share. My Children, this distribution is made by the Authority of the Cherokee Nation, & according to their own rules over which we have no controul. We do our duty in delivering the Annuities to the head men of the Nation and we pretend to no Authority over them, to no right of directing how they are to be distributed. but We will instruct our Agent Colo. Meigs to exhort the Chiefs to do justice to all the parts of their Nation in the distribution of these Annuities & to endeavor that every town shall have it's due share. We would willingly pay these Annuities in money which Could be more equally divided, if the Nation would prefer that, and if we can be assured that the money will not be laid out in strong drink instead of necessaries for your wives & children. We wish to do whatever will best secure your people from suffering for want of clothes or food. it is these wants which bring sickness & death into your families & prevent you from multiplying as we do. In answer to your question relating to the lands we have purchased from your Nation at different times, I inform you that the payments have for the most part been made in money, which has been left, as the Annuities are, to the discharge of your debts & to be distributed According to the rules of the Nation.

You propose My Children, that your Nation shall be divided into two and that your part the Upper Cherokees, shall be separated from the lower by a fixed boundary, shall be placed under the Government of the U.S. become citizens thereof, and be ruled by our laws; in fine, to be our brothers instead of our children. My Children I shall rejoice to See the day when the red men our neighbors become truly one people with us, enjoying all the rights and previleges we do, & living in peace & plenty as we do without any one to make them afraid, to injure their persons, or to take their property without being punished for it according to fixed laws. but are you prepared for this? have you the resolution to leave off hunting for your living, to lay off a farm for each family to itself, to live by industry, the men working that farm with their hands, raising stock or learning trades as we do, & the women spinning & weaving Clothes for their Husbands & Children? all this is necessary before our laws can suit you or be of any use to you. however let your people take this matter into Consideration. if they think themselves prepared for becoming Citizens of the U.S. for living in Subjection to laws and under their protection as we do, let them consult the lower towns, come with them to an agreement of Separation by a fixed boundary, & send to this place a few of the Chiefs they have most confidence in with powers to arrange with us regulations concerning the protection of their persons, punishment of crimes, assigning to each family their Separate farms, directing how these shall go to the family as they die one after another, in what manner they shall be governed, & all other particulars necessary for their happiness in their new condition. On our part I will ask the assistance of our great Council the Congress, whose Authority is necessary to give validity to these arrangements & who wish nothing more sincerely than to render your Condition secure & happy. Should the principal part of your people determine to adopt this alteration, & a smaller part still chuse to continue the hunters life, it may facilitate the settlement among yourselves to be told that we will give to these leave to go, if they Chuse it, & settle on our lands beyond the Missisipi where some Cherokees are already settled, & where game is plenty, and we will take measures for establishing a Store there Among them, where they may obtain necessaries in exchange for their peltries, & we will still continue to be their friends there as much as here.

My Children, carry these words to your people, advise with Colo. Meigs in your proceedings, ask him to inform me from time to time how you go on, & I will further advise you in what may be necessary. tell your people I take them all by the hand; that I leave them free to do as they Chuse, & that whatever Choice they make, I will still be their friend and father.— Th: Jefferson

TJ to Kitchao-Geboway

My Son Kitchao-Geboway.— [21 Dec 1808]

I am happy to receive your visit at the seat of our Government, and to repeat to you the assurances of my friendly dispositions towards your nation. I am the more pleased to see you Again as at your last visit we could not converse together for want of an interpreter. this difficulty is now removed by the presence of Mr. Ryley.

I approve of your disposition my Son, to live at peace with all the world. it is what we wish all our red children to do, and to consider themselves as brethren of the same family, and forming with us but one nation. the great Spirit did not make men that they might destroy one another, and undo what he has done, but to live in peace & friendship with one another doing to each other all the good in their power, and thus filling the Land with happiness instead of misery and murder. this is the way in which we wish all our red children to live with one another, & with us; and this is what I wish you to say to your nation from me, when you deliver to them what I said to you the last winter. I am sorry you have not been able to carry it to them; they would have seen by that that you came here as the friend of your own nation and of all your red brethren. My Son, I take by the hand the Young Man, the son of your friend whom you brought with you. he is now Young and I hope will live to be old, and through his life will be steadfast in encouraging his Nation to live in peace and friendship with their White brethren of the United States.

The Secretary at War will provide for your journey back, and your father Govr. Hull will be glad to see you on your way. he will always give good advice to your nation in my name and will guide them in the paths of peace & friendship with all Men.—

TJ to Hendrick Aupaumut

My Son Capt. Hendrick and my children the Delawares, Mohiccons and Munsies.— 21 Dec 1808

I am glad to see you here, to receive your salutations, and to return them by taking you by the hand, and renewing to you the assurances of my friendship. I learn with pleasure that the Miamis & Poughtewatamies have given you some of their lands on the White River to live on, and that you propose to gather there your scattered tribes, and to dwell on it all your days.—

The picture which you have drawn, my Son, of the increase of our numbers and the decrease of yours is just. the causes are very plain and the remedy depends on yourselves alone. You have lived by hunting the Deer & Buffalo; as these have been driven westward you have sold out on the Sea board & moved Westwardly in pursuit of them. As they became scarce there, your food has failed you, you have been a part of every year without food except the roots and other unwholsome things you could find in the forest. Scanty and unwholsome food produce diseases and death among your children, and hence you have raised few & your numbers have decreased. frequent wars too, and the abuse of spirituous liquors have assisted in lessening your numbers. the whites on the other hand are in the habit of cultivating the earth, of raising stocks of Cattle, hogs and other domestic Animals in much greater numbers than they could kill of Deer & Buffalo. having always a plenty of food and clothing they raise abundance of children, they double their numbers every twenty years, the new swarms are continually advancing upon the country like flocks of Pigeons, & so they will continue to do. Now my Children, if we wanted to diminish our numbers, we would give up the culture of the earth, pursue the Deer and Buffalo & be always at war. this would soon reduce us to be as few as you are, and if you wish to increase your numbers you must give up the Deer & buffalo, live in peace and cultivate the earth. you see then My Children, that it depends on yourselves alone to become a numerous and great people. let me intreat you therefore on the lands now given you, to begin to give every man a farm, let him inclose it, cultivate it, build a warm House on it, and when he dies let it belong to his wife and children after him. nothing is so easy as to learn to cultivate the earth. all your women understand it, and to make it easier we are always ready to teach you how to make ploughs, hoes and other necessary utensils. if the men will take the labour of the earth from the women these will learn to spin & weave and to clothe their families. in this way you will also raise many children, you will double your numbers every twenty years, and soon fill the land your friends have given you, and your children will never be tempted to sell the spot on which they have been born, raised, have laboured and called their own. when once you have property you will want laws & Magistrates to protect your property and persons, and to punish those among you who commit crimes. you will find that our laws are good for this purpose; you will wish to live under them, you will unite yourselves with us, join in our great Councils & form one people with us and we shall

all be Americans, you will mix with us by marriage, your blood will run in our veins, & will spread with us over this great Island. Instead then my children of the gloomy prospect you have drawn of your total disappearance from the face of the earth which is true if you continue to hunt the Deer and buffalo & go to war. you see what a brilliant aspect is offered to your future history, if you give up war and hunting, adopt the culture of the earth and raise domestic Animals: you see how from a small family you may become a great nation by adopting the course which from the small beginning you describe had made us a great Nation.—

My Children, I will give you a paper declaring your right to hold, against all persons, the lands given you by the Miamis & Poutewatamies, and that you never can sell them without their consent. but I must tell you that if ever they & you agree to sell, no paper which I can give you can prevent your doing what you please with your own. the only way to prevent this is to give to every one of your People a farm, which shall belong to him and his family and which the nation shall have no right to take from them & sell. in this way alone can you ensure the lands to your descendants through all generations, and that it shall never be sold from under their feet.— It is not the keeping your lands, which will keep your people alive on them after the deer and buffalo shall have left them. It is the cultivating them alone which can do that—The hundredth part in corn & cattle will support you better than the whole in deer & buffalo.

My Son Hendrick, deliver these words to your people. I have spoken to them plainly, that they may see what is before them and that it is in their own power to go on dwindling to nothing, or to become again a great People. it is for this reason I wish them to live in peace with all people, to teach their Young Men to love agriculture, rather than war & hunting. let these words sink deep in their hearts, and let them often repeat them & consider them.— tell them that I hold them fast by the hand, & that I will ever be their friend to advise and to assist them in following the true path to their future happiness.—

TJ to Henri Grégoire

Sir — Washington Feb. 25. 09.

I have received the favor of your letter of Aug: 17. and with it the Volume you were so kind as to send me on the literature of negroes. Be assured that no person living wishes more sincerely than I do, to see a complete refutation of the doubts I have myself entertained and expressed on the grade of understanding allotted to them by nature, and to find that in this respect they are on a par with ourselves. My doubts were the result of personal observation on the limited sphere of my own State, where the opportunities for the developement of their genius were not favorable, and those of exercising it still less so. I expressed them therefore with great hesitation. But whatever be their degree of talent it is no measure of their rights. Because Sr. I. Newton was superior to others in understanding he was not therefore Lord of the person or property of others. on this subject they are gaining daily in the Opinions of nations, & hopeful advances are making towards their reestablishment on an equal footing with the other colours of the human family. I pray you therefore to Accept my thanks for the many instances you have enabled me to observe of respectable intelligence in that race of men, which cannot fail to have effect in hastening the day of their relief, & to be assured of the Sentiments of high & just esteem & consideration which I tender to your self with all sincerity

Th: Jefferson

TJ to Joel Barlow

Dear Sir — Monticello Oct. 8. 09.

It is long since I ought to have acknoleged the reciept of your most excellent oration on the 4th of July. I was doubting what you could say, equal to your own reputation, on so hackneyed a subject. But you have really risen out of it with lustre, and pointed to others a field of great expansion. A day or two after I recieved your letter to Bishop Gregoire a copy of his diatribe to you came to hand from France. I had not before heard of it. He must have been eagle eyed in quest of offence to have discovered ground for it among the rubbish massed together in the print he animadverts on. you have done right in giving him a sugary answer. but he did not deserve it. for notwithstanding a compliment to you now & then he constantly returns to the identification of your sentiments with the extravagancies of the Revolutionary zealots. I believe him a very good man, with imagination enough to declaim eloquently, but without judgment to decide. he wrote to me also on the doubts I had expressed five or six & twenty years ago, in the Notes on Virginia, as to the grade of understanding of the negroes, & he sent me his book on the literature of the negroes. his credulity has made him gather up every story he could find of men of colour (without distinguishing whether black, or of what degree of mixture) however slight the mention, or light the authority on which they are quoted. the whole do not amount in point of evidence, to what we know ourselves of Banneker. we know he had spherical trigonometry enough to make almanacs, but not without the suspicion of aid from Ellicot, who was his neighbor & friend, & never missed an opportunity of puffing him. I have a long letter from Banneker which shews him to have had a mind of very common stature indeed. as to Bishop Gregoire, I wrote him, as you have done, a very soft answer. it was impossible for doubt to have been more tenderly or hesitatingly expressed than that was in the Notes of Virginia, and nothing was or is farther from my intentions than to enlist myself as the champion of a fixed opinion, where I have only expressed a doubt. St Domingo will, in time, throw light on the question.

I intended, ere this, to have sent you the papers I had promised you. but i have taken up Marshal's 5th volume & mean to read it carefully, to correct what is wrong in it, and commit to writing such facts and annotations as the reading that work will bring into my recollection and which have not yet been put on paper. in this I shall be much aided by my memorandums & letters, and will send you both the old & the new. but i go on very slowly. in truth during the pleasant season I am always out of doors employed, not passing more time at my writing table than will dispatch my current business. but when the weather becomes cold I shall go out but little. I hope therefore to get through this volume during the ensuing winter; but should you want the papers sooner, they shall be sent at a moment's warning. the ride from Washington to Monticello in the stage, or in a gigg is so easy that I had hoped you would have taken a flight here during the season of good roads. whenever mrs Barlow is well enough to join you in such a visit, it must be taken more at ease. it will give us real pleasure whenever it may take place. I pray you to present me to her respectfully, and I salute you affectionately. Th: Jefferson

TJ to John Adams

Dear Sir Monticello June 11. 1812.

By our post preceding that which brought your letter of May 21. I had recieved one from mr Malcolm on the same subject with yours, and by the return of the post had stated to the President my recollections of him. but both of your letters were probably too late; as the appointment had been already made, if we may credit the newspapers.

You ask if there is any book that pretends to give any account of the traditions of the Indians, or how one can acquire an idea of them? some scanty accounts of their traditions, but fuller of their customs & characters are given us by most of the early travellers among them. these you know were chiefly French. Lafitau, among them, and Adair an Englishman, have written on this subject; the former two volumes, the latter one, all in 4to. but unluckily Lafitau had in his head a preconceived theory on the mythology, manners, institutions & government of the antient nations of Europe, Asia, & Africa, and seems to have entered on those of America only to fit them into the same frame, and to draw from them a confirmation of his general theory. he keeps up a perpetual parallel, in all those articles, between the Indians of America, & the antients of the other quarters of the globe. he selects therefore all the facts, and adopts all the falsehoods which favor his theory, and very gravely retails such absurdities as zeal for a theory could alone swallow. he was a man of much classical & scriptural reading, and has rendered his book not unentertaining. he resided five years among the Northern Indians, as a Missionary, but collects his matter much more from the writings of others, than from his own observation.

Adair too had his kink. he believed all the Indians of America to be descended from the Jews: the same laws, usages, rites & ceremonies, the same sacrifices, priests, prophets, fasts and festivals, almost the same religion, and that they all spoke Hebrew. for altho he writes particularly of the Southern Indians only, the Catawbas, Creeks, Cherokees, Chickasaws and Choctaws, with whom alone he was personally acquainted, yet he generalizes whatever he found among them, & brings himself to believe that the hundred languages of America, differing fundamentally every one from every other, as much as Greek from Gothic, have yet all one common prototype. he was a trader, a man of learning, a self-taught Hebraist, a strong religionist, and of as sound a mind as Don Quixot in whatever did not touch his religious chivalry. his book contains a great deal of real instruction on it's subject, only requiring the reader to be constantly on his guard against the wonderful obliquities of his theory.

The scope of your enquiry would scarcely, I suppose, take in the three folio volumes of Latin of De Bry. in these fact and fable are mingled together, without regard to any favorite system. they are less suspicious therefore in their complexion, more original and authentic, than those of Lafitau and Adair. this is a work of great curiosity, extremely rare, so as never to be bought in Europe; but on the breaking up, & selling some antient library. on one of these occasions a bookseller procured me a copy, which, unless you have one, is probably the only one in America.

You ask further, if the Indians have any order of priesthood among them, like the Druids, Bards or Minstrels of the Celtic nations? Adair alone, determined to see what he wished to see in every object, metamorphoses their Conjurers into an order of priests, and describes their sorceries as if they were the great religious ceremonies of the nation. Lafitau calls them by their proper names, Jongleurs, Devins, Sortileges; DeBry praestigiatores, Adair himself sometimes Magi, Archimagi, cunning men, Seers, rainmakers, and the modern Indian interpreters, call them Conjurers & Witches. they are persons pretending to have communications with the devil and other evil spirits, to foretel future events, bring down rain, find stolen goods, raise the dead, destroy some, & heal others by enchantment, lay spells Etc. and Adair, without departing from his parallel of the Jews & Indians, might have found their counterpart, much more aptly, among the Soothsayers, sorcerers and wizards of the Jews, their Jannes & Jambres, their Simon Magus, witch of Endor, & the young damsel whose sorceries disturbed Paul so much; instead of placing them in a line with their High-priest, their Chief priests, and their magnificent hierarchy generally. In the solemn ceremonies of the Indians, the persons who direct or officiate, are their chiefs, elders and warriors, in civil ceremonies or in those of war; it is the Head of the Cabin, in their private or particular feasts or ceremonies; and sometimes the Matrons, as in their Corn feasts. and, even here, Adair might have kept up his parallel, without ennobling his Conjurers. for the antient Patriarchs, the Noahs, the Abrahams, Isaacs & Jacobs, and, even after the consecration of Aaron, the Samuels & Elijahs, and we may say further every one for himself, offered sacrifices on the altars. the true line of distinction seems to be, that solemn ceremonies, whether public or private, addressed to the Great Spirit, are conducted by the worthies of the nation, Men, or Matrons, while Conjurers are resorted to only for the invocation of evil spirits. the present state of the several Indian tribes, without any public order of priests, is proof sufficient that they never had such an order. their steady habits permit no innovations, not even those which the progress of science offers to increase the comforts, enlarge the understanding, & improve the morality of mankind. indeed so little idea have they of a regular order of priests, that they mistake ours for their Conjurers and call them by that name.

So much in answer to your enquiries concerning Indians, a people with whom, in the very early part of my life, I was very familiar, and acquired impressions of attachment & commiseration for them which have never been obliterated. before the revolution they were in the habit of coming often, & in great numbers to the seat of our government, where I was very much with them. I knew much the great Outassetè, the warrior and orator of the Cherokees. he was always the guest of my father, on his journies to & from Williamsburg. I was in his camp when he made his great farewell oration to his people, the evening before his departure for England. the moon was in full splendor, and to her he seemed to address himself in his prayers for his own safety on the voyage, and that of his people during his absence. his sounding voice, distinct articulation, animated action, and the solemn silence of his people at their several fires, filled me with awe & veneration, altho I did not understand a word he uttered. that nation, consisting now of about 2000. warriors, & the Creeks of about 3000. are far advanced in civilization. they have good Cabins, inclosed fields, large herds of cattle & hogs, spin & weave their own clothes of cotton, have smiths & other of the most necessary tradesmen, write & read, are on the increase in numbers, & a branch of the Cherokees is now instituting a regular representative government. some other tribes were advancing in the same line. on those who have made any progress, English seductions will have no effect. but the backward will yeild, & be thrown further back. these will relapse into barbarism & misery, lose numbers by war & want, and we shall be obliged to drive them, with the beasts of the forest into the Stony mountains. they will be conquered however in Canada. the possession of that country secures our women & children for ever from the tomahawk & scalping knife, by removing those who excite them: and for this possession, orders I presume are issued by this time; taking for granted that the doors of Congress will re-open with a Declaration of war. that this may end in indemnity for the past, security for the future, & compleat emancipation from Anglomany, Gallomany, and all the manias of demoralised Europe, and that you may live in health & happiness to see all this, is the sincere prayer of

Yours affectionately
Th: Jefferson

TJ to Jeremiah A. Goodman

Dear Sir — Monticello Dec. 22. 13.

Dick, Solomon and Philip are permitted to go and see their friends, and in returning will help to bring the hogs and beeves. I am in hopes you have procured the beds and given them to the women. in giving out their clothes I forgot the article of hats, which I give every other year; but as it will be more convenient to give about half one year and half another, we will give to the men only, this year, and to the women the next. be so good therefore as to get hats for all the men & lads who labour. we get them here at a dollar & 7/6. clover seed is now at 15.D. and may get higher. at this price we can only afford to sow mr Darnell's lower field which must be sowed at any price. I expect Gill's waggon will be with you about the latter end of the next week, and will bring, when she returns, the residue of the peas which Dick shall not bring. I shall be glad to learn by the return of the bearers what progress is made on the bear creek road and whether the tobacco is sold or got down. were the weather to be very mild in Feb. or Mar. it is possible I might then pay you a visit. Accept my best wishes. Th: Jefferson

[*on address cover:*]
since writing the within Gill is taken very ill, which will delay his coming. Th:J.

TJ to Edward Coles

Dear Sir Monticello Aug. 25. 14.

Your favor of July 31. was duly recieved, and was read with peculiar pleasure. the sentiments breathed thro' the whole do honor to both the head and heart of the writer. mine on the subject of the slavery of negroes have long since been in possession of the public, and time has only served to give them stronger root. the love of justice & the love of country plead equally the cause of these people, and it is a mortal reproach to us that they should have pleaded it so long in vain, and should have produced not a single effort, nay I fear not much serious willingness to relieve them & ourselves from our present condition of moral and political reprobation. from those of the former generation who were in the fulness of age when I came into public life, which was while our controversy with England was on paper only, I soon saw that nothing was to be hoped. nursed and educated in the daily habit of seeing the degraded condition, both bodily & mental, of those unfortunate beings, not reflecting that that degradation was very much the work of themselves & their fathers, few minds had yet doubted but that they were as legitimate subjects of property as their horses or cattle. the quiet & monotonous course of colonial life had been disturbed by no alarm, & little reflection on the value of liberty. and when alarm was taken at an enterprise on their own, it was not easy to carry them the whole length of the principles which they invoked for themselves.

in the first or second session of the legislature after I became a member, I drew to this subject the attention of Colo Bland, one of the oldest, ablest, and most respected members, and he undertook to move for certain moderate extensions of the protection of the laws to these people. I seconded his motion, and, as a younger member, was more spared in the debate: but he was denounced as an enemy to his country, & was treated with the grossest indecorum. from an early stage of our revolution other and more distant duties were assigned to me, so that from that time till my return from Europe in 1789. and I may say till I returned to reside at home in 1809. I had little opportunity of knowing the progress of public sentiment here on this subject. I had always hoped that the younger generation, recieving their early impressions after the flame of liberty had been kindled in every breast, and had become as it were the vital spirit of every American, that the generous temperament of youth, analogous to the motion of their blood, and above the suggestions of avarice, would have sympathised with oppression wherever found, and proved their love of liberty beyond their own share of it. but my intercourse with them, since my return, has not been sufficient to ascertain that they had made towards this point the progress I had hoped. your solitary but welcome voice is the first which has brought this sound to my ear; and I have considered the general silence which prevails on this subject as indicating an apathy unfavorable to every hope. yet the hour of emancipation is advancing in the march of time. it will come; and whether brought on by the generous energy of our own minds, or by the bloody process of St Domingo, excited and conducted by the power of our present enemy, if once stationed permanently within our country, & offering asylum & arms to the oppressed, is a leaf of our history not yet turned over.

As to the method by which this difficult work is to be effected, if permitted to be done by ourselves, I have seen no proposition so expedient on the whole, as that of emancipation of those born after a given day, and of their education and expatriation at a proper age. this would give time for a gradual extinction of that species of labor and substitution of another, and lessen the severity of the shock which an operation so fundamental cannot fail to produce. the idea of emancipating the whole at once, the old as well as the young, and retaining them here, is of those only who have not the guide of either knolege or experience of the subject. for, men, probably of any colour, but of this color we know, brought up from their infancy without necessity for thought or forecast, are by their habits rendered as incapable as children of taking care of themselves, and are extinguished promptly wherever industry is necessary for raising the young. in the mean time they are pests in society by their idleness, and the depredations to which this leads them. their amalgamation with the other colour produces a degradation to which no lover of his country, no lover of excellence in the human character can innocently consent.

I am sensible of the partialities with which you have looked towards me as the person who should undertake this salutary but arduous work. but this, my dear Sir, is like bidding old Priam to buckle the armour of Hector "trementibus aevo humeris et inutile ferrum cingi." no. I have overlived the generation with which mutual labors and perils begat mutual confidence and influence. this enterprise is for the young; for those who can follow it up, and bear it through to it's consummation. it shall have all my prayers, and these are the only weapons of an old man. but in the mean time are you right in abandoning this property, and your country with it? I think not. my opinion has ever been that, until more can be done for them, we should endeavor, with those whom fortune has thrown on our hands, to feed & clothe them well, protect them from ill usage, require such reasonable labor only as is performed voluntarily by freemen, and be led by no repugnancies to abdicate them, and our duties to them. the laws do not permit us to turn them loose, if that were for their good: and to commute them for other property is to commit them to those whose usage of them we cannot controul. I hope then, my dear Sir, you will reconcile yourself to your country and it's unfortunate condition; that you will not lessen it's stock of sound disposition by withdrawing your portion from the mass. that, on the contrary you will come forward in the public councils, become the Missionary of this doctrine truly Christian, insinuate & inculcate it softly but steadily thro' the medium of writing & conversation, associate others in your labors, and when the phalanx is formed, bring on & press the proposition perseveringly until it's accomplishment. it is an encouraging observation that no good measure was ever proposed which, if duly pursued, failed to prevail in the end. we have proof of this in the history of the endeavors in the British parliament to suppress that very trade which brought this evil on us. and you will be supported by the religious precept "be not wearied in well doing." that your success may be as speedy and compleat, as it will be of honorable & immortal consolation to yourself I shall as fervently & sincerely pray as I assure you of my great friendship and respect. Th: Jefferson

P.S. will you give to the inclosed letter the proper address of place to find your brother?

TJ to Jeremiah A. Goodman

Dear Sir Monticello Jan. 6. 15.

Dick arrived here on the 4th with the butter, salt, beef & hogs. one he said had been left at Lynchburg, one tired and was killed on the road, the other 13. have been killed here. their weights were 101. 99. 91. 91. 80. 76. 67. 67. 67. 61. 56. 55. 47. as they would not make bacon at all, being so small they would dry up to nothing, we shall try to make them up into salt pork, in which way they may do for the people. but such a supply of pork, and 14. bushels of wheat a hand carried to market are very damping circumstances. Dick carries with him a pair of the Guinea breed of hogs, of the same which I sent formerly, but which seem to have had no effect. we killed hogs of this breed here this year, not 18. months old weighing 200.℔. and a great part of them 150. & all under that age. yours average 73¾.

I send by Dick 4. ploughs, which with the one sent by James, and a Peacock plough sent formerly, allows three for each place. he brings 2. barrels containing bottled beer, to be put into the cellar, and 2. barrels containing 40.℔ of wool. we can very illy spare it, not having enough for our people here, but we will try a mixture of hemp & cotton for the negro children here, in order to help out for your people. it is indispensably necessary that you take as much care of the lambs & sheep as if they were children. we feel now the misfortune of the loss of so many last year as well as mr Darnell's trespass. the wool sent is half blooded Merino, and very difficult to make any thing of for coarse cloth. you can do nothing with it with wool-cards. it must either be carded with fine cotton cards, or carded at some of the carding machines. it would be better indeed if you could exchange it for common wool with some of the neighbors who want to make fine cloth for their own use. I expected to have recieved by Dick a list of the stock, and now send you blank lists for each place, which I will be glad to have filled up and returned to me by the mail. I must get you to speak to mr Watkins and let him know I depend on his promise to come and make a wheat machine for me. the stuff has been all ready this twelvemonth. if he can make his arrangements to come about the middle of April, it would be in time. I should have an opportunity of seeing him at Poplar Forest the 1st week in April, when I shall be there. Phill Hubard arrived here the 2d day after Christmas. his subject of complaint is exactly what you supposed. he says that he and Dick's Hanah had become husband & wife, but that you drove him repeatedly from her father's house and would not let him go there, punishing her, as he supposes, for recieving him. certainly there is nothing I desire so much as that all the young people in the estate should intermarry with one another and stay at home. they are worth a great deal more in that case than when they have husbands and wives abroad. Phill has been long petitioning me to let him go to Bearcreek to live with his family. and Nanny has been as long at me to let her come to the Poplar forest. we may therefore now gratify both, by sending Phill & his wife to Bear creek, and bringing Nanny and any one of the single men from there, that is to say Reuben, Daniel, or Stephen. no new house will be wanting because Phill can take the house Nanny leaves, and Nanny may take the house which Cate's Hanah leaves. I would wish you to give to Dick's Hanah a pot, and a bed, which I always promise them when they take husbands at home, and I shall be very glad to hear that others of the young people follow their example. a crocus bed may be got from mr Robertson. I would by no means have Phill punished for what he has done; for altho I had let them all know that their runnings away should be punished, yet Phill's character is not that of a runaway. I have known him from a boy and that he has not come off to sculk from his work.—mr Mitchell will take his debt out of the wheat, at the price he pays to others, and the rest must be ground & sent immediately to Richmond. I hope you are getting on with the tobacco. it is very pressing to have that at Richmond. Dick carries the two blankets which were short of the number intended to have been sent by James. let the beer be put into the cellar immediately, for fear of it's freezing, setting the proper head of the barrels uppermost, that the bottles in them may stand with the corks up. Accept my best wishes.

Th: Jefferson

TJ to Joel Yancey

Dear Sir Monticello Jan. 17. 19. Sunday

The waggons arrived here on Wednesday a little after the middle of the day. we were under extreme sufferance for the want of a short job of hauling, and I thought it better to set both about it that they might go back together; and the rather as every day's stay enabled Johnny Hemings to add another plough frame. they will accordingly carry you three made on Thursday, Friday & Saturday, and will start tomorrow morning (Monday) I shall be very glad to recieve the latter peas I liked so much the last year and hope Nace has saved me a full sowing of them. I wrote you the last year that Dick had delivered all his articles safe and thought so at the time. but I learnt afterwards that he did not deliver a bag containing a bushel of dried peaches which [he] said had dropped thro a hole in the bottom of his waggon; altho' no hole was seen which could have let such a mass thr[o'.] this year his soap weighs 38. ℔ instead of 45 ℔. and the bar[rel] of apples is a little more than half full. these repeated accidents cannot but excite suspicions of him, sufficient to make us attentive in future. I will ask the favor of you to send by Jerry the Athenian poplars in the nursery of the garden. you will know them by the stems being ribbed, which distinguishes them from the Lombardy poplars & Aspens in the same place. their roots should be covered very thick with straw, tied firmly on, so that the cold may not reach the roots, which it very certainly kills. the old bacon may remain as I shall pass a great proportion of the ensuing year there. The unproductiveness of our crops which you notice in your letter, is indeed a serious calamity, and the more so to me as 3. years of war, & 4. years of Goodman & Darnell had thrown me into arrears which will require 2. or 3. good crops to extricate me from. yet I do not ascribe it to any want of management in yourself, but to the impoverishment of our fields by constant culture without any aid of manure; and this cause will continue to increase. we must either attend to the recruiting our lands, or abandon them & run away to Alibama, as so many of our countrymen are doing, who find it easier to resolve on quitting their country, than, to change the practices in husbandry to which they have been brought up. straw will do something, good manure more, but nothing short of plaister and clover can recruit our extensive fields. the miracles this is working in this neighborhood can be believed only by those who see them. my fields here, which in my hands produced 4, 5. or 6. bushels to the acre, are now giving my grandson from 15. to 18. after one or two alternations only of plaister & clover. my neighbor Rogers, who while tenant [. . .] [Harv]ey's estate adjoining us, had reduced it to 5. bushels, now that [. . .] proprietor has made this last year from 25. to 30. bushels one thro the whole of his fields, & all by plaister & clover. we must either go into the same course, or run away. if we cannot get the plaister carried up for 10.D. we must give 15. if not for 15. we must give 20. if you can make arrangements therefore for bringing up & grinding and will so inform me, I will write to Capt Peyton of Richmond to procure the plaister. then it may be necessary to buy the clover seed, but I hope never after the 1st year. the mortality among our negroes is still more serious as involving moral as well as interested considerations. they are well fed, and well clothed, & I have had no reason to believe that any overseer, since Griffin's time, has over worked them. accordingly the deaths among the grown ones seem ascribable to natural causes. but the loss of 5. little ones in a year induces me to fear that the overseers do not permit the women to devote as much time as is necessary to the care of their children: that they view their labor as the 1st object and the raising their child but as secondary. I consider the labor of a breeding woman as no object, and that a child raised every 2. years is of more profit than the crop of the best laboring man. in this, as in all other cases, providence has made our interests & our duties coincide perfectly. women too are destroyed by exposure to wet at certain periodical indispositions to which nature has subjected them. with respect therefore to our women & their children I must pray you to inculcate upon the overseers that it is not their labor, but their increase which is the first consideration with us. with respect to yourself my confidence is entire; and I am as well satisfied [t]hat every thing under your eye is going on for the best as if I were there to see the fact. I know that the considerations under which you act are of a high & pure order, and it is a heart felt satisfaction to me to feel as well as to assure you of my sincere friendship & respect Th: Jefferson

Adam Hodgson's Account of a Visit to Monticello

[17 June 1820]

——. I FEAR, however, that I am leaving no room for an account of my very interesting visit to Monticello. I went nearly 25 miles out of my way to obtain a letter of introduction to Mr. Jefferson, from his friend, Judge ——, of Staunton, to whom I was recommended by the late amiable and very popular Governor of the State of Mississippi.

On the 18th instant, I left Hayes's tavern, at the foot of the Blue ridge . . . We shortly afterwards passed through Charlottesville, where General Tarleton was near capturing Mr. Jefferson and the State Legislature, being prevented only by a private intimation, sent by a female relation of one of the officers, a few miles distant, at whose house the General and his suite had invited themselves to breakfast. Here we saw an extensive university, which the State is erecting under Mr. Jefferson's auspices, and to which it is intended to invite the ablest Professors which Europe can supply.

We arrived at Monticello, three miles farther, about eleven o'clock, ascending the South West Mountain, on which the house is situated, by a winding carriage-road through the wood. I sent in my letter to Mr. Jefferson, who soon afterwards came out and gave me a polite reception, leading me through the hall, hung with mammoth bones and Indian curiosities, to a room, ornamented with fine paintings. A young lady was playing on a piano-forte, but retired when we entered. Our conversation turned principally on the Indians, and the fine timber of the United States. With respect to the former, he considers them quite on a level, as respects intellectual character, with the Whites, and attributes the rapid civilization of the Choctaws, compared with that of the Creeks, on whom, perhaps, greater efforts have been bestowed, to the advantages possessed by the former for the growth of cotton, which had gradually induced them to spin and weave. He observed, that notwithstanding the fine specimens which have been preserved of Indian eloquence, the Indians appear to have no poetic genius; and that he had never known an Indian discover a musical taste; that, on the contrary, the Africans almost universally possess fine voices and an excellent ear, and a passionate fondness for music. With this I have often been struck, as I passed through the Southern States, especially when I have seen them assembled at public worship, or packing cotton at New Orleans. Mr. Jefferson said that he never knew a person who had resided long among the Indians, return and settle among the Whites; and I understood him to say also, that he never knew a person who left the coast for the western country, or his descendants, return to the Atlantic States. After sitting about an hour, I rose to take leave, when Mr. J. pressed me to stay to dinner, to which I assented, on condition that he would not allow me to be any restraint upon him. He said he must leave me for an hour to ride, as his health had a few months since begun to fail, for the first time. I found no difficulty, however, in amusing myself in the museum and the grounds and garden. In the former, was the only upper jaw ever yet discovered, as I was told, of a large animal now extinct, and some maps traced by the Indians on leather. The view on every side of the house, except one, where a small arc of the horizon is intercepted by a hill, is very extensive and beautiful. The Blue ridge affords an interesting variety of romantic scenery in a broken curve, extending, I believe, above 100 miles; one peak at the distance, I understood, of more than 120 miles, being sometimes visible. The horizon, on the Atlantic side, is about 40 miles distant; and bounds a flat well-wooded country, which appeared tame, when contrasted with the sublimity of the mountains. These, and especially a hill of the shape and dimensions of the largest pyramid in Egypt, which gives Mr. Jefferson a meridian line of 40 miles, frequently exhibit the phenomenon of looming.

On Mr. Jefferson's return from his ride, we had some interesting conversation respecting the university, and a favourite plan of his of dividing every county into districts, in which there should be schools, and a humble sort of college at convenient distances, a superior college, with every possible advantage, being established in the State. After dinner, when the ladies had retired, and we were quite alone, he expressed his sentiments very freely on the present situation of England, and the character of many of her public men. He then stated the views and feelings which he had entertained with respect to her while President, as well as those which had been generally entertained by the American Government; the various causes which had contributed to the unhappy misunderstanding between the two countries, and the grounds for believing that many of them were of a nature which rendered their recurrence improbable. He then described, with a good deal of spirit and minuteness, the character of the different ministers we have sent to Washington, and concluded with an earnest hope, that as the two Governments at length understood each other perfectly, the people might gradually be soothed into better humour with one another. The particulars of this very interesting conversation, which lasted two hours, and of which I have preserved a memorandum, I will give you when we meet.

Mr. Jefferson's appearance is rather prepossessing. He is tall and very thin, a little bent with age, with an intelligent and sprightly countenance. His manners are dignified, but courteous and gentlemanly; and he enters into conversation with great ease and animation.

After two hours téte-à-téte, I rose about six o'clock to take my leave. He invited me to stay all night; but I thought I had already encroached sufficiently on his time, and I was not sure that wc should withdraw to the ladies, of whom I had just seen enough to feel persuaded that I should have passed a very agreeable evening with them. While sitting with this philosophical legislator and his polished family, in a handsome saloon, surrounded by instruments of science, valuable specimens of the fine arts, and literary treasures of every nation, and every age, I could not help contrasting my situation with some of those which I had occupied during the preceding month, when sleeping on a bear-skin, on the floor of an Indian hut, listening to the traditions of my Chickasaw or Choctaw host, or dandling on my knee a young Indian warrior, with his miniature belt and mocassins, his necklaces and feathers, and his little bow and arrow, doomed to provoke nothing but a smile. In the course of a few weeks, I had passed from deep forests, whose silence had never been broken by the woodman's axe, to a thickly settled country, where cattle were grazing in extensive meadows, and corn fields waving in the wind; where commerce was planting her towns, science founding her universities, and religion rearing her heaven-directed spires. In the same period, I had traced man through every successive stage of civilization, from the roaming savage, whose Ideas scarcely extend beyond the narrow circle of his daily wants, to the statesman who has learnt to grasp the complicated interests of society, and the philosopher, to contemplate the system of the universe.

Crossing the Rivannah, at the bottom of Mr. Jefferson's grounds, the water up to our saddle-skirts, we proceeded to Mr. Boyd's tavern, about eight miles distant. On Monday, the 19th, we resumed our journey . . .

I forgot to say, that at Mr. Jefferson's, I saw the belt and shot pouch of the famous Tecumseh . . .

TJ to John Wayles Eppes

Dear Sir | Monticello June 30. 20.

. . . My commitment for Mr Nicholas is still of uncertain issue. if a compromise, now in negociation, succeeds, of which it is said there is a good prospect, I shall be saved by the time it provides for the disposal of his estate as well as for the preference of bonâ fide creditors. 3. or 4 of the shavers only have held off, and it is believed they are now disposed to concur. this will be known in a few days. if this compromise fails it is very possible I may have to advance the money, and not certain that I shall be ever reimbursed. besides this I have considerable debts of my own, which the fall of produce, likely to be permanent, forbids me to count on paying from annual crops. I had therefore proposed to begin to prepare for these cases by selling some lands; having scruples about selling negroes but for delinquency, or on their own request. but your proposition gets me over these scruples as it is in fact to keep them in the family. and on that ground it will be acceptable, and indeed desirable, with some necessary modifications. for the negroes here being under engagement for 3. or 4. years to come, the sale must be from those in Bedford only. but there I could not part with 10. men without breaking up my plantations. I would spare 20. negroes in all from those plantations, men women and children in the usual proportions: and I should think this really more advantageous for Francis than all men. I know no error more consuming to an estate than that of stocking farms with men almost exclusively. I consider a woman who brings a child every two years as more profitable than the best man of the farm. what she produces is an addition to the capital, while his labors disappear in mere consumption. the agreement you propose therefore, with this modification would be really acceptable to me, and more salutary for my affairs than to sell land only. the selection of the individuals should be made with a fair and favorable eye to the interests of Francis, & the valuation left to any good and unconnected judges. Th: Jefferson

Roll of the Negroes According to Their Ages

1727. ~~Squire~~ d. Mar. 20. 1810
31. ~~Goliah.~~ D May 5.1810
43. ~~Abram~~
~~48.~~ ~~Phill~~ d. Sep. 1810
~~49.~~ ~~Caesar d~~ 1820
~~Molly~~ d Apr. 21. 1811
53. John.
55. Davy.
56. Amy.
57. Doll.
~~58.~~ ~~Isabel.~~ D 1819.
59. Betty Brown
60. Ned.
Lewis.
61. Nance
64. Jenny Ned's
68. Isaac.
Bagwell
Jenny. Lewis's
69. Critta.
70. Peter Hemings.
71. Minerva.
Jame
73. Sally
Rachel
75. John Hemings.
76. Jamey

~~Mary~~ Jerry's d 13.
Rachael
77. Jerry.
79. Cretia
~~[Moses.~~
Eve
80. Mary. Moses's
Joe.
81. Wormley
Dick
82. Shepherd.
83. ~~[Lucy. Phill's~~
Barnaby
Burwell.
84. Davy. Isabel's
85. Charles
Ben.
John Bedfd.
Davy Bedfd.
86. ~~Phill Hubbard~~ movd. 1812
Bartlet
Ned. Jr.
87. Ursula.
Edy.
88. Lewis
Mary. Bagwell's
Fanny.
~~89.~~ ~~Aggy.~~ Charles's d 15
90. Dick
d. ~~Jesse~~ July 16. 15.
Abram.
91. Nanny. Rach's
Lilly
92. Gill.
[Sally. Lew's
Moses. Dianh Bedfd.

58.

1793. [Edwin
~~Amy. Isabel's~~
Virginia. Bagw's
~~[Thenia. Doll's~~
94. Scilla. Ned's
Dolly. Doll's.
Solomon.
95. [Thruston
James. Lew's
Esther.

96. Philip.
Nace.
[James. Ned's.
Sucky. Jerry's
97. Sanco.
Indridge
Evelina.
Maria.
[Bec.
98. [Beverly. Run away 22.
[Aggy. Ned's
~~99.~~ ~~Robert.~~
~~Billy Bedford.~~
1800. ~~John. Cretia's~~
Nanny. Bagw's
Isabel. Lew's
Thrimston. Isabel's
Israel. Ned's
Isaiah. Jerry's
01. [William. Moses. Bedfd.
[Harriet. Sally's run. 22
Mary. Bet's
Joe. Rachael's
d. 16. ~~Lovila. Isabel's~~ 1816.
02. Jerry. Jerry's.
Randal. Cretia's.
03. Davy. Moses's.
Moses. Ned's
04. Jupiter. Jerry's
05. [James. Edy's
Madison. Sally's
Joe. Ursula's
~~[*illegible*]~~
[Henry, Cretia's d. 21
Washington. Mary's
Eliza. Rachael's
Lania. Bedfd. Rachael's
06. Willis. Bagw's
Jossy. Eve's
~~Anderson. Lilly's~~ d. Oct. 1811.
Celia. Moses's
Suckey. Ned's
07. Anne. Ursula's
Milly. Cretia's
Gloster. Rachael's
Maria. Edy's
~~[*illegible*]~~
08. Archy. Bagw's

	Eston. Sally's
	Ellen. Rach's Dec.
09.	Dolly. Ursula's
	Burwell. Eve's
	Stannard. Lilly's
	Lilburn. Cretia's
	Ellen. Fanny's.
10.	Tucker Mary's Apr.
	Patsy Edy's May. 11.
	Jordan Minerva's Sep
	Polly. Aggy's. Aug
	Washington. Rachael's
11.	Lucy. Lilly's. Mar. 12.

60

1811. Apr. 1.	Cornelius. Ursula's	
Sep.	Jamey. Scilla's.	
Dec.	Jenny. Fanny's	
Oct.	Matilda. Cretia's	
Dec. 24.	Robert. Virginia's	
1812. Oct. 27.	Zacharias. Moses's	
Dec. 6.	Betsy-Ann. Edy's	
1813. January.	Lindsay. Esther's	
May.	Edmund. Rachael B.	
~~Sep.~~	~~Fanny. Scilla's~~ d Mar. 1814.	Whoopg.
~~Sep. 10.~~	~~Mary. Cretia's.~~ d. Mar. 1814.	Cough
Oct. 1.	Thomas. Ursula's	
1814. May.	Marshall. Maria's [i.e. Lazaria's]	
~~Molly~~	~~[Molly. Lucy's~~	
d June.	~~Moses. Fanny's~~	
	Cary Anne. Sally's	
1815. June 5.	Peter. Edy's	
July.	James Band. Cretia's	
Aug.	Patsy. Moses's	
Sep.	Amanda. Virginia's	
1816. Jan. 21.	Louisa. Ursula's	
April. 15.	Martin. Maria's	
	Fleming. Bec's	
July	Miles. Scilla's	
	Jennet. Sally's	
	Lindsay. Rachael's B.	
	~~[Melinda. Lucy's~~	
1817. July 11.	~~Melinda Fanny's~~	
Aug.	Fosset. Moses's	
1818	Lovila. Cretia's	
1818.	Jackson. Milly's	
	Bec's	
	Lucy. Scilla's	

	~~[Nicholas. Lucy's~~
	James Hamilton. Maria's
	Caroline. Ursula's
	Lorenzo. Sally's
1819. Jan. 7.	Isabella. Edy's
Apr. 3.	Indridge. Fanny's
Aug.	Nancy. Cretia's
Oct. 15.	Fontaine. Mary Mos's
1820. Jan. 27.	Critta. Ursula's
Mar.	Martha. Beck's
July.	Amy. Isabel's
1821. Apr.	Aggy. Scilla's
May.	Sally's
	William Edy's
Nov.	Virginia's
1822. Sep.	Melinda. Fanny's
Dec.	Gilly. Aggy's
1823	Martha. Maria's (Rachael's]
	Manuel. Eve's
May	Isabella. Sally's Chas.' Wife
	girl Virginia's
	George. Ursula's
1824. Aug.	Another

Thomas Jefferson, Autobiography, *January 6, 1821*

In 1769, I became a member of the legislature by the choice of the county in which I live, & continued in that until it was closed by the revolution. I made one effort in that body for the permission of the emancipation of slaves, which was rejected: and indeed, during the regal government, nothing liberal could expect success. Our minds were circumscribed within narrow limits by an habitual belief that it was our duty to be subordinate to the mother country in all matters of government, to direct all our labors in subservience to her interests, and even to observe a bigoted intolerance for all religions but hers. The difficulties with our representatives were of habit and despair, not of reflection & conviction. Experience soon proved that they could bring their minds to rights on the first summons of their attention. But the king's council, which acted as another house of legislature, held their places at will & were in most humble obedience to that will: the Governor too, who had a negative on our laws held by the same tenure, & with still greater devotedness to it: and last of all the Royal negative closed the last door to every hope of amelioration.

TJ to Lydia Howard Huntley Sigourney

Monticello July 18. 24

I thank you Madam, for the kindness of your letter of June 30. and the partial notice you are so good as to take of the part I bore in our great revolutionary struggle. I was one only of many, very many indeed who exerted their best endeavours in the accomplishment of that change in our condition. its success will make it the greatest event in human history, and although rivers of blood are yet to flow for the general establishment of its principles and its consequences towards the amelioration of the condition of man throughout the universe, they will be finally established. we have had to be sure one great example of retrogradation in the improvement of man, in the extinction by the Northern Barbarians of the science of Greece and Rome. but the art of printing was then unknown. that renders impossible the loss of lights once gained.

I rejoice also in your advocation of the Indian rights. & concur in all your sentiments in their favor. I once had hopes that the Southern tribes were nearly ripe for incorporation with us. the facility with which the cotton plant enables them to clothe themselves renders their civilization easier than that of the Northern tribes, who are obliged to resort to the beasts of the forest for covering. but my hopes in the South are damped by the transactions of the late war which in destroying many of them have produced in the rest so implacable a hatred of us as to revolt them against all counsels coming from us. the happy numbers in which you have so strongly and so feelingly expressed their wrongs will ensure their being read, and felt by breasts which humble prose can rarely touch. reading, they will reflect, and feel the duties we owe to that race of men. I wish that was the only blot in our moral history, and that no other race had higher charges to bring against us. I am not apt to despair; yet I see not how we are to disengage ourselves from that deplorable entanglement, we have the wolf by the ears and feel the danger of either holding or letting him loose. I shall not live to see it but those who come after us will be wiser than we are, for light is spreading and man improving. to that advancement I look, and to the dispensations of an all-wise and all-powerful providence to devise the means of effecting what is right. I pray you to accept assurances of my high and respectful consideration.

Th: Jefferson

"A Book Peddler Invades Monticello," May 31, 1824

. . . Charlottesville, Va. Monday Morn'g, 31 May, 1824. Between 8 and 9 o'clk. called on Mr. Jefferson. The boy conducted and left me at the door and I knocked. Mr. Jefferson came himself. I approached and shook hands with him and he asked me in. I opened by saying I had no introduction to him but a new publication [Mitford's *History of Greece*] for which I was getting subscribers. He replied he never subscribed for anything. I told him of my work and he said it was a very bad work. Mitford misrepresents the Democrats and distorts facts, etc. etc. I turned the subject and we talked about 1st: The right of 'he georgians to the Cherokee lands, 2nd: The character of the Indians, 3rd: The character of the Negroes, 4th: The Tariff, 5th: The disposition of Gt. Britain towards Spain and the United States, 6th: The Being of God, 7th: The character of Christ and His Religion, 8th: The Christian Clergy and Theological Controversy. 1st—He is decidedly opposed to the Georgia Claim. . . . He appears to think the Indians will all dwindle away and be lost in our race by amalgamation. 3rd—Says the south agrees with the Negroes best—that the experiment now making at Hayti is very interesting. He hopes well of their [i.e., Negroes'] minds though has never seen evidence of genius among them, but they are possessed of the best hearts of any people in the world. Great levity of character, etc. On account of the prejudice of our Nation against the black, he would defer treating with the haytians as long as possible, but we must certainly acknowledge their independence . . . I should think him less of a philosopher than a partizan. His manners are much the most agreeable part of him. They are artifical [*sic*], he shrugs his shoulders when talking, has much of the

Frenchman, is rapid, varying, volatile, eloquent, amusing. I should not think him (did I not know his age) much over 60 or 65 years. He alluded to his being troubled with extensive correspondence but said he could read with as much ease and pleasure as ever—Can see in the day time without glasses. When speaking of the Indians he observed that in a conversation with a Chief he had told him that both his daughters married descendents of Pocahontas. This he evidently is proud of.

James Heaton to TJ

Middletown, Butler county,
Ohio, April 20th 1826.

Aged and Honored Sir,

Permit a plain man, a native of Virginia, an admirer of your character, who feels an interest in your fame, and who always has eagerly laid hold of every thing, that he thought ever escaped your pen, as political and moral perfection; I say, permit such a man, to occupy a few minutes of your precious and remaining time—It has for many years been conjectured, that you would favor the world, at some period, with a political treatise, having for one object, the abolition of slavery. If Heaven, in mercy to the blacks, and safety to the whites, and unfading honor to your already great name and fame, should so move you, to leave but one single page, to that effect; many of your devoted friends, and political deciples firmly believe, it would have a more certain, calm, permanent and irrisistible effect, than any, and all things, said, and written thereon since the existence of the american Government—I am well aware, that to ask you to write me your opinion, in detail, on that subject, would be improper, and for me to trouble you with a tedious letter would be impertinent; But my zeal on the subject, together with a long confirmed opinion of the goodness of your heart, and rectitude of your Head, has emboldened me, to pray of you, to give me two lines, expressive of the probability, of your leaving, for the World, your thoughts on that subject.—I fear in making this request, I may be censured for impertinence, or gross ignorance of proper decorum, or both; if however I err, in anyway, I beg forgiveness—And whatever may be the fate of this my request, I shall die, as I have lived, the undeviating friend to the good name, fame and character of Jefferson. James Heaton.

TJ to James Heaton

Dear Sir Monticello May 20. 26.

The subject of your letter of Apr. 20 is one on which I do not permit myself to express an opinion, but when time, place, & occasion may give it some favorable effect. a good cause is often injured more by ill timed efforts of it's friends than by the arguments of it's enemies. persuasion, perseverance, and patience are the best advocates on questions depending on the will of others. the revolution in public opinion which this case requires, is not to be expected in a day, or perhaps in an age. but time, which outlives all things, will outlive this evil also. my sentiments have been 40. years before the public. had I repeated them 40. times, they would only have become the more stale and thread-bare. altho I shall not live to see them consummated, they will not die with me. but living or dying they will ever be in my most fervent prayers. this is written for yourself, and not for the public: in compliance with your request of two lines of sentiment on the subject. accept the assurance of my good will and respect. Th: Jefferson

TJ to Roger Chew Weightman

Respected Sir Monticello June 24. 26

The kind invitation I recieve from you on the part of the citizens of the city of Washington, to be present with them at their celebration of the 50th anniversary of American independance; as one of the surviving signers of an instrument, pregnant with our own, and the fate of the world, is most flattering to myself, and heightened by the honorable accompaniment proposal for the comfort of such a journey. it adds sensibly to the sufferings of sickness, to be deprived by it of a personal participation in the rejoicings of that day. but acquiescence is a duty, under circumstances not placed among those we are permitted to controul. I should indeed, with peculiar delight, have met and exchanged there, congratulations personally, with the small band, the remnant of that host of worthies, who joined with us, on that day, in the bold and doubtful election we were to make, for our country, between submission, or the sword; and to have enjoyed with them the consolatory fact that our fellow citizens, after half a century of experience and prosperity, continue to approve the choice we made. may it be to the world what I believe it will be, (to some parts sooner, to others later, but finally to all.) the Signal of arousing men to burst the chains, under which Monkish ignorance and superstition had persuaded them to bind themselves, and to assume the blessings & security of self government. the form which we have substituted restores the free right to the unbounded exercise of reason and freedom of opinion. all eyes are opened, or opening to the rights of man. the general spread of the light of science has already laid open to every view the palpable truth that the mass of mankind has not been born, with saddles on their backs, nor a favored few booted and spurred, ready to ride them legitimately, by the grace of god. these are grounds of hope for others. for ourselves let the annual return of this day, for ever refresh our recollections of these rights and an undiminished devotion to them.

I will ask permission here to address the pleasure with which I should have met my ancient neighbors of the City of Washington and of it's vicinities, with whom I passed so many years of a pleasing social intercourse; an intercourse which so much relieved the anxieties of the public cares, and left impressions so deeply engraved in my affections, as never to be forgotten. with my regret that ill health forbids me the gratification of an acceptance, be pleased to recieve for yourself and those for whom you write the assurance of my highest respect and friendly attachments.

Th: Jefferson

Theories

Introduction

ALTHOUGH THE SUBJECT did not obsess Jefferson—and there were subjects that did obsess him—he had serious things to say about slavery, about Black people, and about Native Americans. The state of relations between the three racial groups that occupied North America during his lifetime, spanning the colonial period, the revolutionary period, and into the early American Republic, was naturally a matter of concern to him.

Though often troubled, the relationship between Native Americans and Whites was naturally of quite a different character than the relationship between Whites and Blacks. Jefferson knew both Indians and Black people, but he knew them under very different circumstances. He very famously, or one might say infamously, recorded his thoughts about the two groups in *Notes on the State of Virginia*. Jefferson wrote the *Notes* as part of an answer to a series of queries—twenty-two of them—by François Barbé-Marbois, who was in the United States (Philadelphia) serving as the secretary to the French Legation in 1780. He wanted information about the new country, and he sent his questions to officials in each of the newly formed states. A member of the Virginia delegation in Philadelphia sent the questions to Jefferson, who was then governor of Virginia, as the person most likely to be able to answer them. Jefferson rearranged the queries and responded to each, while adding one on climate that Barbé-Marbois had not requested. When he finished, he had a manuscript that was book length. Over the next two years he worked on the *Notes*, expanding it further.

Jefferson writes openly about race in queries that are often quoted and critiqued. Query VI was designed to counter the Compte de Buffon's assertion that every living thing in the New World degenerated over time. Jefferson offers Native Americans' cultural and physical attributes as part of his rebuttal. He expresses generally positive, though patronizing, views about them, drawing on Scottish stadial theory, which identifies four stages of human social development: the hunter stage, the pastoral stage, the agricultural stage, and the commercial stage. Indians were still in the hunter stage, but he expressed confidence that they could progress through to the other stages. He noted what he saw as their reluctance to quit the hunt in favor of farming, and he was deeply critical of cultural practices that sent women to the fields instead of working in the home, as White women did. He insisted that the labor Indian women performed negatively affected their fertility. But the undercurrent of admiration and romanticization, along with the patronizing tone, can be seen in Jefferson's later policy choices as a government official about how to handle the Native American question. Then, in Query XI, he catalogs the various populations of Indigenous people under the heading "Aborigines."

Jefferson raises Black people in the most infamous passages in the *Notes* in Query XIV, "Laws." There he speculates—"venture[s] as a suspicion only"—about the mental inferiority of Black people. Strangely enough it was his criticism of slavery in Query XVIII that worried Jefferson the most. He never intended for the *Notes* to be published, and he was fearful that what he had to say about slavery would make him a pariah among his fellow Virginians. Before it was published, without his authorization, he was careful about with whom he shared the work. There had been a suggestion that it be given to all the students at William and Mary, but that idea was rejected out of fear that the content on slavery might raise the ire of less enlightened people at the school.

It should come as no surprise that Jefferson's comments in Query XIV about Black people have had the most deleterious effect upon his legacy and reputation in our post–Civil Rights era. The interesting thing about the views expressed in the query is that examples from his actions and words in other contexts, as will be demonstrated by some of the documents in this section and the last one, contravene almost everything he has to say in the *Notes*. One example: Jefferson writes that he never heard a Black person utter anything "above the level of plain narration," essentially calling into question their capacity to reason. Yet, Jefferson gave Black people instructions and had them perform tasks that he well knew required more than telling a story, which is what "plain narration" would be. He talked about the intelligence and capacity of individual Black people in letters. He made a Black man, George Granger, the overseer at Monticello and made his son, George Jr., the foreman of Monticello's nailery, both positions requiring capacities beyond repeating stories.

There is little reason to doubt that Jefferson believed that White people were more intelligent than Black people. It must be noted that Jefferson's adherence to Enlightenment thinking shaped his views in this area. Categorization—putting things in order—was an integral part of the Enlightenment approach to science. Categorizing the races was a part of that, and we see Jefferson's pretensions to "science" in the *Notes* on the question of race and intelligence. He says he ventures it as a "suspicion only" that Blacks are less intelligent, but that seems in service of the abundance of caution of a would-be scientist. After all, he had not conducted any experiments or carried out empirical studies. But the sentiment he voiced was widespread in the White community then, and there is evidence that it remains an article of faith among many today. What does this tell us about the nature of the idea of White supremacy and how it progresses in the world?

In the *Notes*, Jefferson was voicing what amounts to a catechism of White supremacy, saying aloud all the things that people were supposed to believe, the agreed-upon fictions that society was to live by. In their heart, people could believe them with varying degrees of strength, from fervently to not at all. The important thing was to say them out loud so that everyone would know what was expected. Those agreements would hold until circumstances warranted acting in contravention of them. When Jefferson needed the services of the Grangers, what he had written in the *Notes* fifteen years earlier about Blacks' mental capacities did not apply.

It is also Jefferson's prescription for solving the problem of slavery that rankles modern-day observers. He spoke, with apparent pride and enthusiasm, about his plan for emancipation that had been rejected by the Virginia legislature. The plan called for educating Black children—boys to the age of twenty-one, girls to the age of eighteen—after which time they would be freed but sent to live outside the United States. The possible destination changed—the western part of the United States, to Africa, to Haiti. But the basic idea was emancipation with expatriation. Jefferson did not think there could be a peaceful multiracial society. Whites would never give up their prejudices against Black people. Black people would never forgive Whites for how they had been treated. The two races would eventually to go war. He offered that "the Almighty has no attribute which can take side with us in such a contest."

In addition to going to war, if Blacks did not leave the country there would be a danger that Blacks and Whites would have children together. Given the revelations about Jefferson's connection to the enslaved Sally Hemings, with whom he had children, this expressed fear seems most poignant. Hemings and Jefferson's wife, Martha, had the same father, John Wayles. Jefferson knew well, from his own family circumstances and from what he knew of Virginia in general, that slavery was a virtual laboratory for racial mixture. He seems to refer to this obliquely in his critique of slavery in Query XVIII in the passage about the "boisterous passions" that enslavers visited upon the enslaved. But propriety and, likely, his family situation prevented him from being more explicit about the nature of the passions exhibited. The closest he comes to commenting upon that was a letter to Francis Gray in which he sets out a mathematical formula explaining when racial mixture resulted in a Black person becoming White. By his reckoning, his children with Sally Hemings were White. Once they were freed, they would be free citizens of the United States.

Jefferson's first three public pronouncements about race and slavery appear in this section as well, though one was when he was acting in his capacity as the lawyer for an enslaved man suing for his freedom in the case of *Howell v. Netherland*. Jefferson was making an argument on behalf of a litigant, but there is no reason to doubt that he believed the sentiment expressed that " all men are born free and equal," his first usage of that idea pre–Declaration of Independence. The second pronouncement can be found in his *Summary View of the Rights of British America*, written in 1774. In first draft of the Declaration of Independence, Jefferson includes language about the evils of the slave trade, referring to it as a "cruel war against human nature" that violated the "most sacred rights of life & liberty in the persons of a distant people who never offended him." He calls Africans "people" and says that they have the right to life and liberty. That would seem to answer the question about whether Blacks were meant to be included in the Preamble to the Declaration stating that "all men are created equal" with the rights to "life, liberty, and the pursuit of happiness," but for the fact that Jefferson lived life as one who enslaved people.

Because of what he wrote in the *Notes* about slavery and African Americans, Jefferson had a number of occasions to correspond with people about both subjects. The letters that are reproduced in this section show, over the span of a long life, that his thoughts on the subjects remained fairly steady. One thing to note about the letters, however, is that it was almost uniformly the correspondent, not Jefferson, who raised the subject. After the *Notes* appeared, to both acclaim and criticism, Jefferson did not volunteer his thoughts about slavery or race out of the blue. By 1790 he was an official in the US government and by the mid-1790s a thoroughgoing politician. It would not have done him any good to press his claims about slavery or race while he was vice president or president. Jefferson was a popular figure in Virginia, but there were always concerns about his views on slavery. The letters he wrote during his retirement—still at the prompting of others—show him resorting to "dreams of the future," what he said he believed would be a better future, to solve the problem of slavery and the problem of race.

Documents

Howell v. Netherland

[April, 1770.]

On behalf of the plaintiff it was insisted, 1st, that if he could be detained in servitude by his first master, he could not be aliened. But 2nd. that he could not be detained in servitude.

1. It was observed that the purpose of the act was to punish and deter women from that confusion of species, which the legislature seems to have considered as an evil, and not to oppress their innocent offspring. That accordingly it had made cautious provision for the welfare of the child, by leaving it to the discretion of the church wardens to choose out a proper master; and by directing, that that master should provide for it sufficient food, clothing, and lodging, and should not give immoderate correction. For these purposes the master enters into covenants with the church wardens; and to admit he had a power after this to sell his ward, would be to admit him a power of discharging himself of his covenants. Nor is this objection answered by saying that the covenants of the first master are transferred to the alienee, because he may be insolvent of the damages which should be recovered against him, and indeed they might be of such a nature as could not be atoned for, either to the servant or to society; such, for instance, would be a corruption of morals either by the wicked precept or example of the master, or of his family. The truth is, the master is bound to the servant for food, raiment, and protection and is not at liberty, by aliening his charge,

to put it out of his own power to afford them when wanting. The servant may as well set up a right of withdrawing from his master those personal services which he, in return, is bound to yield him. Again, the same trust which is created by express compact in favor of the first mulatto, is extended by the law to her issue. The legislature confiding that the choice of a master for the first mulatto, by the church wardens, would be prudent, vest the issue in him also without further act to be done; and the master, at the time he takes the mother, knowing that her issue also is to be under her servitude on the same conditions, does by accepting her, tacitly undertake to comply with those conditions raised by the law in their favor. These servants bear greater resemblance to apprentices than to slaves. Thus, on the death of the first master, they go to his executor as an apprentice would, and not to his heir as a slave. The master is chosen, in both cases, from an opinion of his peculiar propriety for that charge, and the performances of his duty in both cases is secured by mutual covenants. Now it is well known that an apprentice can not be aliened; and that, not from any particular provision of the legislature, but from the general nature of the connection and engagements between them: there being, as was before observed, a trust reposed in the diligence and discretion of the master; and a trust by our law cannot be assigned. It adheres to the person as closely as does his integrity, and he can no more transfer the one than the other to a purchaser. But,

2nd. It was insisted, that the plaintiff, being a mulatto of the third generation, would not be detained in servitude under any law whatever: the grand position now to be proved being that one law had reduced to servitude the first mulatto only, the immediate offspring of a white woman by a negro or mulatto man; that a second law had extended it to the "children" of that mulatto; but that no law had yet extended it to her grandchildren, or other issue more remote than this. To prove this, a general statement of these laws was premised. Act of 1705, c. 49 s. 18. "If any woman servant shall have a bastard child, by a negro or mulatto, or if a free Christian white woman shall have such bastard child by a negro or mulatto; in both the said cases the churchwardens shall bind the said child to be a servant until it shall be of thirty one years of age." In other parts of the act, it is declared who shall be slaves, and what a manumission of them; from sect. 34 to 39. are regulations solely relative to slaves, among which is sect. 36. "Baptism of slaves doth not exempt them from bondage; and all children shall be bond or free according to the condition of their mothers and the particular directions of this act."

Act. 1723. c. 4 s. 22. "Where any female mulatto or Indian, by law obliged to serve till the age of thirty or thirty one years shall, during the time of her servitude, have any child born of her body, every such child shall serve the master or mistress of such mulatto or Indian, until it shall attain the same age, the mother of such child was obliged, by law, to serve unto."

In 1748, the Assembly revising and digesting the whole body of our acts of Assembly, in act 14. s. 4. incorporate the clauses before cited, without any addition or alteration. And in 1753, c. 2. s. 4. 13, the law of 1748, is re-enacted with some new matter which does not effect the present question.

Now it is plain the plaintiff does not come within the description of the act of 1705, s. 18; that only reducing to servitude "the child of a white woman by a negro or mulatto man." This was the predicament of the plaintiff's grandmother. I suppose it will not be pretended that the mother being a servant, the child would be a servant also under the law of nature, without any particular provision in the act. Under the law of nature, all men are born free, every one comes into the world with a right to his own person, which includes the liberty of moving and using it at his own will. This is what is called personal liberty, and is given him by the author of nature, because necessary for his own sustenance. The reducing the mother to servitude was a violation of the law of nature: surely then the same law cannot prescribe a continuance of the violation to her issue, and that too without end, for if it extends to any, it must to every degree of descendants. Puff. b. 6. c. 3. s. 4. 9. supports this doctrine. For having proved that servitude to be rightful, must be founded on either compact, or capture in war, he proceeds to shew that the children of the latter only follow the condition of the mother: for which he gives this reason, that the person and labor of the mother in a condition of perfect slavery, (as he supposes to be that of the captive in war) being the property of the master, it is impossible she should maintain it but with her master's goods; by which he supposes a debt contracted from the infant to the master. But he says in cases of servitude founded on contract, "The food of the future issue is contained or implied in their own maintenance, which their master owes them as a just debt; and consequently their children are not involved in a necessity of slavery." This is the nature of the servitude introduced by the act of 1705, the master deriving his title to the service of the mother, entirely from the contract entered into with the churchwardens. That the bondage of the mother does not under the law of nature, infer that of her issue, as included in her, is further obvious from this consideration, that by the same reason, the bondage of the father would infer that of his issue; for he may with equal, and some anatomists say with greater reason, be said to include all his posterity. But this very law admits there is no such descent of condition from father to child, when it imposes servitude on the child of a slave, which would have been unnecessary, if the condition had descended of course. Again, if it be a law of nature that the child shall follow the condition of the parent, it would introduce a very perplexing dilemma; as where the one parent is free and the other a slave. Here the child is to be a slave says this law by inheritance of the father's bondage: but it is also to be free, says the same law by inheritance of its mother's freedom. This contradiction proves it to be no law of nature.

But the 36th section of the act will perhaps be cited as the entailing condition of the mother on the child, where it says, that "children shall be bond or free according to the condition of the mother, and the particular direction of this act." Now that the word "bond" in this clause relates to "slaves" only, I am justified in asserting, not only from common parlance but also from its sense in other parts of this very act. And that on the other hand it considers those who were to be free after a temporary servitude, as described under the word "free." In this very section, 36, it says, "baptism of slaves does not exempt them from bondage." Here then in the very sentence now under consideration, the word bondage is used to express perpetual slavery; and we cannot conceive they meant to use it in two different senses in the same sentence. So in clause nineteen of the same act, it says, "to prevent that abominable mixture of white men or women with negroes or mulattoes, whatever white man or woman being free, shall intermarry with a negro or mulatto, &c. shall be committed to prison, &c." Now unless the act means to include white servants and apprentices under the denomination of "freemen," then a white servant or apprentice may intermarry with a negro or mulatto. But this is making the act miss of its purpose, which was "to prevent the abominable mixture of white men or women with negroes or mulattoes." But to put it out of dispute, the next clause (twenty) says that "if any minister shall, notwithstanding, presume to marry a white man or woman with a negro or mulatto," he shall incur such a penalty. Here then the prohibition is extended to whites in general, without saying "free whites" as the former clause did. But these two clauses are plainly co-extensive; and consequently the word "free" in the nineteenth, was intended to include the temporary white servants taken in by the twentieth clause, under the general appellation of "white men or women." So that this act where it speaks of bondmen, means those who are "perpetual slaves," and where of "freemen," those who are to be free after a temporary servitude, as well as those who are so now. Indeed to suppose, where the act says, "the children of a bondwoman shall be bond," that it means "the children of a temporary servant shall be temporary servants," would infer too much: for it would make temporary servants of the children of white servant women, or of white apprentice women, which yet was never pretended. The conclusion I draw from this, is, that since the temporary service of a white woman does not take from her the appellation of a freewoman, in the sense of this act, and her children under this very clause are free, as being the children of a free woman, neither does the temporary servitude of a mulatto exclude her from the same appellation, and her children also shall be free under this clause, as the children of a free woman. So that the meaning of this clause is, that children shall be slaves, where slavery was the condition of the mother; and free, where freedom either immediate or remote, was her condition: excepting only the instance of the mulatto bastard, which this act makes a servant, though the mother was free. This is the case alluded to by the last words of the clause, "according to the particular direction of this act." Because in this case, the act had made a temporary servant of the child, though the mother was not so.

Then comes the act of 1723, directing that where any female mulatto or Indian, by law obliged to serve till thirty or thirty one, shall have a child during her servitude, such child shall serve the same master to the same age. This act does itself prove that the child was not obliged to serve under the former law of 1705, which had imposed servitude on the mother; and consequently that the clause "children shall be bond or free, according to the condition of the mother," affected the children of slaves only. For wherefore else was this law made? If the children of a mulatto held in temporary servitude were to follow the condition of the mother, and be temporary servants under the law of 1705, that of 1723 was wholly unnecessary. But on the contrary, when we find an Assembly within eighteen years after the law of 1705, had been passed, the one half or whom would probably be the same members who had passed that law, when we see these people I say, enacting expressly that the children should be temporary servants, it is a strong proof the makers of the first law had not intended they should be so. *Expositio contemporanea est optima*, is a maxim in our law, because such exposition is supposed to be taken from the makers of the law themselves, who best knew their own intention; and it is doubly conclusive, where the makers themselves pass a new act to testify their intention. So that I hold it certain, the act of 1705, did not extend to the children of the first mulatto, or that of 1723, would not have been made.

That the act of 1723, did not extend to the plaintiff, is apparent from its words. "Where any female mulatto by law obliged to serve till thirty one (that is, the plaintiff's grandmother) shall during the time of her servitude, have a child born of her body (that is, the plaintiff's mother) such a child shall serve till thirty one." This act describes the plaintiff's mother then as the subject on which to operate. The common sense of mankind would surely spare me the trouble of proving the word "child" does not include the grandchild, great-grandchild, great-great-grandchild, &c. *in infinitum*. Or if that would not, the act itself precludes me, by declaring it meant only a "child born of her body." So that as the law of 1705, has made a servant of the first mulatto, that of 1723, extends it to her children.

The act of 1748, is the next in course. At this time all our acts were revised and digested, and sent in one volume to receive his

Majesty's approbation. These two laws being found to be on the same subject, were then incorporated without any alteration. This however, could not affect their meaning, which is still to be sought after by considering the component acts in their separate state. At any rate it cannot affect the condition of the plaintiff, who was born in 1742, which was six years before it was made. The same may be said of the law of 1753, which is copied from 1748, with only the addition of some new matter, foreign to the present question. So that on the laws of 1705, and 1723, alone, it is to be determined; with respect to which I have endeavored to shew;

That the first of them subjected to servitude, the first mulatto only.

That this did not, under the law of nature, affect the liberty of the children.

Because, under that law we are all born free.

Because, the servitude of the mother was founded on compact, which implies maintenance of her children, so as to have them under no obligation to the master.

And because, this descent of condition from parent to child, would introduce a contradiction where the one parent is free, and the other in servitude.

That as little are they affected by the words of the act, "children shall be bond or free, according to the condition of the mother."

Because that act uses the word "bond," so as to shew it means thereby those only who are perpetual slaves, and by the word "free" those who are entitled to freedom in *præsenti* or in *futuro*; and consequently calling the mother "free," says her children shall be "free."

Because it would make servants of the children of white servants or apprentices, which nobody will say is right.

And because the passing the act of 1723, to subject the child to servitude, shews it was not subject to that state under the old law.

And lastly, that the act of 1723, affects only "children of such mulattoes," as when that law was made were obliged to serve till thirty-one; which takes in the plaintiff's mother who was of the second generation, but does not extend to himself who is of the third.

So that the position at first laid down is now proven, that the act of 1705, makes servants of the first mulatto, that of 1723, extends it to her children, but that it remains for some future legislature, if any shall be found wicked enough, to extend it to the grandchildren and other issue more remote, to the "*nati natorum et qui nascentur ab illis*."

Money to Samuel Howell

Do. For Jos. Hale ord. Joan. Collins 12/6.
Pd. R. Harvie for R. Woods £15.
At coffee H. 7½d.
Gave pauper client 2/.

Notes on the State of Virginia, Queries VI, XI, XIV, and XVIII

QUERY VI, "A NOTICE OF THE MINES AND SUBTERRANEOUS RICHES; ITS TREES, PLANTS, FRUITS, &C?"

. . . Of the Indian of South America I know nothing; for I would not honor with the appellation of knowledge, what I derive from the fables published of them. These I believe to be just as true as the fables of Æsop. This belief is founded on what I have seen of man, white, red, and black, and what has been written of him by authors, enlightened themselves, and writing amidst an enlightened people. The Indian of North America being more within our reach, I can speak of him somewhat from my own knowledge, but more from the information of others better acquainted with him, and on whose truth and judgment I can rely. From these sources I am able to say, in contradiction to this representation, that he is neither more defective in ardor, nor more impotent with his female, than the white reduced to the same diet and exercise: that he is brave, when an enterprise depends on bravery; education with him making the point of honor consist in the destruction of an enemy by stratagem, and in the preservation of his own person free from injury; or perhaps this is nature; while it is education which teaches us to[1] honor force more than finesse; that he will defend himself

1. Sol Rodomonte sprezza di venire
Se non, dove la via meno è ficura. Ariosto. 14. 117.

against an host of enemies, always chusing to be killed, rather than to surrender,[2] though it be to the whites, who he knows will treat him well: that in other situations also he meets death with more deliberation, and endures tortures with a firmness unknown almost to religious enthusiasm with us: that he is affectionate to his children, careful of them, and indulgent in the extreme: that his affections comprehend his other connections, weakening, as with us, from circle to circle, as they recede from the center: that his friendships are strong and faithful to the uttermost[3] extremity: that his

2. In so judicious an author as Don Ulloa, and one to whom we are indebted for the most precise information we have of South America, I did not expect to find such assertions as the following. 'Los Indios vencidos son los mas cobardes y pusilanimes que se peuden vér:—se hacen inocentes, se humillan hasta el desprecio, disculpan su inconsiderado arrojo, y con las súplicas y los ruegos dán seguras pruebus de su pusilanimidad.—ó lo que refieren las historias de la Conquista, sobre sus grandes acciones, es en un sendito figurado, ó el caracter de estas gentes no es ahora segun era entonces; pero lo que no tiene duda es, que las Naciones de la parte Septentrional subsisten en la misma libertad que siempre han tenido, sin haber sido sojuzgados por algun Principe extrano, y que viven segun su régimen y costumbres de toda la vida, sin que haya habido motivo para que muden de caracter; y en estos se vé lo mismo, que sucede en los del Peru, y de toda la América Meridional, reducidos, y que nunca lo han estado.' Noticias Americanas. Entretenimiento XVIII. §. 1. Don Ulloa here admits, that the authors who have described the Indians of South America, before they were enslaved, had represented them as a brave people, and therefore seems to have suspected that the cowardice which he had observed in those of the present race might be the effect of subjugation. But, supposing the Indians of North America to be cowards also, he concludes the ancestors of those of South America to have been so too, and therefore that those authors have given fictions for truth. He was probably not acquainted himself with the Indians of North America, and had formed his opinion of them from hearsay. Great numbers of French, of English, and of Americans, are perfectly acquainted with these people. Had he had an opportunity of enquiring of any of these, they would have told him, that there never was an instance known of an Indian begging his life when in the power of his enemies: on the contrary, that he courts death by every possible insult and provocation. His reasoning then would have been reversed thus. 'Since the present Indian of North America is brave, and authors tell us, that the ancestors of those of South America were brave also; it must follow, that the cowardice of their descendants is the effect of subjugation and ill treatment.' For he observes, ib. §. 27. that 'los obrages los aniquilan por la inhumanidad con que se les trata.'

3. A remarkable instance of this appeared in the case of the late Col. Byrd, who was sent to the Cherokee nation to transact some business with them. It happened that some of our disorderly people had just killed one or two of that nation. It was therefore proposed in the council of the Cherokees that Col. Byrd should be put to death, in revenge for the loss of their countrymen. Among them was a chief called Silòuee, who, on some former occasion, had contracted an acquaintance and friendship with Col. Byrd. He came to him every night in his tent, and told him not to be afraid, they should not kill him. After many days deliberation, however, the determination was, contrary to Silòuee's expectation,

sensibility is keen, even the warriors weeping most bitterly on the loss of their children, though in general they endeavour to appear superior to human events: that his vivacity and activity of mind is equal to ours in the same situation; hence his eagerness for hunting, and for games of chance. The women are submitted to unjust drudgery. This I believe is the case with every barbarous people. With such, force is law. The stronger sex therefore imposes on the weaker. It is civilization alone which replaces women in the enjoyment of their natural equality. That first teaches us to subdue the selfish passions, and to respect those rights in others which we value in ourselves. Were we in equal barbarism, our females would be equal drudges. The man with them is less strong than with us, but their woman stronger than ours; and both for the same obvious reason; because our man and their woman is habituated to labour, and formed by it. With both races the sex which is indulged with ease is least athletic. An Indian man is small in the hand and wrist for the same reason for which a sailor is large and strong in the arms and shoulders, and a porter in the legs and thighs.—They raise fewer children than we do. The causes of this are to be found, not in a difference of nature, but of circumstance. The women very frequently attending the men in their parties of war and of hunting, child-bearing becomes extremely inconvenient to them. It is said, therefore, that they have learnt the practice of procuring abortion by the use of some vegetable; and that it even extends to prevent conception for a considerable time after. During these parties they are exposed to numerous hazards, to excessive exertions, to the greatest extremities of hunger. Even at their homes the nation depends for food, through a certain part of every year, on the gleanings of the forest: that is, they experience a famine once in every year. With all animals, if the female be badly fed, or not fed at all, her young perish: and if both male and female be reduced to like want, generation becomes less active, less productive. To the obstacles then of want and hazard, which nature has opposed to the multiplication

---

that Byrd should be put to death, and some warriors were dispatched as executioners. Silòuee attended them, and when they entered the tent, he threw himself between them and Byrd, and said to the warriors, 'this man is my friend: before you get at him, you must kill me.' On which they returned, and the council respected the principle so much as to recede from their determination.

of wild animals, for the purpose of restraining their numbers within certain bounds, those of labour and of voluntary abortion are added with the Indian. No wonder then if they multiply less than we do. Where food is regularly supplied, a single farm will shew more of cattle, than a whole country of forests can of buffaloes. The same Indian women, when married to white traders, who feed them and their children plentifully and regularly, who exempt them from excessive drudgery, who keep them stationary and unexposed to accident, produce and raise as many children as the white women. Instances are known, under these circumstances, of their rearing a dozen children. An inhuman practice once prevailed in this country of making slaves of the Indians. It is a fact well known with us, that the Indian women so enslaved produced and raised as numerous families as either the whites or blacks among whom they lived.—It has been said, that Indians have less hair than the whites, except on the head. But this is a fact of which fair proof can scarcely be had. With them it is disgraceful to be hairy on the body. They say it likens them to hogs. They therefore pluck the hair as fast as it appears. But the traders who marry their women, and prevail on them to discontinue this practice, say, that nature is the same with them as with the whites. Nor, if the fact be true, is the consequence necessary which has been drawn from it. Negroes have notoriously less hair than the whites; yet they are more ardent. But if cold and moisture be the agents of nature for diminishing the races of animals, how comes she all at once to suspend their operation as to the physical man of the new world, whom the Count acknowledges to be 'à peu près de mème stature que l'homme de notre monde,' and to let loose their influence on his moral faculties? How has this 'combination of the elements and other physical causes, so contrary to the enlargement of animal nature in this new world, these obstacles to the developement and formation of great germs,'[4] been arrested and suspended, so as to permit the human body to acquire its just dimensions, and by what inconceivable process has their action been directed on his mind alone? To judge of the truth of this, to form a just estimate of their genius and mental powers, more facts are wanting, and great allowance to be made for those

4. XVIII. 145.

circumstances of their situation which call for a display of particular talents only. This done, we shall probably find that they are formed in mind as well as in body, on the same module with the[5] 'Homo sapiens Europæus.' The principles of their society forbidding all compulsion, they are to be led to duty and to enterprise by personal influence and persuasion. Hence eloquence in council, bravery and address in war, become the foundations of all consequence with them. To these acquirements all their faculties are directed. Of their bravery and address in war we have multiplied proofs, because we have been the subjects on which they were exercised. Of their eminence in oratory we have fewer examples, because it is displayed chiefly in their own councils. Some, however, we have of very superior lustre. I may challenge the whole orations of Demosthenes and Cicero, and of any more eminent orator, if Europe has furnished more eminent, to produce a single passage, superior to the speech of Logan, a Mingo chief, to Lord Dunmore, when governor of this state. And, as a testimony of their talents in this line, I beg leave to introduce it, first stating the incidents necessary for understanding it.

In the spring of the year 1774, a robbery and murder were committed on an inhabitant of the frontiers of Virginia, by two Indians of the Shawanee tribe. The neighbouring whites, according to their custom, undertook to punish this outrage in a summary way. Col. Cresap, a man infamous for the many murders he had committed on those much-injured people, collected a party, and proceeded down the Kanhaway in quest of vengeance. Unfortunately a canoe of women and children, with one man only, was seen coming from the opposite shore, unarmed, and unsuspecting an hostile attack from the whites. Cresap and his party concealed themselves on the bank of the river, and the moment the canoe reached the shore, singled out their objects, and, at one fire, killed every person in it. This happened to be the family of Logan, who had long been distinguished as a friend of the whites. This unworthy return provoked his vengeance. He accordingly signalized himself in the war which ensued. In the autumn of the same year, a decisive battle was fought at the mouth of the Great Kanhaway, between the collected forces

5. Linn. Syst. Definition of a Man.

of the Shawanees, Mingoes, and Delawares, and a detachment of the Virginia militia. The Indians were defeated, and sued for peace. Logan however disdained to be seen among the suppliants. But, lest the sincerity of a treaty should be distrusted, from which so distinguished a chief absented himself, he sent by a messenger the following speech to be delivered to Lord Dunmore.

'I appeal to any white man to say, if ever he entered Logan's cabin hungry, and he gave him not meat; if ever he came cold and naked, and he clothed him not. During the course of the last long and bloody war, Logan remained idle in his cabin, an advocate for peace. Such was my love for the whites, that my countrymen pointed as they passed, and said, 'Logan is the friend of white men.' I had even thought to have lived with you, but for the injuries of one man. Col. Cresap, the last spring, in cold blood, and unprovoked, murdered all the relations of Logan, not sparing even my women and children. There runs not a drop of my blood in the veins of any living creature. This called on me for revenge. I have sought it: I have killed many: I have fully glutted my vengeance. For my country, I rejoice at the beams of peace. But do not harbour a thought that mine is the joy of fear. Logan never felt fear. He will not turn on his heel to save his life. Who is there to mourn for Logan?—Not one.'

Before we condemn the Indians of this continent as wanting genius, we must consider that letters have not yet been introduced among them. Were we to compare them in their present state with the Europeans North of the Alps, when the Roman arms and arts first crossed those mountains, the comparison would be unequal, because, at that time, those parts of Europe were swarming with numbers; because numbers produce emulation, and multiply the chances of improvement, and one improvement begets another. Yet I may safely ask, how many good poets, how many able mathematicians, how many great inventors in arts or sciences, had Europe North of the Alps then produced? And it was sixteen centuries after this before a Newton could be formed. I do not mean to deny, that there are varieties in the race of man, distinguished by their powers both of body and mind. I believe there are, as I see to be the case in the races of other animals. I only mean to suggest a doubt, whether the bulk and faculties of animals depend on the side of the Atlantic on which their food happens to grow, or which furnishes the elements of which they are compounded? Whether nature has enlisted herself as a Cis or Trans-Atlantic partisan? I am induced to suspect, there has been more eloquence than sound reasoning displayed in support of this theory; that it is one of those cases where the judgment has been seduced by a glowing pen: and whilst I render every tribute of honor and esteem to the celebrated zoologist, who has added, and is still adding, so many precious things to the treasures of science, I must doubt whether in this instance he has not cherished error also, by lending her for a moment his vivid imagination and bewitching language.

QUERY XI, "ABORIGINES"

A description of the Indians established in that state?

When the first effectual settlement of our coloney was made, which was in 1607, the country from the sea-coast to the mountains, and from Potowmac to the most southern waters of James river, was occupied by upwards of forty different tribes of Indians. Of these the *Powhatans*, the *Mannahoacs*, and *Monacans*, were the most powerful. Those between the sea-coast and falls of the rivers, were in amity with one another, and attached to the *Powhatans* as their link of union. Those between the falls of the rivers and the mountains, were divided into two confederacies; the tribes inhabiting the head waters of Potowmac and Rappahanoc being attached to the *Mannahoacs*; and those on the upper parts of James river to the *Monacans*. But the *Monicans* and their friends were in amity with the *Mannahoacs* and their friends and waged joint and perpetual war against the *Powhatans*. We are told that the *Powhatans*, *Mannahoacs*, and *Monacans*, spoke languages so radically different, that interpreters were necessary when they transacted business. Hence we may conjecture, that this was not the case between all the tribes, and probably that each spoke the language of the nation to which it was attached; which we know to have been the case in many particular instances. Very possibly there may have been anciently three different stocks, each of which multiplying in a long course of time, had separated into so many little societies. This practice results from the circumstance of their having never submitted themselves to any laws, any coercive power, any shadow of government.

Their only controuls are their manners, and that moral sense of right and wrong, which, like the sense of tasting and feeling, in every man makes a part of his nature. An offence against these is punished by contempt, by exclusion from society, or, where the case is serious, as that of murder, by the individuals whom it concerns. Imperfect as this species of coercion may seem, crimes are very rare among them; insomuch that were it made a question, whether no law as among the savage Americans, or too much law, as among the civilized Europeans, submits man to the greatest evil, one who has seen both conditions of existence would pronounce it to be the last: and that the sheep are happier of themselves, than under care of the wolves. It will be said, that great societies cannot exist without government. The savages therefore break them into small ones.

The territories of the *Powhatan* confederacy, south of the Potowmac, comprehended about 8000 square miles, 30 tribes, and 2400 warriors.

Capt. Smith tells us, that within 60 miles of James town were 5000 people, of whom 1500 were warriors. From this we find the proportion of their warriors to their whole inhabitants, was as 3 to 10. The *Powhatan* confederacy then would consist of about 8000 inhabitants, which was one for every square mile; being about the twentieth part of our present population in the same territory, and the hundredth of that of the British islands.

Besides these, were the *Nottoways*, living on Nottoway river, the *Meherrins* and *Tuteloes* on Meherrin river, who were connected with the Indians of Carolina, probably with the Chowanocs.

The preceding table contains a state of these several tribes, according to their confederacies and geographical situation, with their numbers when we first became acquainted with them, where these numbers are known. The numbers of some of them are again stated as they were in the year 1669, when an attempt was made by the assembly to enumerate them. Probably the enumeration is imperfect, and in some measure conjectural, and that a further search into the records would furnish many more particulars. What would be the melancholy sequel of their history, may however be argued from the census of 1669; by which we discover that the tribes therein enumerated were, in the space of 62 years, reduced to about one-third of their former numbers. Spirituous liquors, the small pox, war and an abridgment of territory, to a people who lived principally on the spontaneous productions of nature, had committed terrible havock among them, which generation, under the obstacles opposed to it among them, was not likely to make good. That the lands of this country were taken from them by conquest, is not so general a truth as is supposed. I find in our historians and records, repeated proofs of purchase, which cover a considerable part of the lower country; and many more would doubtless be found on further search. The upper country we know has been acquired altogether by purchases made in the most unexceptionable form.

Westward of all these tribes, beyond the mountains, and extending to the great lakes, were the *Massawomees*, a most powerful confederacy, who harassed unremittingly the *Powhatans* and *Manahoacs*. These were probably the ancestors of tribes known at present by the name of the *Six Nations*.

Very little can now be discovered of the subsequent history of these tribes severally. The *Chickahominies* removed about the year 1661, to Mattapony river. Their chief, with one from each of the tribes of the Pamunkies and Mattaponies, attended the treaty of Albany in 1685. This seems to have been the last chapter in their history. They retained however their separate name so late as 1705, and were at length blended with the Pamunkies and Mattaponies, and exist at present only under their names. There remain of the *Mattaponies* three or four men only, and they have more negro than Indian blood in them. They have lost their language, have reduced themselves, by voluntary sales, to about fifty acres of land, which lie on the river of their own name, and have from time to time, been joining the Pamunkies, from whom they are distant but 10 miles. The *Pamunkies* are reduced to about 10 or 12 men, tolerably pure from mixture with other colours. The older ones among them preserve their language in a small degree, which are the last vestiges on earth, as far as we know, of the Powhatan language. They have about 300 acres of very fertile land, on Pamunkey river, so encompassed by water that a gate shuts in the whole. Of the *Nottoways*, not a male is left. A few women constitute the remains of that tribe. They are seated on Nottoway river, in Southampton county, on very fertile lands. At a very early period, certain lands were marked out and appropriated to these tribes, and were kept

	NORTH.					
WEST.		MANNAHOACS.				
		TRIBES.	COUNTRY.	CHIEF TOWN.	WARRIORS.	
					1607	1669
	Between PATOWMAC and RAPPAHANOC.					
		Whonkenties	Fauquier			
		Tegninaties	Culpeper			
		Ontponies	Orange			
		Tauxitanians	Fauquier			
		Hassinungaes	Culpeper			
	Between RAPPAHANOC and YORK.					
		Stegarakies	Orange			
		Shackakonies	Spotsylvania			
		Manahoacs	Stafford. Spotsylvania			
	Between YORK and JAMES.	MONACANS.				
		Monacans	James R. above the falls	Fork of James R.		30
		Monasiccapanoes	Louisa. Fluvanna			
	Between JAMES and CAROLINA.					
		Monahassanoes	Bedford. Buckingham			
		Massinacaes	Cumberland			
		Mohemenchoes	Powhatan			
	EASTERN SHORE.					
	SOUTH.					

POWHATANS.						EAST.
TRIBES.	COUNTRY.	CHIEF TOWN.	WARRIORS.			
			1607	1669		
Tauxenents	Fairfax	About General Washington's	40			
Patówomekes	Stafford. King George	Patowmac creek	200		By the name of Matchotics. U. Matchodie. Nanzaticos. Nanzatico. Appamatox Matox.	
Cuttatawomans	King George	About Lamb creek	20	60		
Pissasecs	King Geo. Richmond	Above Leeds town	—			
Onaumanients	Westmoreland	Nomony river	100			
Rappahànocs	Richmond county.	Rappahanoc creek	100	30		
Moràughtacunds	Lancaster. Richmond	Moratico river	80	40	by the name of Totuskeys	
Secacaonies	Northumberland	Coan river	30			
Wighcocòmicoes	Northumberland	Wicocomico river	130	70		
Cuttatawomans	Lancaster	Corotoman	30			
Nantaughtacunds	Essex. Caroline	Port tobacco creek	150	60		
Màttapomènts	Mattapony river	———	30	20		
Pamùnkies	King William	Romuncock	300	50		
Wèrowocòmicos	Gloucester	About Rosewell	40			
Payànkatanks	Piankatank river	Turk's Ferry. Grimesby	55			
Youghtanunds	Pamunkey river	———	60			
Chickahòminies	Chickahominy river	Orapaks	250	60		
Powhatàns	Henrico	Powhatan. Mayo's	40	10		
Arrowhàtocs	Henrico	Arrohatocs	30			
Wèanous	Charles city	Weynoke	100	15		
Paspahèghes	Charles city. James city	Sandy point	40			
Chískiacs	York	Chiskiac	45	15		
Kecoughtáns	Elizabeth city	Roscows	20			
Appamàttocs	Chesterfield	Bermuda hundred	60	50	1669	
Quiocohanoes	Surry	About Upper Chipoak	25	3 Pohics	Nottoways	
Wàrrasqeaks	Isle of Wight	Warrasqueac			Meherrics 90	
Nasamònds	Nansamond	About the mouth of West. branch	200	45	Tuteloes 50	
Chèsapeaks	Princess Anne	About Lynhaven river	100			
Accohanocs	Accom. Northampton	Accohanoc river	40			
Accomàcks	Northampton	About Cheriton's	80			

from encroachment by the authority of the laws. They have usually had trustees appointed, whose duty was to watch over their interests, and guard them from insult and injury. The *Monacans* and their friends, better known latterly by the name of *Tuscaroras*, were probably connected with the Maslawomecs, or Five Nations. For though we are told their languages were so different that the intervention of interpreters was necessary between them, yet do we also learn that the Erigas, a nation formerly inhabiting on the Ohio, were of the same original stock with the Five Nations, and that they partook also of the Tuscarora language. Their dialects might, by long separation, have become so unlike as to be unintelligible to one another. We know that in 1712, the Five Nations received the Tuscaroras into their confederacy, and made them the Sixth Nation. They received the Meherrins and Tuteloes also into their protection: and it is most probable, that the remains of many other of the tribes, of whom we find no particular account, retired westwardly in like manner, and were incorporated with one or other of the western tribes.

I know of no such thing existing as an Indian monument: for I would not honour with that name arrow points, stone hatchets, stone pipes, and half-shapen images. Of labour on the large scale, I think there is no remain as respectable as would be a common ditch for the draining of lands: unless indeed it would be the Barrows, of which many are to be found all over this country. These are of different sizes, some of them constructed of earth, and some of loose stones. That they were repositories of the dead, has been obvious to all: but on what particular occasion constructed, was a matter of doubt. Some have thought they covered the bones of those who have fallen in battles fought on the spot of interment. Some ascribed them to the custom, said to prevail among the Indians, of collecting, at certain periods the bones of all their dead, wheresoever deposited at the time of death. Others again supposed them the general sepulchres for towns, conjectured to have been on or near these grounds; and this opinion was supported by the quality of the lands in which they are found, (those constructed of earth being generally in the softest and most fertile meadow-grounds on river sides) and by a tradition, said to be handed down from the aboriginal Indians, that, when they settled in a town, the first person who died was placed erect, and earth put about him, so as to cover and support him; that when another died, a narrow passage was dug to the first, the second reclined against him, and the cover of earth replaced, and so on. There being one of these in my neighbourhood, I wished to satisfy myself whether any, and which of these opinions were just. For this purpose I determined to open and examine it thoroughly. It was situated on the low grounds of the Rivanna, about two miles above its principle fork, and opposite to some hills, on which had been an Indian town. It was of a spheroidical form, of about 40 feet diameter at the base, and had been of about twelve feet altitude, though now reduced by the plough to seven and a half, having been under cultivation about a dozen years. Before this it was covered with trees of 12 inches diameter, and round the base was an excavation of five feet depth and width, from whence the earth had been taken of which the hillock was formed. I first dug superficially in several parts of it, and came to collections of human bones, at different depths, from six inches to three feet below the surface. These were lying in the utmost confusion, some vertical, some oblique, some horizontal, and directed to every point of the compass, entangled, and held together in clusters by the earth. Bones of the most distant parts were found together, as, for instance, the small bones of the foot in the hollow of a scull, many sculls would sometimes be in contact, lying on the face, on the side, on the back, top or bottom, so as, on the whole, to give the idea of bones emptied promiscuously from a bag or basket, and covered over with earth, without any attention to their order. The bones of which the greatest numbers remained, were sculls, jawbones, teeth, the bones of the arms, thighs, legs, feet, and hands. A few ribs remained, some vertebrae of the neck and spine, without their processes, and one instance only of the bone which serves as a base to the vertebral column. The sculls were so tender, that they generally fell to pieces on being touched. The other bones were stronger. There were some teeth which were judged to be smaller than those of an adult; a scull which on a slight view, appeared to be that of an infant, but it fell to pieces on being taken out, so as to prevent satisfactory examination; a rib and a fragment of the under jaw of a person about half grown; another rib of an infant; and part of the jaw of a child, which had not cut its teeth. This last furnishing the most decisive proof of the burial of children here, I was particular in my attention to it. It was part of the right half of the under jaw. The processes, by which it was articulated to the temporal bones, were entire, and the bone itself firm to where it had been broken off, which, as nearly as I could judge, was about the place of the eye-tooth. Its upper edge, wherein would have been the sockets of the teeth, was perfectly smooth. Measuring it with that of an adult, by placing their hinder processes together, its broken end extended to the penultimate grinder of the adult. This bone was white, all the others of a sand colour. The bones of infants being soft, they probably decay sooner, which might be the cause so few were found here. I proceeded then to make a perpendicular cut through the body of the barrow, that I might examine its internal structure. This passed about three feet from its center, was opened to the former surface of the earth, and was wide enough for a man to walk through and examine its sides. At the bottom, that is, on the level of the circumjacent plain, I found bones; above these a few stones, brought from a cliff a quarter of a mile off, and from the river one-eighth of a mile off; then a large interval of earth, then a stratum of bones, and so on. At one end of the section were four strata of bones plainly distinguishable; at the other, three; the strata in one part not ranging with those in another. The bones nearest the surface were least decayed. No holes were discovered in any of them, as if made with bullets, arrows, or other weapons. I conjectured that in this barrow might have been a thousand skeletons. Every one readily seize the circumstances above related, which militate against the opinion, that it covered the bones only of persons fallen in battle; and against the tradition also, which would make it the common sepulchre of a town, in which the bodies were placed upright, and touching each other. Appearances certainly indicate that it has derived both origin and growth from the accustomary collection of bones, and deposition of them together; that the first collection had been deposited on the common surface of the earth, a few stones put over it, and then a covering of earth, that the second had been laid on this, had covered more or less of it in proportion to the number of bones, and was then also covered with earth; and so on. The following are the particular circumstances which give it this aspect. 1. The number of bones. 2. Their confused position. 3. Their being in different strata. 4. The strata in one part having no correspondence with those in another. 5. The different states of decay in these strata, which seem to indicate a difference in the time of inhumation. 6. The existence of infant bones among them.

But on whatever occasion they may have been made, they are of considerable notoriety among the Indians: for a party passing, about thirty years ago, through the part of the country where this barrow is, went through the woods directly to it, without any instructions or enquiry, and having staid about it some time, with expressions which were construed to be those of sorrow, they returned to the high road, which they had left about half a dozen miles to pay this visit, and pursued their journey. There is another barrow much resembling this, in the low grounds of the south branch of Shenandoah where it is crossed by the road leading from the Rockfish gap to Staunton. Both of these have within these dozen years, been cleared of their trees and put under cultivation, are much reduced in their height, and spread in width, by the plough, and will probably disappear in time. There is another on a hill in the Blue ridge of mountains, a few miles north of Wood's gap, which is made up of small stones thrown together. This has been opened and found to contain human bones, as the others do. There are also many others in other parts of the country.

Great question has arisen from whence came those aboriginals of America? Discoveries, long ago made, were sufficient to show that a passage from Europe to America was always practicable, even to the imperfect navigation of ancient times. In going from Norway to Iceland, from Iceland to Groenland, from Groenland to Labrador, the first traject is the widest: and this having been practiced from the earliest times of which we have any account of that part of the earth, it is not difficult to suppose that the subsequent trajects may have been sometimes passed. Again, the late discoveries of Captain Cook, coasting from Kamschatka to California, have proved that if the two continents of Asia and America be separated at all, it is only by a narrow straight. So that from this side also, inhabitants may have passed into America: and the resemblance between the Indians of America and the eastern inhabitants of Asia, would induce us to conjecture, that the former are the descendants of the latter, or the latter of the former: excepting indeed the Eskimaux, who, from the same circumstance of resemblance, and from identity of language, must be derived from the Groenlanders, and these probably from some of the northern parts of the old continent. A knowledge of their several languages would be the most certain evidence of their derivation which could be produced. In fact, it is the best proof of the affinity of nations which ever can be referred to. How many ages have elapsed since the English, the Dutch, the Germans, the Swiss, the Norwegians, Danes and Swedes have separated from their common stock?

Yet how many more must elapse before the proofs of their common origin, which exist in their several languages, will disappear? It is to be lamented then, very much to be lamented, that we have suffered so many of the Indian tribes already to extinguish, without our having previously collected and deposited in the records of literature, the general rudiments at least of the languages they spoke. Were vocabularies formed of all the languages spoken in North and South America, preserving their appellations of the most common objects in nature, of those which must be present to every nation barbarous or civilized, with the inflections of their nouns and verbs, their principles of regimen and concord, and these deposited in all the public libraries, it would furnish opportunities to those skilled in the languages of the old world to compare them with these, now or at any future time, and hence to construct the best evidence of the derivation of this part of the human race.

But imperfect as is our knowledge of the tongues spoken in America, it suffices to discover the following remarkable fact. Arranging them under the radical ones to which they may be palpably traced, and doing the same by those of the red men of Asia, there will be found probably twenty in America, for one in Asia, of those radical languages, so called because, if they were ever the same they have lost all resemblance to one another. A separation into dialects may be the work of a few ages only, but for two dialects to recede from one another till they have lost all vestiges of their common origin, must require an immense course of time; perhaps not less than many people give to the age of the earth. A greater number of those radical changes of language having taken place among the red men of America proves them of greater antiquity than those of Asia.

I will now proceed to state the nations and numbers of the Aborigines which still exist in a respectable and independent form. And as their undefined boundaries would render it difficult to specify those only which may be within any certain limits, and it may not be unacceptable to present a more general view of them, I will reduce within the form of a catalogue all those within, and circumjacent to, the United States, whose names and numbers have come to my notice. These are taken from four different lists, the first of which was given in the year 1759 to general Stanwix by George Croghan, deputy agent for Indian affaires under Sir William Johnson; the second was drawn up by a French trader of considerable note, resident among the Indians many years, and annexed to colonel Bouquet's printed account of his expedition in 1764. The third was made out by captain Hutchins, who visited most of the tribes, by order, for the purpose of learning their numbers in 1768. And the fourth by John Dodge, an Indian trader, in 1779, except the numbers marked, which are from other information.

Northward and Westward of the United States.

TRIBES.	Croghan. 1759.	Bouquet. 1764.	Hutchins. 1768.	Where they reside.
Oswegatchies	—	—	100	At Swagatchy, on the river St. Laurence.
Connasedagoes	—	—	300 (Connasedagoes and Cohunnewagoes together)	Near Montreal.
Cohunnewagoes	—	200		
Orondocs	—	—	100	Near Trois Rivieres.
Abenakies	—	350	150	Near Trois Rivieres.
Little Algonkins	—	—	100	Near Trois Rivieres.
Michmacs	—	700	—	River St. Laurence.
Amelistes	—	550	—	River St. Laurence.
Chalas	—	130	—	River St. Laurence.
Nipissins	—	400	—	Towards the heads of the Ottawas river.
Algonquins	—	300	—	Towards the heads of the Ottawas river.
Round heads	—	2500	—	Riviere aux Tetes boules on the E. side of Lake Superior.
Messasagues	—	2000	—	Lakes Huron and Superior.
Christinaux. Kris.	—	3000	—	Lake Christinaux.

TRIBES.	Croghan. 1759.	Bouquet. 1764.	Hutchins. 1768.	Where they reside.
Assinaboes	—	1500	—	Lake Assinaboes.
Blancs, or Barbus	—	1500	—	
Sioux of the Meadows	10,000	2500	10,000	On the heads of the Missisippi and westward of that river.
Sioux of the Woods		1800		
Sioux	—			
Ajoues	—	1100	—	North of the Padoucas.
Panis. White	—	2000	—	South of the Missouri.
Panis. Freckled	—	1700	—	South of the Missouri.
Padoucas	—	500	—	South of the Missouri.
Grandes eaux	—	1000	—	
Canses	—	1600	—	South of the Missouri.
Osages	—	600	—	South of the Missouri.
Missouris	400	3000	—	On the river Missouri.
Arkanzas	—	2000	—	On the river Arkanzas.
Caouitas	—	700	—	East of the Alibamous.

Within the Limits of the United States.

TRIBES.	Croghan. 1759.	Bouquet. 1764.	Hutchins. 1768.	Dodge. 1779.	Where they reside.
Mohocks	—	—	160	100	Mohocks river.
Onèidas	—	—	300	400	East side of Oneida Lake and head branches Susquehanna.
Tuscaròras	—	—	200		Between the Oneidas and Onondagoes.
Onondàgoes	—	1550	260	230	Near Onondago Lake.
Cayùgas	—	—	200	220	On the Cayuga Lake near the North branch of Susquehanna.
Sènecas	—	—	1000	650	On the waters of Susquehanna, of Ontario, and the heads of the Ohio.
Aughquàgahs	—	—	150	—	East branch of Susquehanna, and on Aughquàgah.

TRIBES.	Croghan. 1759.	Bouquet. 1764.	Hutchins. 1768.	Dodge. 1779.	Where they reside.
Nanticoes	—	—	100	—	Utsanango, Chaghtnet, and Owegy, on the East branch of Susquehanna.
Mohìccons	—	—	100	—	In the same parts.
Conòies	—	—	30	—	In the same parts.
Sapòonies	—	—	30	—	At Diahago and other villages up the North branch of Susquehanna.
Mùnsies	—	—	150	*150	At Diahago and other villages up the North branch of Susquehanna.
Delawares, or Linnelinopies	—	—	150		At Diahago and other villages up the North branch of Susquehanna.
Delawares, or Linnelinopies	600	600	600	*500	Between Ohio and Lake Erie and the branches of Beaver creek, Cayahoga and Muskingum.
Shàwanees	500	400	300	300	Sioto and the branches of Muskingum.
Mìngoes	—	—	—	60	On a branch of Sioto.

Within the Limits of the United States.

TRIBES.	Croghan. 1759.	Bouquet. 1764.	Hutchins. 1768.	Dodge. 1779.	Where they reside.
Mohìccons	—	—		*60	
Cohunnewagos	—	—	300	—	Near Sandusky.
Wyandots	300	300	—		
Wyandots			250	180	Near fort St. Joseph's and Detroit.
Twightwees	300	—	250	—	Miami river near fort Miami.
Miamis	—	350	—	300	Miami river, about fort St. Joseph,

TRIBES.	Croghan. 1759.	Bouquet. 1764.	Hutchins. 1768.	Dodge. 1779.	Where they reside.
Ouiàtonons	200	400	300	*300	On the banks of the Wabash, near fort Ouiatonon.
Piànkishas	300	250	300	*400	On the banks of the Wabash, near fort Ouiatonon.
Shákirs	—	—	200	—	On the banks of the Wabash, near fort Ouiatonon.
Kaskaskias	—	600	300	—	Near Kaskaskia. Mitchigamis?
Illinois	400	300	—		Near Cahokia. Qu. if not the same with Mitchigamis?
Piorias	—	800	—	—	On the Illinois river, called Piaurias, but supposed to mean Piorias.
Pouteòtamies	—	350	300	450	Near fort St. Joseph's and fort Detroit.
Ottàwas	—	—	550	*300	Near fort St. Joseph's and fort Detroit.
Chippawas	—	—	200	—	On Saguinam bay of lake Huron.
Ottawas	—	—	—		On Saguinam bay of lake Huron.
Chippawas	—	—	400	—	Near Michillimackinac.
Ottawas	2000	5900	250	5450	Near Michillimackinac.
Chippawas			400		Near fort St. Mary's on lake Superior.
Chippawas	—	—	—	—	Several other villages along the banks of lake Superior. Numbers unknown.
Chippawas	—	—	—	—	Near Puans bay on lake Michigan.
Shakies	200	400	550	—	Near Puans bay on lake Michigan.
Mynonàmies	—	—	—	—	Near Puans bay on lake Michigan.

Within the Limits of the United States.

TRIBES.	Croghan. 1759.	Bouquet. 1764.	Hutchins. 1768.	Dodge. 1779.	Where they reside.
Ouisconsings	—	550	—	—	Ouisconsing river.
Kickapous	600	300	—	250	On lake Michigan, and between that and the Mississippi.
Otogamies. Foxes	—	—	—	—	
Màscoutens	—	500	4000	—	
Miscòthins	—	—	—		
Outimacs	—	—	—	—	
Musquakies	200	250	—	250	
Sioux. Eastern	—	—	—	500	On the eastern heads of the Mississippi, and the islands of lake Superior.
			Galphin. 1768.		
Cherokees	1500	2500	3000	—	Western parts of North-Carolina.
Chickasaws	—	750	500	—	Western parts of Georgia.
Catawbas	—	150	—	—	On the Catawba river in South-Carolina.
Chacktaws	2000	4500	6000	—	Western parts of Georgia.
Upper Creeks	—	—	3000 (Upper and Lower Creeks)	—	Western parts of Georgia.
Lower Creeks	—	1180			
Natchez	—	150	—	—	
Alibamous	—	600	—	—	Alibama river, in the western parts of Georgia.

The following tribes are also mentioned:

Croghan's Catal.	Lezar,	400	From the mouth of Chio to the mouth of Wabash.
	Webings,	200	On the Missisippi below the Shakies.
	Ousasoys / Grand Tuc.	4000	On White Creek, a branch of the Missisippi.
	Linways,	1000	On the Missisippi.
Bouquet's.	Les Puans,	700	Near Puans Bay,
	Folle Avoine	350	Near Puans Bay.
	Ouanakina,	300	Conjectured to be Tribes of the Creeks.
	Chiakanessou,	350	
	Machecous,	800	
	Souikilas,	200	

Dodge's.	Mineamis,	2000	North-West of L. Michigan, to the heads of Missisippi, and up to L. Superior.
	Piankishas, Mascoutins, Vermillions,	800	On and near the Wabash towards the Illinois.

But apprehending these might be different appellations for some of the tribes already enumerated, I have not inserted them in the table, but state them separately as worthy of further inquiry. The variations observable in numbering the same tribe may sometimes be ascribed to imperfect information, and sometimes to a greater or less comprehension of settlements under the same name.

QUERY XIV, "LAWS"

The administration of justice and the description of the laws? . . . Conveyances of land must be registered in the court of the county wherein they lie, or in the general court, or they are void, as to creditors, and subsequent purchasers.

Slaves pass by descent and dower as lands do. Where the descent is from a parent, the heir is bound to pay an equal share of their value in money to each of his brothers and sisters.

Slaves, as well as lands, were entailable during the monarchy: but, by an act of the first republican assembly, all donees in tail, present and future, were vested with the absolute dominion of the entailed subject.

. . . The mode of acquiring lands, in the earliest times of our settlement, was by petition to the general assembly. If the lands prayed for were already cleared of the Indian title, and the assembly thought the prayer reasonable, they passed the property by their vote to the petitioner. But if they had not yet been ceded by the Indians, it was necessary that the petitioner should previously purchase their right. This purchase the assembly verified, by enquiries of the Indian proprietors; and being satisfied of its reality and fairness, proceeded further to examine the reasonableness of the petition, and its consistence with policy; and according to the result, either granted or rejected the petition. The company also sometimes, though very rarely, granted lands, independently of the general assembly. As the colony increased, and individual applications for land multiplied, it was found to give too much occupation to the general assembly to enquire into and execute the grant in every special case. They therefore thought it better to establish general rules, according to which all grants should be made, and to leave to the governor the execution of them, under these rules. This they did by what have been usually called the land laws amending them from time to time, as their defects were developed. According to these laws, when an individual wished a portion of unappropriated land, he was to locate and survey it by a public officer, appointed for that purpose: its breadth was to bear a certain proportion to its length: the grant was to be executed by the governor: and the lands were to be improved in a certain manner, within a given time. From these regulations there resulted to the state a sole and exclusive power of taking conveyances of the Indian right of soil: since, according to them an Indian conveyance alone could give no right to an individual, which the laws would acknowledge. The state, or the crown, thereafter, made general purchases of the Indians from time to time, and the governor parcelled them out by special grants, conformed to the rules before described, which it was not in his power, or in that of the crown, to dispense with. Grants, unaccompanied by their proper legal circumstances, were set aside regularly by *scire facias*, or by bill in chancery. Since the establishment of our new government, this order of things is but little changed. An individual, wishing to appropriate to himself lands still unappropriated by any other, pays to the public treasurer a sum of money proportioned to the quantity he wants. He carries the treasurer's receipt to the auditors of public accompts, who thereupon debit the treasurer with the sum, and order the register of the land-office to give the party a warrant for his land. With this warrant from the register, he goes to the surveyor of the county where the land lies on which he has cast his eye. The surveyor lays it off for him, gives him its exact description, in the form of a certificate, which certificate he returns to the land office, where a grant is made out, and is signed by the governor. This vests in him a perfect dominion in his lands, transmissible to whom he pleases by deed or will, or by descent to his heirs if he die intestate.

Many of the laws which were in force during the monarchy being relative merely to that form of government, or inculcating principles inconsistent with republicanism, the first assembly which met after the establishment of the commonwealth appointed a committee to revise the whole code, to reduce it into proper form and volume, and report it to the assembly. This work has been executed by three gentlemen, and reported; but probably will not be taken up till a restoration of peace shall leave to the legislature leisure to go through such a work.

The plan of the revisal was this. The common law of England, by which is meant, that part of the English law which was anterior to the date of the oldest statutes extant, is made the basis of the work. It was thought dangerous to attempt to reduce it to a text: it was therefore left to be collected from the usual monuments of it. Necessary alterations in that, and so much of the whole body of the British statutes, and of acts of assembly, as were thought proper to be retained, were digested into 126 new acts, in which simplicity of style was aimed at, as far as was safe. The following are the most remarkable alterations proposed:

. . . To make slaves distributable among the next of kin, as other moveables . . .

To emancipate all slaves born after passing the act. The bill reported by the revisors does not itself contain this proposition; but an amendment containing it was prepared, to be offered to the legislature whenever the bill should be taken up, and further directing, that they should continue with their parents to a certain age, then be brought up, at the public expense, to tillage, arts or sciences, according to their geniuses, till the females should be eighteen, and the males twenty-one years of age, when they should be colonized to such place as the circumstances of the time should render most proper, sending them out with arms, implements of household and of the handicraft arts, seeds, pairs of the useful domestic animals, &c. to declare them a free and independent people, and extend to them our alliance and protection, till they have acquired strength; and to send vessels at the same time to other parts of the world for an equal number of white inhabitants; to induce whom to migrate hither, proper encouragements were to be proposed. It will probably be asked, Why not retain and incorporate the blacks into the state, and thus save the expense of supplying by importation of white settlers, the vacancies they will leave? Deep rooted prejudices entertained by the whites; ten thousand recollections, by the blacks, of the injuries they have sustained; new provocations; the real distinctions which nature has made; and many other circumstances, will divide us into parties, and produce convulsions, which will probably never end but in the extermination of the one or the other race.—To these objections, which are political, may be added others, which are physical and moral. The first difference which strikes us is that of colour. Whether the black of the negro resides in the reticular membrane between the skin and scarf-skin, or in the scarf-skin itself; whether it proceeds from the colour of the blood, the colour of the bile, or from that of some other secretion, the difference is fixed in nature, and is as real as if its seat and cause were better known to us. And is this difference of no importance? Is it not the foundation of a greater or less share of beauty in the two races? Are not the fine mixtures of red and white, the expressions of every passion by greater or less suffusions of colour in the one, preferable to that eternal monotony, which reigns in the countenances, that immoveable veil of black which covers all the emotions of the other race? Add to these, flowing hair, a more elegant symmetry of form, their own judgment in favour of the whites, declared by their preference of them, as uniformly as is the preference of the Oranootan for the black women over those of his own species. The circumstance of superior beauty, is thought worthy attention in the propagation of our horses, dogs, and other domestic animals; why not in that of man? Besides those of colour, figure, and hair, there are other physical distinctions proving a difference of race. They have less hair on the face and body. They secrete less by the kidnies, and more by the glands of the skin, which gives them a very strong and disagreeable odour. This greater degree of transpiration renders them more tolerant of heat, and less so of cold than the whites. Perhaps too a difference of structure in the pulmonary apparatus, which a late ingenious experimentalist has discovered to be the principal regulator of animal heat, may have disabled them from extricating, in the act of inspiration, so much of that fluid from the outer air, or obliged them in expiration, to part with more of it. They seem to require less sleep. A black after hard labour through the day, will be induced by the slightest amusements to sit up till midnight, or later though knowing he must be out with the first dawn of the morning. They are at least as brave, and more adventuresome. But this may perhaps proceed from a want of forethought, which prevents their seeing a danger till it be present. When present, they do not go through it with more coolness or steadiness than the whites. They are more ardent after their female: but love seems with them to be more an eager desire, than a tender delicate mixture of sentiment and sensation. Their griefs are transient. Those numberless afflictions, which render it doubtful whether heaven has given life to us in mercy or in wrath, are less felt, and sooner forgotten with them. In general, their existence appears to participate more of sensation than reflection. To this must be ascribed their disposition to sleep when abstracted from their diversions, and unemployed in labour. An animal whose body is at rest, and who does not reflect, must be disposed to sleep of course. Comparing them by their faculties of memory, reason, and imagination, it appears to me that in memory they are equal to the whites; in reason much inferior, as I think one could scarcely be found capable of tracing and comprehending the investigations of Euclid; and that in imagination they are dull, tasteless, and anomalous. It would be unfair to follow them to Africa for this investigation. We will consider them here, on the same stage with the whites, and where the facts are not apocryphal on which a judgement is to be formed. It will be right to make great allowances for the difference of condition, of education, of conversation, of the sphere in which they move. Many millions of them have been brought to, and born in America. Most of them indeed have been confined to tillage, to their own homes, and their own society: yet many have been so situated, that they might have availed themselves of the conversation of their masters; many have been brought up to the handicraft arts, and from that circumstance have always been associated with the whites. Some have been liberally educated, and all have lived in countries where the arts and sciences are cultivated to a considerable degree, and have had before their eyes samples of the best works from abroad. The Indians, with no advantages of this kind, will often carve figures on their pipes not destitute of design and merit. They will crayon out an animal, a plant, or a country, so as to prove the existence of a germ in their minds which only wants cultivation. They astonish you with strokes of the most sublime oratory; such as prove their reason and sentiment strong, their imagination glowing and elevated. But never yet could I find that a black had uttered a thought above the level of plain narration; never see even an elementary trait of painting or sculpture. In music they are more generally gifted than the whites with accurate ears for tune and time, and they have been found capable of imagining a small catch. Whether they will be equal to the composition of a more extensive run of melody, or of complicated harmony, is yet to be proved. Misery is often the parent of the most affecting touches in poetry.—Among the blacks is misery enough, God knows, but no poetry. Love is the peculiar oestrum of the poet. Their love is ardent, but it kindles the senses only, not the imagination. Religion indeed has produced a Phyllis Whately; but it could not produce a poet. The compositions published under her name are below the dignity of criticism. The heroes of the Dunciad are to her, as Hercules to the author of that poem. Ignatius Sancho has approached nearer to merit in composition; yet his letters do more honour to the heart than the head. They breathe the purest effusions of friendship and general philanthropy, and shew how great a degree of the latter may be compounded with strong religious zeal. He is often happy in the turn of his compliments, and his stile is easy and familiar, except when he affects a Shandean fabrication of words. But his imagination is wild and extravagant, escapes incessantly from every restraint of reason and taste, and, in the course of its vagaries, leaves a tract of thought as incoherent and eccentric, as is the course of a meteor through the sky. His subjects should often have led him to a process of sober reasoning: yet we find him always substituting sentiment for demonstration. Upon the whole, though we admit him to the first place among those of his own colour who have presented themselves to the public judgment, yet when we compare him with the writers of the race among whom he lived and particularly with the epistolary class, in which he has taken his own stand, we are compelled to enroll him at the bottom of the column. This criticism supposes the letters published under his name to be genuine, and to have received amendment from no other hand; points which would not be of easy investigation. The improvement of the blacks in body and mind, in the first instance of their mixture with the whites, has been observed by every one, and proves that their inferiority is not the effect merely of their condition of life. We know that among the Romans, about the Augustan age especially, the condition of their slaves was much more deplorable than that of the blacks on the continent of America. The two sexes were confined in separate apartments, because to raise a child cost the master more than to buy one. Cato, for a very restricted indulgence to his slaves in this particular, took from them a certain price. But in this country the slaves multiply as fast as the free inhabitants. Their situation and manners place the commerce between the two sexes almost without restraint.—The same Cato, on a principle of oeconomy, always sold his sick and superannuated slaves. He gives it as a standing precept to a master visiting his farm, to sell his old oxen, old waggons, old tools, old and diseased servants, and every thing else become useless.

"Vendat boves vetulos, plaustrum vetus, ferramenta vetera, servum senem, servum morbosum, & si quid aliud supersit vendat."

Cato de re rusticâ c. 2. The American slaves cannot enumerate this among the injuries and insults they receive. It was the common practice to expose in the island Aesculapius, in the Tyber, diseased slaves, whose cure was like to become tedious. The emperor Claudius, by an edict, gave freedom to such of them as should recover, and first declared that if any person chose to kill rather than expose them, it should be deemed homicide. The exposing them is a crime of which no instance has existed with us; and were it to be followed by death, it would be punished capitally. We are told of a certain Vedius Pollio, who, in the presence of Augustus, would have given a slave as food to his fish, for having broken a glass. With the Romans, the regular method of taking the evidence of their slaves was under torture. Here it has been thought better never to resort to their evidence. When a master was murdered, all his slaves, in the same house, or within hearing, were condemned to death. Here punishment falls on the guilty only, and as precise proof is required against him as against a freeman. Yet notwithstanding these and other discouraging circumstances among the Romans, their slaves were often their rarest artists. They excelled too in science, insomuch as to be usually employed as tutors to their master's children. Epictetus, Terence, and Phaedrus, were slaves. But they were of the race of whites. It is not their condition then, but nature, which has produced the distinction.—Whether further observation will or will not verify the conjecture, that nature has been less bountiful to them in the endowments of the head, I believe that in those of the heart she will be found to have done them justice. That disposition to theft with which they have been branded, must be ascribed to their situation, and not to any depravity of the moral sense. The man, in whose favour no laws of property exist, probably feels himself less bound to respect those made in favour of others. When arguing for ourselves, we lay it down as a fundamental, that laws, to be just, must give a reciprocation of right: that, without this, they are mere arbitrary rules of conduct, founded in force, and not in conscience: and it is a problem which I give to the master to solve, whether the religious precepts against the violation of property were not framed for him as well as his slave? And whether the slave may not as justifiably take a little from one, who has taken all from him, as he may slay one who would slay him? That a change in the relations in which a man is placed should change his ideas of moral right and wrong, is neither new, nor peculiar to the colour of the blacks. Homer tells us it was so 2600 years ago.

'Emisu, ger t' aretes apoainutai euruopa Zeus Haneros, eut' an min kota doulion ema elesin. Od. 17, 323.

Jove fix'd it certain, that whatever day Makes man a slave takes half his worth away.

But the slaves of which Homer speaks were whites. Notwithstanding these considerations which must weaken their respect for the laws of property, we find among them numerous instances of the most rigid integrity, and as many as among their better instructed masters, of benevolence, gratitude, and unshaken fidelity.—The opinion, that they are inferior in the faculties of reason and imagination, must be hazarded with great diffidence. To justify a general conclusion, requires many observations, even where the subject may be submitted to the anatomical knife, to optical classes, to analysis by fire, or by solvents. How much more then where it is a faculty, not a substance, we are examining; where it eludes the research of all the senses; where the conditions of its existence are various and variously combined; where the effects of those which are present or absent bid defiance to calculation; let me add too, as a circumstance of great tenderness, where our conclusion would degrade a whole race of men from the rank in the scale of beings which their Creator may perhaps have given them. To our reproach it must be said, that though for a century and a half we have had under our eyes the races of black and of red men, they have never yet been viewed by us as subjects of natural history. I advance it therefore as a suspicion only, that the blacks, whether originally a distinct race, or made distinct by time and circumstances, are inferior to the whites in the endowments both of body and mind. It is not against experience to suppose, that different species of the same genus, or varieties of the same species, may possess different qualifications. Will not a lover of natural history then, one who views the gradations in all the races of animals with the eye of philosophy, excuse an effort to keep those in the department of man as distinct as nature has formed them? This unfortunate difference of colour, and perhaps of faculty, is a powerful obstacle to the emancipation of these people. Many of their advocates, while they wish to vindicate the liberty of human nature are anxious also to preserve its dignity and beauty. Some of these, embarrassed by the question

What further is to be done with them?

join themselves in opposition with those who are actuated by sordid avarice only. Among the Romans emancipation required but one effort. The slave, when made free, might mix with, without staining the blood of his master. But with us a second is necessary, description unknown to history. When freed, he is to be removed beyond the reach of mixture.

QUERY XVIII, "MANNERS"

The particular *customs and manners that may happen to be received in that state?*

It is difficult to determine on the standard by which the manners of a nation may be tried, whether *catholic*, or *particular*. It is more difficult for a native to bring to that standard the manners of his own nation, familiarized to him by habit. There must doubtless be an unhappy influence on the manners of our people produced by the existence of slavery among us. The whole commerce between master and slave is a perpetual exercise of the most boisterous passions, the most unremitting despotism on the one part, and degrading submissions on the other. Our children see this, and learn to imitate it; for man is an imitative animal. This quality is the germ of all education in him. From his cradle to his grave he is learning to do what he sees others do. If a parent could find no motive either in his philanthropy or his self-love, for restraining the intemperance of passion towards his slave, it should always be a sufficient one that his child is present. But generally it is not sufficient. The parent storms, the child looks on, catches the lineaments of wrath, puts on the same airs in the circle of smaller slaves, gives a loose to the worst of passions, and thus nursed, educated, and daily exercised in tyranny, cannot but be stamped by it with odious peculiarities. The man must be a prodigy who can retain his manners and morals undepraved by such circumstances. And with what execration should the statesman be loaded, who permitting one half the citizens thus to trample on the rights of the other, transforms those into despots, and these into enemies, destroys the morals of the one part, and the amor patriae of the other. For if a slave can have a country in this world, it must be any other in preference to that in which he is born to live and labour for another: in which he must lock up the faculties of his nature, contribute as far as depends on his individual endeavours to the evanishment of the human race, or entail his own miserable condition on the endless generations proceeding from him. With the morals of the people, their industry also is destroyed. For in a warm climate, no man will labour for himself who can make another labour for him. This is so true, that of the proprietors of slaves a very small proportion indeed are ever seen to labour. And can the liberties of a nation be thought secure when we have removed their only firm basis, a conviction in the minds of the people that these liberties are of the gift of God? That they are not to be violated but with his wrath? Indeed I tremble for my country when I reflect that God is just: that his justice cannot sleep for ever: that considering numbers, nature and natural means only, a revolution of the wheel of fortune, an exchange of situation is among possible events: that it may become probable by supernatural interference! The almighty has no attribute which can take side with us in such a contest.—But it is impossible to be temperate and to pursue this subject through the various considerations of policy, of morals, of history natural and civil. We must be contented to hope they will force their way into every one's mind. I think a change already perceptible, since the origin of the present revolution. The spirit of the master is abating, that of the slave rising from the dust, his condition mollifying, the way I hope preparing, under the auspices of heaven, for a total emancipation, and that this is disposed, in the order of events, to be with the consent of the masters, rather than by their extirpation.

Henry Skipwith to TJ

Dear Sir Hors du Monde January 20th 1784.

Your favor reached me last evening, preceeding the most tremendous Snow storm this country has ever experienced since my rememberance . . .

Previous to my answering (which I do with pleasure) your queries relative to my White negroes I must premise, that exclusive of mine I knew a very stout robust white negroe slave, the pro[perty] of Captain John Butler near Petersburg, who had issue (by a black man) a daughter of the jet hue, about fourteen years of age very handsome. Also that there is now in existence an elderley, tall, stout, white negro *man* slave in the county of Cumberland, about six miles from me, the property of Charles Lee; as this is the only male I ever knew or heard of, I shall postpone sending this letter until the Snow permits me to see Mr. Lee and give you also a particular history of this Phnomenon. In the mean time you have subjoined answers to your Queries, to wit.

I had three female white Negro slaves.

Full sisters.

Their parents have had three whites and two blacks.

Their parents were very healthy.

Their parents are of the ordinary color of blacks (not jet).

The skin of these white negroes is a disagreeable chalky white, their hair perfectly similar to short Sheeps wool, curled like a common negroe.

They have no coloured seams or spots about them.

They are exceedingly well formed, very healthy, strong, and active.

They hear well.

Their eye sight is not strong, their eyes are much affected by the rays of the Sun, and perpetually quiver in their sockets.

Their senses are remarkably perfect, they are very shrewd and quick at repartee.

I know of no instance of this species generating together. Two of mine have generated with black's and each had issue female children of the ordinary complexion of light coloured negroes.

The eldest of the three died in childbed with her second child, at about the age of twenty seven years. The youngest was destroyed at the age of twelve years by lightning from Heaven. The middle one is now alive and well.

Since writing the above I have seen Mr. Lee. He tells me his White Negro man slave was generated between a couple of negro's of the ordinary colour and that he in every respect (the sex excepted) is like my own.

With every sentiment of regard I remain Dear Sir Your afft. friend & Sevt., Henry Skipwith

We request our love may be sent to Patsey by your next letter to her.

TJ to Chastellux

Dear Sir Paris June 7, 1785

I have been honoured with the receipt of your letter of the 2d. instant, and am to thank you, as I do sincerely for the partiality with which you receive the copy of the Notes on my country. As I can answer for the facts therein reported on my own observation, and have admitted none on the report of others which were not supported by evidence sufficient to command my own assent, I am not afraid that you should make any extracts you please for the Journal de physique which come within their plan of publication. The strictures on slavery and on the constitution of Virginia are not of that kind, and they are the parts which I do not wish to have made public, at least till I know whether their publication would do most harm or good. It is possible that in my own country these strictures might produce an irritation which would indispose the people towards the two great objects I have in view, that is the emancipation of their slaves, and the settlement of their constitution on a firmer and more permanent basis. If I learn from thence, that they will not produce that effect, I have printed and reserved just copies enough to be able to give one to every young man at the College. It is to them I look, to the rising generation, and not to the one now in power for these great reformations. The other copy delivered at your hotel was for Monsr. de Buffon. I meant to ask the favour of you to have it sent to him, as I was ignorant how to do it. I have one also for Monsr. Daubenton: but being utterly unknown to him I cannot take the liberty of presenting it till I can do it through some common acquaintance.

I will beg leave to say here a few words on the general question of the degeneracy of animals in America. 1. As to the degeneracy of the man of Europe transplanted to America, it is no part of Monsr. de Buffon's system. He goes indeed within one step of it, but he stops there. The Abbé Raynal alone has taken that step. Your knowlege of America enables you to judge this question, to say whether the lower class of people in America, are less informed and less susceptible of information than the lower class in Europe: and whether those in America who have received such an education as that country can give, are less improved by it than Europeans of the same degree of education. 2. As to the Aboriginal man of America, I know of no respectable evidence on which the opinion of his inferiority of genius has been founded but that of Don Ulloa. As to Robertson, he never was in America, he relates nothing on his own knowlege, he is a compiler only of the relations of others, and a mere translator of the opinions of Monsr. de Buffon. I should as soon therefore add the translators of Robertson to the witnesses of this fact, as himself. Paw, the beginner of this charge, was a compiler from the works of others; and of the most unlucky description; for he seems to have read the writings of travellers only to collect and republish their lies. It is really remarkeable that in three volumes 12mo. of small print it is scarcely possible to find one truth, and yet that the author should be able to produce authority for every fact he states, as he says he can. Don Ulloa's testimony is of the most respectable. He wrote of what he saw. But he saw the Indian of South America only, and that after he had passed through ten generations of slavery. It is very unfair, from this sample, to judge of the natural genius of this race of men: and after supposing that Don Ulloa had not sufficiently calculated the allowance which should be made for this circumstance, we do him no injury in considering the picture he draws of the present Indians of S. America as no picture of what their ancestors were 300 years ago. It is in N. America we are to seek their original character: and I am safe in affirming that the proofs of genius given by the Indians of N. America, place them on a level with Whites in the same uncultivated state. The North of Europe furnishes subjects enough for comparison with them, and for a proof of their equality. I have seen some thousands myself, and conversed much with them, and have found in them a male, sound understanding. I have had much information from men who had lived among them, and whose veracity and good sense were so far known to me as to establish a reliance on their information. They have all agreed in bearing witness in favour of the genius of this people. As to their bodily strength, their manners rendering it disgraceful to labour, those muscles employed in labour will be weaker with them than with the European labourer: but those which are exerted in the chase and those faculties which are employed in the tracing an enemy or a wild beast, in contriving ambuscades for him, and in carrying them through their execution, are much stronger than with us, because they are more exercised. I beleive the Indian then to be in body and mind equal to the whiteman. I have supposed the blackman, in his present state, might not be so. But it would be hazardous to affirm that, equally cultivated for a few generations, he would not become so. 3. As to the inferiority of the other animals of America, without more facts I can add nothing to what I have said in my Notes. As to the theory of Monsr. de Buffon that heat is friendly and moisture adverse to the production of large animals, I am lately furnished with a fact by Doctr. Franklin which proves the air of London and of Paris to be more humid than that of Philadelphia, and so creates a suspicion that the opinion of the superior humidity of America may perhaps have been too hastily adopted. And supposing that fact admitted, I think the physical reasonings urged to shew that in a moist country animals must be small, and that in a hot one they must be large, are not built on the basis of experiment. These questions however cannot be decided ultimately at this day. More facts must be collected, and more time flow off, before the world will be ripe for decision. In the mean time doubt is wisdom.

I have been fully sensible of the anxieties of your situation, and that your attentions were wholly consecrated, where alone they were wholly due, to the succour of friendship and worth. However much I prize your society I wait with patience the moment when I can have it without taking what is due to another. In the mean time I am solaced with the hope of possessing your friendship, and that it is not ungrateful to you to receive assurances of that with which I have the honour to be Dear Sir Your most obedient and most humble servt., Th: Jefferson

Notes on Arthur Young's Letter to George Washington

Notes on Mr. Young's letter.

pa. 3. Is the labour (of negroes @ £9. sterl.) to be commanded in any amount?—If taken by the year it may be commanded in any amount: but not if wanted on particular occasions only, as for harvest, for particular dressings of the land &c.

pa. 4. The labour of a negro Mr. Young reckons cent per cent dearer than the labour of England.—To the hirer of a negro man his hire will cost £9. And his subsistence, cloathing and tools £6. Making £15. sterl. or at the most it may sometimes be £18.—To the owner of a negro his labour costs as follows. Suppose a negro man of 25. years of age costs £75. sterling: he has an equal chance to live 30. years according to Buffon's tables; so that you lose your principal in 30 years. Then say

	£
Int. of £75. annually,	3–15
one thirtieth annually of the principal,	2–10
subsistence, clothes &c. annually,	6
	12– 5

There must be some addition to this to make the labour equal to that of a white man, as I believe the negro does not perform quite as much work, nor with as much intelligence.—But Mr. Young reckons a laboring man in England £8. and his board £16. making £24.

pa. 5. "in the instances of Mountain land, the expressions seem to indicate waste land, unbuilt and uninclosed." If Mr. Young has reference here to the notes which Th:J. gave to the President on the subject of Mountain land, the following explanation is necessary. The lands therein contemplated are generally about one half cleared of the timber which grew on them, say all the land of the first quality and half that of the middling quality. This half is for the most part inclosed with rail fences which do not last long (except where they are of chesnut) but are easily repaired or renewed. The houses on them for the use of the farm are so slight and of so little worth that they are thrown into the bargain without a separate estimate. The same may be said of the farmer's house, unless it be better than common. When it is of considerable value, it adds to the price of the land, but by no means it's whole value. With respect to the soil I saw no uplands in England comparable to it. My travels there were from Dover to London, and on to Birmingham, making excursions of 20. or 30. miles each way. At Edgehill in Warwickshire my road led me over a red soil something like this, as well as I recollect. But it is too long ago to speak with certainty.

pa. 7. "That in America farmers look to labour much more than to land, is new to me."—But it is a most important circumstance. Where land is cheap, and rich, and labour dear, the same labour, spread in a slighter culture over 100. acres, will produce more profit than if concentrated by the highest degree of cultivation on a small portion of the lands. When the virgin fertility of the soil becomes exhausted, it becomes better to cultivate less and well. The only difficulty is to know at what point of deterioration in the land, the culture should be increased, and in what degree.

pa. 10. "can you sell your beef and mutton readily?" The market for them, fresh and in quantity, is not certain in Virginia. Beef well salted will generally find a market, but salted mutton is perhaps unknown.

pa. 11. "mutton dearer than beef."—Sheep are subject to many diseases which carry them off in great numbers. In the middle and upper parts of Virginia they are subject to the wolf, and in all parts of it to dogs. These are great obstacles to their multiplication. In the middle and upper parts of the country the carcase of the beef is raised on the spontaneous food of the forests, and is delivered to the farmer in good plight in the fall, often fat enough for slaughter. Hence it's cheapness. Probably however sheep, properly attended to, would be more profitable than cattle as Mr. Young says. They have not been attended to as they merited.

pa. 13. Mr. Young calculates the employment of £5040. worth of land and 1200£ farmer's capital, making an aggregate capital of £6240. in England, which he makes yeild 5. pr. cent extra, or 10 pr. cent on the whole. I will calculate, in the Virginia way, the employment of the same capital, on a supposition of good management in the manner of the country

1. supposing negro laborers to be hired.
2. supposing them to be bought.

1. Suppose labourers to be hired, one half men @ £18. the other half women @ £14 for labor, subsistence, clothg. (I always mean sterlg. money)

Int. of £4160., for 3310. as. of land @ 25/ pr. acre.	£208–
of 2080. for farmer's capital of stock, tools &c.	104–
6240.	
taxes @ 7d. the acre (I do not know what they are)	96–
hire of 33. labourers @£16.	528–
	936–

Produce to be sold annually.

	£	
Wheat 6600. bushels @ 3/.	990	
meat & other articles @ £5. for each laborer	165	1155–
Net profit over & above the 5. pr. cent above charged		219–
Add annual rise in the value of lands		165–
real profit over & above the 5. pr. cent above charged		385–

which is 6⅕ per cent extra, or 11⅓ pr. cent on the whole capital.

———

2. Suppose labourers to be bought, one half men, & one half women @ sterl. on an average.

				£
Int.	of £3125.	for 2500. as. of land @ 25/		156–
	of 1562–10,	farmer's capital of stock, utensils &c.	£	78–
	of 1500–,	for purchase of 25. laborers.	75	
	£6187–10,	subsistence, clothing &c.	150.	225–

[I allow nothing for losses by death, but on the contrary shall presently take credit 4. pr. cent pr. annum for their increase over & above keepg. up their own numbers.]

Taxes @ 7d. the acre	72–
	532–

Produce to be sold annually

	£	
Wheat 5000. bush. @ 3/	750	
meat & other articles @ £5. for each labourer	125	875– 0
Net profit over & above the 5. pr. cent above charged		342–15
add 5. pr. cent annual rise in the value of lands 156– 5		
4. pr. cent increase of negroes more than keepg. up original number		60– 0
real profit over & above the 5. pr. cent above charged.		559– 0

which is 9. pr. cent extra, or 14. pr. cent on the whole capital. In the preceding estimate I have supposed that 200. bushels of wheat may be sold for every labourer employed, which may be thought too high. I know it is too high for common land, and common management. But I know also that on good land and with good management it has been done thro' a considerable neighborhood and for many years. On the other hand I have overrated the cost of labouring negroes, and I presume the taxes also are overrated. I have observed that our families of negroes double in about 25. years, which is an increase of the capital, invested in them, of 4. per cent over and above keeping up the original number.

I am unable to answer the queries page as to the expence necessary to make an acre of forest land maintain one, two, or three sheep. I began an experiment of that kind in the year 1783. Clearing out the under-growth, cutting up the fallen wood but leaving all the good trees. I got through about 20. or 30. acres and sowed it with white clover and greensward, and intended to have gone on through a forest of 4. or 500. acres. The land was excessively rich, but too steep to be cultivated. In spite of total neglect during my absence from that time to this, most of it has done well. I did not note how much labour it took to prepare it; but I am sure it was repaid by the fuel it yielded for the family. The richness of the pasture to be thus obtained, will allways be proportioned to that of the land. Most of our forest is either midling, or poor. It's enclosure with a wood fence costs little, as the wood is on the spot.

Th: Jefferson
June 18. 1792.

TJ to Madame Plumard de Bellanger

Dear Madam Monticello in Virginia Apr. 25. 1794.

While I remained in public office, it was out of my power to acknolege the receipt of the letters with which you were pleased to honor me. My daily and necessary labours obliged me to deny myself the satisfaction of all private correspondence, which I rigorously did, and without a single exception but in the case of my children. I have now been able to disengage myself from public affairs, and to retire to the bosom of my family, my farm, my books and my neighbors. Among the pleasing circumstances in which I find myself placed, a prominent one is the society of Mr. Derieux, your worthy relation, to whom I sincerely wish the partialities of fortune had been as great as are those of his neighbors and acquaintance, who join, one and all, in their esteem and good wishes towards him. But the casualties of fortune seem rarely to be in his favor. The handsome aid which you were so generous as to give him has been lessened in it's effect by singular circumstances. It found him engaged in a small commerce of West India goods in which he had found a profit which had aided to support his family. He ventured to remit a part of your gift to the islands for a new cargo. The revolution there occasioned it's total loss. He was living in a rented house at Charlottesville where he carried on his commerce. His landlord, having occasion for money, he lent him another part of your gift, for the rent of his house by way of interest, and it was a very high interest, and the landlord mortgaged the house to him as a security for repaiment. I fear he has lost this money, and that the house having in the meantime gone rapidly to decay, will replace but a small part of it. The legacy from his uncle was lessened greatly as you know by the depreciation of the assignats. The prudent measure you recommended of remitting the legacy in merchandize, not money, saved much of his loss, as he gained on the sale of a part of the merchandize, nearly what had been lost by the assignats on that part of the purchase. But still the loss was too much for his circumstances, and the net proceeds of that legacy have been in a degree absorbed by debts which he had been obliged to contract, living in Charlottesville without any means of support but his capital unemployed, and therefore yeilding no profit. I have thought this explanation of his affairs due to you in return for your goodness to him, and due to myself too, to shew you how the views which I laid before you for the employment of the money you gave, have failed. It is indeed one of the circumstances which makes me lament either that I was not here when your aid came to him, or that it had not been postponed till I came. Had either of these been the case, I may, from the confidence he is pleased to repose in me, venture to affirm, that the whole should have been invested in negroes and cattle, or in good land, not leaving a shilling of it to the risk of any casualty, and that with his prudence and turn for agriculture, he would have been placed out of the danger of want. In the present situation of things I confess I look forward for him with disquietude. With his wife and a fine family of children in Charlottesville, he must soon consume the rest of his capital, and tho' extremely anxious to go to a farm, he has not the means of doing it. The house there is all which remains to him, and I fear that is already become by decay a very small resource. Should the favor of his relations be directed towards him in future, and particularly if you should be so good as to give him any further help without incommoding yourself, I think I may pledge myself that it shall be ever farthing of it laid out in lands and negroes, which besides a present support bring a silent profit of from 5. to 10. per cent in this country by the increase in their value. I can assure you from my own knolege of Mr. Derieux that you cannot do favors to a more worthy relation, nor to one in more need of it. But this would be the effect of your own goodness only which is sufficiently marked by what you have already done for him.—I have filled my letter with his subject, as there is no other in this country interesting to you, and those of France are too much unknown to me to say any thing of them, avec connoissance de cause. This scrap of French reminds me that I ought to make an apology for not writing to you in your own language. But the little habit I had of explaining myself in that tongue, is entirely lost, and I have been forced to address you in English or to lose the benefit of doing it at all. I inclose you a letter from Mr. Derieux, and have the honor to be, with sentiments of the most perfect respect & attachment, Dear Madam, Your most obedient & most humble servt Th: Jefferson

Martha Jefferson Randolph and Thomas Mann Randolph to TJ

January 31 1801

I should not have waited for your letter my Dearest Father had it been in my power to have written sooner but incredible as it may appear, that in period of 2 months not one day could have been found to discharge so sacred and pleasing a duty, it is litterally true that the first fort night of your absence excepted and 3 or 4 days of the last week, I have not been one day capable of attending even to my common domestic affairs. I am again getting into the old way with regard to my stomack, totally unable to digest any thing but a few particular vegetables; harrassed to death by little fevers, for 6 week I scarcely ever missed a night having one untill by recurring to my accustomed remedy in such cases, giving up meat milk coffee and a large proportion of the vegetable tribe that have allways been inimical to my constitution I have at last found some relief. it requires some self denial but I find my self so much recruited both in health and spirits, and every transgression so severely punished, that I shall rigorously adhere to it as long as my health requires it.

Cornelia shows the necessity there was for weaning her by her surprising change for the better since that time. the children are all well except Jefferson who cought (that filthiest of all disorders) the itch from a little aprentice boy in the family. he was 6 or seven weeks in constant and familar intercourse with us before we suspected what was the matter with him, the moment it was discovered that the other little boy had it, we were no longer at a loss to account for Jefferson's irruption which had been attributed all along to his covering too warm at night. I am delighted that your return will happen at a season when we shall be able to enjoy your company without interuption. I was at Monticello Last spring 1 day before the arrival of any one, and one day more of interval between the departure of one family and the arrival of another, after which time I never had the pleasure of passing one sociable moment with you. allways in a croud, taken from every useful and pleasing duty to be worried with a multiplicity of disagreable ones which the entertaining of such crouds of company subjects one to in the country, I suffered more in seeing you all ways at a distance than if you had still been in Philadelphia, for then at least I should have enjoyed in anticipation those pleasures which we were deprived of by the concourse of strangers which continually crouded the house when you were with us. I find my self every day becoming more averse to company I have lost my relish for what is usually deemed pleasure, and duties incompatible with it have surplanted all other enjoyments in my breast—the education of my Children to which I have long devoted every moment that I could command, but which is attended with more anxiety now as they increase in age without making those acquirements which other children do. my 2 eldest are uncommonly backward in every thing much more so than many others who have not had half the pains taken with them. Ellen is wonderfully apt. I shall have no trouble with her, but the two others excite serious anxiety with regard to their intellect. of Jefferson my hopes were so little sanguine that I discovered with some surprise & pleasure that he was quicker than I had ever thought it possible for him to be, but he has Lost so much time and will necesarily lose so much more before he can be placed at a good school that I am very unhappy about him. Anne does not want memory but she does not improve. she appears to me to Learn absolutely without profit. adieu my Dear Father we all are painfully anxious to see you. Ellen counts the weeks and continues scoring up complaints against Cornelia whom she is perpetually threatning with *your* displeasure. long is the list of misdemeanors which is to be comunicated to you, amongst which the stealing of 2 potatoes carefully preserved 2 whole days for you but at last Stolen by Cornelia, forms a weighty article. adieu again dearest best beloved Father 2 long months still before we shall see you in the mean time rest assured of the first Place in the heart of your affectionate Child

M. Randolph

P.S. by Th:M.R.
Every thing goes on well at Mont'o.—the Nailers all returned to work & executing well some heavy orders, as one from D. Higinb.m for 30.000. Xd. Moses, Jam Hubbard Davy & Shephard still out & to remain till you order otherwise—Joe cuting nails—I had given a charge of lenity respecting all: (Burwell absolutely excepted from the whip alltogether) before you wrote: none have incurred it but the small ones for truancy & yet the work proceeds better than since George. such is the sound sense cleverness & energy of Lillie.

Second Inaugural Address

[before 4 Mch. 1805]

. . . The Aboriginal inhabitants of these countries I have regarded with the commiseration their history inspires. endowed with the faculties & the rights of men, breathing an ardent love of liberty and independance, & occupying a country which left them no desire but to be undisturbed, the stream of overflowing population from other regions directed itself on these shores. without power to divert, or habits to contend against it, they have been overwhelmed by the current, or driven before it. now reduced within limits too narrow for the hunter-state, humanity enjoins us to teach them agriculture & the domestic arts; to encourage them to that industry which alone can enable them to maintain their place in existence, & to prepare them in time for that state of society, which to bodily comforts adds the improvement of the mind & morals. we have therefore liberally furnished them with the implements of husbandry & houshold use; we have placed among them instructors in the arts of first necessity; and they are covered with the Aegis of the law against aggressors from among ourselves.

But the endeavors to enlighten them on the fate which awaits their present course of life, to induce them to exercise their reason, follow it's dictates, & change their pursuits with the change of circumstances, have powerful obstacles to encounter. they are combated by the habits of their bodies, prejudices of their minds, ignorance, pride, & the influence of interested & crafty individuals among them, who feel themselves something in the present order of things, and fear to become nothing in any other. these persons inculcate a sanctimonious reverence for the customs of their ancestors; that whatsoever they did must be done through all time; that reason is a false guide, and to advance under it's counsel in their physical, moral or political condition is perilous innovation: that their duty is to remain as their creator made them, ignorance being safety, and knolege full of danger. in short, my friends, among them also is seen the action and counteraction of good sense and of bigotry. they too have their Anti-Philosophists, who find an interest in keeping things in their present state; who dread reformation, and exert all their faculties to maintain the ascendancy of habit over the duty of improving our reason, & obeying it's mandates . . .

TJ to Francis C. Gray

Dear Sir, Monticello Mar. 4. 15.

Dispatching to mr Ticknor my packet of letters for Paris, it occurs to me that I committed an error in a matter of information which you asked of me while here. it is indeed of little importance, yet as well corrected as otherwise; and the rather as it gives me an occasion of renewing my respects to you. you asked me in conversation what constituted a mulatto by our law? and I believe I told you 4 crossings with the whites. I looked afterwards into our law, and found it to be in these words. "every person, other than a negro, of whose grandfathers or grandmothers any one shall have been a negro, shall be deemed a mulatto, and so every such person who shall have one fourth part or more of negro blood; shall in like manner be deemed a mulatto." L. Virga. 1792. Dec. 17 the case put in the first member of this paragraph of the law is exempli gratiâ. the latter contains the true Canon, which is that ¼ of negro blood, mixed with any portion of white, constitutes the mulatto. as the issue has one half of the blood of each parent, and the blood of each of these may be made up of a variety of fractional mixtures, the estimate of their compound, in some cases, may be intricate. it becomes a Mathematical problem of the same class with those on the mixtures of different liquors or different metals. As in these therefore, the Algebraical notation is the most convenient & intelligible. Let us express the pure blood of the white in the capital letters of the printed alphabet, the pure blood of the negro in the small letters of the printed alphabet, and any given mixture of either, by way of abridgment in MS. letters.

let the 1st crossing be of **a**, pure negro, with **A**. pure white. the Unit of blood of the issue being composed of the half of that of each parent, will be **a**/2 + **A**/2 call it, for abbreviation, h (half-blood)

let the 2d crossing be of h. and **B**. the blood of the issue will be h/2 + **B**/2, or substituting for h/2 it's equivalent, it will be **a**/4 + **A**/4 + **B**/2. call it q (quarteroon) being ¼ negro blood

let the 3d crossing be of q. and **C**. their offspring will be

q/2 + **C**/2 = **a**/8 + **A**/8 + **B**/4 + **C**/2. call this e. (eighth) who having less than ¼ of **a**. or of pure negro blood, to wit ⅛ only, is no longer a mulatto. so that a 3d cross clears the blood.

from these elements let us examine other compounds.

for example, let h. and q. cohabit. Their issue will be

h/2 + q/2 = **a**/4 + **A**/4 + **a**/8 + **A**/8 + **B**/4 = ⅜ + ⅜ + **B**/4 wherein we find ⅜ of **a**. or of negro blood.

Let h. and e. cohabit. their issue will be

h/2 + e/2 = **a**/4 + **A**/4 + **a**/16 + **A**/16 + **B**/8 + **C**/4 = 5**a**/16 + 5**A**/16 + **B**/8 + **C**/4 wherein 5/16**a**. makes still a mulatto.

Let q. and e. cohabit. the half of the blood of each will be

q/2 + e/2 = **a**/8 + **A**/8 + **B**/4 + **a**/16 + **A**/16 + **B**/8 + **C**/4 = 3**a**/16 + 3**A**/16 + ⅜ + **C**/4 wherein 3/16 of **a** is no longer mulatto.

and thus may every compound be noted & summed, the sum of the fractions composing the blood of the issue being always equal to Unit. it is understood in Natural history that a 4th cross of one race of animals with another gives an issue equivalent for all sensible purposes to the original blood. thus a Merino ram being crossed 1st with a country ewe, 2dly with this daughter, 3dly with this grandaughter, and 4thly with the great grandaughter, the last issue is deemed pure Merino, having in fact but 1/16 of the country blood. our Canon considers 2. crosses with the pure white, and a 3d with any degree of mixture, however small, as clearing the issue of the negro blood. but observe that this does not reestablish freedom, which depends on the condition of the mother, the principle of the civil law, partus sequitur ventrem, being adopted here. but if e. be emancipated, he becomes a free white man, and a citizen of the US. to all intents and purposes—so much for this trifle, by way of correction.

TJ to John Holmes

Monticello Apr. 22. 20.

I thank you, Dear Sir, for the copy you have been so kind as to send me of the letter to your constituents on the Missouri question. it is a perfect justification to them. I had for a long time ceased to read newspapers or pay any attention to public affairs, confident they were in good hands, and content to be a passenger in our bark to the shore from which I am not distant. but this momentous question, like a fire bell in the night, awakened and filled me with terror. I considered it at once as the knell of the Union. it is hushed indeed for the moment. but this is a reprieve only, not a final sentence. A geographical line, coinciding with a marked principle, moral and political, once concieved and held up to the angry passions of men, will never be obliterated; and every new irritation will mark it deeper and deeper. I can say with conscious truth that there is not a man on earth who would sacrifice more than I would, to relieve us from this heavy reproach, in any practicable way. the cession of that kind of property, for so it is misnamed, is a bagatelle which would not cost me a second thought, if, in that way, a general emancipation and expatriation could be effected: and, gradually, and with due sacrifices, I think it might be. but, as it is, we have the wolf by the ear, and we can neither hold him, nor safely let him go. justice is in one scale, and self-preservation in the other. of one thing I am certain, that as the passage of slaves from one state to another would not make a slave of a single human being who would not be so without it, so their diffusion over a greater surface would make them individually happier and proportionally facilitate the accomplishment of their emancipation; by dividing the burthen on a greater number of co-adjutors. an abstinence too from this act of power would remove the jealousy excited by the undertaking of Congress; to regulate the condition of the different descriptions of men composing a state. this certainly is the exclusive right of every state, which nothing in the constitution has taken from them and given to the general government. could congress, for example say that the Non-freemen of Connecticut, shall be freemen, or that they shall not emigrate into any other state?

I regret that I am now to die in the belief that the useless sacrifice of themselves, by the generation of '76. to acquire self government and happiness to their country, is to be thrown away by the unwise and unworthy passions of their sons, and that my only consolation is to be that I live not to weep over it. if they would but dispassionately weigh the blessings they would throw away against an abstract principle more likely to be effected by union than by scission, they would pause before they would perpetrate this act of suicide on themselves and of treason against the hopes of the world. to yourself as the faithful advocate of union I tender the offering of my high esteem and respect. Th: Jefferson

TJ to Jared Sparks

Dear Sir Monticello Feb. 4. 24.

I duly recieved your favor of the 13th and, with it, the last No of the N. A. Review. this has anticipated the one I should recieve in course, but have not yet recieved under my subscription to the new series. the article on the African colonisation of the people of colour, to which you invite my attention, I have read with great consideration. It is indeed a fine one, and will do much good. I learn from it more too than I had before known of the degree of success and promise of that colony.

In the disposition of these unfortunate people, there are two rational objects to be distinctly kept in view. 1. the establishment of a colony on the coast of Africa, which may introduce among the Aborigines the arts of cultivated life, and the blessings of civilisation and science. by doing this, we may make to them some retribution for the long course of injuries we have been committing on their population. and considering that these blessings will descend to the "nati natorum, et qui nascentur ab illis," we shall, in the long run, have rendered them perhaps more good than evil. to fulfil this object the colony of Sierra leone promises well, and that of Mesurado adds to our prospect of success. under this view the colonization society is to be considered as a Missionary society, having in view however objects more humane, more justifiable, and less aggressive on the peace of other nations than the others of that appellation.

The 2d object, and the most interesting to us, as coming home to our physical and moral characters, to our happiness and safety, is to provide an Asylum to which we can, by degrees, send the whole of that population from among us, and establish them under our patronage and protection, as a separate, free and independant people, in some country and climate friendly to human life and happiness. That any place on the coast of Africa should answer the latter purpose, I have ever deemed entirely impossible. and, without repeating the other arguments which have been urged by others, I will appeal to figures only, which admit no controversy. I shall speak in round numbers, not absolutely accurate, yet not so wide from truth as to vary the result materially. there are in the US: a million and a half of people of colour in slavery. to send off the whole of these at once nobody concieves to be practicable for us, or expedient for them. Let us take 25. years for it's accomplishment, within which time they will be doubled. Their estimated value as property, in the first place, (for actual property has been lawfully vested in that form, and who can lawfully take it from the possessors?) at an average of 200. D. each, young and old, would amount to 600. millions of Dollars, which must be paid or lost by somebody. to this add the cost of their transportation by land & sea to Mesurado, a year's provision of food and clothing, implements of husbandry and of their trades which will amount to 300. millions more, making 36. millions of Dollars a year for 25. years, with ensurance of peace all that time, and it is impossible to look at the question a second time. I am aware that at the end of about 16. years, a gradual detraction from this sum will commence, from the gradual diminution of breeders, and go on during the remaining years. calculate this deduction, and it is still impossible to look at the enterprize a second time. I do not say this to induce an inference that the getting rid of them is for ever impossible. for that is neither my opinion, nor my hope. but only that it cannot be done in this way. there is, I think, a way in which it can be done, that is, by emancipating the after-born, leaving them, on due compensation, with their mothers, until their services are worth their maintenance, and then putting them to industrious occupations, until a proper age for deportation. this was the result of my reflections on the subject five and forty years ago; and I have never yet been able to concieve any other practicable plan. it was sketched in the Notes on Virginia, under the 14th Query. The estimated value of the new-born infant is so low (say 12½ Dollars) that it would probably be yielded by the owner gratis, and would thus reduce the 600, millions of Dollars, the first head of expence, to 37. Millions & a half. leaving only the expences of nourishment while with the mother, and of transportation. and from what fund are these expences to be furnished? Why not from that of the lands which have been ceded by the very states now needing this relief? and ceded on no consideration, for the most part, but that of the general good of the whole. these cessions already constitute one fourth of the states of the Union. it may be said that these lands have been sold, are now the property of the citizens composing those states, and the money long ago recieved and expended. But an equivalent of lands in the territories since acquired, may be appropriated to that object, or so much, at least, as may be sufficient; and the object, altho' more important to the slave-states, is highly so to the others also, if they were serious in their arguments on the Missouri question. the slave-states too, if more interested, would also contribute more by their gratuitous liberation, thus taking on themselves alone the first and heaviest item of expence. In the plan sketched in the Notes on Virginia no particular place of asylum was specified; because it was thought possible that, in the revolutionary state of America, then commenced, events might open to us some one within practicable distance. this has now happened. St. Domingo is become independant, and with a population of that colour only; and, if the public papers are to be credited, their Chief offers to pay their passage, to recieve them as free citizens, and to provide them employment. this leaves then for the general confederacy no expence but of nurture with the mother a few years, and would call of course for a very moderate appropriation of the vacant lands. suppose the whole annual increase to be of 60 thousand effective births. 50. vessels of 400. tons burthen each, constantly employed in that short run, would carry off the increase of every year, & the old stock would die off in the ordinary course of nature, lessening from the commencement until it's final disappearance. in this way no violation of private right is proposed. voluntary surrenders would probably come in as fast as the means to be provided for their care would be competent to. looking at my own state only, and I presume not to speak for the others, I verily believe that this surrender of property would not amount to more annually than half our present direct taxes, to be continued fully about 20. or 25. years, and then gradually diminishing for as many more until their final extinction: and even this half tax would not be paid in cash, but by the delivery of an object which they have never yet known or counted as part of their property: and those not possessing the object will be called on for nothing. I do not go into all the details of the burthens and benefits of this operation. and who could estimate it's blessed effects? I leave this to those who will live to see their accomplishment, and to enjoy a beatitude forbidden to my age. but I leave it with this admonition to rise and be doing. a million and a half are within their controul; but 6. millions (which a majority of those now living will see them attain) and one million of these fighting men, will say "we will not go."

I am aware that this subject involves some constitutional scruples, but a liberal construction, justified by the object, may go far, and an amendment of the constitution the whole length necessary. the separation of infants from their mothers too would produce some scruples of humanity. but this would be straining at a gnat, and swallowing a camel.

I am much pleased to see that you have taken up the subject of the duty on imported books. I hope a crusade will be kept up against it until those in power shall become sensible of this stain on our legislation, and shall wipe it from their code, and from the remembrance of man, if possible. I salute you with assurances of high respect and esteem. Th: Jefferson

John Finch's Account of a Visit to Monticello

[before 5 Apr. 1824]

The Ex-President accompanied me two miles on my route, and I now directed my course to Monticello, the seat of Mr. Jefferson. I came to the banks of the Rivanna, and passed over in a boat to the opposite shore. Advancing towards the mansion, I was struck with the appearance of the negro huts; which, as in all Virginia estates, are placed at a small distance from the residence of the proprietor.

The ravines on the side of the hill were covered by the Ulex Europæus, or prickly gorse, which Mr. Jefferson had been at the trouble of importing from England. I recognized it as an old acquaintance. By its dark green leaves and bright yellow flowers, it concealed the ravages which the torrents had made.

Monticello is situated upon one of the south-west mountains, and commands an extensive view. From the lofty mountaintop, you see the Rivanna pursuing its peaceful, meandering course, and again concealed from view by the trees which overshadow its bank. At the distance of a few miles, it nearly encircles the tumuli of some ancient Indian chieftains—the immense forests—the cultivated plains—the Blue Mountains which bound the horizon—Charlotteville—the university reared under the auspices of Mr. Jefferson.

In the centre of the house is a hall, adorned with a museum, containing the bones of a mastodon, a collection of fossil shells, Indian trophies, and various curiosities. The drawing-room is an octagon, and has glass folding-doors, which lead on one side into the hall, on the other to the garden and shrubberies. The walls are covered with paintings. I was delighted to see the pictures of Locke, Bacon, Newton; of the discoverers of America—Columbus, Americus, Cabot, and Sir Walter Raleigh; also portraits of the Presidents of the United States. Besides these, there were several paintings of the Flemish and Italian schools.

I was shewn by the servant into the drawing-room, and waited with some anxiety for the moment when I should see Mr. Jefferson. In a few minutes he came, welcomed me to Monticello, and began to converse with as much ease as if we had been acquainted for years. Mr. Jefferson was at this time nearly eighty years of age, tall, slender, and stooped very slightly; he retained all the vivacity of a much younger period of life. The pictures of Mr. Jefferson as President do not give a correct idea of his countenance. The profile by Stuart, and the likeness by Colonel Trumbull, in the picture of the Signing of the Declaration of Independence, are the most correct. It would be impossible to paint the genius and fire which appeared in the expression of his eyes.

Mr. Jefferson's favorite topic of conversation was the University; on my expressing a wish to see it, Mr. Jefferson said he would give me a distant view of it. He led the way to a terrace in the garden, and pointed out the buildings, which made a prominent figure in the landscape.

But at this time I scarce paid any attention to the scene at a distance, I was so engaged in listening to every word Mr. Jefferson spoke, and watching the expression of his countenance. I was standing by the side of the philosopher and statesman, whose name is forever enrolled in the page of his country's history; who had written and signed the Declaration of Independence of the United States of North America. I was conversing with an individual upon whom his country had conferred all the honors she had to bestow. Mr. Jefferson had been successively Representative, Senator, and Governor of Virginia; Ambassador to France; Secretary of State; Vice-President, and President of the United States; the friend of Washington, of La Fayette, and the heroes who achieved the liberty of America.

On returning to the drawing-room, we had a conversation which continued three hours, and the following were some of the sentiments Mr. Jefferson expressed:—

"Bonaparte was a man of great talents, but totally without principle, except that of self-aggrandisement. When in France, I traced every large river from its mouth to its source; I was thus certain of seeing the most fertile land. I was on foot, and visited the farms to see the agriculture of the country; the farmers were very civil, and answered my questions with great readiness. The laborers in France consume very little animal food.

"I walked along the canal of Languedoc, having hired a boat to carry my baggage. I experienced no difficulty except at the taverns, which were generally filled with a low description of persons. In England I obtained a list of the principal gardens within one hundred miles of London, and made a tour to visit them. I called at many farm-houses, but the farmers were not so conversable as those in France.

"At Nismes, I spent several hours a day, for three weeks, examining the Temple, and sent the plan to Virginia; the State House at Richmond is built after this model.

"I was acquainted with Condorcet, Mirabeau, and several members of the National Convention. I often dined with the Count de Buffon, who talked without ceasing, but with great eloquence, on subjects connected with natural history.

"I played with Dr. Franklin at chess, and was equal to him at the game.

"Kosciusko came to America in 1798, to arrange some accounts with Congress. He kept his room six months, and gave as a reason, that the Empress of Russia would have him assassinated if she knew where he was.

"The old Virginian Assembly was the most dignified body of men ever assembled to legislate.

"Henry spoke wonderfully—call it oratory or what you please, but I never heard any thing like it. He had more command over the passions than any man I ever knew; I heard all the celebrated orators of the National Assembly of France, but there was none equal to Patrick Henry. It was his profound knowledge of human nature, and his manner of speaking, more than the matter of his orations. After listening with the utmost attention, I sometimes endeavoured to recollect what he had been saying, but never could succeed.

"The negroes are better fed than the agricultural laborers on the continent of Europe. They appear to be a different race of people to the whites. Any planter who treated his negroes cruelly would be shunned by his neighbors. The plan of sending the negroes to Africa will not succeed; they should go to St. Domingo; they would be gladly received, and they might all be exported.

"The black children should be set free the moment they are born. A black child is worth five pounds sterling, and there is no planter but would give that sum to get rid of the nuisance. The children should be kept by their parents till they were ten years of age, and then sent off.

"Some members of the old Congress opposed the separation from Great Britain in the most strenuous manner; but when it was passed, they supported the measure with unanimity.

"Rhode Island is the smallest but boldest State in the Union. She sometimes opposes all the other States, without regarding the size of her territory.

"Franklin never spoke in Congress more than five minutes at a time; then he related some anecdote which applied to the subject before the House.

"The States are sovereign for domestic purposes, they are allied for foreign relations.

"Nature makes men Whigs or Tories, Federalists or Democrats. Those who are strong and fearless by nature are never afraid of their fellowmen, and take the side of the people. Those who have weak constitutions are always nervous and timid, and advocate the cause of government.

"No one can have any idea of the strength of party feeling, unless they had seen America in 1798.

"We are various by station, but equally men."

Mr. Jefferson informed me, he had invited several neighbors to dine with him; the guests arrived, and dinner was announced. Mr. Jefferson led the way and placed himself at one side of the table, and we were invited to sit down without any formality. Mr. Jefferson said, that when he was President, he had a contest about punctilio with an ambassador from Europe. He detested ceremony, and when they came to the usual entertainments, he never took the trouble to ascertain whether France, England, Holland, or Spain, had the seat of honor. One envoy would not visit him, because he had not his proper seat. Mr. Jefferson sent a message inviting him as a gentleman and a friend, but even this language could not soften the obduracy of his etiquette.

I was introduced to Governor Randolph and his lady, and their family. Mrs. Randolph was daughter to Mr. Jefferson.

On the following day, Mr. and Mrs. Madison were expected on a visit for a week, and their arrival spread universal joy. I had the pleasure of witnessing the interview between the two Ex-Presidents, who had been friends for half a century. It was the most interesting evening I ever passed; I was in company with two of the most celebrated men of America.

Charlotteville University is one mile from a town of the same name, and has been founded and endowed by the Legislature of Virginia. The State have granted large sums of money for the support of professors, and it has now two hundred students. The buildings were just completed: it is built on an advantageous site.

On the following morning I prepared to depart. Mr. Jefferson urged me to stay, but as I had already passed two days at Monticello, I thought it would be trespassing on hospitality; I therefore took leave, and proceeded towards Richmond.

Actions and Interactions

Introduction

OVER THE COURSE OF HIS LIFE, Jefferson enslaved more than six hundred people. As a boy and as a man, he was often in circumstances in which he and his legal family were greatly outnumbered by people of African descent. In his private life he had to make decisions about the people whom he enslaved, and he had numerous interactions with them. While in public office, he had to make decisions about the lives of Black people in general.

Jefferson had fewer daily interactions with Native peoples, but as president of the United States he certainly took actions that affected their lives. After purchasing Louisiana, he was responsible for setting policy about the westward expansion of, largely, White settlers. Some see him as having set in motion the process of Indian Removal, which would be taken up more strenuously by President Andrew Jackson almost three decades later. We will see Jefferson writing to and about Native peoples, including the public controversy over his rendering of "Logan's lament," a speech by a chief of the Mingo people that he attached to *Notes on the State of Virginia.*

Because of his association with the Declaration of Independence and because of what he had to say on the subject of Black people in *Notes on the State of Virginia*, Jefferson drew the attention of Black people, who saw him as the member of the founding generation with whom they could most profitably engage. His antislavery position, as well as his reputation as a radical, suggested that he might be amenable to their calls for justice. The most famous communication between Jefferson and a Black person is his exchange of letters in August 1791 with Benjamin Banneker, which led to correspondence with others in which Jefferson references Banneker. These letters reveal Jefferson's complicated dance on the question of African American people. He clearly wanted to be seen by fellow adherents to the Enlightenment of his time as a liberal on the question of Black people. But he could not escape his prejudices and "suspicion" about their talent.

Jefferson corresponded with less well-known Black people. His most frequent correspondent was John Hemmings, the master carpenter at Monticello. Jefferson and Hemmings, the half-brother of Sally Hemings, were almost in daily contact as Hemmings carried out Jefferson's carpentry needs at Monticello. Jefferson put his three sons Beverley, Madison, and Eston under the tutelage of Hemmings so they could learn carpentry and joining. We get a sense of the boundaries Jefferson set for interactions between the races in these letters and from Jefferson's correspondence with and about free Blacks. In less well-known letters, we see Jefferson hiring a free Black man to take care of his property at the Natural Bridge, meaning making sure there were no squatters and that taxes were paid on time. In his *Memorandum Book*, the records of all of his daily monetary transactions, we see him using honorifics for free Black people that he did not use for enslaved Blacks.

Because of his reputation, Jefferson also drew the attention of Whites who wanted to work to end slavery. This section contains his correspondence with people like St. George Tucker, the Virginia jurist who in the wake of the Haitian Revolution created a gradual emancipation plan (so gradual that the last slave would not be free until sometime in the twentieth century) that he wanted Jefferson to support. There is also the case of Tadeusz Kościuszko, the Polish patriot who left a sum of money to buy the freedom of a group of enslaved people, with Jefferson as the executor of the will. The correspondence details the reasons Jefferson, in the end, refused to serve as executor. Among those, he learned that Kościuszko had written three wills, and the matter was likely to be resolved only after protracted litigation, which turned out to be what happened. The case went all the way to the Supreme Court about twenty years after Jefferson's death. The Court surveyed the numerous wills, one of which explicitly repudiated the will that had provided for the emancipation of enslaved people, and determined that the bequest was void. There are other letters and documents that show Jefferson responding to the high expectations that people had of him.

The most revealing, poignant, and maddening documents are those of Jefferson as a slaveholder. He gave orders to enslaved people, borrowed money from them, decided who would be punished and how, noted who would be sold or given away, or allowed to quietly leave. What comes across most clearly is that one family dominated these records in every respect: the Hemings-Wayles family. These six men and women, who were the half-siblings of Jefferson's wife, were the face of slavery and race for him. He interacted the most with them, and wrote the most about them and to them. Because he treated them differently, gave them more privileges than other enslaved people, Jefferson could think of himself as that archetype we moderns reject: a benevolent enslaver. The men of the first generation of Hemingses were allowed free movement. They hired themselves out to work as valets and travel guides and kept their own money. The Hemings women were never required to go to the fields.

We will see that his treatment of James and Sally Hemings while in Paris—paying them fair wages—established a practice that he followed once he returned to the United States. Anytime he lived away from Monticello—in New York, Philadelphia, or Washington—he paid enslaved people working in the household wages along with White workers. This undoubtedly lessened the tension that would otherwise be present with one set of people getting paid and the other not. This was a boon to the conflict-averse Jefferson. It also presented him with the opportunity to see himself as a "good" person, one who refused to take a liberty that he could have taken.

It cannot be included in its entirety, of course, but Jefferson's *Farm Book*, in which he kept records of the people and operations on his plantations over the course of fifty years, also shaped Jefferson's attitude about himself in relation to slavery and the enslaved. We see him decide who lived where, what rations families and individuals would receive, who died, who was born, and who was sold. We think about the power given to one man to decide the fates of others in such an intense and arrogant way. We recoil at the situation, but there is little reason to doubt that Jefferson saw these notations in the *Farm Book* as establishing himself as a responsible patriarch. The longer he acted in this role, the harder it became to think of being out of it.

This section also takes up Jefferson's will. When he died in 1826 at age eighty-three, Jefferson was $107,000 in debt. Monticello was sold not long after that, and 135 enslaved people were sold to help pay his debts. The patriarch, because of bad decisions, bad luck, and bad economic times, ended up failing his dependents. His last will, however, contains one last gesture to five African American enslaved people. He freed Burwell Colbert, Joseph Fossett, John Hemmings, and Madison and Eston Hemings. The last two people were his youngest sons with Sally Hemings. Virginia had passed a law in 1806 requiring all emancipated slaves to leave the state within one year or they would be sold back into slavery, unless they received permission from the state to remain. Jefferson petitioned the legislature to allow these men to stay in Virginia, where their "families and connections" were. Of course, this action was in contravention of the plan for emancipated slaves that Jefferson long talked about in his formal statements about the policy that should be followed regarding freed people. He knew these men, and one could say that in his own way, he loved them. There was no requirement that they leave Virginia and the United States to go to Liberia, a stipulation that was beginning to appear in wills in Virginia. These men deserved to remain in place because of their ties of affection to the location, which, of course, was the reason all African Americans when freed should have been allowed to remain in the only country they had ever known. Once again, there was a gap between public performance and private feelings and action.

Documents

Advertisement for a Runaway Slave

[7 September 1769]

Run away from the subscriber in *Albemarle*, a Mulatto slave called *Sandy*, about 35 years of age, his stature is rather low, inclining to corpulence, and his complexion light; he is a shoemaker by trade, in which he uses his left hand principally, can do coarse carpenters work, and is something of a horse jockey; he is greatly addicted to drink, and when drunk is insolent and disorderly, in his conversation he swears much, and his behaviour is artful and knavish. He took with him a white horse, much scarred with traces, of which it is expected he will endeavour to dispose; he also carried his shoemakers tools, and will probably endeavour to get employment that way. Whoever conveys the said slave to me in *Albemarle*, shall have 40 s. reward, if taken up within the county, 4 l. if elsewhere within the colony, and 10 l. if in any other colony, from

Thomas Jefferson.

Testing Martin Hemings, 1774

Mar. 1. My sister Elizabeth was found last Thursday being Feb. 24

√ 4. Sent my mother a quarter of stalled beef 118 ℔ weighed by Mr. Bryan for which charge @ 20/ comes to 23/8.

6. A flood in the Rivanna 18 I. higher than the one which carried N. Lewis's bridge away & that was the highest ever known except the great fresh in May 1771.

7. √ Sold my two old book cases to Mr. Clay for £5. of which credit him 40/ for performing the funeral service this day on burying my sister Elizabeth, & 40/ more for preaching Mr. Carr's funeral sermon, which last sum charge to D. Carr's estate. The other 20/ is a gratuity.

10. It appears Barksdale made me the following paimts. for my lands on Tye river.

	£
when he bought	10
1765. Nov. 30.	41
1766. Jan. 4.	10
Apr. 27.	15
	£76

√ Pd. Robert Harris for D. Carr's estate which charge 5/4.
Pd. Mr. Cole's Ned for a galln. of peas 5/.
Took admn. of E. Jefferson's estate.

14. Pd. Mrs. Dudley a midwife's fee for Ursula 10/3.
Recd. from the Forest 4 doz. 10 bott. of Jamaica rum (Note I shall keep a tally of these as we use them by making a mark in the margin in order to try the fidelity of Martin.

TJ to John Page

Dear Page — Philadelphia Aug. 5. 1776.

I am sorry to hear that the Indians have commenced war, but greatly pleased you have been so decisive on that head. Nothing will reduce those wretches so soon as pushing the war into the heart of their country. But I would not stop there. I would never cease pursuing them while one of them remained on this side the Misisippi. So unprovoked an attack and so treacherous a one should never be forgiven while one of them remains near enough to do us injury. The Congress having had reason to suspect the Six nations intended war, instructed their commissioners to declare to them peremptorily that if they chose to go to war with us, they should be at liberty to remove their families out of our settlements, but to remember that they should not only never more return to their dwellings on any terms but that we would never cease pursuing them with war while one remained on the face of the earth: and moreover, to avoid equivocation, to let them know they must recall their young men from Canada, or we should consider them as acting against us nationally. This decisive declaration produced an equally decisive act on their part: they have recalled their young men, and are stirring themselves with anxiety to keep their people in quiet, so that the storm we apprehended to be brewing there it is hoped is blown over. . . . Adieu

TJ to George Rogers Clark

Sir Williamsburg Jan. 1. 1779. [i.e., 1780]

The late assembly having made some alteration in the Western force as stated to you in my former letter, I think it necessary to apprize you of it. They have directed your battalion to be completed, 100 men to be stationed at the falls of the Ohio under Majr. Slaughter, and one only of the additional battalions to be completed. Major Slaughter's men are raised, and will march in a few days, this letter being to go by him. The returns which have been made to me do not enable me to say whether men enough are raised to make up the additional battalion; but I suppose there must be nearly enough. This battalion will march as early in the spring as the weather will admit. I hope that by this time the Spaniards have relieved us from the Natchez and Mansiack. I know therefore of but two objects between which you can balance for your next summer's operations. These are 1. an expedition against Detroit. or 2. against those tribes of Indians between the Ohio and Illinois rivers who have harrassed us with eternal hostilities, and whom experience has shewn to be incapable of reconciliation. Removed at such a distance as we are, and so imperfectly informed, it is impossible for us to prescribe to you. The defences at Detroit seem too great for small arms alone. And if that nest was destroyed the English still have a tolerable channel of communication with the Northern Indians by going from Montreal up the Utawas river. On the other hand, the Shawanese, Mingoes, Munsies, and the nearer Wiandots are troublesome thorns in our sides. However we must leave it to yourself to decide on the object of the campaign. If against these Indians, the end proposed should be their extermination, or their removal beyond the lakes or Illinois river. The same world will scarcely do for them and us. I suppose it will be best for the new battalion to act with you all the summer, aided by a considerable part of Slaughter's men, and in the fall to fortify the posts we propose to take on the Ohio, and remain in them during the succeeding winter. The posts which have been thought of are the mouth of Fishing cr., Little Kanhaway, Gr. Kanhaway, Sioto, Great Salt lick, and Kentucky. There being posts already at Pittsburg, the mouth of Weeling, and the Falls of Ohio, these intermediate ones will form a chain from Pittsburg to the falls. I have then only to wish that your post was at the mouth of Ohio, which would complete the line.

I am Sir with great respect Your very humble servt.

Money to James Hemings to Go to Rouen; Change Back from the Journey, and Other Transactions

Aug. 1. Pd. barber 1f4 coffee 14s. for an Umbrella 19f.
Gave James to bear expences &c. to Rouen 72f.
2. Pd. for cord 3s. fruit 2s. ribban 1f6 coffee 1f barber 12s.
3. Pd. for 4. Portmanteau straps 6f4—gave servts. 7f12.
Pd. Entertt. at Mahon's (l'aigle d'or) 102f8—coffee 12s. servt. 12s.

Pd. Posthorses to	la Botte	7f10
	Bolbec	5f12½
	Aliquerville	3f15
	Yvetot	5f12½
	Barentin	7f10
	Rouen	7f10

Gave the several postilions 13f1.
Gave in charity 15s.
Recd. Back from James of the money given him 36f.

Doctor James Hemings, October 7, 1784

4. Pd. Linen merchant's acct. 192f.
5. Pd. for handirons 1. Pr. 70f.

		f s
6. Pd. Marc for	traiteur Sep. 27–Oct. 3 inclus.	143– 2
	hhd. Expen. Sep. 27–Oct. 3.	157–15
	Household furniture	36– 9
	Washing	18– 6
	Fuel	24–10
	Gazettes	45–
		425– 2

Do. for James 9f6.
Pd. bookbinder 45f10—paid for books 8f10.
8. Pd. for 59 bottles Bourdeaux 208f—Molini for books 21f.
11. Pd. bookbinder 26f18. ₶

Pd. Marc for traiteur	81–16
hhd. Expences	101–15
	183–11

Oct. 25. Paid Royez for books 40f10.

26. Pd. for a fountain & cistern 100f.

Pd. for colours 12f.

Pd. for 11. First livraisons of the Encyclopedie 295f10.

Pd. for a Hercules in plaister 36f.

Pd. for books 39f.

27. Pd. Marc from Oct. 18–29. To wit

	₶
Postage	20–15
fitting house	18–10
potences for a table	24–18
Traiteur	60–
hhd. Exp.	136–17
	261

28. **Pd. Doctr. McMahon for attendg. James 120f.**

Paid for James Hemings's training

Gave a garçon 1f10.

5. Pd. for sword chain 6f.

Pd. Mr. Williamos	things bought for A. S. Jefferson	556f
	do. bought for my children &c.	771f
		1327

Dec. 6. Pd. an Eboniste balce. for night table 60f.

Pd. Mending Chess-men 18f.

8. Pd. Marc Nov. 29–Dec. 6. viz.

	f s
thermometer	2– 8
fuel	5– 8
dress	6– 8
bathing	17– 4
hhd. Furniture	23– 2
Traiteur	144–
hhd. Exp.	107–11
	306– 1

Recd. by Mr. Williamos from Le Couteux on Mr. Adams's bill on Holland 2000f.

The balance still due is 940f–7s–6d.

Gave Patsy 6f.

9. Pd. W. T. Franklin balce. for copying press &c. 88f2.

13. Pd. for books from Royez 97f paid bookbinder 113f12.

16. Pd. Marc. Dec. 6–12 viz.

	f S
washing	6–11
postage	2–12
Charity	9–
Traiteur	152–
hhd. Exp.	164–4–6
	334–7–6

Pd. the Traiteur 150f being the half of what I am to pay him for teaching James, the other half to be paid when he is taken away.

TJ to Paul Bentalou

Sir Paris Aug. 25. 1786.

I am honoured with your favour of the 9th. inst. and am to thank you for your care of the packet from Mr. McHenry, and congratulate yourself and Mrs. Bentalou on your safe arrival in France. I have made enquiries on the subject of the negro boy you have brought, and find that the laws of France give him freedom if he claims it, and that it will be difficult, if not impossible, to interrupt the course of the law. Nevertheless I have known an instance where a person bringing in a slave, and saying nothing about it, has not been disturbed in his possession. I think it will be easier in your case to pursue the same plan, as the boy is so young that it is not probable he will think of claiming freedom. This plan is the more adviseable, as an unsuccessful attempt to procure a dispensation from the law might produce orders which otherwise would not be thought of. Nevertheless should you find that you shall lose the possession of the boy unless protected in it, if you will be so good as to inform me of the facts, I will try whether a dispensation can be obtained. I would rather avoid asking this if you can, by any means, keep the boy without it. I have the honour to be with sentiments of much respect, Sir, your most obedient humble servant,

Th: Jefferson

TJ to Nicholas Lewis

Dear Sir Paris July 11. 1788.

. . . I shall give orders at Havre relative to the bacon whenever it arrives. But in future it will not be worth while to send me any, because it's importation is prohibited, and I have never yet been able to obtain any article of this kind from the Custom house. I thank Mrs. Lewis kindly for the ears of corn and the seeds accompanying them which are safely come to hand. The homony corn is a precious present. The corn of this country and of Italy, as far as I have seen it, cannot be eaten, either in the form of corn or of bread, by any person who has eaten that of America. I have planted some grains which may perhaps come to maturity as we have still 3 months and a half to frost.—One word more on my leases. I think the term should not exceed three years. The negroes too old to be hired, could they not make a good profit by cultivating cotton? Much enquiry is made of me here about the cultivation of cotton; and I would thank you to give me your opinion how much a hand would make cultivating that as his principal crop instead of tobacco. Great George, Ursula, Betty Hemings not to be hired at all, nor Martin nor Bob otherwise than as they are now. I am sensible, my dear Sir, how much trouble and perplexity I am giving you with my affairs. The plan of leasing will in a great measure releive you. I know Mrs. Lewis's goodness too and her attentions to them. I tender you both the feelings of the most heart felt gratitude. My daughters are well and join me in affectionate remembrance to yourself, Mrs. Lewis and family. I pray you both to accept assurances of my sincere affection, and of the sentiments of esteem & attachment with which I am Dear Sir your friend & servant,

Th: Jefferson

Passports Issued by TJ, 1785–1789

1787	Jan	17.	Colo. Franks 2.m.
	Feb.	6.	——Warner 2.m.
		7.	Davd. S. Franks. 2.m.
			John Bannister. 2.m.
		18	Colo. Blagden 2.m.
			M. Mumford 2.m.
			Burrill Carnes 2 m.
		1.	**Petit, Polly J. & Sally Hemings 2.m.**

TJ to Thomas Mann Randolph Sr.

My dear Sir — Monticello Feb. 4. 1790.

The marriage of your son with my daughter cannot be more pleasing to you than to me. Besides the worth which I discover in him, I am happy that the knot of friendship between us, as old as ourselves, should be drawn closer and closer to the day of our death. I am perfectly contented to leave to yourself the provision for your son. What you propose is liberal. I feel myself tied up by the demand of Farrell & Joneson Mr. Wayles's representatives, and the jealousy they would entertain, as well as my co-representatives were I to follow the dictates of my heart on this occasion. Under these circumstances I propose to give to my daughter immediately my best plantation in Bedford, of 1000 acres of the Poplar forest tract, and 25. negroes little and big. But whatever we do, my dear friend, let us do it for them effectually. This cannot be, if we pass over the moment of their marriage. Marriage is in law a valuable consideration, and will protect them against any demand from any other quarter, or on any other consideration (unless indeed there were a prior mortgage). Your letter to me, and this to you, would be good against you and me: but nothing can be good against all the world but a deed duly executed and recorded. Come then, my dear Sir, and let us place them in security before their marriage. As soon as they shall have agreed on the day you shall know it (perhaps your son can tell it you now) and let me intreat you to come some days before it. Your anxiety for your son's future welfare will I am sure reconcile you to the temporary inconveniences of the journey, which may be lessened by making short stages. The last must be from the point of fork, where you can be well lodged, and from whence the road is good. Should ill health or any other accident put off your coming, it will be better for them on the whole to delay the ceremony. My dcparturc cannot possibly be prolonged an hour after the last day of this month. I am, with the most sincere esteem & attachment, Dr. Sir, your affectionate friend & servant,

Th: Jefferson

Jefferson's Vocabulary of the Unquachog Indians

[14 June 1791]
Unquachogs. About 20. souls. They constitute the Pusspátock settlement in the town of Brookhaven S. side of Long island.

The language they speak is a dialect differing a little from the Indians settled near Southampton called Shinicocks and also from those of Montock called Montocks. The three tribes can barely understand each other.

Quadrupeds cow. Čowsen
horse. Hosses
sheep sheeps.
hog. hog.
dog. Arsúm
—fox. sqúirrútes
—squirrel. moccás.
—rabbet móh-tux
—deer. Hátk

Birds —bird. aswássas.
—crow. concónchus.
gull. Arráx
—goose. hakénah
—eagle wéquaran.
—duck. nanásecus.
—dove. má-owks.
—fish hawk. manamáquas.
—quail. ohócotees
—partridge. ápacus
whippoorwill. whácorees.

Insects —snake. Skwk
—bug seukr
worm. húquer
—fly. muchávwas.
musketo. murráquitch

Plants —tree. péewye.
—pine. Cw
—oak. húchemus.
—hiccory. wusqúat
appletree. appeesanck.
peach tree. péachesanck
cherry tree. chérrysanck.
—grape. cátamenón.
plumb tree. sassémenac.
strawberries. wotáhomon.
—mulberry tree. accacúmenoc.
rose. wósowancon.
Indn. corn. sowháwmen.
—woman. squah.
—child. Peewútstut
—boy. macúchax.
lad. rungcump.
—girl. squásses.
lass. yúnksquas.
—head. okéyununc.
—hair. wé-usk
—eyes. skésuc.
—nose. Cochóy

—turkey nahiam.
chicken. kekeeps.
potato. panac.
squash. Áscoot
wheat. Maróomar
—bread. ap.
mouse. poquáttas
rat. no name.
rye. Rye
—oats. oats.
tobacco. tobac.
hominy. samp.
meat. wéeows.
—stone. sun.
—clay. { púckwe / squoint }
sand yaac
—water. núp
—dirt. puckwé
the whole world. wáame-pámakíu.
—sky. ke-isk
—cloud. pamayaúxen
—rain. súkerun
—snow. soáchop
—ice. copátn
—hail. mosécan
—sun. háquaqua
—moon. neépa.
—star. aráqusac
—fire. ruht. yuht.
whale oil. púttapapúm.
greese. pum.
whale. púttap.
—fish. opéramac.
oyster. apóonahac.
clam. poquahoc.
—a man. run.
—husband. ks-hamps
—wife. keé-us
gr. child. cówhees
—milk. wampachú-unk
peas. no name.
beans. mais-cusseet
—black. shickayo.
—white. wámpayo
—red. sqúayo
—yellow. weesa-wayo

—mouth. Cúttoh
—teeth. Képut
—lips. kussissit.
—chin. cotuḿpcan
—cheek. Canánno
—ear. catáwoc.
—neck. keésquish.
shoulder. Péquan
—arm. copút-te
elbow. keésquan.
—hand. Coŕitché
—finger. coŕitcheus.
—nail. Cocássac
—back. Cúpsquan
skin. Cuttaqúras
—belly. Cráckish
hip. Corúcan
—thigh. Copómac
knee. Cucúttuc
—leg. coráun.
—foot. Cussed
—grt. toe. cumsquáusseet
—little toe. Peewasticonseet
—father cẃs
—mother cẃca
—brother contàyux
—sister. Keéssums
—child. neechuntz.
aunt cacácas
uncle nisséis
Gr father numpsoonk
Gr. mother. Nánnax
—to run. Quáquees
—to break. pẃksa
—to bend. co-unkarúnneman
to cut with a knife.
poquesímman.
to cut with an axe.
poquatáhaman
—to kill. wúhnsa.
war. Ayutówac
—peace. Weéhsaac
to hunt. peénsaac.
—I. née
—you. Kee
—he. naácum.
<*she. wéena*>
—small peéwátsu
—blue. seewamp-wayo
—green. uscusquáyo
—rainbow papuhmúncsunc
bow. atúmp.
arrow. neep.
tomahawk. chékenas.
a pot. coquées
a bed. apúnna
a blanket. aquéewants.
axe. ochégan.
—house. weécho.
door. squnt.
chimney. hamánek
gourd. <*quai*> whorámmok.
watermelon. Waghti-
whorámmok
wampum. whampump.
mocassens. mocússenus
—good. woréecan
—bad. mattateáyuh.
—clever. weáyuh.
—handsome. woreeco.
—ugly. neeho wuchayuk
a cross <*angry*> fellow.
cheeáscota.
—a river seépus
—ocean. cutstúk
a bay. petápagh
—to walk. copumusah
—to stand. cotofer
—to lie down. cutchéepur
—to sit. kiummatap.
10. payac.
11. nápan-naquut
12. napan-ees
13. napan-us
14. napan-yóut
15. napan-napá
16. napan-nacuttah.
&c. to 19.
20. neésun-chog
21. neesun chognaquut
30. Sowunchog
40. Yauhwunchóg
50. napáatsunchóg.
60. nacúttahtsunchog
70. tumpawatsunchog.
&c.

1. Naqúut	<*100 norit sunchog*>
2. Nées	—100. noquut pasit
3. Nus	—200. nees pasu
4. Yaut	<*300*>
5. pa [or] napáa	<*god*> god. mánto.
6. nacúttah [or] cúttah	a great god. masakéetmúnd.
7. Túmpawa	devil. máttateáshet
8. swah.	—thunder. pataquáhamoc.
9. nẃre	—lightening. wowosúmpsa.

The orthography is English. This Vocabulary was taken by Th: J. June 13. 1791. in presence of James Madison and Genl. Floyd. There remain but three persons of this tribe now who can speak it's language. These are old women. From two of these, brought together, this vocabulary was taken. A young woman of the same tribe was also present who knew something of the language.

TJ to Nicholas Lewis

Dear Sir　　　　Philadelphia Apr. 12. 1792.

Unremitting business must be my apology, as it is really the true one, for my having been longer without writing to you than my affections dictated. I am never a day without wishing myself with you, and more and more as the fine sun shine comes on, which seems made for all the world but me. Congress will rise about the 21st. They have past the Representation bill at one for 33,000. which gives to Virginia 19. members. They have voted an army of 5000. men, and the President has given the command to Wayne, with 4. brigadiers, to wit Morgan, Brooks, Willet, and Wilkinson. Congress is now engaged on the ways and means of raising money to pay this army. A further assumption of state debts has been proposed by the Secretary of the Treasury, which has been rejected by a small majority: but the chickens of the treasury have so many contrivances and are so indefatigable within doors and without, that we all fear they will get it in yet some way or other. As the doctrine is that a public debt is a public blessing, so they think a perpetual one is a perpetual blessing, and therefore wish to make it so large as that we can never pay it off.

I must ask the favor of you to send the bonds taken at my sale, to Mr. Eppes, who will deliver them to Hanson, and take a proper receipt, so as to clear me of the paiments of July next and July twelvemonth. I imagine Mr. Randolph may be going to Richmond soon, in which case he can take charge of them so far, and find safe means of sending them over to Mr. Eppes. Should he not be going soon, then I must ask you to send them by such other safe means as can be procured. In every case I shall be obliged to you to keep a copy of one of the bonds, and a list of the whole, naming the sums, times of paiment, purchaser, security and the negroes for which each bond was given. I have written to Mr. Randolph on the subject of contriving the bonds to Mr. Eppes.—I am not certain whether I gave you power to dispose of Mary according to her desire to Colo. Bell, with such of her younger children as she chose. If I did not, I now do it, and will thank you to settle the price as you think best. The 1st. day of July in every year being near my days of payment, his might be fixed to that day of the present year and the next, just as you can agree. The bonds to be sent in like manner to Hanson. Be pleased to present my affectionate respects to Mrs. Lewis, and to accept yourself assurances of the sincere esteem with which I am Dear Sir Your friend & servt, Th: Jefferson

TJ to Thomas Mann Randolph Jr.

Dear Sir Philadelphia Oct. 12. 1792.

Your favor of the 1st. inst. came to hand on the 9th. and brought me the welcome news that you were all well, about which I was anxious, having left Martha not quite as well as I wished. The short proceeds of my sale the last year obliged me to a small one this year, which would have been unnecessary had the other yeilded as was reasonably expected. I therefore, while at home, sent orders to Bedford to sell a dozen negroes from thence, taking the opportunity of some sale in the neighborhood to carry them to. In Albemarle I have concluded to sell Dinah and her younger children, and wrote to my brother to find a purchaser in his neighborhood, so as to unite her to her husband, the circumstance which determined me to fix on her. I am sorry I did not know your wish, as I would have arranged my matters otherwise, so as to have sold the two you mention, and especially Caesar, notorious for his rogueries. On the contrary they are now engaged with the overseers for the crop. Would it not be practicable for you to sell their families at private sale in the neighborhood? Mr. E. Carter sold a great number in this way, and advantageously.—I have been considering that it would be better to floor my stables with slabs from Henderson's. In this case the edges of the slabs must be taken off to a sufficient substance with a drawing knife, and the sleepers should be so laid, as that the end of the slab under the manger may be a couple of inches higher than that at the front.—I think you told me that none of the turneps came up in the ground below the lower roundabout. Would it not be well to make them remove their cowpen to that inclosure? as it will be a preparation for St. foin which I intend for that.—I am giving you a great deal of trouble with my little memorandums. My distance must excuse it, and the prospect that I shall ere long be in the way to do my own business.

Maria is living with a Mrs. Fullerton, whom, as far as I have seen, I like much. She is soon to remove nearer to me. Maria will only come to see me on Sundays. She promises that she will then write to Monticello, and I shall endeavor to make her do it. My love to my dear Martha, with my best compliments to Miss Jane, P. C. and my neighbors. I am with sincere esteem & attachment my dear Sir Your's affectionately Th: Jefferson

TJ to Martha Jefferson Randolph

My dear daughter Philadelphia Oct. 26. 1792.

Having not received a letter by yesterday's post, and that of the former week from Mr. Randolph having announced dear Anne's indisposition, I am under much anxiety. In my last letter to Mr. Randolph I barely mentioned your being recovered, when somewhat younger than she is, by recurrence to a good breast of milk. Perhaps this might be worthy of proposing to the Doctor. In a case where weakness of the digesting organs enters into the causes of illness, a food of the most easy digestion might give time for getting the better of the other causes, whatever they may be. I think it should however be some other than your own, if a breast of milk is to be tried.—I hope you are perfectly well and the little one also, as well as Mr. Randolph to whom present my sincere regards. Adieu my dear your's affectionately Th: Jefferson

TJ to Daniel L. Hylton

Dear Sir Philadelphia Nov. 22. 1792.

I am to acknolege the receipt of your favor of the 10th. and am puzzled what to say on the subject. My first object is to be sure of the price. The mortgage of the Green briar lands I consider as almost nothing, so distant, probably so worthless, so difficult to be got at by the law, and so little likely to be sold for even any thing. I do not know Dr. Taylor's circumstances: but Mr. Eppes tells me he is sure he could get good security. Now if I could have two good persons (say Dr. Taylor and some other responsible one) bound personally, I would accept the Greenbriar mortgage in supplement. Observe that when I ask for *two responsible* persons, I do not count Mr. Banks as one. This being in Dr. Taylor's power, I think he cannot in candour hesitate to agree to it. If he refuses, I must leave it to yourself altogether to consider whether he is himself in such circumstances as to make me sure of the money.—I really wish to sell the land that I may wind up with Mr. Hanson. As some alterations of the deeds I sent you may be necessary, I pray you to get it done by some able lawyer.—I have another task for your friendship. Martin and myself disagreed when I was last in Virginia insomuch that he desired me to sell him, and I determined to do it, and most irrevocably that he shall serve me no longer. If you could find a master agreeable to him, I should be glad if you would settle that point at any price you please: for as to price I will subscribe to any one with the master whom he shall chuse. Any credit may be given which shall be desired in reason. Perhaps Martin may undertake to find a purchaser. But I exclude all idea of his own responsibility: and I would wish that the transaction should be finished without delay, being desirous of avoiding all parley with him myself on the subject.—You see, my dear Sir, what free use I make of your good dispositions. I can only say that placed in any situation where I could be useful to you, I should do as much for you. But your troubles are approaching their end, because I approach the term when

I shall be in a situation to do my own business.—Mr. Banks wrote me a letter from Alexandria on the subject of the Elkhill lands. If you will be so good as to tell him that I leave the matter wholly to you, it will save me the necessity of writing a letter to him, and a letter saved is a relief to me. My affectionate respects to Mrs. Hylton & am with great & sincere esteem Dr. Sir your friend & servt Th: Jefferson

Minutes of a Conference with the Illinois and Wabash Indians

[1–4 Feb. 1793]

Feb. 1. 1793. The President having addressed the Chiefs of the Wabash and Illinois Indians, John Baptist De Coin, chief of Kaskaskia, spoke as follows.

Father. I am about to open to you my heart. I salute first the Great Spirit, the master of life, and then you.

I present you a black pipe on the death of our chiefs who have come here and died in your bed. It is the calumet of the dead. Take it and smoke in it in remembrance of them. The dead pray you to listen to the living and to be their friends. They are gone, we cannot recall them, let us then be contented; for, as you have said, tomorrow perhaps it may be our turn. Take then their pipe, and as I have spoken for the dead, let me now address you for the living. [He delivered the black pipe]

[Here Three-legs, a Piankishaw chief, came forward and carried round a white pipe from which every one smoked.]

John Baptist De Coin spoke again.

Father. The sky is now cleared. I am about to open my heart to you again: I do it in the presence of the Great Spirit, and I pray you to attend.

You have heard the words of our father General Putnam. We opened our hearts to him, we made peace with him, and he has told you what we said.

This pipe is white. I pray you to consider it as of the Wiatonons, Piankeshaws, and the people of Eel river.

The English at Detroit are very jealous of our father. I have used my best endeavors to keep all the red men in friendship with you: but they have drawn over the one half, while I have kept the other. Be friendly then to those I have kept.

I have long known you, General Washington, the Congress, Jefferson, and Sinclair. I have laboured constantly for you, to preserve peace.

You see your children on this side: [pointing to the friends of the dead chiefs] they are now orphans. Take care then of the orphans of our dead friends.

Father, your people of Kentuckey are like Musketoes, and try to destroy the red men: the red men are like Musketoes also, and try to injure the people of Kentuckey. But I look to you as to a good being. Order your people to be just. They are always trying to get our lands. They come on our lands. They hunt on them; kill our game and kill us. Keep them then on one side of the line, and us on the other. Listen, father, to what we say, and protect the nations of the Wabash and Missisipi in their lands.

The English have often spoken to me, but I shut my ears to them. I despise their money. It is nothing to me. I am attached to my lands. I love to eat in tranquility, and not like a bird on a bough.

The Piankeshaws, Wiatenons, Piorias and all the Indians of the Missisipi and Wabash, pray you to open your heart and ears to them, and as you befriend them, to give them Capt. Prior for their father. We love him, men, women and children of us, he has always been friendly to us, always taken care of us, and you cannot give us a better proof of your friendship than in leaving him with us.

[Here Three legs handed round the White pipe to be smoked]

De Coin then, taking a third pipe, proceeded.

This pipe, my father, is sent you by the great chief of all the Wiaws, called Crooked legs. He is old, infirm, and cannot walk. Therefore he is not come. But he prays you to be his friend and to take care of his people. He tells you there are many red people jealous of you. But you need not fear them. If he could have walked he would have come; but he is old, and sick and cannot walk. The English have a sugar mouth: but Crooked legs would never listen to them. They threatened us send the red men to cut off him and his people, and they sent the red men who threatened to do it unless he would join the English. But he would not join them.

The Chiefs of the Wabash, father, pray you to listen. They send you this pipe from afar. Keep your children quiet at the Falls of Ohio. We know you are the head of all. We appeal to you. Keep the Americans on one side of the Ohio from the Falls downwards, and us on the other; that we may have something to live on according to our agreement in the treaty which you have. And do not take from the French the lands we have given them.

Old crooked legs sends you this pipe [here he presented it] and he prays you to send him Capt. Pryor for his father, for he is old and you ought to do this for him.

Father, I pray you to listen. So far I have spoken for others, and now will speak for myself. I am of Kaskaskia, and have always been a good American from my youth upwards. Yet the Kentuckians take my lands, eat my stock, steal my horses, kill my game, and abuse our persons. I come far with all these people. My nation is not numerous. No people can fight against you father, none but the Great god himself. All the red men together cannot do it. But have pity on us. I am now old. Do not let the Kentuckians take my lands nor injure me; but give me a line to them to let me alone.

Father, the Wiatonons, Piankeshaws, Piorias, Powtewatomies, Musketons, Kaskaskias have now made a road to you. It is broad and white: take care of it then and keep it open.

Father, you are powerful. You said you would wipe away our tears. We thank you for this. Be firm and take care of your children.

The hatchet has been long buried. I have been always for peace, I have done what I could, given all the money I had, to procure it.

The half of my heart, father, is black. I brought the Piorias to you, half of them are dead. I fear they will say it was my fault. But father, I look upon you, my heart is white again and I smile.

The Shawanese, the Delawares, and the English are always persuading us to take up the hatchet against you, but I have been always deaf to their words.

[Here he gave a belt]

Great Joseph, who came with us, is dead. Have compassion on his neice, his son in law, and his chiefs [pointing to them]. It is a dead man who speaks to you, father, accept therefore these black beads. [Here he presented several strands of dark coloured beads]

I have now seen Genl. Washington, I salute and regard him next after the Great Spirit.

Como, a Poughtewatomy chief then said that as the President had already been long detained, and the hour was advanced, he would reserve what he had to say to another day.

Shawas, the little Doe, a Kickapou chief, tho' very sick, had attended the Conference, and now carried the pipe round to be smoked. He then addressed the President.

Father. I am still very ill and unable to speak. I am a Kickapou, and drink of all the waters of the Wabash and Missisipi. I have been to the Wabash and treated with General Putnam: and I came here, not to do ill, but to make peace. Send to us Capt. Prior to be our father, and no other. He possesses all our love.

Father, I am too ill to speak. You will not forget what the others have said.

Feb. 2. The day being cloudy, the Indians did not chuse to meet.

Feb. 4. The morning was cloudy. They gave notice that if it should clear up they would attend at the President's at 2. aclock. Accordingly, the clouds having broke away about Noon, they attended a little after two; except Shawas and another who were sick, and one woman.

Como, a Powtewatomy chief spoke.

Father, I am opening my heart to speak to you. Open yours to recieve my words. I first address you from a dead chief, who, when he was about to die, called us up to him and charged us "never to part with our lands so I have done for you, my children, and so do you for yours. For what have we come so far? Not to ruin our nation, nor yet that we might carry goods home to our women and children: but to procure them lasting good, to open a road between them and the Whites. Sollicit our father to send Capt. Prior to us. He has taken good care of us and we all love him."

Now, father, I address you for our young people. But there remains not much to say; for I spoke to you through Genl. Putnam, and you have what I said on paper. I have buried the hatchet for ever: so must your children. I speak the truth and you must believe me. We all pray you to send Capt. Pryor to us, because he has been so very kind to us all.

[Here he delivered strands of dark colored beads.]

Father, hear me and believe me. I speak the truth and from my heart; recieve my words then into yours. I am come from afar, for the good of my women and children, for their present and future good. When I was at home in the midst of them, my heart sunk within me, I saw no hope for them. The heavens were gloomy and lowering and I could not tell why. But General Putnam spoke to us, and called us together. I rejoiced to hear him, and determined immediately to come and see my father. Father, I am happy to see you. The heavens have cleared away, the day is bright, and I rejoice to hear your voice. These beads [holding up a bundle of white strands] are a road between us. Take you hold at one end. I will at the other, and hold it fast. I will visit this road every day, and sweep it clean. If any blood be on it, I will cover it up; if stumps, I will cut them out. Should your children and mine meet in this road they shall shake hands and be good friends. Some of the Indians who belong to the English will be trying to sow harm between us: but we must be on our guard and prevent it.

Father, I love the land on which I was born, the trees which cover it, and the grass growing on it. It feeds us well. I am not come here to ask gifts. I am young, and by hunting on my own land, can kill what I want and feed my women and children in plenty. I come not to beg. But if any of your traders would wish to come among us, let them come. For who will hurt them? Nobody. I will be there before them.

Father, I take you by the hand with all my heart, I will never forget you; do not you forget me.

[Here he delivered the bundle of white strands]

The Little beaver, a Wiatonon, on the behalf of Crooked legs, handed round the pipe, and then spoke.

Father, listen now to me, as you have done to others. I am not a very great chief: I am a chief of war, and leader of the young people.

Father, I wished much to hear you: you have spoken comfort to us, and I am happy to have heard it. The sun has shone out, and all is well. This makes us think it was the great spirit speaking truth through you. Do then what you have said: restrain your people if they do wrong, as we will ours if they do wrong.

Father, we gave to our friend (Pryor) who came with us, our name of Wiatonon, and he gave us his name of American. We are now Americans. Give him then to us for a father. He has loved us and taken care of us. He had pity on our women and children and fed them. Do not forget to grant us this request. You told us to live in quiet and to do right. We will do what you desire. Then do you what we desire, and let Pryor come to us.

Now that we are come so far to hear you, write a line to your people to keep the river open between us, that we may go down it in safety, and that our women and children may work in peace. When I go back, I will bear to them good tidings, and our young men will no longer hunt in fear for the support of our women and children.

Father, all of us who have heard you, are made happy. All are in the same sentiment with me; all are satisfied. Be assured that, when we return, the Indians and Americans will be one people, will hunt, and play, and laugh together. For me, I will never depart one step from Pryor.

We are come from afar to make a stable peace to look forward to our future good. Do not refuse what we sollicit. We will never forget you.

Here I will cease. The father of life might otherwise think I babbled too much; and so might you. I finish then, in giving you this pipe. It is my own and from myself alone. I am but a warrior. I give it to you to smoke in. Let it's fumes ascend to the great Spirit in heaven.

[He delivered the pipe to the President.]

The wife of the Souldier, a Wiatonon, speaks.

Father I take you by the hand with all my heart because you have spoken comfort to us. I am but a woman: yet you must listen.

The Village-chiefs, and Chiefs of war have opened their bodies and laid naked their hearts to you. Let them too see your heart and listen to them.

We have come, men and women, from afar to beseech you to let no one take our lands. That is one of your children [pointing to

Genl. Putnam] it was he who persuaded us to come. We thought he spoke the truth: we came, we hope that good will come of it.

Father. We know you are strong. Have pity on us. Be firm in your words. They have given us courage. The father of life has opened our hearts on both sides for good.

He, who was to have spoken to you, is dead, great Joseph. If he had lived, you would have heard a good man, and good words flowing from his mouth. He was my uncle, and it has fallen to me to speak for him. But I am ignorant. Excuse then these words. It is but a woman who speaks.

[She delivers white strands]

Three legs, a Piankasha spoke.

I speak for a young chief whom I have lost here. He came to speak to you, father, but he had not that happiness. He died. I am not a Village-chief, but only a chief of war.

We are come to seek all our good, and to be firm in it. If our father is firm we will be so. It was a dark and gloomy day in which I lost my young chief. The master of life saw that he was good, and called him to himself. We must submit to his will.

[He gave a black strand]

I pray you all who are present to say, as one man, that our peace is firm, and to let it be firm. Listen to us if you love us. We live on the river; on one side, and shall be happy to see capt. Pryor on the other, and to have a lasting peace.

Here is our father Putnam. He heard me speak at Au Poste. If I am false, let him say so.

My land is but small. If any more be taken from us, I will come again to you and complain, for we shall not be able to live. Have pity on us father. You have many red children there and they have little whereon to live. Leave them land enough to labour, to hunt and to live on: and the lands which we have given to the French, let them be to them for ever.

Father, we are very poor. We have traders among us, but they sell too dear. We have not the means of supplying our wants at such prices. Encourage your traders then to come, and to bring us guns, powder and other necessaries: and send Capt. Prior also to us.

[He gave a string of white beads.]

De Coin spoke.

Jefferson, I have seen you before, and we have spoken together.

Sinclair, we have opened our hearts to one another.

Putnam, we did the same at Au Poste.

Father, you have heard these three speak of me, and you know my character. The times are gloomy in my town. We have no commander, no souldier, no priest. Have you no concern for us father? If you have, put a magistrate with us to keep the peace. I cannot live so. I am of French blood. When there are no priests among us, we think that all is not well. When I was small we had priests. Now that I am old, we have none. Am I to forget then how to pray? Have pity on me and grant what I ask. I have spoken on your behalf to all the nations. I am a friend to all, and hurt none. For what are we on this earth? But as a small and tender plant of corn;—even as nothing. God has made this earth for you as well as us: we are then but as one family, and if any one strikes you, it is as if he had struck us. If any nation strikes you father, we will let you know what nation it is.

Father, we fear the Kentuckians. They are headstrong, and do us great wrong. They are not content to come on our lands to hunt on them, to steal and destroy our stocks, as the Shawanese and Delawares do, but they go further and abuse our persons. Forbid them to do so. Sinclair, you know that the Shawanese and Delawares came from the Spanish side of the river, destroyed our corn and killed our cattle. We cannot live, if things go so.

Father, you are rich, you have all things at command, you want for nothing. You promised to wipe away our tears. I commend our women and children to your care.

[He gave strands of white beads]

The President then assured them that he would take into consideration what they had said, and would give them an answer on another day, whereupon the Conference ended for the present.

American Philosophical Society's Instructions to André Michaux

[ca. 30 Apr. 1793]

To Mr. Andrew Michaud.

Sundry persons having subscribed certain sums of money for your encouragement to explore the country along the Missouri, and thence Westwardly to the Pacific ocean, having submitted the plan of the enterprize to the direction of the American Philosophical society, and the Society having accepted of the trust, they proceed to give you the following instructions.

They observe to you that the chief objects of your journey are to find the shortest and most convenient route of communication between the US. and the Pacific ocean, within the temperate latitudes, and to learn such particulars as can be obtained of the country through which it passes, it's productions, inhabitants and other interesting circumstances.

As a channel of communication between these states and the Pacific ocean, the Missouri, so far as it extends, presents itself under circumstances of unquestioned preference. It has therefore been declared as a fundamental object of the subscription, (not to be dispensed with) that this river shall be considered and explored as a part of the communication sought for. To the neighborhood of this river therefore, that is to say to the town of Kaskaskia, the society will procure you a conveyance in company with the Indians of that town now in Philadelphia.

From thence you will cross the Missisipi and pass by land to the nearest part of the Missouri above the Spanish settlements, that you may avoid the risk of being stopped.

You will then pursue such of the largest streams of that river, as shall lead by the shortest way, and the lowest latitudes to the Pacific ocean.

When, pursuing these streams, you shall find yourself at the point from whence you may get by the shortest and most convenient route to some principal river of the Pacific ocean, you are to proceed to such river, and pursue it's course to the ocean. It would seem by the latest maps as if a river called Oregan interlocked with the Missouri for a considerable distance, and entered the Pacific ocean, not far Southward of Nootka sound. But the Society are aware that these maps are not to be trusted so far as to be the ground of any positive instruction to you. They therefore only mention the fact, leaving to yourself to verify it, or to follow such other as you shall find to be the real truth.

You will, in the course of your journey, take notice of the country you pass through, it's general face, soil, rivers, mountains, it's productions animal, vegetable, and mineral so far as they may be new to us and may also be useful or very curious; the latitude of places or materials for calculating it by such simple methods as your situation may admit you to practice, the names, numbers, and dwellings of the inhabitants, and such particularities as you can learn of their history, connection with each other, languages, manners, state of society and of the arts and commerce among them.

Under the head of Animal history, that of the Mammoth is particularly recommended to your enquiries. As it is also to learn whether the Lama, or Paca of Peru is found in those parts of this continent, or how far North they come.

The method of preserving your observations is left to yourself, according to the means which shall be in your power. It is only suggested that the noting them on the skin might be best for such as are most important, and that further details may be committed to the bark of the paper birch, a substance which may not excite suspicions among the Indians, and little liable to injury from wet, or other common accidents. By the means of the same substance you may perhaps find opportunities, from time to time, of communicating to the society information of your progress, and of the particulars you shall have noted.

When you shall have reached the Pacific ocean, if you find yourself within convenient distance of any settlement of Europeans, go to them, commit to writing a narrative of your journey and observations and take the best measures you can for conveying it by duplicates or triplicates thence to the society by sea.

Return by the same, or such other route, as you shall think likely to fulfill with most satisfaction and certainty the objects of your mission; furnishing yourself with the best proofs the nature of the case will admit of the reality and extent of your progress. Whether this shall be by certificates from Europeans settled on the Western coast of America, or by what other means, must depend on circumstances.

Ignorance of the country thro' which you are to pass and confidence in your judgment, zeal, and discretion, prevent the society from attempting more minute instructions, and even from exacting rigorous observance of those already given, except indeed what is the first of all objects, that you seek for and pursue that route which shall form the shortest and most convenient communication between the higher parts of the Missouri and the Pacific ocean.

It is strongly recommended to you to expose yourself in no case to unnecessary dangers, whether such as might affect your health or your personal safety: and to consider this not merely as your personal concern, but as the injunction of Science in general which expects it's enlargement from your enquiries, and of the inhabitants of the US. in particular, to whom your Report will open new feilds and subjects of Commerce, Intercourse, and Observation.

If you reach the Pacific ocean and return, the Society assign to you all the benefits of the subscription beforementioned. If you reach the waters only which run into that ocean, the society reserve to themselves the apportionment of the reward according to the conditions expressed in the subscription.

They will expect you to return to the city of Philadelphia to give in to them a full narrative of your journey and observations, and to answer the enquiries they shall make of you, still reserving to yourself the benefits arising from the publication of them.

Agreement with James Hemings, September 15, 1793

Having been at great expence in having James Hemings taught the art of cookery, desiring to befriend him, and to require from him as little in return as possible, I do hereby promise and declare, that if the said James shall go with me to Monticello in the course of the ensuing winter, when I go to reside there myself, and shall there continue until he shall have taught such person as I shall place under him for that purpose to be a good cook, this previous condition being performed, he shall be thereupon made free, and I will thereupon execute all proper instruments to make him free. Given under my hand and seal in the county of Philadelphia and state of Pennsylvania this 15th. day of September one thousand seven hundred and ninety three.

Th: Jefferson
Witness
Adrien Petit

Deed of Manumission for Robert Hemings, December 24, 1794

This indenture witnesseth that I Thomas Jefferson of the county of Albemarle have manumitted and made free Robert Hemings, son of Betty Hemmings: so that in future he shall be free and of free condition, with all his goods and chattels and shall be discharged of all obligation of bondage or servitude whatsoever: and that neither myself, my heirs executors or administrators shall have any right to exact from him hereafter any services or duties whatsoever. In witness whereof I have put my seal to this present deed of manumission. Given in Albemarle this twenty fourth day of December one thousand seven hundred and ninety four.

Th: Jefferson
Signed, sealed and
delivered
in presence of
D: Carr

TJ's Record of the Productivity of the Enslaved Boys Working in the Nailery

Estimate of the actual work of the autumn of 1794

	lb.
Moses wastes	15 in the €
Shepherd	18.
Barnaby	22.
Davy	18.2
Jamey	29.83
Ben	28.
	131. in 600.
	22 in 100.
Joe	19
Wormeley	16.25
Burwell	29.
	64.25
	21.4 in 100.

the day's work of each	VI.	VIII.	X.	XII.
	lb.	lb.	lb.	lb.
Moses, Shepherd, Barnaby	4	4½	5	5½
Davey, Jamey, Ben, Joe, Wormeley	2½	3	3½	4

size	quantity	market price	cost of iron	clear profit
		s d	s d	s d
Vis.	24½ lb.	1–4–6	0–10–2½	0–14–3½
VIII.	28½	1–6–9½	0–11–10½	0–14–11
Xs.	32½	1–9–9	0–13–6½	0–18–2½
XIIs.	36½	1–11–1	0–15–2½	0–15–10½
average	30½	1–8 -0	0–12–8½	0–15–4
290. days or a year	8845	406–0–0	184–5–5	222–7–0
deduct allowance to George of 3. per cent on the nails sold, or 6. per cent on the clear profits				13–6–8
				209–0–4

TJ to Thomas Mann Randolph

Dear Sir Monticello Dec. 26. 94.

Your chariot was ready to have set off the day after Zachary arrived here; but an unlucky use of the permission you had given me respecting your waggon, has prevented it's departure. The post after you left us, I received information *from Philadelphia* that my nail-rod had been lodged in Richmond before the last week in November, and could not be forwarded here for want of a conveyance. I immediately went to Colo. Bell to advise on the prospect of a conveyance from Richmond. He assured me it was desperate, as all the return waggons were engaged by the merchants. I was therefore obliged to avail myself of your kind permission to send your waggon, and having desired Robinson to get a load for her down, Billy set off with her for Richmond on Thursday, and expected to be back here on Thursday again, which was yesterday. I did not suppose however he could be back till to-day. Nor is he as yet arrived, but the moment he arrives, Zachary may set out. I would have sent one of my horses, if we could have made up another, but Zachary says that Billy is as essential as the horses.—Before the receipt of your letter, we had taken up our Asparagus bed, and after replanting had given the spare roots to a neighbor. We have however done our best to send Mrs. Fleming what more could be spared or collected. Patsy wrote for Artichoke roots. But I presume she meant *Asparagus*, as our artichokes are but newly planted, and are most of them of so indifferent a kind that, as soon as we can distinguish them, we mean to dig them up and throw them away.—If you can hire the four negromen for me at the hiring in Richmond Jan. 1. on advantageous terms, I shall be obliged to you, provided they are from the country, and not of the town from whence I should not chuse any mixture with my own negroes. This would be so far adviseable as those of your father's estate may go too high. Otherwise I should have preferred these as they will think themselves still in the family and will be more contented and controuled by your presence.—You will find by the inclosed that Bob's business has been hastened into such a situation as to make it difficult for me to reject it. I had certainly thought it just that the person whom I suppose to have debauched him from me, as well as the special inconvenience of my letting him go for 2. or 3. years to come, and a total abandonment of his services for 11. or 12 years past should have been known and operated in estimating his value as a mulct on Mr. S. However all that has been kept out of view, and I have too much respect for the gentlemen who have valued him to have the subject revised. It remains therefore only to receive the money and deliver the deed, which you will find inclosed in the letter to Mr. Stras. I have made it to Bob himself, because Mr. Stras mentions it is for his freedom he is to advance the money, and his holding the deed will sufficiently secure the fulfilment of Bob's engagements to him. When you shall have received the money, be so good as to pay £41–16 currency of it to Mr. Lyle with the sum delivered you before, and hold up the balance, as I expect in 2. or 3 posts from Philadelphia to learn whether I owe it there or am to apply it to certain purposes here. Stras's letter and the valuation to be returned to me.—Derieux removes to Wood's ordinary within a week. The children are and have been constantly well. I shall not close my letter till Billy arrives.

Dec. 27. half after one. Billy arrived half an hour ago. I had told him that you would be at Richmond about the time of his being there. He mistook this for a direction to wait for you, and says he stayed two days there expecting you. I am endeavoring to get them off this afternoon if it be only for 8. or 10. miles as that will enable them to reach Rockcastle tomorrow. Billy has to go to Edgehill for clothes.—The old lady at Bearcastle is dead; by which the sons of Mr. D. Carr come into immediate possession of their lands, about 1500. as. ⅓ of which are low grounds. There will be about 40 negroes to divide among the children of their grandfather and their representatives. I think Peter Carr will take the whole of his father's share, and of his uncle Sam Carr's. Tho as to this last it is more questionable, Mr. Wythe and Mr. Pendleton having differed in opinion. The question will lie between Peter and his uncles and aunts, and not between him and his brothers and sisters, who I think have no title under any hypothesis.

Billy has brought me 1500. ℔. of nailrod. The rest is at Manchester, and has been there above a month by Swan's own information to Lownes in Philadelphia, and communicated by Lownes to me. I shall endeavor to get the Milton boats to bring it up. If you were to fall in with any of them while you are in Richmond, be so good as to lend a hand to their getting it. But do not go out of your way to do it, as I shall be pretty sure of having it done.—We are all well and concerned for the impediments of your journey, and the state of your's and Patsy's health. My best affections attend you both always.

P.S. Pray lodge nine dollars of the money to be received of Stras in the hands of Colo. Harvie for J. Taylor to pay for the drill plough. I shall give Taylor notice that it is done. My groceries from Colo. Gamble's are come up.

TJ to Jean Nicolas Démeunier

DEAR SIR Monticello. Virginia Apr. 29. 95

. . . In our private pursuits it is a great advantage that every honest employment is deemed honorable. I am myself a nail-maker. On returning home, after an absence of ten years, I found my farms so much deranged, that I saw evidently they would be a burthen to me instead of a support till I could regenerate them; and consequently that it was necessary for me to find some other resource in the mean time. I thought for a while of taking up the manufacture of pot-ash, which requires but small advances of money. I concluded at length however to begin a manufacture of nails, which needs little or no capital, and I now employ a dozen little boys from 10. to 16. years of age, overlooking all the details of their business myself, and drawing from it a profit on which I can get along till I can put my farms into a course of yielding profit. My new trade of nail-making is to me in this country what an additional title of nobility, or the ensigns of a new order are in Europe.—

Th: Jefferson

Deed of Manumission for James Hemings, February 5, 1796

This indenture made at Monticello in the county of Albemarle and commonwealth of Virginia on the fifth day of February one thousand seven hundred and ninety six witnesseth that I Thomas Jefferson of Monticello aforesaid do emancipate, manumit and make free James Hemings, son of Betty Hemings, which said James is now of the age of thirty years so that in future he shall be free and of free condition, and discharged of all duties and claims of servitude whatsoever, and shall have all the rights and privileges of a freedman. In witness whereof I have hereto set my hand and seal on the day and year above written, and have made these presents double of the same date, tenor and indenture one whereof is lodged in the court of Albemarle aforesaid to be recorded, and the other is delivered by me to the said James Hemings to be produced when and where it may be necessary. Th: Jefferson

Signed, sealed and
delivered
in presence of
John Carr
Francis Anderson

TJ to Jean Baptiste Ducoigne

My good friend & brother

John Baptist De Coigne [21 June 1796]

This letter will be delivered you by Mr. Volney, my friend, [and a] countryman of old France. He proposes to go to your country and to be acquainted with you, because good people love to know one another. I therefore recommend him to you, and ask you to be his friend, to take ca[re of] him, and to render him all the services he needs while he is at Kaskaskia. [He] came to visit me at my own house in Virginia, where I had the pleasure of seeing you 15. years ago, when my name sake Jefferson was at his mother's breast. Now he is grown up to be a man, strong and young, and I am become old and infirm, or I should go to your country, as I have a gr[eat] friendship for our elder brothers the Indians who first inhabited this country, and a very great one for you in particular. I wish you and them all peace and happiness, and never to be disturbed in your lands. Perhaps I may come some day yet and smoke the pipe of friendship with you and your friends. You told me your son would come to see me. I shall be very glad to recieve him here, and to be always his father and friend, for I am sure that your lessons and your example will make him always deserve it. My children too will make him very welcome and consider him as their brother, and their children and his will be always brothers and friends.

Farewell my good brother. Continue to esteem me always as I shall you, and shall always be your affectionate friend

Th: Jefferson

Enclosure: Memorandum for Samuel Arnold

Memorandum for mr Arnold.

I left with old George written directions about the accomodation of mr Arnold. I also pointed out to him the place where I left written directions for his employment. I think it was on the top of the glass clock-case in the parlour.

I would have mr Arnold first prepare the architraves mentioned in those instructions, for the Alcoves & doors of all the rooms; because that will enable us to close them & make them inhabitable. then he may go on with the other work in the order mentioned in that paper, except the doors which are to be the last thing done.

John Hemings may work with him till I come home; and I think had better be employed in dressing the flooring plank got from Calvert and such other of the plank as will do tolerably for flooring. particularly some short plank sawed by Haden's people, which will do well to floor the alcoves, as they must be first floored.

No work is to be put up till I come home.

Th: Jefferson Apr. 12. 98.

Preliminary Will of Tadeusz Kościuszko

[before 5 May 1798]

I beg Mr. Jefferson that in case I should die without will or testament he should bye out of my money So many Negroes and free them. that the restante Sums should be Sufficient to give them aducation and provide for thier maintenance. that is to say. each should know before; the duty of a Cytysen in the free Government. that he must defend his Country. against foroign as well internal Enemies who would wish to change the Constitution for the worst. to inslave them by degree afterwards. to have good and human heart Sensible for the Sufferings of others. each must be maried and have 100. Ackres of Land. wyth instruments. Cattle for tillage and know how to manage and Gouvern it as well to know behave to neybourghs. always wyth Kindnes. and ready to help them to them selves frugal. to ther Children give good aducation i mean as to the heart, and the duty to ther Country, in gratitude to me to make thems'elves hapy as possible. T Kosciuszko

Will of Tadeusz Kościuszko

5th day of May 1798

I Thaddeus Kosciuszko being just in my departure from America do hereby declare and direct that should I make no other testamentory disposition of my property in the United States I hereby authorise my friend Thomas Jefferson to employ the whole thereof in purchasing Negroes from among his own or any others and giving them Liberty in my name, in giving them en education in trades or othervise and in having them instructed for their new condition in the duties of morality which may make them good neigh bours good fathers or moders, husbands or vives and in their duties as citisens teeching them to be defenders of their Liberty and Country and of the good order of Society and in whatsoever may Make them happy and useful, and I make the said Thomas Jefferson my executor of this T. Kosciuszko

TJ to Thomas Mann Randolph

Th:J. to TMR Philadelphia June 14. 98.

I wrote you last on the 7th. inst. since which yours of the 3d. is recieved. I shall certainly leave this on the 20th. and be at Fredericksburg on the 23d. consequently one day before my horses, which in my last I desired might set out Saturday the 23d. & be there

Sunday the 24th. in the mean time I thank you for putting an end to the cultivation of tobacco as the peculium of the negroes. I have ever found it necessary to confine them to such articles as are not raised for the farm. there is no other way of drawing a line between what is theirs & mine.

The new naturalization bill is passed. it requires 14. years to make a citizen. the bill for suspending intercourse with the French is signed by the President. this will lessen the English captures, for they have for some time been more considerable than the French. they take all trading with French, Spanish or Dutch colonies. our bill will prevent the odium which would have attended their captures of those bound to the French: and the friends of it would have extended it to Spanish & Dutch if they could have found any pretext, merely to screen the English from censure. a bill is brought in to allow the President to recieve any number of armed vessels (not over 12. in number) and carrying not less metal than 22. nine-pounders, which may be built in the US. and to agree to such paiments of the interest & principal of their cost as he thinks proper. mr Harper has also brought in resolutions to authorize the President to borrow whatever money may be necessary for the expences of this year over & above the taxes. the bill for assessing lands, houses, & slaves is passed the H. of R. that for levying 2. millions on them, is still before that house. it is not yet decided when they will adjourn. Innes is still living. he is sent into the country. my warmest affections to my dear Martha, and the little ones. cordial Adieu to yourself.

P.S. mr Lott will furnish money for Jupiter's road expences. 4. or 5. dollars will be enough. perhaps he can find it himself & recieve it from me.
Flour at Baltimore 4.50. D here 5. D

TJ's Notations on Orchards

PASTURE

In the neighborhood of Philadelphia, butchers pay ⅓ of a dollar a week for pasturing their fattening bullocks.

fields which are in a course of culture should never be pastured, as that injures them as much as rest would recruit them.

ORCHARDS

Straw about the roots of trees prevents the growth of grass & weeds too near the tree, & manure & lighten the ground.

96. Sep. 4. mr Eppes examines my North orchard and says it consists of Clarke's pear -mains, Golden wilding, & red Hughes. he says the Golden wilding must not be mellowed before pressed, it will yeild nothing. it must be pressed as soon as gathered. mixed with the red Hughes the make the best cyder & yeild best.

99. Nov. 1. 70. bushels of the Robinson & red Hughes (about half of each) have made 120. gallons of cyder. George says that when in a proper state (there was much rot among these) they ought to make 3. galls. to the bushel, as he knows from having often measured both.

see 11. Bibl. Phys. econ. apple mill.

1824. Apr. Genr. Cocke says the Peach tree worm is hatching all July, Aug. Sep. and lays its egg immediately on being hatched. it may be seen & taken out from Mar. to June. it should always be done before harvest.

TJ to Thomas Mann Randolph

Th:J. to TMR. Washington Jan. 29. [1801]

Your's of the 24th. came to hand last night. on application to the Postmaster Genl. it seems that I should have put my letters into the office here on the Thursday, instead of Friday. this accordingly goes to the office this day, which is Thursday, and therefore ought to get to you on Thursday next. it may very likely therefore go with my letter of the 23d.

I am very glad indeed to find that Lilly has got so strong a gang, independant of yours & the nailers. with respect to yours I wish you to do exactly what is most for your own interest, either keeping them yourself, or putting any of them with mine as best suits your own convenience. I still think it will be better that such of the nailers as may be able to handle the axe should be employed with it till April, that is to say till Powell comes. it will be useful to them morally and physically, and I have work enough of that kind, with the canal & road to give them full employment. perhaps, as the blowing to be done in the canal will be tedious, it might be worth while to keep Joe & Wormely employed on that in all good weather. if you think so, they should work separately, as I think that one hand to hold the auger & one to strike, is throwing away the labour of one. there should be force enough kept in the nailery to supply our standing customers. there is another reason for employing only the weaker hands in the nailery. I do not believe there is rod to employ the whole any length of time; and none can be got to them till April. I should be glad mr Lilly or mr Dinsmore would count the faggots on hand, & inform me of the quantity by return of post; as I have forgotten the state of the supplies on hand, when I left home.—mr Wilson Nicholas and myself have this day joined in ordering clover seed from New York, where it is to be had, it is said, at 12 dollars. I have ordered 5. bushels for you. I believe I have none to sow myself. mr Jefferson informs me two small casks of wine are forwarded for me to Milton. out of this I wish you to take what I borrowed of you: and I will be thankful to you to inform me as soon as you can of the size of the casks, that I may know how to proportion the equivalent to mr Yznardi. it should be stored in the Dining room cellar, & that secured by double locks, as I presume it is.—with respect to the election, there is no change of appearance since my last. the main body of the Federalists are determined to elect B. or to prevent an election. we have 8. states certain, they 6. and two divided. there are 6. individuals, of moderate dispositions, any one of which coming over to us, will make a 9th. vote. I dare not trust more through the post. my tender love to my ever dear Martha, and to the little ones. I believe I must ask her to give directions to Goliah & his senile corps to prepare what they can in the garden; as it is very possible I may want it. accept assurances of my sincere affection. Adieu.

TJ to William Evans

Dear Sir Washington Feb. 22. 1801.

You mentioned to me in conversation here that you sometimes saw my former servant James, & that he made his engagements such as to keep himself always free to come to me. could I get the favor of you to send for him & to tell him I shall be glad to recieve him as soon as he can come to me? Francis Sayes who also lived with me formerly and, since that, with you, came here some time ago to offer himself to me. he had begun to drink a little before he left me, & I fear he continues it. he moreover says that his wife has good custom in Baltimore as a washer, & particularly your [custom]. I represented to him the inexpediency of removing from an established [house] of business & running the risk of business for her here: for tho' I might possibly give him a birth, yet I could not employ or take in his family, and I endeavored to throw cold water on his proposition. he seemed however so desirous, that I told him if I should be able to employ him, I would write to him: & he returned to Baltimore on this ground. in truth I would rather he would decline it. should he be with you, or fall into your way, I would thank you to discourage him from the idea. he was an affectionate & honest servant to me, which makes me unwilling to reject him absolutely; and yet the fear of his drinking and of his getting his family into distress by removing them, induces me to wish rather that he would decline the thought.—I owe you many apologies for troubling you with these small things: but the truth is that I am so much embarrassed in composing a good houshold for myself, as in providing a good administration for our country.—accept assurances of the esteem with which I am Dear Sir

Your most obedt. servt Th: Jefferson

TJ to Philippe de Létombe

Dear Sir Washington Feb. 22. 1801.

I fear you will consider me as taking much too great a liberty in what I am now about to ask of you; and yet I have had such experience of the friendliness of your disposition, and feel such a consciousness of a reciprocal disposition to serve you, that I am emboldened to go on. being now obliged to fix myself here, I find as great difficulty in composing my houshold, as I shall probably find in composing an administration for the government. you know the importance of a good maitre d'hotel, in a large house, & the impossibility of finding one among the natives of our country. I have imagined that such a person might be found perhaps among the French in Philadelphia, that no one would be more likely to know it than yourself, & that no one would be a better judge of his qualifications. honesty & skill in making the dessert are indispen[sable] qualifications. that he should be good humored & of a discreet, steady disposition is also important. if there be such a one within the compass of your knolege, will you have the goodness to engage him to come to me immediately? and to drop me a line of information whether I stand a chance to get one? if you could, by saying a word about price, fix him to some reasonable demand, it would add to the obligation: as he might on arriving here & seeing my distress take advantage from it to extort what would be unreasonable. you have sometimes given me apprehensions you meant to leave us soon. I should sincerely regret it, as I know the comfort of doing business with a person so rational & accomodating as yourself. it is a blessing to both nations to have such a person placed between them. should however any circumstances lead you to persist in this purpose, I should be happy if you would leave me the legacy of your Maitre d'hotel on your departure, if you think he has the necessary qualifications. I have a good cook: but it is pour l'office, & to take charge of the family that I am distressed. accept assurances of my great & cordial esteem and respect.

Th: Jefferson

Francis Say to TJ

Sir Baltimor Febuary 23 1801

I have spoke to James according to your Desire he has made mention again as he did before that he was willing to serve you before any other man in the Union but sence he understands that he would have to be among strange servants he would be very much obliged to you if you would send him a few lines of engagement and on what conditions and what wages you would please to give him with your own hand wreiting—and I myself should be very much obliged to you if you let me know How soon you would want me I should myself wish to serve you before any other man I have already refused some good employment on acount of yours since Mr. Randolph has made mention to me when he came from Philadelphia. you know very well that I am a poor man

I remain with due respest your Humble Servant

Francis Say

William Evans to TJ

Honored Sir/ Baltimore Feby. 27th. 1801

Your favour of the 22d instant came Duly to hand. that part of the contents of which relative to your former Servant James I Immediately communicated to him, he told that he was under an engagement with Mr Peck, a Tavern Keeper, of this place, which he said was out of his power to relinquish for a few days, I requested him to be particular In mentioning the time he could be in readiness to go you, he gave me for answer that he would make up his mind in the course of the evening and let me Know his determinations, but on finding that he did not call agreeable to promise I sent for him a second time, the answer he returned me, was, that he would not go untill you should write to himself—I will endeavour to persuade Francis from the idea of getting into your employ as I am rather inclined to believe that, he would not answer your purposes from his being overly fond of liquor, permit me Honored Sir to congratulate you on being promoted to the Chief Majestry of America, and believe me with every Sentiment of respect your obedient Servant

William Evans

TJ to William Evans

Dear Sir Washington Mar. 31. 1801.

Being in the moment of departure for Monticello where it is necessary for me to be two or three weeks previous to my final settlement here, I cannot go without thanking you for the trouble you were so good as to take as to James & Francis. I supposed I saw in the difficulties raised by James an unwillingness to come here, arising wholly from some attachment he had formed at Baltimore; for I cannot suspect an indisposition towards me. I concluded at once therefore not to urge him against inclination, and wrote to Philadelphia, where I have been successful in getting a cook equal to my wishes. I am glad Francis remains there, as I cannot bear a servant who drinks, & on the whole am supplied to mind. I would wish James to understand that it was in acquiesance to what I supposed his own wish that I did not repeat my application, after having so long rested on the expectation of having him. Accept assurances of my best wishes & sincere esteem. Th: Jefferson

TJ to Henry Rose

Dear Sir Washington Oct. 23. 1801.

Your's of the 19th. is at hand. soon after my arrival at Monticello in Aug. I recieved from Dr. Waterhouse of Boston some vaccine matter of his own taking and some from Dr. Jenner of England just then come to hand. both of them took well, and exhibited the same identical appearances in the persons into whom they were inserted. I inoculated about 70 or 80 of my own family, my two sons in law as many, in Aug. & Sep. all had kernels under the arms, and a single pustule, to wit that made by the insertion. one or two of the whole number had very sore arms and 4. or 5 pustules on the arm. about 1 in 4. or 5. or 6. had slight feverish dispositions for an evening or two. none of them changed their regimen, & few intermitted their ordinary occupations. the inoculation of the mother in no instance gave it to the child which sucked her. being cautioned by Dr. Waterhouse to be particularly attentive to the state of the matter with which I inoculated, I was so & believe that I preserved the disease in it's genuine form. I found that taking the premature &

the tardy cases of maturation, there was one day which both comprehended, to wit, the 8th. (say 8. times 24. hours) from the time of inoculation. at that point of time I do not know that I ever saw the matter in any patient either unformed, or shewing a commencement of maturation. I brought some matter to Dr. Gantt here who now inoculates from it, & means to try the variolous inoculation on some of his patients. I had no opportunity of doing that. I sent some matter to Doctr. Waterhouse, & I shall have his opinion in due time whether it had been continued genuine. from the trials I made, the Cowpox can hardly be called a disease. it produces no more inconvenience than a burn or blister of a quarter of an inch diameter.

I propose some Saturday morning to ride & explore the road you described to me. if I knew on what Saturday I should find you at home, I would breakfast with you, and take your further directions to find it. Accept my best wishes for your health & happiness.

Th: Jefferson

TJ to William Evans

Dear Sir — Washington Nov. 1. 1801.

I recieved some days ago a very fine rock fish by the stage which, by a card of address accompanying it I percieved to have come from you. It was indeed a remarkeably fine one and I pray you to accept my thanks for it. a report has come here through some connection of one of my servants that James Hemings my former cook has committed an act of suicide. as this whether true or founded will give uneasiness to his friends, will you be so good as to ascertain the truth & communicate it to me. Accept my best wishes for your health & happiness. Th: Jefferson

William Evans to TJ

Sir/ — Baltimore Novr. 5th. 1801

I received your favour of the 1st Instant, and am sorry to inform you that the report respecting James Hennings Having commited an act of Suicide is true. I made every enquiry at the time this melancholy circumstance took place, the result of which was, that he had been delirious for Some days previous to his having commited the act, and it was the General opinion that drinking too freely was the cause, I am Sir

Your obedient Servant

William Evans

TJ to Thomas Mann Randolph

Dear Sir Washington Dec. 4. 1801.

A gentleman here has occasion for a particular purpose to consult the Preliminary discourse written by Dalembert to the antient encyclopedia, which was in fact a developement of Bacon's Arbor scientiae. it is in one of the volumes (the 1st. I believe) of the Melanges de literature in 5. vols. 12. mo. which you will find in the press on the right side of the cherry sash door in my cabinet. I must trouble you to get it from Monticello whenever convenient, & to send it on by post well wrapped in stout paper. I will pray you at the same time to send me Philidor on chess, which you will find in the book room, 2d. press on the left from the door of entrance: to be wrapped in strong paper also. I wrote on the 27th. to my dear Martha. I recieved about that time a letter from mr Eppes. their little one had borne the journey well, tho' it was still under the height of it's whooping cough. Maria's health had suffered sensibly. she had had a rising in her breast which broke the first day after applying the root she had before used. the letter was dated Nov. 21. from Eppington where they expected to remain a fortnight.

I send you a pamphlet giving an account of a water-proof cloth now used in England, which will probably be of value. I have a surtout coat of it, which I have had no opportunity of trying but by dipping it. I inclose you also a specimen of coarse paper, one half of which is water proof, the other not. you recieved the news of peace by the last post probably. in a letter by that post to mr Dinsmore I gave him an account of the tragical end of James Hemmings. I have been expecting mr Craven to Alexandria, who was to have brought a box of books for me. if he is not come & is still coming, that would be a better opportunity than the post for sending the two books above written for. hoping to hear on Tuesday how the children are this day, I conclude with my tender love to my dear Martha & affectionate esteem to yourself. Th: Jefferson

Plan for Work Life of Enslaved People

Labourers.

Build the Negro houses near together that the fewer nurses may serve
& that the children may be more easily attended to by the super-annuated women.
children till 10. years old to serve as nurses.
from 10. to 16. the boys make nails, the girls spin.
at 16. go into the ground or learn trades.
a barrel of flour yields 17. pecks of flour, & the labourers prefer 1. peck
of flour to 1½ peck of Indian meal.
a barrel of fish, costing 7.D. goes as far with the laborers as 200. lb of pork 14.D.
a side of upper leather & a side of soal make 6. pr shoes, & take ½ lb thread, so
that a hide & 1. lb of thread shoe 6. Negroes.

Worth of a pair of shoes. Upper leather 3/ soal leather 1½ lb 3/ thread 6 d. making 2/

1801 Negroes Leased to J. H. Craven

Bagwell. 68.
Minerva. 71.
Mary. 88.
Virginia. 93.
Esther. 95.
Bec. 97.
Ned. 60.
Jenny. 64.
Ned. 86.
[Fanny 88.

Dick 90.
Gill 92.
Scilla 94.
James 96.
Aggy. 98.
Isabel
Aggy 89.
Lilly 91.
Amy 93.
Thruston 95.
Eldridge 97.
James. 76
~~Patty~~ 81 d. Sep. 06
Beverly
Jenny 68.
Jesse 90.
Sally 92.
Jamy 95.
Evelina. 97.
Doll 57.
Thenia. 93.
Dolly 94
Rachael 76.
Nancy 91.
Abram 94.
Larana 97.
Squire 27.
~~Belinda.~~ 39. d. 08
Molly 49.
Mary 76.
Suckey 96.
Amy
d Betty
Caesar. 49.
~~Toby~~ 53. d. July 05.
~~Frank.~~ 57. d. Jul. 09.
~~June.~~ d. 1801

Negroes retained

~~Betty~~ Hemings. 35. d. 07.
Peter Hemings. 70
Betty Brown 59.
Edwin 93
Robert. 99. Dec.
Nance. 61.
Critta. 69.
Jamy 87. run away Apr. 04
Sally 73.
Beverly 98.
Ursula. 87.
Edy 87
Fanny 88
Burwell 83.
Moses 79.
Joe. 80.
Wormly 81.
Jame Hubbard 83.
Barnaby 83.
Isabel's Davy 84.
~~Brown~~ 85. sold 1806
Bedford John 85.
Bedford Davy 85.
Ben. 85.
Cary. 85. sold 1803.
Phill Hubbard 86.
Bartlet 86.
Lewis. 88.
John Hemings 75
Davy 55.
Lewis 60.
Abram. about 1740.
Jerry 77.
John 53.
Goliah 31.
~~Mingo~~ d. 1802.

~~Fanny.~~ 36. d. 1802
Phill wagg. 40.
~~Tom.~~ d. 1801.
~~Phill shoem.~~ d. July 2d 1809.
Shepherd. 82
Isaac 70.
Charles. 81.
~~Martin~~ d. 07.

Negroes in Bedford. July 1805

Jame Hubbard
Cate. abt. 1747.
Armistead. 71.
Nace. 73
Sarah. 88. Aug.
~~Naney~~ 91. Sep.d. abt. 05
Rachael. Oct. 73.
~~Burrel.~~ 94. d. 1808
Cate. 97. Aug.
Joe. 1801.
Lania. 1805
Maria. 76.
Nace 96. Aug.
Nisy. 99.
Johnny 1804. Sep.
Eve. 79.
Sanco. 97. Mar.
Will.smith
Abbey.
Jesse. 72. Nov.
Dick. 81. Oct.
Fanny. 88 Aug.
Edy. 92. Apr.
Armistead. 94. (Manuel)
Amy. 97. Jan
Sal. 77. Nov.
~~Isabel.~~ June 95 d 07

Milley. 97. Mar.
Betty 1801. Jan.
Abbey. 1804. Nov.
Flora. 83.
Gawen. 1804. July
Hanah. (Cate's) 70. Jan.
Lucinda. 91. June
Reuben. 93
Solomon. 94.
Sally 98.
Billy 99.
Jamey 1805. Aug.
Bess. (Guinea Will's)
Hal. (smith) 67. Sep.
Caesar. 74. Sep.
Suck (Bess's) 71. May
Cate 88. Mar.
Daniel 90. Sep.
Stephen. 94.
Philip. 96
Ambrose 99.
Prince. 1804.

~~Hercules.~~ abt. 1733. d. 180
Bet.
Austin. 75. Aug.
Gawen. 78. Aug.
Cate 88. Mar. 8.
Mary. 92. Jan.
Hercules. 94. Nov. 20.
~~Jupiter.~~ 1800. Mar. d. 1809.
Dick. 67.
Dinah. 66.
John 85. Nov.
Aggey. 89. Mar.
Moses. 92. Jan.
Evans. 94.

Hanah. 96. Aug.
Lucy 99.
Jamey. 1802.
Judy (old)
Nanny (Phill's) 78. July.
Maria. 98. Feb. 24.
Phill. 1801. Aug.
~~Polly.~~ 1804. July. d. 1807.
Lucy. (Phill's) 83. July
Robin. 1805.

List of Inoculations at Monticello, 1801 and 1802

List of Inoculations 1801

Inoculns

Aug.	7.	Burwell	
		Joe	
		<*Brown*>	
		<*Jamy*>	
		<*Critta*>	
		<*Thenia*> Melinda. Taken	
	13.	Brown	
		Jamy 21.	
		Taken	
		Critta. 21. q.	
		<*Thenia*> Thenia.	
		Lavinia. 21. Taken	
	16.	Nancy Jeff. From	Joe & Burw. 21. Taken
		Elen.	Joe & Bur. 21. Joe's inflamd.
		Cornelia.	Bur. Failed
		Priscilla.	Bur. 21. Taken
		Wormely	Bur. 21. Taken
		Edwin.	Bur. 21. Taken
		Philip Ev.	Bur. & Joe 21. Taken
		Thenia.	Joe & B. taken
		Ben	Joe & B.
		Cary	Joe & B.
		B. Davy	Joe & B. 21. Taken
		B. Phill	Joe & B. 21. Taken
		Bartlet	Joe. 21. Taken
		John.	Joe & B. 21. Taken
	21.	mr Chisolm	

		Lewis	
		mrs Carr	
	23.	Betsy	
		Sandy	
	30.	Lilly's family	
Sep.	1.	<*Jame Hub.*>	from Betsy.
		Barnaby	do.
		Bedfd. John	do.
		Shepherd.	Do.
		Moses.	Do.
	9	Esther	
		Bec	Bagwell's
		Jenny	
		Scilla	
		James	Ned's
		Aggy	
		Thruston	
		Eldridge	Isabel's
		Thrimston	
		Beverly.	Patty's
		Sally	
		Evelina.	Lewis's
		Isabel	
		Dolly.	Doll's
		Abram	Rachael's
		Lazaria	
		Suckey.	Jerry's
	17.	Jame Hubbard	
		Isab's Davy	
		Jamey. Lewis's	

List of Inoculations 1802

1802		Vaccinations with the thread.	
May.	10.	<*John Hemings.*> failed	
		John Perry	
		<*his apprentice.*> failed	
		<*Henrietta.*> failed	

19.	John	Hem.
	Perry	
	Henrietta.	
	Virginia Rand.	
	Critta's child	
26.	Ned's	Fanny
	Gill	
	Israel	
	Isabel's	Amy
	Lovilo	

Minerva's	Nanny
Jack	
Mary's Isaiah	
mr Drake.	
Sally's	**Beverly**
Harriet	
Betty Brown's Bob.	

TJ to Mary Jefferson Eppes

My Dear Maria Washington July 2. 1802.

My letter of yesterday had hardly got out of my hand, when yours of June 21st. and mr Eppes's of the 25th. were delivered. I learn with extreme concern the state of your health & that of the child, and am happy to hear you have got from the Hundred, to Eppington, the air of which will aid your convalescence, and will enable you to delay your journey to Monticello till you have recovered strength to make the journey safe. with respect to the measles they began in mr Randolph's family about the middle of June; and will probably be a month getting through the family; so that you had better, when you go, pass on direct to Monticello, not calling at Edgehill. I will immediately write to your sister, & inform her I have advised you to this. I have not heard yet of the disease having got to Monticello, but the intercourse with Edgehill being hourly, it cannot have failed to have gone there immediately; and as there are no young children there but Bet's & Sally's, and the disease is communicable before a person knows they have it, I have no doubt those children have past through it. the children of the plantation being a mile & a half off, can easily be guarded against. I will write to Monticello and direct that should the nail boys or any others have it, they be removed to the plantation instantly on your arrival. indeed none of them but Bet's sons stay on the mountain: and they will be doubtless through it. I think therefore you may be there in perfect security. It had gone through the neighborhood chiefly when I was there in May; so that it has probably disappeared. You should make enquiry on the road before you go into any house, as the disease is now universal through the state & all the states. present my most friendly attachments to mr & mrs Eppes. Tell the latter I have had her spectacles these 6. months waiting for a direct conveyance. my best affections to mr Eppes if with you & the family, and tender & constant love to yourself. Th: Jefferson

P.S. I have always forgotten to answer your apologies about Critta, which were very unnecessary. I am happy she has been with you & useful to you. at Monticello there could be nothing for her to do; so that he being with you is exactly as desireable to me as she can be useful to you.

TJ to Martha Jefferson Randolph

My dear Martha Washington July 2. 1802.

I yesterday I letters from mr Eppes & Maria. she has been for a considerable time very unwell, with low but constant fevers, and the child very unwell also. mrs Eppes had gone there and staid with her till she was well enough to be removed to Eppington, where the air & the bark had already produced a favorable effect. she wishes to proceed to Monticello as soon as she is strong enough, but is in dreadful apprehensions from the measles. not having heard from you she was uninformed whether it was in your family. I have this day informed her it is there, and advised her when she goes, to pass directly on to Monticello; and that I would ask the favor of mr Randolph & yourself to take measures for having the mountain clear of it by the 15th. of this month, by which time she may possibly arrive there, or by the 20th. at farthest. after that date should any one on the mountain have it they must remove. Squire's house would be a good place for the nail boys, should they have it, and Betty Hemings's for Bet's or Sally's children. there are no other children on the mountain. I shall be at home from the 25th. to the 28th. my affectionate esteem to mr Randolph and tenderest love to yourself.

Th: Jefferson

Memorandum for Henry Dearborn on Indian Policy

Hints on the subject of Indian boundaries, suggested for consideration

An object, becoming now of great importance, is the establishment of a strong front on our Western boundary, the Missisipi, securing us on that side, as our front on the Atlantic does towards the East. our proceedings with the Indians should tend systematically to that object, leaving the extinguishment of title in the interior country to fall in as occasions may arise. the Indians being once closed in between strong settled countries on the Missisipi & Atlantic, will, for want of game, be forced to agriculture, will find that small portions of land well improved, will be worth more to them than extensive forests unemployed, and will be continually parting with portions of them, for money to buy stock, utensils & necessaries for their farms & families.

On the Missisipi we hold at present from our Southern boundary to the Yazoo. from the Yazoo to the Ohio is the property of the Chickasaws, a tribe the most friendly to us, & at the same time the most adverse to the diminution of their lands. the portion of their territory of first importance to us, would be the slip between the Missisipi on the West, and on the East the Yazoo and the ridge dividing the waters of the Missisipi & Tenissee. their main settlements are Eastward of this. I believe they have few within this slip & towards the Missisipi. the methods by which we may advance towards our object will be 1. to press the encouragements to agriculture, by which they may see how little land will maintain them much better, and the advantage of exchanging useless deserts to improve their farms. 2. to establish among them a factory or factories for furnishing them with all the necessaries & comforts they may wish (spirituous liquors excepted) encouraging them, & especially their leading men, to run in debt for these beyond their individual means of paying; & whenever in that situation they will always cede lands to rid themselves of debt. a factory about the Chickasaw bluffs, would be tolerably central, and they might admit us to tend corn for feeding the factory & themselves when at it, and even to fix some persons there for the protection of the factory from the

Indians West of the Missisipi & others. after a while we might purchase there, and add to it from time to time. 3. we should continue to nourish and increase their friendship & confidence, by every act of justice and of favor which we can possibly render them. what we do in favor of the other Indians, should not constitute the measure of what we do for these, our views as to these being so much more important. this tribe is very poor; they want necessaries with which we abound; we want lands with which they abound; & these mutual wants seem to offer fair ground of mutual supply.

The country between the Missisipi & Illinois on one side, & the Ohio & Wabash on the other, is also peculiarly desirable to us, and is in a situation at this moment which renders it particularly easy for us to acquire a considerable portion of it. it has belonged to the Kaskaskias, Cahokias and Piorias. the Cahokias (of whom the Michigamis were a part) have been extirpated by the Sacs, the Piorias driven off, & the Kaskaskias reduced to a few families. Governor Harrison, in his letter of Nov. 28. 1802. says the Pioria chief has offered the right of his nation to these lands for a trifle. we should not fail to purchase it immediately. the Cahokias being extirpated, we have a right to their land, in preference to any Indian tribe, in virtue of our paramount sovereignty over it. he also says that De Coigne, the Kaskaskia chief would make easy terms with us. I think we should be liberal in our offers to the Kaskaskians. They are now but a few families, exposed to numerous enemies, & unable to defend themselves, and would cede lands in exchange for protection. We might agree to their laying off 100. acres of the best soil for every person young & old of their tribe, we might inclose it well for them, in one general inclosure, give to every family utensils, & stock sufficient for their portion of it, & give them an annuity in necessaries, on their ceding to us their whole country, or retaining for themselves only a moderate range around their farms for their stock to range in; & we might undertake to protect them from their enemies. having thus established ourselves in the rights of the Kaskaskias, Cahokias & Piorias, we should have to settle the boundaries between them, & the Kickapoos, Poutawatamies and Weaws. we should first gain the good will of these tribes by friendly acts, & of their chiefs by largesses, and then propose to run the line between us, to claim whatever can be said to be doubtful, offering them a liberal price for their pretensions, and even endeavoring to obtain from them a cession of so much of their acknoleged territory as they can be induced to part with.

As to the country on the Missisipi above the mouth of the Illinois, it's acquisition is not pressing in the present state of things. it might be well to be enquiring into titles, and to claim whatever may have been abandoned or lost by it's native owners, so as to prevent usurpation by tribes having no right: as also to purchase such portions as may be found in the occupation of small remnants of tribes nearly extinct & disposed to emigrate.

For the present it is submitted to the consideration of the Secretary at war, whether instructions should not be immediately given to Governor Harrison to treat with the Pioria & Kaskaskia chiefs. as to the latter, which is most important, it would be easy to sollicit & bring over by presents every individual of mature age.

Th: Jefferson
Dec. 29. 1802.

TJ to William Henry Harrison

Dear Sir — Washington Feb. 27. 1803.

While at Monticello in August last I recieved your favor of Aug. 6. and meant to have acknoleged it on my return to the seat of government at the close of the ensuing month. but on my return I found that you were expected to be on here in person, & this expectation continued till winter. I have since recieved your favor of Dec. 30.

In the former you mentioned the plan of the town which you had done me the honour to name after me, and to lay out according to an idea I had formerly expressed to you. I am thoroughly persuaded that it will be found handsome, & pleasant, and I do believe it to be the best means of preserving the cities of America from the scourge of the yellow fever which being peculiar to our country must be derived from some peculiarity in it. that peculiarity I take to be our cloudless skies. in Europe, where the sun does not shine more than half the number of days in the year which it does in America, they can build their towns in a solid block with impunity. but here a constant sun produces too great an accumulation of heat to admit that. ventilation is indispensably necessary. experience has taught us that in the open air of the country the yellow fever is not only not generated, but ceases to be infectious. I cannot decide from the drawing you sent me, whether you have laid off streets round the squares thus or only the diagonal street therein marked. the former was my idea, and is, I imagine, most convenient.

You will recieve herewith an answer to your letter as President of the Convention: and from the Secretary at War you recieve from time to time information & instructions as to our Indian affairs. these communications being for the public records are restrained always to particular objects & occasions. but this letter being unofficial, & private, I may with safety give you a more extensive view of our policy respecting the Indians, that you may the better comprehend the parts dealt out to you in detail through the official channel, and observing the system of which they make a part, conduct yourself in unison with it in cases where you are obliged to act without instruction. our system is to live in perpetual peace with the Indians, to cultivate an affectionate attachment from them, by every thing just & liberal which we can do for them within the bounds of reason, and by giving them effectual protection against wrongs from our own people. the decrease of game rendering their subsistence by hunting insufficient, we wish to draw them to agriculture, to spinning & weaving. the latter branches they take up with great readiness, because they fall to the women, who gain by quitting the labours of the field for those which are exercised within doors. when they withdraw themselves to the culture of a small piece of land, they will perceive how useless to them are their extensive forests, and will be willing to pare them off from time to time in exchange for necessaries for their farms & families. to promote this disposition to exchange lands which they have to spare & we want, for necessaries, which we have to spare & they want, we shall push our trading houses, and be glad to see the good & influential individuals among them run in debt, because we observe that when these debts get beyond what the individuals can pay, they become willing to lop th[em off] by a cession of lands. at our trading houses too we mean to sell so low as merely to repay us cost and charges so as neither to lessen or enlarge our capital. this is what private traders cannot do, for they must gain; they will consequently retire from the competition, & we shall thus get clear of this pest without giving offence or umbrage to the Indians. in this way our settlements will gradually circumbscribe & approach the Indians, & they will in time either incorporate with us as citizens of the US. or remove beyond the Missisipi. the former is certainly the termination of their history most happy for themselves. but in the whole course of this, it is essential to cultivate their love. as to their fear, we presume that our strength & their weakness is now so visible that they must see we have only to shut our hand to crush them, & that all our liberalities to them proceed from motives of pure humanity only. should any tribe be fool-hardy enough to take up the hatchet at any time, the seizing the whole country of that tribe & driving them across the Missisipi, as the only condition of peace, would be an example to others, and a furtherance of our final consolidation.

Combined with these views, & to be prepared against the occupation of Louisiana by a powerful & enterprising people, it is important that setting less value on interior extension of purchases from the Indians, we bend our whole views to the purchase and settlement of the country on the Missisipi from it's mouth to it's Northern regions, that we may be able to present as strong a front on our Western as on our Eastern border, and plant on the Missisipi itself the means of it's own defence. we now own from 31.° to the Yazoo, & hope this summer to purchase what belongs to the Choctaws from the Yazoo up to their boundary, supposed to be about opposite the mouth of Acanza. we wish at the same time to begin in your quarter, for which there is at present a favorable opening. the Cahokias being extinct, we are entitled to their country by our paramount sovereignty. the Piorias we understand have all been driven off from their country, & we might claim it in the same way; but as we understand there is one chief remaining, who would, as the survivor of the tribe, sell the right, it will be better to give him such terms as will make him easy for life, and take a conveyance from him. the Kaskaskias being reduced to a few families, I presume we may purchase their whole country for what would place every individual of them at his ease, & be a small price to us. say by laying off for each family wherever they would chuse it as much rich land as they could cultivate, adjacent to each other, inclosing the whole in a single fence, and giving them such an annuity in money or goods for ever as would place them in happiness. and we might take them also under the protection of the US. thus possessed of the rights of these three tribes, we should proceed to the settling their boundaries with the Poutewatamies & Kickapoos; claiming all doubtful territory, but paying them a price for the relinquishment of their concurrent claim, and even prevailing on them if possible to cede for a price such of their own unquestioned territory as would give us a convenient Northern boundary. before broaching this, and while we are bargaining with the Kaskaskias, the minds of the Poutewatamies & Kickapoos should be soothed & consiliated by liberalities and sincere assurances of friendship. Perhaps by sending a well qualified character to stay some time in Decoigne's village as if on other business, and to sound him & introduce the subject by degrees to his mind & that of the other heads of families, inculcating in the way of conversation all those considerations which prove the advantages they would recieve by a cession on these terms, the object might be more easily & effectually obtained than by abruptly proposing it to them at a formal treaty. of the means however of obtaining what we wish you will be the best judge; and I have given you this view of the system which we suppose will best promote the interests of the Indians & of ourselves, & finally consolidate our whole country into one nation only, that you may be enabled the better to adapt your means to the object. for this purpose we have given you a general commission for treating. the crisis is pressing. whatever can now be obtained must be obtained quickly. the occupation of New Orleans, hourly expected, by the French, is already felt like a light breeze by the Indians. you know the sentiments they entertain of that nation. under the hopes of their protection, they will immediately stiffen against cessions of land to us. we had better therefore do at once what can now be done.

I must repeat that this letter is to be considered as private & friendly, & is not to controul any particular instructions which you may recieve through the official channel. you will also percieve how sacredly it must be kept within [your] own breast, and especially how improper to be understood by the Indians. [for] their interests & their tranquility it is best they should see only the present age of their history. I pray you to accept assurances of my esteem & high consideration. Th: Jefferson

Thomas Mann Randolph to TJ

Dear Sir Edgehill May 30. 1803

Your favor of the 5th. instant arrived regularly, and I made the communications from it intended for Monticello, without delay. An accident happened in the nailery at Lillies on Friday last which presented a shocking prospect at first but promises now an issue very different from the dismal end at first expected. The boy Cary, irritated at some little trick from Brown, who hid part of his nail rod to teaze him, but restored it as soon as he found him angry, took a most barbarous revenge; approaching him by stealth he struck him with his whole strength upon the skull, very near the longitudinal suture, on the left side, midway between the horizontal & perpendicular faces of the skull bone, when the body is erect. The skull yielded to the face of the hammer in its whole circumference but was driven in only about ⅔ of it, bending the other part & fracturing no where else. The instantaneous suspension of life did not continue longer than a minute: for an hour no damage was suspected but at the end of that time violent convulsions took place which were quickly succeeded by Coma & its usual symptoms, the leaden eye and apoplectic stupor: the patient was sensible of what was done to him and answered reasonably yet to my astonishment when the pressure was removed had no recollection at all of any circumstance from the blow to that moment. Wardlaw & myself arriving nearly at the same time I acted as his assistant in the operation which he performed by means of the trephine (the saw which works both ways or with the motion of the wrist only) with the greatest boldness, steadiness and skill. The boy is as well as we could have expected today, and will, no doubt I think, in a month, be as well as ever. The other, I committed to jail till Browns fate is determined.

TJ to Thomas Mann Randolph

Dear Sir Washington June 8. 1803.

Your's of May 30. has been recieved. should Brown recover so that the law shall inflict no punishment on Cary, it will be necessary for me to make an example of him in terrorem to others, in order to maintain the police so rigorously necessary among the nailboys. there are generally negro purchasers from Georgia passing about the state, to one of whom I would rather he should be sold than to any other person. if none such offers, if he could be sold in any other quarter so distant as never more to be heard of among us, it would to the others be as if he were put out of the way by death. I should regard price but little in comparison with so distant an exile of him as to cut him off compleatly from ever again being heard of. I have written this to mr Lilly and will thank you to advise & aid him in procuring a sale. in the mean time let him remain in jail at my expence, & under orders not to permit him to see or speak to any person whatever.

Instructions for Meriwether Lewis

To Meriwether Lewis esquire, Captain of the 1st Regiment of infantry of the United States of America.

Your situation as Secretary of the President of the United States has made you acquainted with the objects of my confidential message of Jan. 18. 1803. to the legislature: you have seen the act they passed, which, tho' expressed in general terms, was meant to sanction those objects, and you are appointed to carry them into execution . . .

The object of your mission is to explore the Missouri river, & such principal stream of it, as, by it's course & communication with the waters of the Pacific ocean, may offer the most direct & practicable water communication across this continent, for the purposes of commerce.

Beginning at the mouth of the Missouri, you will take observations of latitude & longitude, at all remarkeable points on the river, & especially at the mouths of rivers, at rapids, at islands & other places & objects distinguished by such natural marks & characters of a durable kind, as that they may with certainty be recognised hereafter. the courses of the river between these points of observation may be supplied by the compass, the log-line & by time, corrected by the observations themselves. the variations of the compass too, in different places, should be noticed.

The interesting points of the portage between the heads of the Missouri & the water offering the best communication with the Pacific ocean, should also be fixed by observation, & the course of that water to the ocean, in the same manner as that of the Missouri.

Your observations are to be taken with great pains & accuracy, to be entered distinctly, & intelligibly for others as well as yourself, to comprehend all the elements necessary, with the aid of the usual tables, to fix the latitude and longitude of the places at which they were taken, & are to be rendered to the war office, for the purpose of having the calculations made concurrently by proper persons within the US. several copies of these, as well as of your other notes, should be made at leisure times, & put into the care of the most trustworthy of your attendants, to guard, by multiplying them, against the accidental losses to which they will be exposed. a further guard would be that one of these copies be written on the paper of the birch, as less liable to injury from damp than common paper.

The commerce which may be carried on with the people inhabiting the line you will pursue, renders a knolege of those people important. you will therefore endeavor to make yourself acquainted, as far as a diligent pursuit of your journey shall admit,

with the names of the nations & their numbers;

the extent & limits of their possessions;

their relations with other tribes or nations;

their language, traditions, monuments;

their ordinary occupations in agriculture, fishing, hunting, war, arts, & the implements for these;

their food, clothing, & domestic accomodations;

the diseases prevalent among them, & the remedies they use;

moral & physical circumstances which distinguish them from the tribes we know;

peculiarities in their laws, customs & dispositions;

and articles of commerce they may need, or furnish, & to what extent.

And, considering the interest which every nation has in extending & strengthening the authority of reason & justice among the people around them, it will be useful to acquire what knolege you can of the state of morality, religion & information among them; as it may better enable those who endeavor to civilize & instruct them, to adapt their measures to the existing notions & practices of those on whom they are to operate. . . .

In all your intercourse with the natives treat them in the most friendly & conciliatory manner which their own conduct will admit; allay all jealousies as to the object of your journey, satisfy them of it's innocence, make them acquainted with the position, extent, character, peaceable & commercial dispositions of the US. of our wish to be neighborly, friendly & useful to them, & of our dispositions to a commercial intercourse with them; confer with them on the points most convenient as mutual emporiums, & the articles of most desireable interchange for them & us. if a few of their influential chiefs, within practicable distance, wish to visit us, arrange such a visit with them, & furnish them with authority to call on our officers, on their entering the US. to have them conveyed to this place at the public expence. if any of them should wish to have some of their young people brought up with us, & taught such arts as may be useful to them, we will recieve, instruct & take care of them. such a mission, whether of influential chiefs, or of young people, would give some security to your own party. carry with you some matter of the kine-pox; inform those of them with whom you may be, of it's efficacy as a preservative from the small pox; and instruct & encourage them in the use of it. this may be especially done wherever you winter.

As it is impossible for us to foresee in what manner you will be recieved by those people, whether with hospitality or hostility, so is it impossible to prescribe the exact degree of perseverance with which you are to pursue your journey. we value too much the lives of citizens to offer them to probable destruction. your numbers will be sufficient to secure you against the unauthorised opposition of individuals, or of small parties: but if a superior force, authorised or not authorised, by a nation, should be arrayed against your further passage, & inflexibly determined to arrest it, you must decline it's further pursuit, and return. in the loss of yourselves, we should lose also the information you will have acquired. by returning safely with that, you may enable us to renew the essay with better calculated means. to your own discretion therefore must be left the degree of danger you may risk, & the point at which you should decline, only saying we wish you to err on the side of your safety, & to bring back your party safe, even if it be with less information.

As far up the Missouri as the white settlements extend, an intercourse will probably be found to exist between them and the Spanish posts at St. Louis, opposite Cahokia, or St. Genevieve opposite Kaskaskia. from still further up the river, the traders may furnish a conveyance for letters. beyond that you may perhaps be able to engage Indians to bring letters for the government to Cahokia or Kaskaskia, on promising that they shall there recieve such special compensation as you shall have stipulated with them. avail yourself of these means to communicate to us, at seasonable intervals, a copy of your journal, notes & observations of every kind, putting into cypher whatever might do injury if betrayed. . . .

Given under my hand at the city of Washington this 20th. day of June 1803

Th: Jefferson
Pr. US. of America

Thomas Harris of Connecticut to TJ

Sterling Connecticut, March 26th. 1804.

May it Please your Excellency: Encouraged by the consideration of the benevolence and philanthropy of your character, which induces you to consider as children of one common parent, all the human race; and that amazing greatness of mind by which you are enabled, and induced to look down with contempt on the distinctions of colour, birth and wealth, among men: I, Thomas Harris, a free black man, of Sterling in the State of Connecticut, have presumed thus to address your Excellency.

I was for many years a slave, fought for American freedom, and by that mean obtained my own; married a woman of my own colour, and had had by her five children, (a family as large as by my labour I thought I could maintain), when in the 53d. year of my age and on the third of March instant, my wife presented me with a pair of *twin boys*. A pair of *black twin boys*, are Sir, I belive no common sight, such a pair however claim protection and support from me, which I fear I shall not be able to afford them. But Sir, as a testimony of my gratitude, for those principles of Justice and humanity by you so boldly advanced and ably advocated; and of the very great respect in which I hold the Father of his Country, the friend of freedom and equal rights, the benefactor of mankind, and of people of colour in particular; I have named one of my twins *Thomas*, and the other *Jefferson*. Deign Sir to accept this humble tribute of respect, trifling indeed, but the greatest in my power to offer. The consideration that my boys, (should I be able to support them in existance) are under your Excellency's government, a government which at once secures to all, whithe rich or poor, white or black, thier equal rights and priviliges, is comforting and encouraging. I cannot find words to express the pleasure I feel, that under your Excellency's government and the prevalence of your principles, my boys are safe from slavery, if not from cold and hunger. It shall be my study to instill into the minds of my children, that veneration for your Excellency's person; character; and government; which the most disinterested exertions for the good and happiness of the distressed and enslaved of all mankind, demand.

For the many benefits our race in particular have received from your Excellency, I as an individual of them, have only my gratitude to offer and when so fair an opportunity presented of expressing it, I thought it a duty so to do. But the reward of conceous virtue is your Excellency's and the only one you seek.

Be pleased to pardon this trespass on your Excellency's patience, by the Humblest of all your Humble Servants, whose earnest wish and prayer is, that your Excellency may long live the defender of freedom and sheild of the oppressed.

Thomas harris

John Freeman to TJ

Sir [18 Apr. 1804]

I am sorye to trubel you with a thing of this kind tho tho I am forced to do it: for I have been foolish anofe to in gage myself to melindors and I was in hops of when i came to Virginia this time to get hir Misstress consent with yours I have got the Consent of hir parence Tho I fear the deth of hir mistress: will make us meresibel unless you will be so good as to keep us botch: as to what I spoke to you about some time ago I am verye willing to doe anye thing in reasion I am willing to bound myself by my word to serve you faithful: I have undoutlye been treated with a great deal of hospilitie in your familye and you yourself more pertickeler infenaitlye more then i have any reason to expect

i am Your humbel Servant
John F

Contract for Purchase of John Freeman

William Baker
to
Thomas Jefferson

Recorded March 8th. 1809 at the request of Negro John

In pursuance of the annexed power of attorney Know all men by these presents that I Philip Thomas Baker of the district of Columbia and County of Washington for and in consideration of the sum of four hundred dollars, money of the United States to me in hand paid by Thomas Jefferson at or before the sealing and delivery of these presents the receipt whereof I do hereby acknowledge, have granted bargained and sold, and by these presents do grant bargain and sell unto the said Thomas Jefferson his executors Administrators and assigns a negroe man by the name of John, at this time in the service of the aforesaid Thomas Jefferson, and is the person alluded to in the subjoined power of attorney, To have and to hold the said negroe John, to the aforesaid Thomas Jefferson, his executors administrators & assigns for and during the term of eleven years from the date hereof and no longer, at the end and expiration of the aforesaid Term of eleven years—I Philip Thomas Baker in pursuance of the authority vested in me by the annexed power of attorney by these presents do liberate manumit and set free, the aforesaid negroe John, to be effected according to the true intent and meaning of the power of attorney hereunto subjoined, and not otherwise, that is to say—The meaning of these presents are that the aforesaid Negroe John shall belong to, and be the property of the aforesaid Thomas Jefferson his executors administrators and assigns, for and during the term of eleven years, and that after the expiration of the aforesaid term of eleven years, the said negro John shall cease to be the property of the said Thomas Jefferson, and of all other persons, and shall be free and that the said Thomas Jefferson purchases, the said negroe John upon this condition, and upon no other and the said Philip Thomas Baker as attorney for William Baker, for myself my heirs, executors administrators and assigns, the said negroe man John to the aforesaid Thomas Jefferson, his executors administrators and assigns against every person or persons whatsoever, will warrant & forever defend by these presents—In witness whereof I have hereunto set hand, and affixed my seal, this twenty third day of July in the year of our lord, one thousand eight hundred & four

P T Baker seal

Witness John Oakley

District of Columbia County of Washington sct. Be it remembered that, on this twenty third day of July, in the year Eighteen hundred and four, before me, the subscriber a justice of the peace aforesaid personally appears P T Baker named in the annexed power of attorney, and acknowledges the aforegoing instrument of writing to be his act and deed and that the negroe therein mentioned is the right title and property, of the aforesaid Thomas Jefferson during the term of eleven years, according to the true intent & meaning thereof & of the power of attorney thereto, annexed acknowledged before,— John Oakley

To all whom these presents shall come, Know ye, that I have empowered and by these presents constitute ordain & appoint my son Philip Thomas Baker, my lawful attorney in fact to sell convey and lawfully make over to any person my negroe man John, now in the service of the president of the United States, for and during the term of eleven years, from the day he shall be sold and no longer, and my said attorney is authorised and required, to enter into such covenant with the purchaser, as shall secure the said negroe John his emancipation, at the expiration of eleven years aforementioned, and my said attorney is hereby empowered, to do all things in the premises that I might or could do was I personally present. Given under my hand this 10th. day of July 1804.

Wm Baker
Witness Mary Hoxon
True Copy from the original
Wm A Burwell

This is to certify and declare, that this paper contains, true copies of two deeds, the Originals of which are in my possession which deeds are hereby assented to ratified and confirmed, and the said negro man John therein named, is hereby declared to be entitled to his freedom, on the 22nd day of July, which shall be in the year, one thousand eight hundred & fifteen given under my hand, this 6th day of October 1804 Th: Jefferson

Witness William A Burwell

James Oldham to TJ

Sir— Richmond november 26th. 1804.

. . . Ingraiv'd on my mind, Sir, and must there remain until I am no more, the moast savage treatment which I receiv'd from Gabrail Lilley and John perry a few days before I left Albermarl and for no caws whatever as I solemly decleare to heaven, but Lilley says he acted from an athority given to him by your Honourable self, and in Substance it is no less than to consider me as one of the moast vilest reches on earth, Lilley says his orders reciv'd from you was to inform me that it was your wish that I shoul,d not put my foot on monticello or eaven on your Land and swore that he woul,d blow me thro if I a tempted to pass, Seconded by his purgerd brother-in Law John perry, who swore that he woul,d shoot the men that ware in the cart if they attempted to pass, mr. craven had Lent me his cart for the purpose of removeing my Tools to milton and I proceeded along the plain road apprehending no danger when those men stop,d me and exercisd there othority as they say? a few days previous to this I had ast the favour of Lilley to Let his cart or waggon to remove my Tools, when he answer,d me that he woul,d ce me and the Tools all in Hell first, upon this I turnd of from him: Upon the honour of a man Mr. Jefferson had I of thot or coul,d I yet think that my going on any part of your possessions woul,d of given you any offence moast certainly Sir, woul,d never of done it, but thro choice woul,d of Left every rag of clothes and every tool that I posses,d; These men, Sir, for a considerable time past have united themselves and straind every nerve to Injour me but little indeed did I regard it, Had I, Sir of gon into your cellars with these men and others and there of got Beastly drunk, I shoul,d of bin in there sight a clever fellow besi'd geting a few bottles of wine; Had I of Sind my naim to perry,s bill of Lumber and also to his account of the days workes which he charg,d you with it woul,d Still of been all well, but in preference to acting dishonestly I Strove to do Justice to these men as also to your Honourable self. can it be possable, Sir, that you have never hurn of Lilley,s going into the cellar and getting drunk and to be oblig,d to be carried home. it is a well nown fact that Lilly fell out with me within Six weeks after I first went to monticello, becaus I woul,d not assist him to punnish Luis, nor have any thing to do with him, This mr. Randolph nows well; Luis went of from me Twice but it is well nown that I never punnishd him, and have a many a time wish,d that I had of never of seen him; I much question if mr Lilley ever acquainted you how-much flower and poark he fornishd his friends with the first year that he had the supplying of us and her did he supply the Last year with corn.

The Barbarity that he maid use of with Little Jimmy was the moast cruel, to my noledge Jimmy was sick for thre nights and the moast part of the time I raly thot he woul,d not of Liv,d he at this time slep,d in the room with me, I inform,d Lilly the boy was not able to worke and Beg,d him not to punnish him, but this had no affect he whip,d him three times in one day, and the boy was raly not able to raise his hand to his Head?

it has been a constant song with Lilly and perry and by them aserted that I was dischargd on there account and owl,d Stuart,s, be it as it may it is out of my power to prevent it and the all wise provedence knows my persecutions have been grait, but never the Less I pray for my persecutors to be forgiven and fill happy in a seperation, and with a clear contience can say that was alway rady and willing to serve you. A Due and may

Heaven Bless You With
Respect Your Obt Servt.
James Oldham.

TJ to Henry Dearborn

Th: Jefferson to Genl. Dearborne. Dec. 16. 04.

The letter of the Little Turtle to Genl. Wilkinson is so serious, that I suppose it should be answered. among other things I imagine it will be proper to have said to him that tho' the US. will always protect the Indians in the right to their lands so long as they chuse to keep them, yet they have also always professed themselves ready to buy whenever the Indians chuse to sell. that it will certainly be convenient for us to own a given breadth of country on the right bank of Ohio and on the Wabash, that our citizens descending those rivers may find accomodation & safety through their whole length. that the Delawares being in possession of the country in the fork of the rivers, & desirous to sell, we bought: but the Piankeshaws also claiming the same lands & willing to sell their right, we purchased their right also. that we have never heard that any other tribe has any right in them, nor do we believe they have: but that if a right can be proved in any other, & that we have bought from those who had no right, we will do justice to those having the right, & demand justice from those who have sold us what was not theirs. if on the other hand the right to these lands was in the Delawares & Piankeshaws we shall permit no other tribe to intermeddle with their right to sell and ours to buy. every tribe shall be master of their own lands, to keep or to sell them as they please without controul from any other.

I do not know on what grounds the Little Turtle interferes, unless the Miamis have any claim to that country, which I believe they have not. I presume Harrison's success in extinguishing Indian title is at the bottom of the Turtle's dislike of him. the late purchase from the Sacs & Reynards is important as it fortifies our right to keep the British off from the Missisipi. I should suspect Brough to be of a discontented temper, which discolours to his mind whatever is done by others. Affectionate salutns

Th: Jefferson

TJ to William A. Burwell

Dear Sir Washington Jan. 28. 05.

Your letter of the 18th. has been duly recieved and mr Coles consents to remain here till the 4th. of March, when I shall leave this place for Monticello and pass a month there. consequently if you can join me here the second week in April it will be as early as your absence could affect my convenience. I have long since given up the expectation of any early provision for the extinguishment of slavery among us. there are many virtuous men who would make any sacrifices to effect it. many equally virtuous who persuade themselves either that the thing is not wrong, or that it cannot be remedied. and very many with whom interest is morality. the older we grow, the larger we are disposed to believe the last party to be. but interest is really going over to the side of morality. the value of the slave is every day lessening; his burthen on his master dayly increasing. interest is therefore preparing the disposition to be just; and this will be goaded from time to time by the insurrectionary spirit of the slaves. this is easily quelled in it's first efforts; but from being local it will become general, and whenever it does it will rise more formidable after every defeat, until we shall be forced, after dreadful scenes & sufferings to release them in their own way which, without such sufferings we might now model after our own convenience. Accept my affectionate salutations.

Th: Jefferson

James Oldham to TJ

Sir Richmond July 16th. July 05.

Your favor of the 10th. was duly receivd. I did not now at the Time of riteing you the last letter that Cpt. Andrews still remaind in New Yorke: have since heard from him. also receivd some ornaments: the Turning you have pleased to order am very thankful for it is very difficult to get such Little Triffles done in Richmond.

Mr. John Payton came a cross Jimmy as he was passing roud the Bason. he consulted me wheather it would be best to plaice him in confinement. I considerd it would be best not to do it: as he was willing to stay with me until he could heare from you: he is desirous you should now his wish is to Serve you provided he is not plaisd under the direction of Lilley as he says the seveare treatment which he experiencd was the onley cause of his going of. from what he tels me I finde he has bin a Taylor for 4 or 5 months the last fall, from this to norfolke. & since has bin Liveing at bent Creek, with a Mr. Jams. Right. It seams he has bin in the habet of running the river in a boat this spring with Jams. Garven & Jams. Griffin boath of Linchburge.

With Respct. Your moas
Humb Servt
James Oldham

P.S. Mr. Payton will give you further information.

TJ to James Oldham

Dear Sir Monticello July 20. 05.

I am informed that James Hemings my servant has put himself under your superintendance until he can hear from me on the subject of his return. I can readily excuse the follies of a boy and therefore his return shall ensure him an entire pardon. during my absence hereafter I should place him with Johnny Hemings and Lewis at house-joiner's work. if you will get him a passage in the Richmond stage I will get mr Higginbotham to pay his fare on his arrival at Milton. accept my best wishes

Th: Jefferson

TJ to Daniel Bradley

Sir Washington Oct. 6. 05.

I was yesterday informed that you had in custody in the Jail of Fairfax a negro man of mine who run away from my estate in Albemarle about 3 or 4 weeks ago. he is about 20-years of age, very stout, is a nailer by trade & called Jame Hubbard. my informant says he confessed at once the truth of his case, that he had three passes which he said had been given him by the son of mr Lilly my manager. mr George Swink who gives me this information, & goes about the middle of this month on a visit to Albemarle, agrees to take this man with him to whom therefore I will ask the favor of you to deliver him when called for, & in the mean time to keep him in jail. your bill for fees, whenever you shall be so good as to send it to me by post, shall be remitted through the same channel. it would be important for me to recieve the passes immediately because mr Lilly sets out on Thursday for Kentucky, & if he can get the passes into his hands before he goes I am sure he will probe the forgery to the bottom. it is chiefly to obtain them by return of the bearer that I send him express, and shall thank you to send them as our post goes off tomorrow. Accept my salutations.

Th: Jefferson

TJ to Joseph Dougherty

Th: Jefferson to mr. Dougherty Monticello. July 31. 06.

In the first place say not a word on the subject of this letter but to mr Perry, the person who delivers it to you. he comes in pursuit of a young mulatto man, called Joe, 26. years of age, who ran away from here the night of the 29th. inst. without the least word of difference with any body, & indeed having never in his life recieved a blow from any one. he has been about 12. years working at the blacksmith's trade. we know he has taken the road towards Washington, & probably will be there before the bearer. he may possibly trump up some story to be taken care of at the President's house till he can make up his mind which way to go; or perhaps he may make himself know to Edy only, as he was formerly connected with her. I must beg of you to use all possible diligence in searching for him in Washington & George town, and if you can find him, have aid with you to take him as he is strong & resolute; & have him delivered to mr Perry. as the latter is a stranger, & would not know how to seek for him, I have advised him to take quarters where you can see him often, but to keep within doors himself, lest he should be seen by the runaway. relying on your exertions on this occasion I tender you my best wishes. Th: Jefferson

Pseudonym: "A Slave" to TJ

Sir, 30th Nov. 1808.

In looking over Mr. Duane's politicks for Farmers and Mecanicks, I was not a little surprised to hear him bosting of his happy country, & the pacifick measures of this government, and decrying all others as barbarous and oppressive. I wrote to him in Sept. last and requested his friendship, & desir'd him to lay before you our exquisit torment, and the inhuman conduct of our masters; but I have not as yet hear'd, any thing from him.

Our burdens are heavy & call loud for justice! call loud for mercy! I Therefore, take the liberty Sir, to address you myself upon the subject of slaviry, and ask you a few questions respecting Mr. Duane's politicks. What does he mean by this? Young as our country is, in the political world, says he, it has furnish'd a world of useful experience; and that we are, thank Providence, the only nation that has yet profited by our education. If to spit in the face, cudgel in the streets, fight dewils, quarrel in the law, make laws & violate them, oppress & enslave mankind, take away all the honest labours & genius of one part of the community to riot upon, and to aggrandize the rest, gamble, drink to excess, wallow in debauchery, violate the chastity of women, betray publick trust, waist the funds, deceive the people, bely other nations, enslave their citizens, & your own, aggrandize one part of the citizens at the expence of the others, nurse, educate, & exercise children in tyranny and oppression, support a knot of idle hypocritical priest & rapacious lawyers, to loung & strut about the country, divide the people into supersticious hostile sectaries; then setting these poor ignorant people to quarrel in the law one with the other, that they may fall an easy prey to their rapacity; and may more vices of a like heighnous nature; can be said to be a world of useful experience, & a profitable eduction, America can vie with any nation on earth

Yet, with all these vices stareing him bold in the face, he has the vanity to say, that we are, thank Providence, the only nation that has yet improved by our education; & the impiety to call out to God to save his country from the afflictions of war; but above all from the example of England.—

What is this mighty uproar about England? Was there ever any thing in her example, more inhuman, ireligious, or damning, than slavery? Is any nation capable of commiting a more heighnous crime in the sight of God, or more insulting to fellow-man?

What said Mr. Wilkinson respecting slavery in '95? why, believing, said he, that a faithful history of slavery with all its consequences, would be of all others, the darkest pages in the annals of manking. What said you sir, in '81? see notes on Virginia. Well then, if as Wm. asserts, Britain has got three thousand Amerian citizens in slavery on board her ships of war: Has not America, likewise, got in slavery 2,000000 of the former citizens of Africa? If 1,000000 of the subjects of Britain are starving in her work-houses; are not 2,000000 of the citizens of America, running almost naked, starved and abused in a most inhuman and bruital manner, in her fields & kitchens. If Britain takes away one fifth of the labour of her subjects for taxes: Does not the tyrants of America take away the whole of the labour of 2,000000 of the most industerious citizens to riot upon?

I cannot give you a fairer picture of our unfortunate condition sir, then in the words of Esqr. Pigott. Among men, says he, you see the ninty and nine toyling to git a heep of superfluities for One; gitting nothing for themselves all this while, but a little of the coursests of the provisions which their own labour produces; and this One too, oftentimes is the worst of the whole set; a child, a woman, a madman or a fool; looking quiettly on while they see the fruits of all their labours spent on spoiled; and if one of them take a single particle of it, the others join against, and hang him for the theft. What say you sir, to this? can you plead ignorance in these vices and follies; and in this inhuman slavery? If not, what can be your reasons (since you have been rais'd to the highest office in the government) for suffering us to be used in this bruital manner? Can any man who is not over-aw'd by a tyrant, sway'd by prejudice, in love with slavery & oppression, or who lives him self in idleness, drunkenness & debauchery, say, that there is either, honour, honesty, humanity, piety, charity, virtue, or religion in such conduct? O! merciful God, is this humanity? is this concistant with thy holy law, and agreeable to thy divine will? "But hold my impious toungue, its only Christian Charity." Its quite good enough for Negroes, who the sainted pilgrims say, are only a black beast of the Manilla class, with a flat nose, thick lips, woolly head, ivory teeth; and with a face somewhat resembling the human, but clearly not a human being. To prove our human-nature, sir, and our rights as citizens of these states, we have only to appeal to the Declaration of Independence, which says, We hold these truths self-evident; that all men, (not all white men) are created equal; that they are endued by their Creator with inherent & unalienable rights; that among these are life, liberty & the pursuit of happiness. What think you now sir, are we men, or are we beasts? If this is not sufficient to prove our human-nature; our right and our citizenship, take another section from the original draft of the same authority: In speaking of the oughtrages commited by the king of england you say, He has waiged cruel war against human-nature itself, violating its most sacred rights of life & liberty in the persons of a distant people, who never offended him, captuating and carrying them into slavery in another hemisphere or incur miserable death in their transportation thither: this piratical warfare, the approbum of infidal powers, in the warfare of the Christian king of Great Britain—Determined to keep open a market where MAN shall be bought and sold. This is sufficient one would suppose, to convince any unprejudiced mind; but it seem that it has not carried conviction into the flinty hearts of the sainted pilgrims in America, & I fear nothing will but the sword.

Whatever may be the mode of any government, either civil or religious, says the friend of justice & mercy, if it cannot exist and prosper without affecting the peace & harmony of a neighbouring nation, is unjust: Much more must that government be unjust, which aggrandizes one half, or less, of a community, at the expence of the other. The monarchies & aristocracies which have been so often decryed by polititions, as oppressive and violent, are states of independence in comparison of that statee of bondage in which the American black-man is kept.

Is this the fruits of your education Sir? is this that pacifick policy, that frigal and honest policy, which Wm, says, renders equal justice to all men, and to all societies of men, which leaves no room for anger? Is this of all others the pacifick policy inculcated by religion? say, Does the happyness & prosperety of a country concist in slavery? does piety concist in belying a neighbouring nation; and in enslaveing the citizens of another & reducing them below the characters of the bruites? If this is your Christian Charity Sir this your piety and religion. Great God! pleas to come quickly in thy wrath and send thy thunder-bolts & dash these sainted monsters into dust. Again, in the midst of all these complicated horrors, Wm. has the affrontry to call upon the farmers of this land, and upon all the simple honest labouring classes of people, to look at this happy country, and be proude that there is no lord or lordlings to put them from their path of industry, nor to tare from them the fruits of their honest labour and genius.

In the name of God! what does Wm. mean by this? Where has he spent his time? In what cellar has he been shut since the year '76? Does he not know nor did he never hear, that the greatest part of all the manual labour that is done in the southern states is performed by slaves, and that they in general git nothing for it (except kicks and curses) and that their haughty lordling masters live in idleness, drunkenness and debauchery, and aggrandize themselves and families at the expence of the honest labours of the unfortunate people? Can he plead ignorance in all this? If not, by what name does he call such men, who have got four of five hundred slaves at their heels? whom they beat, scurge and abuse in a most inhuman manner, and take away all their honest labours and industry to riot upon?

Again, he adds, that a nation must be oppossed by some overwhelming necessity, some irresistable evil not to be avoided or guarded against, if she can be at all justified in deviating from the principles which ensure happiness—which are the causes of prosperity—which are the fundamental principles of religion. Do for mercy sake sir tell us, what this country is opposed by, which has caused her to deviate from all these principles—Is not slavery & its long train of calamities, a presumptive violation of all these principles? What can a nation do more readily to destroy happiness, prosperity and religion, than to enslave her citizens? Is it not a species of every evil which a nation can be guilty of to distroy all these principles? Let us hear what Mr. Wilkinson says. I cannot but consider says he, the accomplishment of absolute slavery as the greatest evil committed on the stage of this world. Consult upon this subject, the weighter matters of the law; by a friend to justice & mercy. Slavery is unjust says he, because it is tyrannical; it is incompatible with equity & civil rights; it is the greatest of all tyranny. Heavy taxes have been complain'd of as a burden too intolerable to be borne by the unhapy victims of an oppressive government; but the wretched peasant is left at liberty to consult his own sensation of pain & fatigue, & use his ingenuity to pay the exorbitant demands of his oppressor; mean while he can enjoy at short intervals some delightful interchanges of love & duty with his family; without being under the watchful eye of a cruel task-master. Laws to be just & equitabe, should protect the weak & ignorant, & diffuse blessings upon all with a liberal hand. Just laws give vigor and proportion to every part of the body; but slavery aggrandizes one part of the community at the expence of the other. Under its pernicious influence, the head grows to an enormous size, while the inferior members are impoverished & wither away. Like some fatal disorders, it not only destroys the beauty of the body, but its first & best principles, its sympathy and harmony. Slavery is unjust, because it destroys the rites of women & children. It is a mere state of barberism, in which neither the delicacy and chastity of sex, nor the debility & ignorance of little children are regarded. The situation of the female slave is more deplorable & degrading than that of the untutored savage. For littl as savages respect the rights of women & children, their women have exemption from labour, & protection from insult during those delicate & painful periods which are peculiar to their sex; & their children are instructed in all the knowledge which is by them deem either useful or ornamental. The degree of servitude to which savage women are bound, is trifling in comparison with the task of a female slave; and inasmuch as their husbands & children reap the fruits of their labour, & in some measure repay it by acquireng a superior skill in hunting & war, their labour becomes rather a pleasure than a burden. But what is to mitigate the labour of the poor female slave, with the precious burden of her affections at her breast? Slavery is unjust, as it destroys all the physical & commercial distinctions of labour & property. It is a mere monopoly of men, and all their abilities and services.

He who contributes by manual labour to the great stock of wealth, must in justice be entitled to some reward; but in vain does the wretched slave fell the forests, clear the grounds, prepare them for seed; watch & cultivate the tender plant, reap down & geather in the harvest, & bear it to the market.—

Our inhuman tyrants take the whole to riot in drunkenness & debauchery upon, & to aggrandize themselves & families, and we who have bourn the heat and burden of the day, git nothing but kicks and curses, for all our labour. "With what execration should the states man be loaded, who permiting one half the citizens thus to trample on the rights of the other, transforms those into despots, & these into enemies, destroys the morals of the one part, and the amor patria of the other. With the morals of the people, their industry also is destroy'd; for in a warm climate, no man will labour for himself who can make another labour for him." This sufficiently proves my assertions, and justifies me in saying, that a majority of the American agents in the Southern States, are a set of inhuman scoundrils, and ought to be tar'd and feather'd and tyed to the tale end of a dung cart, and horse-whipt throughout the country, from state to state, and forever after banished from human society.

If slavery has become so firmly established in this country, as not to be avoided or garded against, or is such a pleasing object, as to be no longer odious and irreligious, but a source of happiness and prosperity, its high time for America to give up all pretentions to liberty & freedom, & acknoledge herself at once, a joint heir with Jno Bull.

But we have not lost all hopes; we can't yet believe, sir, that you have become so deprav'd as to be in love with slavery, or have done reflecting upon the wrath of a just God, or that his justice cannot sleep forever. Yet there appears to me something in your administration, sir, very misterious. What your reasons can be for keeping open that execrable market where MAN shall be bought and sold, which you wrote so warmly against in the year '76, and condemn'd as a mark of disgrace, of the deepist dye in the Christian king of G. Britain, I cannot conceive. Is a crime of this execrable nature any more criminal in the Christian Crown of Britain, than in the Christian Executive of America? If not, what are your reasons, sir, for suffering us since 30th. Nov. '81 to be troden under foot & abused in such an inhuman & bruital manner? Are not Our rites as well secured to us by every law of natures God as any man's in the universe? we think so; therefore, sir, we consider ourselves, intitled to our yearly wages from that very hour, and no man in the government (except a tyrant) can dispute our demand a single moment. And you may depend on this sir, that we shall never be recconciled to this government till we git it, & our freedom with it.—I think sir, you can't do yourself & your country a greater honour, nor your unfortunate country men a greater piece of justice and mercy, then by freeing your slaves & paying them their yearly wages from '81 to this day. And then, if any slave-holder in America shall here after refuse or neglect so to do, let him or them be made an example of, and their heads be hung in gibbets for an everlasting monument; & a terror to tyrants & evil doers. O! Thomas, you have had a long nap, and spent a great number of years in ease & plenty, upon our hard earned property, while we have been in the mean time, smarting under the cow-hide and sweating in the fields to raise provision to nurse tyrants to cut your throat and perpetuate our own bonds.

Why you should wish, in a free republick, to nurs, educate and exercise your children in such a tyrannical manner, I cannot conceive; since you so early saw, and confes'd the error; and must long ere this most severly have felt the effects of your folly. If not, fold your arms, and lull yourself into a slumber a little longer, and then see how the pig will eat the grapes.—

It is strange, but not more so than true, says Esqr Pigott, that all nations, without exception, are subject to, and the slaves of some error or superstition which is the fundiment of unhapiness to the people. Experience, knowledge, history, in vain afford them lessons, what path to follow and what to shun. Blinded by the warring passions, and stupified by the love of sensuality they rush on head long into the abys of vice and folly, and think to extricate themselves from these pittfalls by heaping crime upon crime till they find themselves even with the rest of the world, that is, flat on their back, see England. And America will soon follow, & fall into the same fatal pitt, if some speedy means cannot be devized to abolish this inhuman slavery, and stop the carreer of those renegaders—I mean the British emissaries and their adhearents, the Lawyers, warmly federalists, and methodist & catholick priests, for I find to my great astonishment, that they are all bound together in one infarnal league, to subvert the constitution, and build up, upon its ruins, one simular to that of the British—

Bees were never more busy abou't a hive than these inhuman monsters are with the people of colour, and all other ignorant classes of people, irretiating their minds agains't the government, and against the French nation:—persuaiding us to believe, that the agents of this government are influenced by France, and that the French people are all either atheists or deists, and that their Chief is a tyrant, and is striveing to over through every religious systim in the Old world and that he is makeing preperation to come to America and give Laws to this country, &c, &c.—

What does all this mean? What end do these monsters in the creation expect to answer by these base lies? Has not France been friendly to this country ever since the revolution? Has she not been fighting these many years, in order to give a universal spread to liberty & freedom? And have not almost all the powers of the earth oppos'd her, and strove to perpetuate slavery? Yea, have not even the Americans themselves, done every thing within their power, or that their malice could suggest to disturb the peace and tranquility of France?

What can all this mighty uproar be for, but to establis some selfish ends to the debtriment of France? What else can they wish, but to over turn the constitution, and stick up some idle debauche for a Duke, Lord, or King, in order to perpetuate our bonds? What else can we expect from such inhuman scoundrels? These wretches have become so dareingly bold, that its no uncomon thing to see them day after day cheek by jole one with the other; calling all who differ from them in polyticks damn'd rascals and wishing them in hell, &c. &c.

"The grand & steadfast enemies to the happiness of mankind are religion and government; The first is the offspring of fear; the latter, the child of depravity; and if it were not for priests & tyrants, who always play into each others hands, mankind would still have had to bless the halcyon days of a natural government and a natural religion.

Its worthy of remark that a standard of truth is errected by every little tyrant, in every little state and tho' truth is immutable, she is a very Proteus, deversifying and varigating her m[any] garb in every soil, in every clime, and in every age. What is a virtue in one country, is a crime in another—what is a truth in one, is falshood in the next—what is justice here, is injustice there—what utility here, injury there—what laudable here, culpable there," &c.—In the name of God, what does this mean? how is a child to learn truth from error? "Has God the heart of a mortal, with passions ever changing? Is he like them, agitated with vengence or compassion, with wrath or repentance? According to them it would seem that God, whimsical and capricious, is angered or appeased as a man: That he loves and hates by turns; that he punishes or favours; that weak or wicked, he broods over hatred; that contradictory or perfedious, he lays snares to entrap; that he punishes the evils he permits; that he foresees, but hinders not crimes; that like a corrupt judge, he is bribed by offerings; like an ignorant despot, he makes laws and revoks them, that like a savage tyrant, he grants or resumes favours without reason, and is flexible only to baseness."

"Thus the ax and the halter, the rack and the wheel, the faggot & the crucifix, are the infallible umpires, unerring oricles; the unchangable standards of truth; the grand determiners of right and rong!

Treason and Integrity, Religion and Superstition, Reason and Error, go hand in hand in the world, and the tyrant & the priest of every pitiful teritory arbitrarily decide by law, which is truth & which is error."—

This is just the pitiful case in Ameria, by her divisions into Republican & Federal, Tyrant and Slave, Priest-craft & Law-craft; day after day, upbraiding each other with lying & deceiving, corruption & error, ignorance & superstition, cheating and defrauding, sedition & knavery, blasphemy & cowardice, envy & tale-bearing, &c. &c. What a world of useful experience! what a happy country! what a genteel education! what a wise & holy people! Examples truly from God; and really worth while to cross the Atlantick, to teach these holy examples to that impious French nation, which Wm. says have not made any improvements in these pious examples. This being the deplorable case, where are we to look for virtue? In what nation? Among what class of people? Who can answer these importent questions? Why, here I have them, already answer'd twenty six years past. Those who labour in the earth, says you, are the chosen people of God, if ever he had a chosen people, whose breast he has made his peculiar deposit for substaintial and genuine virtue.

It is the focus in which he keeps alive that sacred fire, which otherwise might escape from the face of the earth.—

Huzza! this is some consolation, if we are afflicted by tyrants & oppressors in this life, it seem we are not to be troubled with them after death. But hush! what madness is this? what, God made choice of clod-hoppers for his peculiar people? is their breasts the only safe deposit for genuine virtue? What, no trust nor virtue in the priest-hood? No virtue in Burr's best blood of America? Nor in any of Jno. Adams' Nobility? In the name of God Thomas! what do you mean by this? Do you mean to people the heavens with clod-hoppers, the very scum of the creation! For mercy sake! what a sort of a heaven will this make?

How will God look moping abou't in heaven with farmers & mecanicks? How must he feal to see the Devil struting in hell with this long train of nobility, birth, blood & extraction?

Is it possable that God can make such a choise? Have we any other authority to justify such a belief? Why, truly, what says scripture, and even the priest-hood: why, that the unjust shall not see God. Huzza! got by, birth, blood, & extraction, you are the Devils chickerys. Hush! hush! Who beside the Devil could induce people to talk in this manner? How do you expect sir, to answer for these blasphemious speechies to this Noble race of birth, blood & extraction, who stile themselves the most noble, wise, honest, human, pious, charitable, virtuous people in the univers: Yea, the very elect of God, to whom he has given all things on earth, and promised everlasting joys in heaven? If this be true, what becomes of your clodhoppers, sir, and how are you to make atonement to this noble house of birth, blood & extraction, for dooming them to hell? I'll tell you sir, with your head; and that in a few months too, unless you speedily awake from your slumbers. Your enemies are almost ready to begin the massacree, and our strength is to be made use of to complet the inhuman deed. Pause sir, pause, for justice & mercy sake pause, we must fight for, or against you.—

Its high time for you sir, to decide, whether or not you will any longer use us in this brutal manner, or adopt us as brethren, for, in our opinion; or this single circumstance alone, depends the future prosperity, or distruction of these states, and the safty of your own life in perticular.

If ever virtue was in danger of escapeing the continent of America, it is at this time, for its an insult upon human understanding to say, that there is a single spark left in the breasts of any of Burr's best blood of America—in the priest-hood's, or in any of Jno. Adams' Nobility, knaves or fools.

There cannot come a stranger among us from any part of the world or the continent; be him ever so virtuous, useful & well inform'd; but the moment he discovers himself to be a Republican, and opposed to this inhuman slavery, he is spurn'd at, & froun'd upon by our haughty tyrannical masters & excluded from all society, and call'd all the lying damn'd rascals that their malis can invent; even the Clarks in Congress are of this No. & those who pass for republicans. And we their poor unfortunate slaves are beaten, without intermission, and troden underfoot in a most inhuman and bruital manner. Yea, it has come to this, that our lives are no longer safe, for our inhuman masters and over-seers, publickly say that they would as soon take away our lives as that of a dog's, and that they will do it, if we should happen to offend them again, even in the most trifleing offence. And the right of over wives, during those delicate & painful periods which are peculiar to their sex, and which the most savage nations respect, are disregarded by our cruel masters, over-seers, & even by our misterses, & are driven like cattle from their beds in the morning at early dawn, & foursed into the fields almost naked, & there oblidged to labour in the heat of the scorching sun dureing the whole live long day, and many times, even in these painful moment, when eight or nine months gone in pregnancy, they are beaten down & tronden under foot in a most inhuman manner.

These are painful truths which no person can deny, who has ever lived three months among slave-holders. This being our unhappy condition, we humbly beseech you, sir, to lay our cause before the agents of this government, & request them to interpose between us & our inhuman tyrants, or other-wise, necessity will ere long oblidge us to seek our own safty, by takeing away the lives of our tyrants, & freeing ourselves at once from such inhuman monsters.

"Please to cast your eye on the hevens sir, that gives you light, and on the earth that gives you food: Since they offer the same bountie to us all; since from the power that gives them motion, we have all received the same life, the same organs; have we not likewise all received the same right to enjoy its benefits? has it not hereby declared us all equal & free?" Let me once more request you sir, to lay our grievances before the sovreign people of these states—Don't neglect it sir, unless you take delight in tyranny & oppression, or are thursting after blood—if you be, your appytite may ere long git glutted. God forbid that I should have such a thougt; or should live to see another drop of human blood unjustly spilt in America.

O! rouse up the brave sons of '76, and the children of those heros who bleed & died to free their country from foreign foes, & from bondage, that we & our children might live free from foreign, as well as domestick tyrants—Don't let their labours be lost—Don't let so much blood be spilt in vain, and so much treasure be bartered for a whistle—for Spanih folly, or for British knavery and pride. O! rouse, rouse quickly, and snatch your wepons, & unite your strength, & let us banish all tyrants, tyranny and oppression from North America, and let us who surv[ive] the fatal shock, "form but one society, one great family." "And since human-nature has but one constitution, let there in future (at least in America) exist but one law; that of nature; but one code; that of reason; but one throne; that of justice and but one alter; that of union. Then might the sons and aughters of America set under their vines and fruit-trees, and enjoy the fruits of their labour, and the friendship of the whole human family. Then might they set down in the joy of their hearts and sing with the birds in the following beautiful lines, viz.

Love & Liberty.
1. In bri'ry dell, on thicket brown,
On mountain high, in lowly vale,
Or where the thistle sheds its down,
And sweet-fern sents the passing gale,
There hops the birds from bush to tree,
    Love fills their throats,
    Love swells their notes,
Their song is love and Liberty.
2. No tyrant bird shall love direct,
His fair he seeks in plumy throng,
Caught by the plumage of her neck,
Or kindred softness of her song.
They sing and bill from bush to tree,
    Love fills their throats,
    Love swells their notes,
Their song is love and Liberty.—
3. Some airy songster feather'd shape,
O! could my love & I assume;
The ring Dove's glossy neck, he take,
And I the modest turtle's plume,
O! then we'd sport from bush to tree,
    Love fills our throats,
    Love swell our notes
Our song to love and Liberty.—

Religion, justice and humanity apart, the slave trade, says Mr. Wilkinson, is an indignity offered to human-nature, that ought to be resented by the whole world.

"Inquire around, the nations all accord,
That man is nature's delegated Lord;
To lift his lot above the beasts that die,
His God commission'd Justice from the sky,
Humanity, & mil'd Religion down,
His life to govern & his end to crown.
By these directed & by these approv'd,

He lives a blessing, & he dies belov'd;
Earth smiles in peace beneath his righteous hands,
And heaven for him her joyful gales expands.
If these neglected, leave their stubborn charge,
He raves a monster thro' the world at large;
Waste marks his way, his feet in blood are dy'd,
As on he stalks, the slave of lust & pride.
Humanity! thou loveliest power below,
Thou kind consoler of the breast of woe!
A virgin's softest bloom thy cheeks supplies,
Gifts fill thy hands, compassion fills thine eyes.
'Tis short with thee, if thy sweet influence reign
In Afric's blood no more our hands we stain;
But if the publick guardians of this land,
Bid yet the sail of slavery expand,
Thy gentle form a trembling victim lies,
Bleeds by her agints & by her seamen dies.
O Thou! the high & holy Lord of all,
Who form'd for glorious ends this spacious ball
Peopl'd its plains with beings formed to know
The vast extremes of happiness and woe,
Bid human race live inocent and free,
And rise to happiness in serving thee:
All this in Wisdom! & in each design,
The good thy creatures & the glory thine!
While musing thus my adoration spring,
To thee, thou first, best, everlasting King!
But when thou view'st the labour of thy hand,
Thus foul with lust & blood, and let's tit stand,
My finite views in wonder lost remain
The myst'ries of thy mercy to explain.
Yet, be my soul resign'd! & if the pray'rs
Of humble dust may reach thy holy ear;
O! teach the people of this high-favour'd land,
And hold from Afric's blood their guilty hand"!

Once more let me repeat it, as no subject can be dwelt upon which borders so strong on justice & mercy as the abolition of slavery; I say, sir, you cannot do yourself, & country so great an honour, nor your countrymen a greater kindness; nor will virtue in no act of your life shine so conspicuous as in the freedom of your slaves, & by separation for the insult offered them.

Such an example, is a cause of so much magnitude to human-nature, must inevitable throw such a luster on your character that no diamond in the universe could out shine it. And I flatter myself, that such an example in a man of your character, would have such an influence on the minds of slave-holders in general in Ameria, and in perticular upon Messrs Clinton & Madison that they would not only free their own, but would make use of all their influence to effect a general immancipation; and free their country from this inhuman slaviry & disgrace.

"That unexhausted power they nature call,
Which forms, produces, & provdes for all:
Did it, or did its Lord, by deed assign
The negro's life a sacrifice to thine?
Was he but born to contemplate the sky,
Yet know no joy, but toil for thee & die?
To feel in youth a premature decay,
And drop by drop to wear his strengh away;
Oppress'd abus'd, not live out half his days,
That thou mayst riot, & thy villan raise.
Say, do the sweets, the pleasures of the board,
Which the poor negro's life of toil afford,
In heaven's impatial scale of good & ill,
Balance the pains his wretched being fill?
Couldst thou of both thy just proportion know:
Or all the pleasure feel, and all the woe:
Then wouldst thou still the self same system hold
Of want, profusion, wretchedness & gold;
By justice weigh'd, how must the scale decline,
His all the pain, & all the pleasure, thine!
But are thy joys, thy pleasures all sincere?
Tho' hard the heart, a smile the face may wear;
But such a smile's no deeper than the skin,
No man is bless'd till things are well within.
Let sympathy thy clouded soul refine,

Religion warm thee with a fire divine;
Virtue thy lawless appetites command,
And sacred justice guide thy erring hand;
So to thy bosom, peace shall find its way,
No transient guest, but ever, ever stay.

Which God of his infinites mercy grant shall ever be the prayer of sir, yours (then) to serve. A Slave

NB. If you should think these observations worth your notice Sir, & are desirous to heal a fatal wound, & should think it prudent to communicate a few thoughts to console the afflicted heart & wounded body of one of the moust unfortunate of all the human species, you can make such as your wisdom may hereafter dictate in the National Intelligencer, and it will soon come to hand—

Your complyance sir, will revive the expanding hopes of two millions of the most miserable of all the human race—Never was men more inhumanly use'd in no Government under heaven!—than the slaves are in this country.

The foregoing hints have been on paper some days, but kept back for the birth of your message. Since that has issued without takeing any notice of our unhappy cituation, we begin to loos all hopes of haveing our grievences address'd by the present agents of America

But before we quite despond, we conclude to wait & see the issue of Congress. We hope at least sir, that you will deign to make known our miserable condition to the agents of the sovreign people of these states, that we may shortly hear whether, or not they will interpose between us and our inhuman masters, in order if possable, to mitigate our pains, ease our burthens, heal our smarting wounds.

TJ to Edmund Bacon

Sir Washington Dec. 26. 08.

I have not heard whether Jerry is returned from Bedford with his waggon, but I expect he is, and that except bringing home your corn, you have little waggoning to do. it will be well therefore to have both waggons in order, and to proceed to waggoning dung to the garden. that from Milton should be first brought, and for this purpose it will be worth your while to put the road along the river side in order, I mean that on the South side. as this would be to be put into good order as soon as I come home, it will be better to do it now, that you may have the benefit of it in the job of bringing the dung from Milton. 6. waggon loads are first to be laid on the old asparagus bed below the wall, which Wormley must immediately spread even & then fork it in with the threepronged garden fork, taking care not to fork so deep as to reach the crown of the Asparagus roots. then begin at the S.W. end of the garden, and drop a good waggon load of dung every five yards along a strait line through the middle of the garden from the S.W. to the N.E. end. This will take between 60. & 70. loads in the whole, which will do for the first year.

As it will be necessary that we make preparation for clothing our people another year, we must plant a large cotton patch, say two acres at the least. a light sandy soil is best. I suppose therefore it should be in the low grounds at the mill dam. seed can be procured from those who have cotton gins. the present method of cultivating cotton is very little laborious. it is done entirely with the plough. next, to secure wool enough, the negroes dogs must all be killed. do not spare a single one. if you keep a couple yourself it will be enough for the whole land. Let this be carried into execution immediately. since writing the above Davy has delivered me your letter of the 21s. My best wishes attend you.

Th: Jefferson

TJ to Indian Nations

My Children Chiefs of the
Wiandots, Ottawas, Chippeways,
Poutewatamies & Shawanese. Jan. 10. 1809.

This is the first time I have had the pleasure of seeing the distinguished men of our neighbors the Wiandots, Ottawas & Chippeways at the Seat of our Government. I welcome you to it as well as the Poutewatamies & Shawanese and thank the great Spirit for having conducted you hither in safety & health. I take you and your people by the hand and salute you as my Children; I consider all my red children as forming one family with the whites, born in the same land with them, and bound to live like brethren, in peace, friendship, & good neighborhood. in former times, my Children, we were not our own Masters, but were governed by the English. then we were often at war with our red neighbors. ill blood was raised, & kept up, between us, and in the war, in which we threw off the English Government, many of the red people, mistaking their brothers & real friends, took side with the English against us: & it was not, till many years after we made peace with the English, that the treaty of Grenville closed our last wars with our Indian Neighbors. from that time, My Children, we have looked on you as a part of ourselves, and have cherished your prosperity as our own. we saw that three things were wasting away your numbers to nothing. that the intemperate use of ardent Spirits produced poverty, troubles & murders among you. your wars with one another were lessening your numbers: & attachment to the hunter life, after game had nearly left you, produced famine sickness & deaths among you in the Scarce Season of every year. it has been our endeavor therefore like your true fathers and brothers to withold strong liquors from you, to keep you in peace with one another, & to encourage, & aid you in the culture of the earth, & raising domestic Animals, to take place of the wild ones. this we have done, my Children, because we are your friends, & wish you well. if we feared you, if we were your enemies, we should have furnished you plentifully with whisky, let the men destroy one another in perpetual wars, & the women & children waste away for want of food and remain insensible that they could raise it out of the Earth.

we have been told, my Children, that some of you have been doubting whether we or the English were your truest friends. what do the English do for you? they furnish you with plenty of whiskey, to keep you in idleness, drunkenness, & poverty; and they are now exciting you to join them in war against us, if war should take place between them and us. but we tell you to stay at home in quiet, to take no part in quarrels which do not concern you. the English are now at war with all the world but us, and it is not yet known whether they will not force us also into it. they are Strong on the water, but weak on the land. we live on the land, & we fear them not. we are able to fight our own battles; therefore we do not ask you to Spill your blood in our quarrels: much less do we wish to be forced to Spill it with our own hands. you have travelled through our Country from the Lakes to the tide waters. you have seen our numbers in that direction: and were you to pass along the Sea Shore, you would find them much greater. you know the English numbers, their Scattered forts and String of people, along the borders of the Lakes & the St. Lawrence how long do you think it will take us to sweep them out of the Country?—&, when they are swept away, what is to become of those who join them in their war against us? My Children, if you love the land in which you were born, if you wish to inhabit the earth which covers the bones of your fathers, take no part in the war between the English & us, if we should have war. never will we do an unjust Act towards you. on the contrary we wish to befriend you in every possible way. but the tribe which shall begin an unprovoked war against us, we will extirpate from the Earth, or drive to such a distance, as that they shall never again be able to strike us. I tell you these things My Children, not to make you afraid. I know you are brave men & therefore cannot fear. but you are also wise men, & prudent men. I say it therefore, that, in your wisdom & prudence, you may look forward. that you may go to the graves of your fathers and say "fathers shall we abandon you?" that you may look in the faces of your wives & children & ask "shall we expose these our own flesh & blood to perish from want in a distant country and have our race & name extinguished from the face of the Earth"?. think of these things my Children, as wise men, & as men loving their fathers, their wives & children & the name & memory of their Nation. I repeat that we will never do an unjust act towards you. on the contrary we wish you to live in peace, to increase in numbers, to learn to labor, as we do, and furnish food for your increasing numbers, when the game shall have left you. we wish to see you possessed of property, & protecting it by regular laws. in time you will be as we are; you will become one people with us; your blood will mix with ours; & will spread, with ours, over this great Island. hold fast then, my Children, the Chain of friendship, which binds us together; & join us in keeping it forever bright & unbroken.—

I invited you to come here, my Children, that you might hear, with your own ears, the words of your father; that you might see, with your own eyes, the sincere dispositions of the U.S. towards you. in your journey to this place you have seen great numbers of your white brothers; you have been received by them as brothers, have been treated kindly & hospitably, & you have seen & can tell your people that their hearts are now sincerely with you. this is the first time I have ever addressed your Chiefs, in person, at the Seat of Government. it will also be the last. sensible that I am become too old to watch over the extensive concerns of the Seventeen States & their territories, I requested my fellow Citizens to permit me to retire to live with my family and to chuse another President for themselves, and father for you. they have done so; and in a short time I shall retire & resign into his hands the care of your and our Concerns. be assured, my Children; that he will have the same friendly dispositions towards you which I have had, & that you will find in him a true and affectionate father. indeed this is now the disposition of all our people towards you. they look upon you as brethren, born in the same land, & having the same interests. tell your people therefore, to entertain no uneasiness on account of this change; for there will be no change as to them. deliver to them my Adieux, and my prayers to the Great Spirit for their happiness. tell them that, during my administration, I have held their hand fast in mine; & that I will put it into the hand of their New father, who will hold it as I have done.— Th: Jefferson

TJ to James Madison

Dear Sir Monticello Apr. 19. 09.

Cents	D
392. bushels of coal @ .25	98.
100. bottles of Madeira	100.
36. do Noyau	36.
expences filling the ice-house	77.205
a horse	200.
months months D	
John Freeman. 76½ out of 132 @ 400.	231.81
	743.015

the deed for John is inclosed.

Enclosure: Deed of John Freeman's Indenture to James Madison

I hereby assign & convey to James Madison President [of the Uni] ted States the within named servant, John, otherwise called John Freeman during the remaining term of his service from the 11th day of March last past when he was delivered to the said James for the consideration of two hundred and thirty one Dollars 81. cents. Witness m[y hand] this 19th day of April 1809. at Monticello in Virginia. Th: Jefferson

TJ to Benjamin Smith Barton

Dear Sir Monticello Sep. 21. 09.

I recieved last night your favor of the 14th and would with all possible pleasure have communicated to you any part or the whole of the Indian vocabularies which I had collected, but an irreparable misfortune has deprived me of them. I have now been thirty years availing myself of every possible opportunity of procuring Indian vocabularies to the same set of words: my opportunities were probably better than will ever occur again to any person having the same desire. I had collected about 50. and had digested most of them in collateral columns and meant to have printed them the last year of my stay in Washington. but not having yet digested Capt Lewis's collection, nor having leisure then to do it, I put it off till I should return home. the whole, as well digest as originals were packed in a trunk of stationary & sent round by water with about 30. other packages of my effects from Washington, and while ascending James river, this package, on account of it's weight & presumed precious contents, was singled out & stolen. the thief being disappointed on opening it, threw into the river all it's contents of which he thought he could make no use. among these were the whole of the vocabularies. some leaves floated ashore & were found in the mud; but these were very few, & so defaced by the mud & water that no general use can ever be made of them. on the reciept of your letter I turned to them, & was very happy to find that the only morsel of an original vocabulary among them was Capt Lewis's of the Pani language of which you say you have not one word. I therefore inclose it to you, as it is, & a little fragment of some other, which I see is in his handwriting, but no indication remains on it of what language it is. it is a specimen of the condition of the little which was recovered. I am the more concerned at this accident as of the 250 words of my vocabularies and the 130. words of the great Russian vocabularies of the languages of the other quarters of the globe, 73. were common to both, and would have furnished materials for a comparison from which something might have resulted. altho I believe no general use can ever be made of the wrecks of my loss, yet I will ask the return of the Pani vocabulary when you are done with it. perhaps I may make another attempt to collect, altho' I am too old to expect to make much progress in it.

I learn with pleasure your acquisition of the pamphlet on the astronomy of the antient Mexicans. if it be antient & genuine, or modern & rational it will be of real value. it is one of the most interesting countries of our hemisphere, and merits every attention.

I am thankful for your kind offer of sending the original Spanish for my perusal. but I think it a pity to trust it to the accidents of the post, & whenever you publish the translation, I shall be satisfied to read that which shall be given by your translator, who is, I am sure, a greater adept in the language than I am. Accept the assurances of my great esteem & respect.

Th: Jefferson

Roll of the Negroes 1810 Albemarle

Burwell. 83.
Edwin 93
Edy. 87.
  James Jan. 7. 05.
  Maria. Oct. 27. 07.
  Patsy. 10. May 11.
Fanny. 88.
  Ellen. 09. Aug. 22
~~Amy 93.~~
  Jenny. 11. Nov.
Critta. 69
Sally. 73.
  Harriet. 01. May
  Madison. 05. Jan
  Eston. 08. May 21.
Betty Brown. 59.
  Robert. 99. Dec.
  Mary. 01. Oct.
Peter Hemings. 70.
Nance. 61.
Mary. perhaps abt. 80.
  William 01. Mar.
  Davy. 03. Feb.
  Celia. 06
  Tucker. 10. Apr.

John Hemings. 75
Lewis. abt. 60
Davy. 55.
Shepherd. 82.
Abram. abt. 1740.
Joe. 80.
Moses. 79.
Davy. Isb's 84. Sep.
Thruston. 95 July 5.
James. Lew's 95 Apr.
Phill. 96. (Suck's
Nace. 96. Aug. Maria's
Sanco. 97. Eve's.
Beverley. 98. Apr. 1.
~~Jame Hubbard 83.~~
Jerry. 77.
Jame. 76.
Barnaby. 83.
Wormley 81.
John 53.
Ned 60.
James (Ned's) 96. June 14.

22

John Bedfd. 85.
Bardet. 86
Isaac. abt. 68.
Isabel. probly. abt. 58
  Thrimton. 1799. June 22
  Lovilo. 01. Oct. 27.
  ~~[*illegible*]~~
Amy. John probly. abt. 56.
Jenny. Ned's 64.
  Aggy. 98 Oct. 25
  Israel. 1800. Dec. 28
  Moses. 03. Jul. 28.
  Sucky. 06. Dec. 21
Jenny. Lew's. 68.
  Isabel. 1800. May.
Doll. 57.
~~Molly. 89.~~
~~Mary.~~ Jerry's 76. d.13
  Isaiah. 1800. Dec. 31.
  Jerry. 02. Jan. 14.
  Jupiter. 04. Jan. 15.
~~Goliah. 31.~~ d 1810
~~Phill. 40.~~ d 1810
~~Squire. 27.~~ d. 1810.

~~22~~ 19

Bagwell. 68.
Caesar. 49.
Ben. 85.
Phill. Hubd. 86.
Ned. 86.
Dick. 90.
Gill. 92.
~~Jesie. 90.~~
Abram. 94.
Minerva. 71.
Virginia. 93
Esther. 95. Mar. 19
  Nanny. 00. Apr. 10
  Willis. 06. Jan. 6
  Archy. 08 Feb. 3
  Jordan. 10
Mary. **Bagw.** 88
  Washington. 05. Mar 1.
Rachael. 76.
  Eliza. 05. Sep. 30
  Ellen. 08. Dec. 18
Nancy. 91.
Thenia. 93.
Dolly. 94.
Lilly 91.

~~[*illegible*]~~
Charles. abt. 85
Lewis. 66.
Davy Bedfd. 85.
Aggy. 89
Polly. 10 Aug.
Sally Lew's 92
Scilla. Ned's 94
  Jamey. 11. Sep

7

Ursula. 87.
  Joe. 05. Jan
  Anne 07. Feb.
  Dolly. 09. Feb.
  Cornelius 11. Apr. 1.
Cretia. abt. 79
  John. 1800.
  Randal. 02.
  Henry. 05.
  Milly 07.
  Lilburn 09.
Sucky. Jerry's 96.
Bec. Bagwell's 97
Indridge 97. Mar. 30.
Evelina. Lewis' 97. Oct. 24.
Larana. Rach's 97. Mar. 22.

37
37
22
19
26
7
111

d. ~~Andersen. 06. July. 30~~
  Stannard. 09. Jun. 22.
  Lucy. 11. Mar. 12.

26

Roll of the Negroes 1810 Bedford

POPLAR FOREST.

Hal. Bess's. smith 67. Sep
+ Hanah. Cate's. 70. Jan.
Sally. 98.
Billy. 99.
Jamy. 05.
Phill. 08.
Edmund. 09.
+ Nace. Cate's. 73.
+ Lucinda. Hanah's. 91. June
Melinda. 09. Aug. 8.
Will. smith. abt. 53.
+ Abbey. Judy's. abt. 53.
+ { Dick. Will's. 81. Oct.
+ Austin. isld. Betty's 75. Aug.
+ Flora. Will's. 83.
Gawen. 04. July.
Aleck. 06. Sep.
Billy. 08. Oct.
+ Fanny. Will's. 88. Aug.
Rachael. 07. Feb.
Doreas. 09. May. 1.
d. Jan. 28. 11
Edy. Will's. 92. Apr.
+ Manuel. Will's. 94.
Amy. Will's. 97. Jan.
+ Bess. Guinea Will's. abt. 47.
+ Caesar. Bess's. 74. Sep.
+ Suck. Bess's. 71. May.
+ Stephen 94.
Ambrose. 99.
Prince. 04.
Joe. 06. May.
Shepherd. 09. Apr.
+ Cate. Suck's. 88. Mar.
Davy. 06. June.
+ Betty. isld. abt. 49.
+ Cate Betty's. 88. Mar. 8.
+ Mary. Betty's. 92. Jan.
+ Hercules. Betty's. 94. Nov. 20.
+ Jesse. Indn. camp. Will's. 72. Nov.
+ Dick. Aggey's. 67.
+ Dinah. 66.
+ Moses. Dinah's. 92. Jan.
+ Evans. Dinah's. 94.
Hanah. Dinah's 96. Aug

Lucy. do. 99.
Jamy. do. 02.
Bryley. 05. Dec.
47

\+ Aggy. Dinah's.89. Mar.
\+ Nanny. Phill's.78. July
Maria.98. Feb. 24.
Phill.01. Aug.
Milly.06. May.
George Dennis.08. May
\+ Lucy. Phill's 83. July.
Robin.05.
Sandy.07. Nov. 25.

old Judy.abt. 1728.

47
10
~~28~~ 29 29
~~85~~ 86

BEAR CREEK.

Jame. Hubbard.abt. 43
Cate. Sall's.abt. 47.
\+ Armistead. Hubbard's.71.
\+ { Jame. purchd. 72.
\+ { Rachael Cate's 73. Oct.
Cate.97. Aug.
{ Joe.01.
Lania.05.
Gloster.07. Dec. 25.
Washington.10. May 26
\+ Reuben. Hanah's.93.
\+ { Solomon. Hanah's 94
\+ Maria. Cate's.76. Oct.
Nisy.99.
Johnny.04. Sep.
Isaac.09. Nov.
\+ Eve. Cate's 79.
Jossy.06. July.
Burwell.09. May.
\+ Sally. Cate's 78. Aug.
Billy.08. Mar.
\+ Gawen. isld. Betty's 78. Aug.
\+ Sal. Will's.77. Nov.
19. d Milly 97. Mar.
Betty.01. Jan.
Abby.04. Nov.

	Edy.06. Aug.
	Martin.09. Jan. 31.
+	Daniel. Bess's.90. Sep.

DEATHS SINCE 1801

1805.	Nancy. Cate's.	born 1791.
07.	Isabel. Sall's.	95.
	Polly. Nanny's.	04.
	Hercules.	
08.	Burrel. Rachael's	94.
09.	Jupiter. Hercules'	1800.
	Dick. Aggy's.	09.
	Jenny. Cate's	09.

TJ's Conveyance of James Hubbard to Reuben Perry

This deed poll and bipartite made between Thomas Jefferson of the county of Albemarle of the one part and Reuben Perry of the county of Bedford of the other part witnesseth that the said Thomas hath sold and now conveys to the said Reuben a negro man slave called Jame Hubbard aged about twenty seven years, who has lately, and is at this time absconded from his habitation in Albemarle, for the considerations following, that is to say, of the sum of three hundred Dollars which the said Reuben covenants to pay to the said Thomas or his assigns, whether the said Jame be recovered or not. and of the further sum of two hundred Dollars in addition to the sd 300. Dollars before mentioned, to be paid whenever he shall be recovered to the possession of the sd Reuben. and the sd Thomas agrees that, in satisfaction of both the said sums of 300. and 200. Dollars, he or his assigns will accept of such work to those amounts in Carpentry or House-joinery, to be performed by the sd Reuben, and on such part of the lands called the Poplar Forest in Bedford, as the said Thomas or his assigns shall indicate. Provided that if the said Reuben, within six months after such indications, shall not commence any parcel of work so to be indicated, and continue at it steadily, and with all his force until compleated, that then he shall be bound to pay the deficiency in money: and Provided also that all such work shall be estimated at the prices which have been settled by agreement or practice for similar work done between John Perry brother of the sd Reuben & the said Thomas. In witness whereof the sd Thomas & Reuben have hereto set their hands & seals this day of February 1811.

Witness
Th: Jefferson
Reuben Perry

It is agreed between the parties within named that the sd Reuben Perry shall transfer his obligation to do work for the sd Thomas Jefferson at Poplar forest, to the county of Albemarle in consideration whereof the sd Thomas abates fifty Dollars from the sum due for the within named slave Jame Hubbard according to the within agreement. witness their hands this 3d day of September 1812.

Th: Jefferson
Reuben Perry

Elijah Fletcher's Account of a Visit to Monticello

[8 May 1811]

Wednsday 8th I started again for Monticello—Mr Kelly when I g[ot t]o Char. went with me. When we arrived at the foot of the hill, we wound a side way, circutous course to avoid the steapness in getting the house, which was immediately upon the top of the mountain. We rode up to the front gate of the door yard [a] servant took our horses—Mr. Jefferson appeared at the door. I was introduced to him—and shook hands with him very cordially—We went into the drawing room—wines and liquers were soon handed us by the servant—He conversed with me very familiarly & he gratified my curiosity in showing me his Library—Museum of curiosities Philosophical apparatus &c Mr. Jefferson is tall, spare, straight in body. his face not handsome but savage—I learnt he was but little esteemed by his neighbers. Republicans as well as federalists in his own County dislike him and tell many anecdotes much to his disgrace—I confess I never had a very exalted opinion of his moral conduct—but from the information I gained of his neighbors, who must best know him—I have a much poorer one—The story of black Sal is no farce—That he cohabits with her and has a number of children by her is a sacred truth—and the worst of it is, he keeps the same children slaves—an unnatural crime which is very common in these parts—This conduct may receive a little palliation when we consider that such proceedings are so common that they cease here to be disgraceful—

TJ's List of Landholdings and Monticello Slaves

[ca. 1811–1812]

[1000].	a.s patd 1735.	
27½	purchd from	N. Lewis
25¼		Overton
470½	part of 483.	Carter
40.		Wells
61¼		Brown
3.	bed of road. Brown	
150.	Tufton. patd 1755.	
150.	Portobello patd 1740.	
[1]927½	the Montico tract	
[1]162¼	the Hendersons	
222.	on Henderson's bra.	
196.	Ingraham's.	
[1]580¼	the Milton tract.	
400.	as Shadwell	
819¼.	Lego.	
485.	Shadwell mountn	
400.	Pouncey's	
4.	Limestone. Sharp's	
133⅓	do Hardware	
5749⅓		

Bedford & Campbell

214.	Dan. Robinson
2650.	part of Pop. For.
[2]864.	N. of Tomahawk.
534.	part of Pop. For.
380.	Callaway's pat.
183.	Jno Robinson's
800.	Buffalo.
1897.	S. of Tomahawk
29.	Johnson
[4]790	

1743.	Abram.
49.	Caesar.
53.	John.
55.	Davy.
56.	Amy.
57.	Doll.
58.	Isabel.
59.	Betty Brown.
60.	Ned.
	Lewis.
61.	Nance.
64.	Jenny. Ned's
68.	Isaac.
	Bagwell.
	Jenny. Lewis'.
69.	Critta.
70.	Peter Hemings.
71.	Minerva.
72.	Jame Bedfd
73.	Sally. Hem.
	Rachael B. Oct.
75.	John Hem.
76.	James. Isab's.
	Mary. Jerry's.
	Rachael. Doll's.
77.	Jerry.
79.	Cretia.
	Moses. Isab's.
	Eve.
80.	Mary. Moses'.
	Joe.
81.	Wormly.
	Dick. Bedf.
82.	Shepherd.
83.	Lucy. Phill's.

[85.] [Charles.]
Ben.
John Bedf. Dinah's
Davy Bedf.
86. Bartlet.
Ned.
87. Ursula
Edy.
88. Lewis jr
Mary. Bagw's.
Fanny.
89. Aggy. Charles's
90. Dick. Ned's
Jesse.
Abram jr
91. Nancy. Rach's
Lilly.
92. Gill.
Sally Lew's
Moses. Bedf. Dinah's.
93. Edwin.
Virginia.
Thenia.
94. Scilla.
Dolly. Doll's
Solomon.
95. Thruston.
James. Lew's
Esther.
96. Philip. Suck's
Nace. Maria's
James. Ned's
Suckey.
97. Sanco. Eve's.
Indridge.
Evelina.
Lazaria.
Bec.
[98.] [Bev]erly.
[Aggy. Ned's.]

Barnaby.
Burwell.
84[.] Davy[.] Is[ab's.]
1799. Robert.
1800. John. Cretia's.
Nanny. Bagw's.
Isabel. Lew's.
Thrimson. Isab's
Israel. Ned's
Isaiah. Jerry's
01. William. Moses'.
Harriet. Sally's
Mary. Bet's
Lovilo. Isab's.
Joe. Rachael's
02. Jerry. Jerry's
Randal. cretia's.
03. Davy. Moses's.
Moses. Ned's
04. Jupiter. Jerry's.
05. James. Edy's
Madison. Sally's.
Joe. Ursula's.
Robin. Lucy's.
Henry. Cretia's.
Washington. Mary B's.
Eliza. Rach's
Lania. Bedf. Rachael's[6]
06. Willis. Bagw's
Jossy. Eve's.
Calia. Moses'.
Sucky. Ned's
07. Anne. Ursula's.
Milly. Cretia's
Maria. Edy's
Sandy. Lucy's
Gloster. B. Rachael's[7]
08. Archy. Bagw's.
Eston. Sally's.
Ellen. Rach's.
09. Dolly. Ursula's
Burwell. Eve's.
Stannard. Lilly's.
Lilburn. Cretia's.
Ellen. Fanny's.
[10.] [Tucker. Mary's]
Patsy. Edy's.
Jordan. Bagw's.

Polly. Aggy's.
Washington B. Rachael's.
11. Lucy. Lilly's.
Cornelius. Ursula's
Jamey. Scilla's.
[Matilda.] Cretia's.
Jenny. Fanny's.

Conveyance of Sally Goodman from TJ to Jeremiah A. Goodman

Know all men by these presents that I Thomas Jefferson of the county of Albemarle do hereby sell and convey to Jeremiah A. Goodman now of the county of Bedford a certain negro girl slave named Sally, being the daughter of Aggy one of the slaves of the sd Thomas, which said Girl Sally is about three years of age in consideration of the sum of one hundred and fifty Dollars to me the sd Thomas, by the sd Jeremiah in hand paid: to hold & to own the sd girl Sally in absolute property free of all uses, trusts, or other incumbrances: and the said slave Sally I do hereby warrant to the sd Jeremiah A. Goodman his executors, administrators & assigns for ever. Witness my hand this 30th day of November one thousand eight hundred and fifteen.

Th: Jefferson
Witness
Rolin Goodman

The sd girl Sally remains in my possession by agreement in the care of her mother until either the sd Jeremiah Goodman or myself chuses that she shall be taken into his possession

Th: Jefferson

William Caruthers to TJ

Sir Lexington 2nd June 1817

Patrick Henry a free Man of Coular requested me to Write You that he Will Rent What land is Cultivatable On the Bridge Tract—Which is perhaps about 10 Acres all of Which is to Clear off & Enclose & for Which he is Willing to pay a fair Value—

Patrick is a Man of Good Behavior and as the Neighbours are Destroying Your Timber Verry much it Might not be Amiss to Authorise him—to Take care of it in Order to Which it Might be Well to have the lines Run by the Surveyor of the County

Accept My Best Respects Wm Caruthers

TJ to William Caruthers

Sir Monticello June 11. 17.

I recieved yesterday your favor of the 2d inst. and I readily consent that Patrick Henry, the freeman of colour whom you recommend, should live on my land at the Natural bridge, and cultivate the cultivable lands on it, on the sole conditions of paying the taxes annually as they arise, and of preventing trespasses. I some time since saw the tract advertized for sale by the US. Collector, and immediately sent him the taxes. but I do not know how it is with the state taxes. I cannot find that I have paid them myself since 1813. nor do I know if Dr Thornton has paid them. I requested him verbally to pay up any arrears due and place it in account between us, which he promised to do, but I am uninformed whether it is done or not. should it be at all jeopardised as to the state taxes, I would hope your kindness would drop me a line of information. if they are unpaid now, on recieving a line of information, I would immediately remit them to you by mail. I expect to be at the bridge in September, and probably in that season every year as it is but 28. miles from my place in Bedford where I pass at different times about three months in the year. I salute you with great esteem and [resp]ect

Th: Jefferson

TJ to Jeremiah A. Goodman

Sir Monticello July 20. 17.

with respect to the girl Sally, the fair thing is to consider the bargain as annulled, and for me to repay you the sum allowed for her, 150.D. with interest till repaid: but I cannot undertake the repayment but in all May 1819. I had as live pay in May 18. as in Aug. 18.

but I could not do this conveniently, this with the repayment of her clothing comes to something more than you propose. I tender you my best wishes Th: Jefferson

P.S. July 30. 17. the only contribution you have given to the clothing or subsistence of the child being the sum of 15.D. allowed me for corn in a subsequent account, I mean that that shall also be repaid with interest.

TJ: Agreement with Jeremiah A. Goodman

Having at the date of a settlement of Nov. 30. 1815. with Jeremiah A. Goodman sold to him a negro girl called Sally for the sum of 150. Dollars, for which sum I was then allowed a credit in account; it is now agreed with the sd Jeremiah that that sale shall be annulled; that the said negro girl Sally shall now become my property, and that I shall repay to him the said sum of 150.D. with interest thereon from the sd 30th of November 1815. until repaid; and also that I shall repay him the sum of fifteen Dollars allowed me in account on the 16th day of December 1816. for subsistence for the sd girl with interest thereon from the sd 16th of Dec. 1816. until payment and that these payments of the sd sums of 150.D. & of 15.D. with their respective interests shall be made in the month of May eighteen hundred and nineteen. Witness my hand this 30th day of July 1817.

Th: Jefferson

I agree to the above and have delivered up the deed for the negro girl who has always been in the possession of the sd Thomas.

Jeremiah A Goodman

Andrew Alexander to TJ

Sir Lexington Augt 4th 1817

Your letter of the 11th June to Mr Caruther, (whose death we have to lament!) was recd after his death

Patrick Henry the free man of colour is very willing to accept of your land at the Natural bridge on the terms you propose—but he does not know the boundery—and wishes you to send him a copy of the courses &c—as he supposes trespasses have been committed—

I enquired of the Sherif he informed me there are three years taxes due on your land—$2.91

For future trespasses if they should be made—perhaps it might be well to direct Patrick Henry how to proceed—

Yours &c
Andw Alexander

Paid Patrick Henry for Taxes, November 14, 1817

Cate for 3. turkey polts 1.
Recd. from Joel Yancey 18.25 in part proceeds of a hhd. tobo. of mine he has sold at Lynchbg. @ 8½ D. pr. Cwt.
Gave E. W. Randolph at Greenlee's 2.D.
Natural Bridge. pd. to Patrick Henry 4D. to be pd. to the Sher. of Rockbridge for taxes past & toc om.—gave him 1.D.

Tadeusz Kościuszko to TJ

Editors' Translation

My dear Respectable Friend Solothurn 15. September 1817.

We are all getting older, which is why, my dear and respectable friend, I am asking if you would arrange (since you have the full power) that, after the death of our worthy friend Mr. Barnes, someone just as honest takes his place, so that I will punctually receive the interest on my capital, of which you know the unchanging destination after my death. As for the present, do as you think best. I much appreciate and am very grateful for your kind invitation, but my country is quite dear to my heart, as are my friends and acquaintances, and it pleases me to advise them sometimes. I am the only real Pole in Europe; all the others, because of their circumstances, are subject to different powers. You may perhaps tell me that this is the most miserable condition. Yes, without a doubt, but that is precisely why they need advice. My dear and respectable friend, one can be independent anywhere when one thinks well, reasons well, has a good heart, is humane, and has a firm, upright, and open character, which always confounds the most astute diplomat and the most deceitful, cunning, and base people. You are aware of the proclamations in which the powers promise liberal constitutions to their people. They keep making pledges that will vanish like dust carried off by the wind. Your canal from Lake Erie to the Hudson River astonishes everyone in Europe but me, who knows your fellow citizens so well. I have always known them to be great in everything they do. You are happier than Europeans, thanks to your government, which is closer to human nature, and to the immense distance separating you from the other powers. This should not prevent the establishment of a large civil-military school in your country under the immediate supervision of a congressional commission. Pay my respects to Mr. Monroe, your president. I do not tire of repeating to him the absolute necessity for this school.

I embrace you a thousand times, not in the French way, but from the bottom of my heart. Accept the assurance of my high consideration T Kosciuszko

John Armstrong to TJ

Dear Sir Red Hook 4 Jan 1818.

Some years before I left Paris Gen. Kosciuszko put into my hands the paper, of which the enclosed is a copy. Understanding that it was not to be used 'till the General's death, it has been in my cabinet unopened from that day 'till this & is now recurred to on the information brought by the mails of the day that the Genl had died in Switzerland on the 15th of Oct last & that his funeral was celebrated in Paris on the 31st of that month. I beg to know from your kindness, whether you have any information from Switzerland or France, in relation to this event & (if it corresponds with mine) what other steps if any besides furnishing the original documents will be necessary or proper to give effect to the Generals will so far as my son is concerned? The young man is now fifteen or sixteen years old.

I beg you Sir, to accept assurances of my great respect and esteem (Signed) John Armstrong

Enclosure: Will of Tadeusz Kościuszko

Know all men by these presents that I Tharde Kosciusko formerly an officer of the United States of America in their Revolutionary War against Great Britain, & a Native of Lituanie in Poland, at present residing at Paris do hereby will & direct that at my decease the sum of Three thousand seven hundred & Four Dollars Currency of the aforesaid United States shall of right be possessed by & delivered over to the full enjoyment & use of Kosciusko Armstrong the son of Genl John Armstrong Minister Plenipotentiary of said States at Paris; for the security & performance whereof, I do hereby instruct and authorize my only lawful Executor in the said United States, Thomas Jefferson President thereof to reserve in trust for that special purpose, of the Funds he already holds belonging to me, the aforesaid sum of Three thousand seven hundred & four Dollars in principal to be paid by him the said Thomas Jefferson immediately after my decease to him the aforesaid Kosciusko Armstrong & in case of his death to the use & benefit of his surviving Brothers.

Given under my hand & seal at Paris this twenty eighth day of June One thousand eight hundred & six.

Thade Kosciuszko
In presence of
Charles Carter,
James M Morris

TJ to Edward Graham

[Sir] Monticello Mar. 10. 18.

I am indebted to you for your favor of Jan. 24. and the courses of my lands at the Natural bridge. I will certainly be there in autumn with a view to the running and settling my lines with my neighbors, and shall ask your assistance; but as there is no reason why you should lie till then out of the fee for your past service, I now inclose you a five dollar bill, which I trust will go safe by mail.

I take the liberty of putting under the protection of your cover a letter for Patrick Henry, living near the bridge, in the hope he may get it safely from Lexington. I pray you to accept the assurance of my esteem & respect. Th: Jefferson

TJ to Patrick Henry (of Rockbridge County)

Th: Jefferson to mr Patrick Henry. Monticello Mar. 10. 18.

Having recieved no answer from Dr Thornton to my offers to let him off of the lease of the Bridge, I consider the lease as continuing. I pray you therefore to do nothing with any of his works in consequence of my conversations with you while I expected he would give up the lease and to consider those works as still at his sole command. I shall certainly be with you in autumn to get my lines settled. I salute you with my best wishes.

Peter J. Zeltner to TJ

Editors' Translation

Sir, [received 30 Oct. 1818]

Having had the privilege of enjoying for more than twenty years the very special friendship of the illustrious deceased, who spent more than fifteen years in my home, I could not ignore the amicable relationship he cultivated with you. A friendship based on mutual respect could not help but endure; I am therefore certain that the news of his unexpected death will distress you. In response to the wishes of the Emperor of Russia, he had left in May 1815 to confer with him in Vienna regarding the fate of Poland. From Vienna he came back to Solothurn, Switzerland, where he stayed at my brother's house while waiting on circumstances to decide whether he should go to his homeland or return here to the refuge he had selected for himself. He was about to choose the latter when death took him away from both his homeland and his numerous friends, among whom I know you are in the first rank. This consideration has made it my duty to announce this sad news to you directly.

As General Kosciuszko has disposed of most of his fortune in favor of my children, nieces, brothers, and sister-in-law, and since

I am, moreover, very close to his relatives, whom I intend to visit in Poland, I ask that you please send me the details of the funds he left in your hands and other effects of which you may have knowledge; you will be greatly obliging one who has the honor to be, with esteem and high consideration

Sir Your very humble and
obedient servant
P J Zeltner

Hannah to TJ

Master November 15th 1818

I write you a few lines to let you know that your house and furniture are all safe as I expect you would be glad to know I heard that you did not expect to come up this fall I was sorry to hear that you was so unwell you could not come it greive me many time but I hope as you have been so blessed in this that you considered it was god that done it and no other one we all ought to be thankful for what he has done for us we ought to serve and obey his commandments that you may set to win the prize and after glory run

master I donot my ignorant letter will be much encouragement to you as know I am a poor ignorunt creature, this leaves us all well

adieu, I am your humble sarvant

Hannah

John V. Henry (for Patrick Henry [of Rockbridge County]) to TJ

Sir Lexington April 25th 1819

by request of my Brother Patrick Henry I write to inform you of his Dissagreeable situation respecting the house in which he lives. by your permision after your land was run by Mr Grahan & Mr Douthat he built him the house mention within a hundred & fifty yards of the Bridge and is now theatend by oltletree ares of haveing it taking from him to which he has devoted two years laber but he is satisfied in hopeing of seeing you soon he would come to your house but being so bisy plowing on the place Joining your land which he has rented prevents his comeing.

All best Your obedient
Servant
for Patrick Henry
Jno. V. Henry

TJ to John H. Cocke

Dear General Monticello May 3. 19.

It is really scandalous, after so liberal a supply of fish from you to ask a second donation. yet I am forced to it by the stupidity of the servant who in my absence was entrusted with the mission. instead of never stopping till he got home, night overtook him on the road, he encamped, and the water being unchanged thro' the night, he found the fish all dead on his awakening in the morning. my ponds being all in readiness, and the spawning season hastening away, I am obliged to renounce all modesty and ask your aid a second time. the servant now sent can be relied on never to stop till he delivers them into the pond.

Mr Stack is arrived from Philadelphia and will open his grammar school in Charlottesville this week. we have procured the female academy in which he will have a schoolroom, & Laporte will take the rest of it for a boarding house. I believe you may be assured he is the ablest classical teacher in America, and seems to be an amiable modest man. if your son is disengaged it is impossible to find a better situation for him. mr Brockenbrough is arrived and relieves my shoulders from a burthen too much for them. I propose to prove Kosciuzko's will in the district court on Monday and hope you will relieve me from that task. ever and affectionately yours

Th: Jefferson

John H. Cocke to TJ

Dear Sir, Bremo May 3d 1819

. . . I have also to inform you, that the difficulties which seem to stand in the way of carrying the design of Genl Kosiuscos will into execution—in the first place from the scarcity of Schools about me & 2dly from the prejudices to be encounterd in obtaining admission for negroes—to say nothing of the effect which might be produced on the minds of my own people—must induce me to decline the undertaking. I presume the terms of the Will give you no discretion that wou'd admit of your directing the fund to the accomplishment of the object in the way set forth in the inclosed paper—I however send you the paper, as I shou'd be glad to know your opinion as to the practicability of the scheme of the Colonization Society—I suppose you are in possession of the late information collected by Messrs Mills & Burgess on the Coast of Africa with a view to this object.—I am Sir Yours respectfully

J. H. Cocke

TJ to William Wirt

Dear Sir Monticello June 27. 19.

My letters of Jan. 5. and Nov. 10. of the last year had informed you generally that Genl Kosciuzko had left a considerable sum of money in the funds of the US. and had, by a will deposited in my hands, disposed of i[t] to a charitable purpose: & I asked the favor of your opinion in what court the will should be proved. according to that opinion, expressed in your favor of Dec. 28. I proved the will in our district court, renouncing the execut[or]ship. the purport of the will is that his whole funds in this country shall be laid out in the purchase of young negroes, in their education & their emancipation. I had formerly intended to get an admr appointed here with the will annexed, and to have the trust placed entirely under the direction of the court; but circumstances since occurring change my view of the case. Genl Armstrong, on behalf of his son Kosciuzko

Armstrong has a claim to 3704.D. which is well founded. a mr Zoeltner of Soleure [th]e friend in whose house Kosciuzko lived and died claims the wh[ole u]nder a will deposited with him. this I am persuaded will appear no[t to] reach the property here. a relation of the General's, has lately, through the minister of Russia, mr Poletika, claimed the whole also in right of his relationship. these claimants being all foreigners, or of another state, have a right to place the litigation in a federal court; and I have supposed the most convenient one to them would be the district court of Columbia: and my wish is to transfer it there, if that court will take cognisance and charge of it. I suppose they would name an Admr with the will annexed, and that he would require the claimants to interplead, that the court might decide the right. I wish therefore in the first place to constitute you general Counsel for the trust. you would draw your compensation of course from the funds of the testator, and that you would advise me in what form I must apply to the court to effect the transfer. I suppose by a petition to them in Chancery, delivering to them the will, and the original certificates, which are in my hands, and amount to 17,159.63 D, and praying to be entirely relieved and discharged from all further concern or responsibility. mr Barnes, who has been the agent in fact, will settle his account of transactions during the life of the General. I have none to settle: having never acted but thro' mr Barnes, and not meaning to charge little incidcntal disbursements incurred. will you undertake this my dear Sir, and inform me how I am to proceed? I shall be at Poplar Forest near Lynchburg before you recieve this, and shall be there 3. months. but your answer will reach me there, and I mention it only to explain beforehand the greater delays in the correspondence which the greater distance of that place may occasion. in the hope therefore of hearing from you as soon as convenient, and of your aid in getting relief from this charge, now become too litigious for [me,] I salute you with constant friendship and respect

Th: Jefferson

Ellen W. Randolph (Coolidge) to Martha Jefferson Randolph

Poplar Forest July 28th 1819

I received your letter of the 24th yesterday evening, my dearest Mother, three days after date, and this circumstance is particularly comforting to me, at a time when your state of health will keep me constantly anxious to hear of & from you regularly, and without any post-office delays. I have been thinking what an unpleasant day we spent on the road, the friday after leaving you, and at that time I thought nothing could have increased the discomforts of my situation; but how totally all personal considerations would have been forgotten, if I could then have known that you were in a state of sickness and suffering.

Jefferson's attentions are just what I should have expected from his devoted attachment to you; an attachment which all your children feel to a degree that makes it a ruling passion—how much pleasure it gives me, especially when I am separated from you, to recollect all the claims which you have to our devoted gratitude and affection & to feel that your cares are repaid, as far as our utmost tenderness can repay them; and "still paying still to owe" is the most delightfull of all obligations in such a case as this. Grandpapa and myself are in the habit of sitting, some time after dinner, in conversation, upon different subjects, and it was but the other day, that, speaking of education, & the influence exerted by mothers over their children, he paid to his grandchildren the compliment of all others the most valuable, that of alluding indirectly to what he considers their excellences, and ascribing them to education and the influence of example.

Cornelia and myself have been quite industrious since we arrived here, and the pleasure we take in each others society, our free & unrestrained conversations, are the best proofs of the slow—but sure advancement of the union you have sometimes spoken to me of and considered so desirable. had it taken place sooner or more suddenly between characters and tempers so different, it would have been a plant of forced and perhaps sickly growth, but its gradual development will give time for the roots to strike deep; I do not think the firmest attachments are those which are the affect of habit, and that sort of consciousness of the excellencies of the object, which arises rather from their never having been disputed by others, than by any investigation of our own. I have never under-valued Cornelia, although she perhaps may have thought so, and mistaken eagerness of manner and impetuosity of temper for an affectation of superiority—if these suspicions have ever existed, time and the development of character on each side, will do them away, thus removing real injustice on one side and the appearance of it on the other.

With all my wishes and all my efforts to make the best use of my time whilst here, I have not yet done much. we have had some interruptions from company, and one, much more serious, from the dangerous illness of Burwell. the little house-keeping which this threw on our hands, was too trifling to be taken into the account of time, but I lost many hours from real anxiety, I might almost say unhappiness, for the life of a servant so faithfull, so attached and so usefull to my dear Grandfather, was of sufficient value to justify very acute feelings. the complaint was an obstruction in the bowels which refused to give way to any remedies, untill Dr Steptoe tried bleeding him untill he fainted or very nearly fainted. I never saw any one suffer more; he had been sick some time before he gave up his usual employments, and then it was some days before a physician could be procured. our simple remedies & those recommended by Dr Steptoe, (whilst Burwell was still well enough to go to his house to consult him,) thinking it an ordinary cholic, had all failed—he had been two nights without closing his eyes; on the third I sent him a small dose of laudanum, (the doctor had told him he might make use of it to abate the violence of the pain), and it appeared to me impossible for any body to suffer such agonies for such a length of time without danger of inflammation and mortification; this produced the desired effect of giving him a quiet night, but the cause was not removed, the pain returned, and a day or two after, the doctor found the danger so pressing as to devote almost two days to him, although his own brother was very ill at the time. I never saw any body more uneasy than Grandpapa, and his constant anxiety by convincing me still more of his extraordinary value for Burwell, increased my own fears and feelings to a degree that surprized even myself. I had taken it into my head from the beginning that the disease was a billious cholic and consequently very serious—but I did not know what was necessary to be done, no help was at hand, and I thought very frequently, good god! if he should perish for want of assistance. He is still weak from the effects of the bleeding, but I hope completely out of danger & has gone to work glazing again, although he cannot do much at any thing as yet. John Hemmings paid him attentions which were really affecting, I always believed him an excellent creature but I think better of him now then ever. I really believe that at one time his advice and application of a warm bath, by the temporary relief it procured, enabled Burwell to stand against the violence [of the] complaint untill the doctor's assistance was at last obtained. I d[o think] Grandpapa Cornelia and myself make as complete a trio of ignoram[us]es as I do know. and I do not believe our three heads combined contain as much medical knowledge as would save a sparrow. I am determined to qualify myself for taking a degree as soon as I go home. I must not forget to tell you that Israel has shone, during B.s illness—has kept himself as clean and genteel as possible, and in the pride of being chief waiter has followed Miss Edgeworth's Hamilton's rules, of doing every thing in its proper time, putting every thing to its proper use, and every thing in its proper place, with as much exactness, as if he had studied them with every desire of edification. Grandpapa is quite delighted, and I am obliged to abuse Israel every day to prevent him from thinking hereafter, that the complaints I have no doubt we shall have cause to make, are without foundation—is not this being very prudent and shewing great judgement and forethought.

Mrs Radford has as usual been very attentive to C—and myself. Mrs Yancey is lying in with her sixth child, (which with the other five) enjoys good health and a prospect of life. she is but six and twenty and likely to share in the glory of the fair young lady mentioned by lady Montague who having brought forth thirty living children, was so unfortunate as to be stopped short in her career, by the corpulence of too gross health. Mrs Y. is not likely to be checked by the same cause.

Adieu my dearest Mother my letters are too too long, and as much as I regret this defect, I almost despair of ever correcting it, although I know it is one of those things to which I should force myself; for an indefatigable pen, is full as impertinent as too long a tongue. I must however thank you for all the trouble you have taken about the Folia; I only wish I could put it to immediate profit. Be so good as to send us some ink & paper by the carpenters; our latin exercises, spanish verbs &c take a great deal independent of letter writing. Kiss my precious George for me and give my love to all the girls and boys. I shall write to Aunt R—if I have time. Remember me to Jane & Jefferson, and if Sarah has come up offer her my sincerest congratulations on her returning health. Remember me also to Mrs Trist & Aunt Marks, a great deal of love to my dear Papa and kisses to Septimia. for yourself my dearest Mother you know too well what my feelings are to render any expression of them necessary.

TJ to Martha Jefferson Randolph

My dearest Martha Pop. For. July 28. [1819]

I have just learned from the Enquirer the death of my old & valuable friend Cathalan of Marseilles, an important loss to me, & at this time particularly requiring attention, as my orders are now on the way to him for the supplies of the year, & the money to pay for them. but I can do nothing without his papers which I request you to send me. in my Cabinet, & in the window on the right of my writing table you will see 4. or 5. cartoons of papers. the 2d & 3d of these contain a compleat set of alphabeted papers, and in the 2d where the alphabet begins you will find Cathalan's papers in one or more bundles, for I believe they are in more than one. the latest of these in point of date is the one I want. if it includes the present & last year or two it will be sufficient. be so good as to send it by the 1st mail of which the girls apprise you. we should have felt great uneasiness at your sickness had not the same letter informed us of your convalescence. we have been near losing Burwell by a stricture of the upper bowels; but he has got about again and is now only very weak. bless all the young ones for me, and be blessed yourself.

Th: Jefferson

John Hemmings to TJ

Dear Sir poplar forest sunday Sep. 26th 1819

i am veary sorrowey to inform you that the flat roof over the hall Lakes veary bad wensday 22th we had a raine for 24 ourers Cleard off on thursday at sun rise and naver stop driping untill 10 oClock in the day the havyis leake is in the Center and Coms out right at the face of the trimmng Sir remember that the bothom of the guttur joists is Lavell on the under side and now is swaged from 2 to 3 inches in the Center and i think the water will make its way to the lowis place it Cawis one leak in the Parlour and allso in the north west Lodging room i am in hopes it may bee freed at the ends by Copper or Cheet iron but it is much trubbel to remove the Plinth for that is naild to the floer all had better Stand till you Coms

I am your obedient Sirvent
John Hemmings

John Hemmings to TJ

dear sir wnsday oct. 20. 19 Popler forest

i hav fenich the ballourstrating and the hanging of the Partitons doors. and bed room. I am now abut the shetters i hav pine enough for stils and reals of 6 windowrs i have got them al radey to put togatehear that is the motison and tenionten i am now giting the in sid suff reddy we hav anough poplar but have it to slit with the saw but as it is seaisond we reather have it for fear of scrinking that is all the pine plank we hav hear Mr yeancey sayes that he cand get som that is enough to do the remandour I shell go on as farst as possebil—the roof has never leake is bad sence the first rain but that was vary havy but at the same time the house had bin dry on the hold it may git better of it self by weating on it awhill

I am your servent
John hemmings

John Hemmings to TJ

Sir popler forest Nov. 2th 19

I am going on as you request with the blinds one paire at a time I am now got 20 single flights radey for hangin these is only aenugh to cloes 4 windours I hav pine enugh to do the hol of them. mr yancey sent 50 feet & 40 fe we found in the north portico. I dont thinke you evr get the locks & hinges for these starway doors ef you hav you did not lev them out hear. the sheet iron cheese & cracers is come saff & Put away we hav had no rain to make its way though the celing senc the first & seiont I am veary douptfull of the hinges anywear in a good Perpurs you mad mentaion of hangin or waiting 2 of Them toghether the windours veary so much as to wedth from ¼ to ¾.I ef these put on 1 sirfest tha will be trubblesom to git right ef tha ant made with much corecness & at the best it will be a pussel nase says that he is de Prived of garding seed by the hale wishes you to be hented of them i hav spent a grat deel of Dissatisfaction by you not being able to return but i hop you will soon get the better of it

I am
John hemings your
Servents

TJ to John Hemmings

Th: Jefferson to John Hemings. Nov. 14. 19.

Your letter of the 2d got to Charlottesville last night only. with respect to the doors of the stairways I have the locks & bolts at Poplar Forest, but they cannot be got at in my absence. I have not hinges, and therefore request mr Yancey to get them and screws at Lynchburg, and I would have you hang the doors immediately. the locks may be put on next year, and you had better screw the hinges to the doorposts rather slightly that they may be the easier taken down hereafter to let in the locks. in the meantime you can make a temporary fastening by bars so as not to deface the door or architrave

In your letter of Octob. 20. you say you had blinds for 6. windows in hand, and in that of Nov. 2. you say 4 are done. 2 of these I suppose are for the parlour, & the other 2. should be for the girls room which needs them most. the cart now carries you the irons, and you had better hang the 4. that are done immediately; and then finish what others you have in hand and hang them. ¾ Inch wood screws must be got from Lynchburg. my bedroom will want the next blinds after the girls room. if you will fix a day by which you can be sure to have the work in hand finished I will then send for you; that is to say when the stair doors shall be hung, th[e] blinds already finished hung, and those in hand finished & hung. the cart carries a map which must have the straw taken off & the map pu[t] into one of the close rooms where the rats cannot get at it. it is to bring down the dried fruit, one firkin of butter, and the cheese which went there from Richmond, which would not keep to the spring. the cart must stay but one day there. Farewell

John Hemmings to TJ

Dear sir Poplar Forest Nov. 18th 19.

i resev your Latter thise evning with grat Pleasure. I hav got 7 saets don radey for hangin, & al the rest put to gather, & pind up; that is for 12 windows wich ar exspoesd to Dangeour. i am now geting the in side stuff rady for them all I Dont think it wold be wll for me to take my hands off of them, untill I fenish them all. for i heav al my tools in odder fore doing them. i am in hopes to hav all rady in side of 10 Days. as soon as I can range the besness, i shold hav the stuff got fore the Doors, & do them. night before Last, about mid night, tha came up a brisk rain, & it awoked me, & i got up, & Lite a candel, & wnte up stars, & it was Lekin badly, & i sot up until Day Light, & went on the roofe of the house & take off the shuters, & rased up the Plank, & examond for the vner, but it raind so hard al Day, untill we got so weet, that we had to cum down, & middol of the Day it hild up, & at et we went agin, & the Places that Lake was 7 of the gutter gists. these being dug out by a parsel of wood munders, with out cear or tention; I made them a gagh, wich oddard in deapth 2.I.¼ all the way from one end to the other, & in stide of thist, i find 6. of them at the sholders 4.I.½ and at the outer end the 2.I.¼. I begind at the outter end, as well as i could, & dige them out, beginning at 2.I.¼ & running out to nothing, that is to the sholder. thist bearly freed the water off. for pruf the weater was. 2.I. in deph at the sholdar, & dry at the outter end. i freed them all and, by Diging the gutter out, unttil the weater folard me. i Put under the ends of sum, reamalents of sheet iron, that we had here, with out cuting the new atal. at the sholdars i find sum cracs; those i buthd with toe & puttey. thars not one drop of water cums in no whear about the sash. the water cant be sents off better. the woodin work, al round the sash, was as Dry as Punk. i am in hops you will take this as on eye witness. now, with what has bin don with others, I may be able to Put a stop to it. here is one thing you may wish to know, wither the water over floes the sholders, or no, bifore i Dug them out, i toke up a bucket of water, & pourde in preatey bresk, & it cam up Levl with the top, and begand to run over; but affter i finish in Digeing of them, i bringes all out at the end, & Lev the shoulder Dry. this is a true statement of the detestable vner.—

i hav put the mape a way safe in the young Ladis room

I remand your servent
John hemings

TJ to John Hemmings

Th: Jefferson to John Hemings. Monticello Nov. 27. 19.

Your letter by Henry is recieved, and I am very glad indeed that the cause of the leak is discovered—miss no opportunity of every possible further search whenever rain falls, because if the cause can be unquestionably ascertained, we can remedy i[t.] I would have you first hang the blinds which are finished, that is the 7-sets which you say are done. then finish and hang the remaining 5. which you had put together. hang also the stair doors as before directed, and put the spinning machine into perfect good order. this last is the most important of all, as the want of it obliges me this year to buy some hundreds of yards of shirting which that might have spun.

Write to me every Wednesday, & put your letter the same day into the post office of New London or Lynchburg & it will be sure to be in Charlottesville on Saturday evening. in these letters state to me exactly what work is done, & what you will still have to do, and endeavor to guess at a day by which you think it may all be finished, that I may be ready to send for you by that day. if after all is finished, you should have a little time to spare before the cart arrives, employ yourself on the 2. blinds of the North Portico. these will need only half blinds, to wit, over the lower sash to prevent people seeing into the rooms. fare[well.]

let me know how the window irons answer.

John Hemmings to TJ

Dear sir Poplar forest Dec. 2th 19

I hav close the 12 windows & put all the fastenings on them I am now going on with the doors those i am in hops to finish by Sunday 12th i hav examiond the spining mechin and the is nothing weanting in the world but Cleaning the gum of of the sildinders wich the spindels run in tha wants oil our travileng cart wheels has bin going from time to time that tha at thist time ont bear thear own weight I shold be detaind a Day or so about them but that is concluded in the time apinted i shold repare them so as to bring us Down ef possible i expect to get Don on the 11th Sunday which is 12th i should be puting evry thing a way & Pacting up my things i should be ready for starting on monday at Day Light Sir pleas to put henry in mind of one collar & one Pair of hames for the muel that draws be fore an exelente pair he will jit by replying to Priscilla hangin up in my Cabin the collar he will git els where al the rest of the gear is here

I am you obedient servent
John Hemings

John Hemmings to TJ

Dear sir Poplar forest Dec 8th 19.

your letter of nov. 27th got to me on Dec. 3. with respect to the windows al the irons answers very well exept the one in the center wich the pin passes thro that dos not go free the one puls contrary to the other but it is oing to the rughness of them as yet but when the com to weare a lettle tha will fit better as to the opening back to the wall tha Lays flat agins the face of the weall & Lays well to the face of the sash I think tha ar rether to slender ef the across tassels had one hold mor be tewen the socket & the other three tha wold be much studer but tha dose very well as the is the openings of these doors weare 48. Is: & the doors only 44. I hav got new gambes of 2. inchs thickness & flush them out to resore both door & sash I have put up the gambes and the architravs but tha can not return on the top on the out side fore fear of being obstructive to the Light of the sash tha runs up from the bothom to the top & buts agains the Plaster as it is I had to reduse the emposts down to 3 inches on the inside tha shoe 3 inchs but the out side only 2. inchs i am readey for feting up the doors and hanging them I still keep the Day in vue of seting out from Poplar forest for monticello that is on the 13th. I expect Henry is near Poplar forest by thist time I shuld do the spining machine at eny rate what it wants don to it

I am your obedient servent
John Hemings

TJ to William Wirt

Dear Sir Monticello Feb. 5. 20.

It would require a longer letter than my health enables me to write, to detail to you the obstacles which have so long delayed the transmission to you of the papers of Genl Kosciuzko. ill health on my part has had it's share, unsuccesful efforts to withdraw the original will in the General's own handwriting from the court in which it was recorded, and other untoward obstacles, have never till yesterday permitted me to recieve finally an official copy of the will with the necessary authentications. I hasten to get rid of it, and to place it under your management altogether. I inclose also the papers which will explain to you three claims on the property which have been presented to me. Genl Armstrong's for 3704.D. given to his son, mr Zeltner's for the whole property, and that for the whole property also of a Majr Estko of Polan[d], a nephe[w] of Genl Kosciuzko. the property consists of 4600.D. [in s]hares of the bank of Columbia; of two sums of 11,363.63 D and 1136.36 D of 6. percent stock of the US. in all 17,100.D. and 2. or 3. years dividends or intere[st] on that sum; the certificates of which are in my possession. of these I shall be happy to be relieved as soon as possible by their delivery to any person who shall be authorised to recieve them by whatev[er] court you shall place this case in. I acted for the General under a very full power of Attorney, which (as my vocations did not permit me to undertake details) authorised me to constitute an attorney or agent under me. I accordingly appointed mr John Barnes, who has done the whole business from the beginning: and who, with his vouchers, being on the spot with you, will render to the admr who shall be appointed with the will annexed, a full account of our administrati[on.] in this I have had no part but in the way of general advice & instruction. that his conduct in every thing has been pure faithfull & diligent his accounts as well as character will sufficiently prove

I must pray you to read my letter to mr Politika (who acts for Majr Estko by instructions from his government) which, with what I have formerly written to you, will, as a supplement to this letter, give you a compleat account of the course I have pursued since the death of Genl Kosciuzko. the original letter from him to me of Sep. 15. 1817. quoted in mine to mr Politika, is deposited in the court with the original will as additional proof, by similitude of handwriting, that the will is autograph.

I salute you with affectionate esteem & respect.
Th: Jeffers[on]

TJ to Patrick Henry (of Rockbridge County)

Sir — Poplar Forest. Oct. [22]. 21.

I should long ago have been at the Natural bridg[e] to have my lines there ascertained, but that during the years 19. and 20. I was in a state of low health which rendered it impossible. I am now as well as usual, altho not absolutely well. but if no change occurs I shall try to go to the bridge. I shall set out for Albemarle in 3 days; where however I shall stay not more than a week and endeavor to be back here about the 6th or 7th of November, and on the 11th I will be at mr Greenlee's perhap[s] in time to go on to the bridge and take measures for sendi[ng] to ask mr Graham's attendance with as little delay as possible for my stay will be short. these dates may be varied a little by bad weather.

If the dam below the bridge has not been opened so as to let off the stagnant water and clear the bridge of it below, I shall ask your aid in procuring what laborers you think necessary to do it while I am there. I salute you with my best wishes.

Th: Jefferson

John Hemmings to TJ

dear sir Poplar forest Nov 29th 1821

I am sorry to complain to you so near the close of my worck above all things on earth I hate complants but I am bledg I hav bin going to Poplar forest sevrield falls and that is not the seson for raseing eny kind of vegetable and the very moment your back is turnd from thee Place nace takes evry thing out of the garden and carries them to his cabin and buryis them in the grownd and says that tha ar for the use of the house I dont set up my self for the things thats made for your table but as common a thing as greens wich we ar suffering for tha ware mour or Lest of 2000. I replyd three or four tims and it Perveald not the pipel tels me that he makes market of them at the first oppertunity all ways that is the resond he ont giv eny such conduct as this is to wrongfully and unjustly commeted in my setuation I am at worck in the morning by the time I can see and the very same at night I have got the cornest nealy don I am bout the tow Last members dentels and quearter rownd I shuld Put an architrav on the skie Light frame befour I take the scafful down it will be 16 inchs Leving the first fase on the frame and Planting on the twelve inches this is ½ Inch thick and the og Planted on it Sir Plese to answear this by writing to mr Yeancey Sir I aam your faithful sirvent John Hemmings

John Hemmings to TJ

sir Dec tusday 11th 21

Plese to examon the boy befor he Leves hear that he starts right he must Carey the same mules a collar fore each and one Pair of tuge harnes all the rest of the things is at Poplar forest I shul be ready to Leave poplar forest on the 18th ate any rate I shud wish the boy to gite to popla forest on the 17th earley a noughf fore an earley starte the naxe day puting the architrave on the skey Light has made all the in provement amagenible I have fenish the roome all to a Little of the ser base which I shul geit Done in 2 days mour the boys is Dressing the shingels and the othar gobs be four me

sir
I am your servant
John Hemings

TJ to John Hemmings

Th Jefferson to John Hemings Tuesday Dec. 18. 21.

Your letter was dated Tuesday the 11th. came in the mail to Charlottesville Saturday night the 15th. I recieved it the next day 16th and it requested the mules to be at Poplar Forest on Monday (yesterday) the 17th which was impossible. it moreover rained all day yesterday and last night. the boys set off this morning.

I desired Jefferson to tell you to make out a bill of scantling for exactly such another barn as that at Poplar Forest that the stuff might be carried immediately to Capt Martin's to be sawed. the Carpenters will go up in the spring to build it. Lilburne has a hurt on his leg which will disable him from walking back. Eston must drive the cart therefore and Lilburne stay and come in the waggon.

Anonymous to TJ

Sir Boston July 20th 1821

Excuse me of taking the liberty to send you one of the papers inclosed within concerning the African Abolition of Slave Trade

ENCLOSURE: ANONYMOUS DESCRIPTION OF "CELEBRATION OF FREEDOM" BY AFRICAN AMERICANS IN BOSTON, JULY 16, 1821

On Monday the Africans, and descendants of Africans, in this town, held their annual commemoration of the commencement of measures for the abolition of the Slave Trade. A respectable procession passed through many streets, (which were nearly as much thronged as they are on Election and Independent days, or as when President Monroe, and some of our Naval Worthies passed them in procession) to the African meeting-house. The Rev. Hosea Ballou delivered the discourse this year. A dinner was served up in the African school-house. The blessing was craved by the Rev. Thomas Paul and thanks returned by Mr. Samuel Snowden. Every thing was conducted with decency and order, and the company retired to their homes two hours before sunset.

The following Toasts were given:—

Wilberforce, Pitt, Fox, Clarkson, Grenville, Benezet, Woolman, Dickson, Marquis de la Fayette, Brissot, Claviere, Washington, Franklin, Adams, Hancock, Jefferson, Madison, Monroe—Names in the old and new world, which Africans and descendants of Africans will long have reason to remember.

The ever memorable vote for the Abolition of the Slave Trade in 1807. *which was carried in the House of Lords in the affirmative,* 100 *to* 16 *and in the Commons* 286 *to* 16. The deed is registered in Heaven—the mandate is gone forth—Africa must and shall be free.

Africa.—She is free—when a nation of Africans can vindicate their claims to mental equality in the community of civilized man.

The late report of the Legislature of Massachusetts on the subject of "Free Blacks." We wish the Gentlemen Committee a better acquaintance with us.—For our characters, we refer to the merchants of Long, Central, and India wharves, and to those citizens, in whose families many of us have lived a great number of years, and from all whom we derive support for ourselves, our wives and our little ones.

The Orator of the day.—He has discoursed to us upon the principles of our Independence. May we at all times be found acting in accordance with them.

The memory of Abiel Smith—Through his munificence, aided by the School Committee of the town of Boston, ample provision is made for our African Free School.

His Excellency Gov. Brooks.—Long may he live to enjoy the gratitude of the people of this great State.

His Honor Lt. Gov. Phillips—The charity meetings held in our African Church have witnessed, that his high station does not prevent him from worshiping at the same altar, and casting in of his abundance to the same box with Africans.

The Christian Religion—It is shewn in its true spirit when Ministers of every denomination cheerfully take their turns to discourse to us upon the great events which terminated in breaking the fetters of slavery.

Our Procession this day.—A proof of the good order of the inhabitants of the Head Quarters of correct principles.

The Municipal Authorities of this ancient metropolis.—Able administrators of wise and wholesome regulations—may we never be found deficient in a due observance of them.

The Laws of the Land.—As good subjects, may Africans strive to live peaceably with all men—render unto Caesar the things which are Caesar's and unto God the things which are God's.

The Report of the Committee on "Free Blacks."—Africans may securely rest under their own vine and their own fig tree, when their cause is in the hands of that elegant, spirited, and Christian, "*L'Ami des Noirs.*" Boston, July 16th, 1821.

Benjamin Lear to TJ

Sir, Washington 19 Sept 1821.

Mr Wirt has probably informed you that he had transfered to me the papers wh: you sent him relative to the Estate of Genl Kosciuszko, and requested me to administer upon it, as you had desired him to transfer it to Some other person, if he could not himself conveniently undertake it.—

I have now the honor to inform you; Sir, that I have received Letters of administration with the will annexed, after having given

Bond with the most Satisfactory Security for the faithful performance of the trust. my object therefore in troubling you with this letter, Sir, is to request that you will be so good as to furnish me with the certificates of the Stock held by Genl K. both in the Public funds & the Bank of Columbia, that I may lay them before the appraizers appointed by the Orphan's Court, to ascertain the value of the personal Estate left by Genl K.

As this is a trust of considerable importance, & one in wh: you, Sir, must feel Some interest, I will avail myself of this occasion, (altho' I may obtrude a longer letter upon you than I ought,) to mention the manner in wh: I intend to proceed. As I am sensible that nothing so much embarrasses the faithful execution of such trusts, as the converting property into money & then suffering the funds to mingle indiscriminately with others, & become liable to be divested to other uses, until they are at length irretrievable, I have resolved, upon receiving the Certificates of Stock, & after an appraizment of it, to deposit them in the hands of one of my sureties in the Bond & there let them remain till the Court shall order a sale of some of the Stock. I shall thus place the funds far enough out of my own reach, to avoid the embarrassment above mentioned, and what is scarcely less dangerous, in these peculiar days of immoral influences, the temptation wh: no one ought to encounter unnecessarily, since we have seen how many strong men have yielded.—

In addition to the public notice in the newspapers of my administration, I have, already written to Genl Armstrong & he has appointed Counsel to prosecute his claim in the Orphan's Court here.—I shall notify Mr Politica, on his return to this place, to take a similar step in behalf of Major Estuo, the nephew of Genl K.—& shall write by the first opportunity to Mr Zeltner, to prosecute his claim.—For I am resolved to decide nothing myself in relation to the several claims but let them interplead & contest them in the Orphan's Court, taking appeals if they please, to a superior tribunal, & not to pay one Dollar to any one, without the authority & order of the Court, that I may exonerate myself & sureties from all future responsibility not only legal but moral.—

If none of the claims shd be allowed by the Court, then a question may arise how far the will can be executed compatibly with the Laws of Virginia & Maryland,—wh: regard with jealousy the education of that description of persons, to the extent provided for by the Will. If the will shd be defeated on such ground, the funds would probably be subject to a Law of Maryland wh: provides, that all funds remaining in the hands of Executors or administrators & wh: cannot be appropriated legally to any other purpose, shall go into the fund for the support of schools.—In any event I shall always avail myself of the Counsel of my good friend Mr Wirt, and your own, if you will permit me, Sir, to do so, not only in this particular, but in any other emergency wh: may arise in the progress of the business.—

I called to day upon the worthy Mr Barnes. He offers me Every facility in his power & promises me an account of his transactions, in the business, as soon as I shall receive the Certificates of Stock. He speaks with enthusiasm of Genl Kosciuszko, and gave me as kind a reception as if I had been his relation, instead of his mere legal representative.— With the highest respect & esteem, I am, Sir, Your faithful & most ob: St:
Benjamin L. Lear

Example of Annual Gratuities to Burwell Colbert and John Hemmings

Oct. 1. Hhd. exp. 10.D.

2. Drew on B. Peyton for 50.D. favr. Jas. Leitch. See Aug. 16. Sep. 11.
Drew on do. for 70.D. in favor of Wolfe & Raphael.
Recd. of Isaac Raphael 50.D.
Pd. T. W. Maury 40.D. for Ben & Lewis. Entd. them Sep. 17.

Drew on B. Peyton for 145.44 favr. of Sheriff. taxes	137.44
Meeks's order	8.
	145.44

Recd. from Wm. Wertenbaker 68.20 in full of Gilmore's rent.
Gave ord. on Wolfe & Raphael for 20.D. favr. A. Garrett for my subscription to Mr. Hatch for the current year.
Cash in hand 94.26.
Gave my note to Pasquil Fretwell for 45.D. for a mule, payable at next court, viz. Nov. 5. Note this was pd. by Th:J.R. with money recd. from Dr. Everett.

3. Ned sewers 1.D. V. W. Southall a fee v. Gilmore's estate 5.D. Hhd. xp. 1.D.

4. Ellen for vales 2.D.
   Warren. Cobbs ferrge. & lodging 4.55.
5. Mrs. Flood's breakfast 2.50 Hunter's lodging &c. 5.87½.
   My taxes in Bedford this year are 139.54.
13. **Burwell gratuity 10.D.**
22. Drew on Colo. B. Peyton in favr. Sheriff of Bedford for 139.54 my taxes here now due.
25. **Gave J. Hemings gratuity 20.D.**

TJ to Joseph C. Cabell

Dear Sir Monticello July 4. 23.

About a month before the reciept of your favor of June 24. I had been requested to draw the plan of a jail for the county of Cumberland adapted to the requisitions of the late law. I send you a copy of it, with estimates of the cost. some articles of it are left blank, because I had no ready means of coming at their value; but this may be as well obtained with you as here. there is only one article of the estimate which may not be exact, to wit, the laying down the sheet iron floor. we had no experience of the expence of rivets, of which each floor will require 8. or 900, at 2.I. apart. as iron is rolled into sheets of various lengths, you should get them of 7.f as these will work up without waste and with fewest rivets.

The Literary board agreed to hold back 20. M. D. till Xmas. the Rotunda is rising nobly. the marble capitels for the Pavilions are now on their passage from New York to Richmond. they cost at the quarry 100 D. round. the expences by the time they get here will be 50. p. c. on that. the duty was 315.60D ever & affectly yours

Th: Jefferson

Enclosures: Drawing and Specifications for a Jail

[before 4 July 1823]

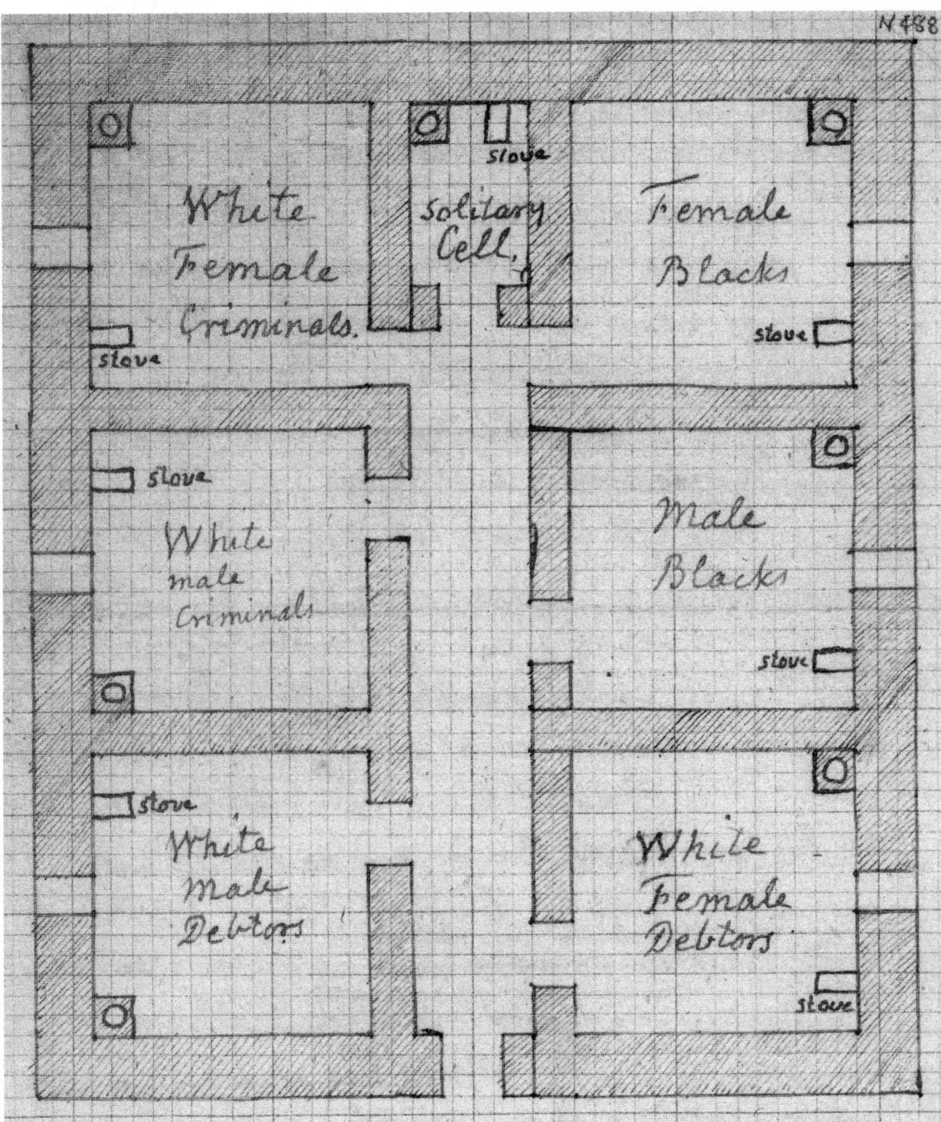

The necessary in each room should be a box with a hole in the top, and covered more over by a tight lid. behind it in the external wall should be an arch high & wide enough to draw out the ordure occasionally, which arch should be secured by a grated iron door. lime should almost daily be thrown into the feces to neutralise them.

a solitary cell is proposed to put ill behaved prisoners into occasionally, as a punishment.

The best way of securing the floors of the Criminal apartments is with blocks of rough stone 2. or 3. feet long, set up an end, in as even, close & solid order as possible, the interstices then filled with grout and gravel, and the top made smooth with mortar & gravel for the floor, and, for further security as well as cleanliness lay the floor over with sheet iron, it's edges lapped on one another and well riveted together.

A covering of tin costs 10.D. a square and will last for centuries. the cover of this building would be of 25. squares if of pediment pitch, to wit 10.f

suppose the foundation of the walls 3 f. the walls 9 f high.
let the outer walls be, their foundation 3½ bricks thick
their upper walls 3 br. thick
the partition walls their foundation 2½ bricks thick
their upper walls 2 br. thick
the outer walls 180 f. running measure
inner do 154 f.
they will take 137,844 bricks.
the floors of the 4. criminal rooms at 2 f depth take 45. perch stone and 584. sq. f. of sheet iron @ 18.D. pr sq.

	the iron.	105.D.
puttg on @ 4.D		23.36
		128.36

6. stoves open @ 15.D.

Will and Codicil of Thomas Jefferson, 1826

I Thomas Jefferson of Monticello in Albemarle, being of sound mind and in my ordinary state of health, make my last will and testament in manner and form as follows.

I give to my grandson Francis Eppes, son of my dear deceased daughter Mary Eppes, in fee simple all that part of my lands at Poplar Forest lying West of the following lines, to wit, Beginning at Radford's upper corner near the double branches, of Bear creek and the public road, & running thence in a straight line to the fork of my private road, near the barn, thence along that private road (as it was changed in 1817.) to it's crossing of the main branch of North Tomahawk creek, and, from that crossing, in a direct line over the main ridge which divides the North and South Tomahawk, to the South Tomahawk, at the confluence of two branches where the old road to the Waterlick crossed it, and from that confluence up the Northernmost branch (which separates McDaniel's and Perry's fields) to it's source, & thence by the shortest line to my Western boundary. And having, in a former correspondence with my deceased son in law John W: Eppes contemplated laying off for him with remainder to my grandson Francis, a certain portion in the Southern part of my lands in Bedford and Campbell, which I afterwards found to be generally more indifferent then I had supposed, & therefore determined to change it's location for the better; now to remove all doubt, if any could arise on a purpose merely voluntary & unexecuted, I hereby declare that what I have herein given to my sd grandson Francis is instead of, and not additional to that I had formerly contemplated.

I subject all my other property to the payment of my debts in the first place.

Considering the insolvent state of the affairs of my friend & son in law Thomas Mann Randolph, and that what will remain of my property will be the only resource against the want in which his family would otherwise be left, it must be his wish, as it is my duty, to guard that resource against all liability for his debts, engagements or purposes whatsoever, and to preclude the rights, powers and authorities over it which might result to him by operation of law, and which might, independantly of his will, bring it within the power of his creditors, I do hereby devise and bequeath all the residue of my property real and personal, in possession or in action, whether held in my own right, or in that of my dear deceased wife, according to the powers vested in me by deed of settlement for that purpose, to my grandson Thomas J. Randolph, & my friends Nicholas P. Trist, and Alexander Garrett & their heirs during the life of my sd son in law Thomas M Randolph, to be held & administered by them, in trust, for the sole and separate use and behoof of my dear daughter Martha Randolph and her heirs. and, aware of the nice and difficult distinctions of the law in these cases, I will further explain by saying that I understand and intend the effect of these limitations to be, that the legal estate and actual occupation shall be vested in my said trustees, and held by them in base fee, determinable on the death of my sd son in law, and the remainder during the same time be vested in my sd daughter and her heirs, and of course disposable by her last will, and that at the death of my sd son in law, the particular estate of the sd trustees shall be determined, and the remainder, in legal estate, possession and use become vested in my sd daughter and her heirs, in absolute property, for ever.

In consequence of the variety and undescribableness of the articles of property within the house at Monticello, and the difficulty of inventorying and appraising them separately and specifically, and it's inutility, I dispense with having them inventoried and appraised; and it is my will that my executors be not held to give any security for the administration of my estate. I appoint my grandson Thomas Jefferson Randolph my sole executor during his life, and after his death, I constitute executors my friends Nicholas P. Trist and Alexander Garrett, joining to them my daughter Martha Randolph after the death of my sd son in law Thomas M. Randolph.

Lastly I revoke all former wills by me heretofore made; and in witness that this is my will, I have written the whole with my hand on two pages, and have subscribed my name to each of them this 16th day of March one thousand eight hundred and twenty six

Th: Jefferson

I Thomas Jefferson of Monticello in Albemarle make and add the following Codicil to my will, controuling the same so far as it's provisions go.

I give to my good, affectionate, and faithful servant Burwell his freedom, and the sum of three hundred Dollars to buy necessaries to commence his trade of painter and glazier, or to use otherwise as he pleases. I give also to my good servants John Hemings and Joe Fosset their freedom at the end of one year after my death: and to each of them respectively all the tools of their respective shops or callings: and it is my will that a comfortable log-house be built for each of the three servants so emancipated on some part of my lands convenient to them with respect to the residence of their wives, and to Charlottesville and the University, where they will be mostly employed, and reasonably convenient also to the interests of the proprietor of the lands; of which houses I give the use of one, with a curtilage of an acre to each, during his life or personal occupation thereof.

I give also to John Hemings the service of his two apprentices, Madison and Eston Hemings until their respective ages of twenty one years, at which period respectively, I give them their freedom. and I humbly and earnestly request of the legislature of Virginia a confirmation of the bequest of freedom to these servants, with permission to remain in this state where their families and connections are, as an additional instance of the favor, of which I have received so many other manifestations, in the course of my life, and for which I now give them my last, solemn, and dutiful thanks.

In testimony that this is a Codicil to my will of yesterday's date, and that it is to modify so far the provisions of that will, I have written it all with my own hand, in two pages, to each of which I subscribe my name this 17th day of March one thousand eight hundred and twenty-six Th: Jefferson

Thomas Jefferson Randolph's Newspaper Advertisement for the Poplar Forest and Monticello Estate Sales

mr. jefferson's estate

We cannot forbear inviting the attention of the reader to the advertisement of the intended sale of Mr. Jefferson's property—We understand all that the Executor can controul has been brought forward for sale; and that the residue of the lands will be offered as soon as legal authority can be obtained for their disposition.— We are prompted to depart from our usual course, and to notice this advertisement. The sale which it announces is of no ordinary description!

executor's sale

will be sold on the premises, on the first day of January, 1827, that well known and valuable estate called Poplar Forest, lying in the counties of Bedford and Campbell, the property of Thomas Jefferson, dec. within eight miles of Lynchburg and three of New London;

also about 70 likely and valuable negroes, with stock, crops, &c. The terms of sale will be accommodating and made known previous to the day.

On the fifteenth of January, at Monticello, in the county of Albemarle; the whole of the residue of the personal property of Thomas Jefferson, dec., consisting of 130 valuable negroes, stock, crop, &c. household and kitchen furniture. The attention of the public is earnestly invited to this property. The negroes are believed to be the most valuable for their number ever offered at one time in the State of Virginia. The household furniture, many valuable historical and portrait paintings, busts of marble and plaister of distinguished individuals; one of marble of Thomas Jefferson, by Caracci, with the pedestal and truncated column on which it stands; a polygraph or copying instrument used by Thomas Jefferson, for the last twenty-five years; with various other articles curious and useful to men of business and private families. The terms of sale will be accommodating and made known previous to the day. The sale will be continued from day to day until completed. These sales being unavoidable, it is a sufficient guarantee to the public that they will take place at the times and places appointed.

Thomas J. Randolph
Executor of Th. Jefferson,
dec.

Published in the Richmond *Enquirer*, 3 Nov. 1826, and running unaltered until 20 Jan. 1827.

APPENDIX

RECOLLECTIONS OF PEOPLE ENSLAVED AT MONTICELLO

"Life of Isaac [Granger] Jefferson of Petersburg, Virginia, Blacksmith"

CHAP. 1

Isaac Jefferson was born at Monticello: his mother was named Usler (Ursula*) but nicknamed Queen, because her husband was named George & commonly called King George. She was pastry-cook & washerwoman: Stayed in the laundry. Isaac toated wood for her: made fire & so on. Mrs. Jefferson would come out there with a cookery book in her hand & read out of it to Isaac's mother how to make cakes tarts & so on.

Mrs. Jefferson was named Patsy Wayles,** but when Mr Jefferson married her she was the widow Skelton, widow of Batter (Bathurst) Skelton. Isaac was one year's child with Patsy Jefferson: she was suckled part of the time by Isaac's mother. Patsy married Thomas Mann Randolph.† Mr. Jefferson bought Isaac's mother from Col. Wm Fleming of Goochland. Isaac remembers John Nelson, an Englishman at work at Monticello: he was an inside worker, a finisher. the blacksmith was Billy Ore; (Orr?) the carriage-maker Davy Watson: he worked also for Col. Carter of Blenheim, eight miles from Monticello. Monticello-house was pulled down in part & built up again some six or seven times. One time it was struck by lightning. It had a Franklin rod at one eend. Old master used to say, "If it hadn't been for that Franklin the whole house would have gone." They was forty years at work upon that house before Mr Jefferson stopped building.

* There was a work published in 1862 by C. Scribner at New York, entitled: "The Private Life of Thomas Jefferson" from entirely new materials with numerous facsimiles, edited by Rev. Hamilton W. Pierson D. D. President of Cumberland College, Kentucky. This work consists of the reminiscences of a Captain Edmund Bacon who was overseer for Mr. Jefferson at Monticello for 20 years. The Captain's reminiscences were taken down from his lips by Dr. Pierson. The Captain mentions Ursula among the house-servants & says—: "She was Mrs. Randolph's nurse. She was a big fat woman. She took charge of all the children that were not in school. If there was any switching to be done. She always did it. She used to be down

at my house a great deal with those children. They used to be there so much that we often got tired of them: but we never said so. They were all very much attached to their nurse: they always called her 'Mammy.[']" Isaac in 1847 by his estimate upwards of seventy years old, was a big fat robust black man.

** Martha youngest daughter of John Wayles, a native of Lancaster, England, a lawyer, who lived at "the Forest" in Charles City county, Va. He was married three times & dying in May 1773 left three daughters one of whom married Francis Eppes, (Father of John W. Eppes who married Maria daughter of Thomas Jefferson) & the other Fulwar Skipwith. Mr. Jefferson inherited the Shadwell & Monticello estates. The portion that he acquired by marriage was encumbered with a (British) debt & resulted in a heavy loss. Martha Skelton was 23 years old in 1772 when she married Mr. Jefferson.

† Sometime Governor of Virginia.

CHAP. 2

Mr Jefferson came down to Williamsburg in a phaeton made by Davy Watson. Billy Ore did the iron-work.* That phaeton was sent to London & the springs &c was gilded. This was when Mr Jefferson was in Paris. Isaac remembers coming down to Williamsburg in a wagon at the time Mr Jefferson was Governor. He came down in the phaeton: his family with him in a coach & four. Bob Hemings drove the phaeton: Jim Hemings was a body-servant: Martin Hemings—the butler. These three were brothers: Mary Hemings & Sally, their Sisters. Jim & Bob bright mulattoes, Martin, darker. Jim & Martin rode on horseback. Bob went afterwards to live with old Dr Strauss in Richmond & unfortunately had his hand shot off with a blunderbuss. Mary Hemings rode in the wagon. Sally Hemings' mother Betty was a bright mulatto woman & Sally mighty near white: she was the youngest child. Folks said that these Hemingses was old Mr Wayles' children. Sally was very handsome: long straight hair down her back. She was about eleven years old when Mr Jefferson took her to France to wait on Miss Polly. She & Sally went out to France a year after Mr Jefferson went. Patsy went with him at first, but she carried no maid with her. Harriet one of Sally's daughters was very handsome. Sally had a son named Madison, who learned to be a great fiddler. He has been in Petersburg twice: was here when the balloon went up—the balloon that Beverly sent off.

Mr Jefferson drove faster in the phaeton than the wagon. When the wagon reached Williamsburg Mr Jefferson was living in the College (of Wm & Mary). Isaac & the rest of the servants stayed in the Assembly-house—a long wooden building. Lord Botetourt's picture (statue) was there. The Assembly-house had a gallery on top running round to the College. There was a well there then: none there now. Some white people was living in one eend of the house: a man named Douglas was there: they called him Parson Douglas.**

Mr Jefferson's room in the College was down stairs. A tailor named Giovanni an Italian lived there too: made clothes for Mr Jefferson & his servants. Mrs Jefferson was there with Patsy & Polly. Mrs Jefferson was small: she drawed from old Madam Byrd† several hundred people & then married a rich man (Bathurst Skelton). Old Master had twelve quarters seated with black people: but mighty few come by him: he want rich himself—only his larnin. Patsy Jefferson was tall like her father; Polly low like her mother & longways the handsomest: pretty lady jist like her mother: pity she died—poor thing! She married John W Eppes—a handsome man, but had a hare-lip.

Jupiter and John drove Mr Jeffersons coach & four: one of em rode postilion: they rode postilion in them days. Travelling in the phaeton Mr Jefferson used oftentimes to take the reins himself & drive. Whenever he wanted to travel fast he'd drive: would drive powerful hard himself. Jupiter & John wore caps & gilded bands. The names of the horses was Senegore, Gustavus, Otter, Remus, Romulus & Caractacus Mr Jefferson's riding-horse.

* Capt. Bacon says: John Hemings made most of the wood-work & Joe Fosset made the iron-work.

** The Rev. Wm Douglas in a school at Shadwell near Monticello, instructed young Jefferson in the rudiments of Greek, Latin & French.

† Robert Beverley the historian married Ursula Byrd of Westover, from whom the Monticello Ursula may have derived her name.

CHAP. 3

After one year the Government was moved from Williamsburg to Richmond. Mr Jefferson moved there with his servants, among em Isaac. It was cold weather when they moved up. Mr Jefferson lived in a wooden house near where the Palace (Governor's house) stands now. Richmond was a small place then: not more than two brick houses in the town: all wooden houses what there was. At that time from where the Powhatan house now stands clear down to the Old Market was pretty much in pines. It was a wooden house shedded round like a barn on the hill, where the Assembly-men used to meet, near where the Capitol stands now. Old Mr Wiley had a saddler-shop in the same house. Isaac knew Billy Wiley mighty well—a saddler by trade: he was doorkeeper at the Assembly. His wife was a baker & baked bread & ginger-cakes. Isaac would go into the bake-oven & make fire for: She had a great big bake oven. Isaac used to go way into the oven: when he came out Billy Wiley would chuck wood in. She sometimes gave Isaac a loaf of bread or a cake. One time she went up to Monticello to see Mr Jefferson. She saw Isaac there & gave him a ninepence & said, "This is the boy that made fires for me." Mr Jefferson's family-servants then at the palace were Bob Hemings, Martin, Jim, house-servants, Jupiter & John drivers, Mary Hemings & young Betty Hemings seamstress & house-woman, Sukey, Jupiter's wife the cook.

CHAP. 4

The day before the British (under Arnold) came to Richmond Mr Jefferson sent off his family in the carriage. Bob Hemings & Jim drove[.] When the British was expected (Jan. 6, 1781) old master kept the spy-glass & git up by the sky-light window to the top of the palace looking towards Williamsburg. Some Other gentlemen went up with him, one of them old Mr Marsdell: he owned where the basin is now & the basin-spring. Isaac used to fetch water from there up to the palace. The British reached Manchester about 1 o'clock.* Isaac larnt to beat drum about this time. Bob Anderson a white man was a blacksmith. Mat Anderson was a black man & worked with Bob. Bob was a fifer Mat was a drummer. Mat bout that time was sort a-makin love to Mary Hemings. The soldiers at Richmond, in the camp at Bacon Quarter Branch would come every two or three days to salute the Governor at the Palace, marching about there drumming & fifing. Bob Anderson would go into the house to drink; Mat went into the kitchen to see Mary Hemings. He would take his drum with him into the kitchen & set it down there. Isaac would beat on it & Mat larnt him how to beat.

* They didn't come by way of Manchester.

CHAP. 5

As soon as the British formed a line three cannon was wheeled round all at once & fired three rounds. Till they fired the Richmond people thought they was a company come from Petersburg to join them: some of em even hurraed when they see them coming: but that moment they fired every body knew it was the British. One of the cannon-balls knocked off the top of a butcher's house: he was named Daly not far from the Governor's house. The butcher's wife screamed out & hollerd & her children too & all. In ten minutes not a white man was to be seen in Richmond: they ran as hard as they could stave to the camp at Bacon Quarter Branch. There was a monstrous hollering & screaming of women & children. Isaac was out in the yard: his mother ran out & cotch him up by the hand & carried him into the kitchen hollering. Mary Hemings, she jerked up her daughter the same way. Isaac run out again in a minute & his mother too: she was so skeered, she didn't know whether to stay indoors or out. The British was dressed in red. Isaac saw them marching. The horsemen (Simcoe's cavalry) was with them: they come arter the artillery-men. They formed in line & marched up to the Palace with drums beating: it was an awful sight: seemed like the day of judgment was come. When they fired the cannon old master called out to John to fetch his horse Caractacus from the stable & rode off.

CHAP. 6

Isaac never see his old master arter dat for six months. When the British come in, an officer rode up & asked "Whar is the Governor?" Isaac's father (George) told him:—"He's gone to the mountains."

The officer said, "Whar is the keys of the house?" Isaac's father gave him the keys: Mr Jefferson had left them with him. The officer said: "Whar is the silver?" Isaac's father told him, "It was all sent up to the mountains." The old man had put all the silver about the house in a bed-tick & hid it under a bed in the kitchen & saved it too & got his freedom by it. But he continued to sarve Mr Jefferson & had forty pounds from old master & his wife. Isaac's mother had seven dollars a month for lifetime for washing, ironing, & making pastry. The British sarcht the house but did'nt disturb none of the furniture: but they plundered the wine-cellar, rolled the pipes out & stove em in, knockin the heads out. The bottles they broke the necks off with their swords, drank some, threw the balance away. The wine-cellar was full: old master had plenty of wine & rum—the best: used to have Antigua rum—twelve years old. The British next went to the corn-crib & took all the corn out, strewed it in a line along the street towards where the Washington tavern* is now (1847) & brought their horses & fed them on it: took the bridles off. The British said they did'nt want anybody but the Governor: did'nt want to hurt him; only wanted to put a pair of silver handcuffs on him: had brought them along with them on purpose. While they was plunderin they took all of the meat out of the meat-house; cut it up, laid it out in parcels: every man took his ration & put it in his knapsack. When Isaac's mother found they was gwine to car him away she thought they was gwine to leave her: She was cryin & hollerin when one of the officers came on a horse & ordered us all to Hylton's. Then they marched off to Westham. Isaac heard the powder-magazine when it blew up—like an earthquake. Next morning between eight & nine they marched to Tuckahoe, fifteen miles: took a good many colored people from Old Tom Mann Randolph. He was called "Tuckahoe Tom." Isaac has often been to Tuckahoe—a low-built house but monstrous large. From Tuckahoe the British went to Daniel Hylton's. They carred off thirty people from Tuckahoe & some from Hylton's. When they come back to Richmond they took all old master's from his house: all of em had to walk except Daniel and Molly (children of Mary the pastry-cook) & Isaac. He was then big enough to beat the drum: but could'nt raise it off the ground: would hold it tilted over to one side & beat on it that way.

* At East end of Grace St—now (1871) the Central Hotel.

CHAP. 7

There was about a dozen wagons along: they (the British) pressed the common wagons: four horses to a wagon: some black drivers, some white: every wagon guarded by ten men marching alongside.

One of the officers give Isaac name Sambo: all the time feedin him: put a cocked hat on his head & a red coat on him & all laughed. Coat a monstrous great big thing: when Isaac was in it could'nt see nothing of it but the sleeves dangling down. He remembers crossing the river somewhere in a periauger [piragua]. And so the British carred them all down to Little York (Yorktown.) They marched straight through town & camped jist below back of the battle-field. Mr Jefferson's people there was Jupiter, Sukey the cook, Usley (Isaac's mother) George (Isaac's father) Mary the seamstress & children Molly, Daniel, Joe, Wormley, & Isaac. The British treated them mighty well, give em plenty of fresh meat & wheat bread. It was very sickly at York: great many colored people died there, but none of Mr Jefferson's folks. Wallis (Cornwallis) had a cave dug & was hid in there. There was tremendous firing & smoke: seemed like heaven & earth was come together: every time the great guns fire Isaac jump up off the ground. Heard the wounded men hollerin: when the smoke blow off you see the dead men laying on the ground. General Washington brought all Mr Jefferson's folks & about twenty of Tuckahoe Tom's (Tom Mann Randolph's) back to Richmond with him & sent word to Mr Jefferson to send down to Richmond for his servants. Old master sent down two wagons right away & all of em that was carred away went up back to Monticello. At that time old master & his family was at Poplar Forest his place in Bedford. He stayed there after his arm was broke, when Caractacus threw him. Old master was mightly pleased to see his people come back safe & sound (Although "All men by nature are free & equal.") & to hear of the plate.

CHAP. 8

Mr Jefferson was a tall strait-bodied man as ever you see, right square-shouldered: nary man in this town walked so straight as my old master: neat a built man as ever was seen in Vaginny, I reckon or any place—a straight-up man:* long face, high nose.

Jefferson Randolph (Mr Jefferson's grandson) nothing like him, except in height—tall, like him: not built like him: old master was a straight-up man. Jefferson Randolph pretty much like his mother. Old master wore Vaginny cloth and a red waistcoast, (all the gentlemen wore waistcoats in dem days) & small clothes: arter dat he used to wear red breeches too.** Governor Page used to come up there to Monticello, wife & daughter wid him: drove four-in hand: servants John, Molly & a postilion. Patrick Henry visited old master: coach & two: his face for all the world like the images of Bonaparte: would stay a week or more. Mann Page used to be at Monticello—a plain mild-looking man: his wife & daughter along with him. Dr Thomas Walker lived about ten miles from Monticello—a thin-faced man. John Walker (of Belvoir), his brother, owned a great many black people.†

* Capt. Bacon describes him as "Six feet two & a half inches high, well proportioned & straight as a gun-barrel. He was like a fine horse: he had no surplus flesh.[")

** Capt. Bacon says: "He was always very neat in his dress: wore short breeches & bright shoe-buckles. When he rode on horseback he had a pair of overalls that he always put on.["]

† John Walker member of Congress during the Revolution.

CHAP. 9

Old master was never seen to come out before breakfast—about 8 o'clock. If it was warm weather he would'nt ride out till evening: studied upstairs till bell ring for dinner. When writing he had a copyin machine: while he was a-writin he would'nt suffer nobody to come in his room: had a dumb-waiter: when he wanted anything he had nothing to do but turn a crank & the dumb-waiter would bring him water or fruit on a plate or anything he wanted. Old master had abundance of books: sometimes would have twenty of 'em down on the floor at once: read fust one, then tother. Isaac has often wondered how old master came to have such a mighty head: read so many of them books: & when they go to him to ax him anything, he go right straight to the book & tell you all about it. He talked French & Italian. Madzay* talked with him: his place was called Colle. General Redhazel (Riedesel) stayed there. He (Mazzei) lived at Monticello with old master some time: Didiot a Frenchman married his daughter Peggy: a heavy chunky looking woman—mighty handsome: She had a daughter Frances & a son Francis: called the daughter Franky. Mazzei brought to Monticello Antonine, Jovanini, Francis, Modena & Belligrini, all gardiners. My old master's garden was monstrous large: two rows of palings, all round ten feet high.

* Philip Mazzei—an Italian—author of "Recherches Sur Les Etats-Unis," 3 vols. published at Paris, in 1788.

CHAP. 10

Mr Jefferson had a clock in his kitchen at Monticello; never went into the kitchen except to wind up the clock. He never would have less than eight covers at dinner—if nobody at table but himself: had from eight to thirty two covers for dinner: plenty of wine, best old Antigua rum & cider: very fond of wine & water. Isaac never heard of his being disguised in drink. He kept three fiddles: played in the arternoons & sometimes arter supper. This was in his early time: when he begin to git so old he didn't play: kept a spinnet made mostly in shape of a harpsichord: his daughter played on it. Mr Fauble a Frenchman that lived at Mr Walker's—a music-man, used to come to Monticello & tune it. There was a forte piano & a guitar there: never seed anybody play on them but the French people. Isaac never could git acquainted with them: could hardly larn their names. Mr Jefferson always singing when ridin or walkin: hardly see him anywhar out doors but what he was a-singin:* had a fine clear voice, sung minnits (minuets) & sich: fiddled in the parlor. Old master very kind to servants.

* Capt. Bacon says: "When he was not talking he was nearly always humming some tune; or singing in a low tone to himself."

CHAP. 11

The fust year Mr Jefferson was elected President, he took Isaac on to Philadelphia: he was then about fifteen years old: travelled on horseback in company with a Frenchman named Joseph Rattiff & Jim Hemings a body-servant. Fust day's journey they went from Monticello to old Nat Gordon's, on the Fredericksburg road, next day to Fredericksburg, then to Georgetown, crossed the Potomac there, & so to Philadelphia: eight days a-goin. Had two ponies & Mr Jefferson's tother riding-horse Odin. Mr Jefferson went in the phaeton: Bob Hemings drove: changed horses on the road. When they got to Philadelphia Isaac stayed three days at Mr Jefferson's house: then he was bound prentice to one Bringhouse a tinner: he lived in the direction of the Water-works. Isaac remembers seeing the image of a woman thar holding a goose in her hand—the water spouting out of the goose's mouth. This was at the head of Market Street. Bringhouse was a short mighty small neat-made man: treated Isaac very well: went thar to larn the tinner's trade: fust week larnt to cut out and sodder: make little pepper-boxes & graters & sich, out of scraps of tin, so as not to waste any till he had larnt. Then to making cups. Every Sunday Isaac would go to the President's House—large brick house, many windows: same house Ginral Washington lived in before when he was President. "Old master used to talk to me mighty free & ax me, how you come on Isaac, larnin de tin-business?" As soon as he could make cups pretty well he carred three or four to show him. Isaac made four dozen pint-cups a day & larnt to tin copper & sheets (sheet-iron)—make 'em tin. He lived four years with old Bringhouse. One time Mr Jefferson sent to Bringhouse to tin his copper-kittles & pans for kitchen use: Bringhouse sent Isaac & another prentice thar—a white boy named Charles: cant think of his other name. Isaac was the only black boy in Bringhouse's shop. When Isaac carred the cups to his old master to show him he was mightily pleased: said, "Isaac you are larnin mighty fast: I bleeve I must send you back to Vaginny to car on the tin-business. You is growin too big: no use for you to stay here no longer."

Arter dat Mr Jefferson sent Isaac back to Monticello to car on the tin-business thar. Old master bought a sight of tin for the purpose. Mr Jefferson had none of his family with him in Philadelphia.

Polly his daughter stayed with her aunt Patsy Carr: she lived seven or eight miles from old master's great house. Sam Carr was Mr Jefferson's sister's child. There were three brothers of the Carrs—Sam, Peter & Dabney. Patsy Jefferson while her father was President in Philadelphia stayed with Mrs Eppes at Wintopoke: Mrs Eppes was a sister of Mrs Jefferson:—mightily like her sister. Frank Eppes was a big heavy man.

Old master's servants at Philadelphia was Bob & Jim Hemings; Joseph Rattiff a Frenchman—the hostler. Mr Jefferson used to ride out on horseback in Philadelphia. Isaac went back to Monticello. When the tin came they fixed up a shop. Jim Bringhouse came on to Monticello all the way with old master to fix up the shop & start Isaac to work: Jim Bringhouse stayed thar more than a month.

CHAP. 12

Isaac knew old Colonel (Archibald) Cary mighty well: as dry a looking man as ever you see in your life. He has given Isaac more whippings than he has fingers & toes. Mr Jefferson used to set Isaac to open gates for Col. Cary: there was three gates to open, the furst bout a mile from the house: tother one three quarters; then the yard-gate, at the stable three hundred yards from the house. Isaac had to open the gates. Col. Cary would write to old master what day he was coming. Whenever Isaac missed opening them gates in time, the Colonel soon as he git to the house, look about for him & whip him with his horsewhip. Old master used to keep dinner for Col. Cary. He was a tall thin-visaged man jist like Mr Jefferson: he drove four-in-hand. The Colonel as soon as he git out of his carriage, walk right straight into the kitchen & ax de cooks what they hab for dinner? If they did'nt have what he wanted—bleeged to wait dinner till it was cooked. Col. Cary made freer at Monticello than he did at home: whip anybody: would stay several weeks: give servants money, sometimes five or six dollars among 'em. Tuckahoe Tom Randolph married Colonel Cary's daughter Nancy. The Colonel lived at Ampthill on the James river where Colonel Bob Temple lived arterwards. Edgehill was the seat of Tom Mann Randolph father of Jefferson Randolph: it was three miles from Monticello.

CHAP. 13

Isaac carred on the tin-business two years:—it failed. He then carred on the nail-business at Monticello seven years: made money at that. Mr Jefferson had the first (nail) cutting machine 'twas said, that ever was in Vaginny—sent over from England: made wrought nails & cut-nails, to shingle & lathe: sold them out of the shop: got iron rods from Philadelphia by water: boated them up from Richmond to Milton a small town on the Rivanna: wagoned from thar.

CHAP. 14

Thomas Mann Randolph had ten children.* Isaac lived with him fust & last twenty six or seven years: treated him mighty well: one of the finest masters in Virginia: his a wife mighty peacable woman: never holler for servant: make no fuss nor racket: pity she ever died! Tom Mann Randolph's eldest daughter Ann: a son named Jefferson, another James & another Benjamin.

Jefferson Randolph married Mr Nicholas'** daughter (Anne). Billy Giles† courted Miss Polly old master's daughter. Isaac one morning saw him talking to her in the garden, right back of the nail-factory shop: she was lookin on de ground: all at once she wheeled round & come off. That was the time she turned him off. Isaac never so sorry for a man in all his life: sorry because everybody thought that she was going to marry him. Mr Giles give several dollars to the servants & when he went away dat time he never come back no more. His servant Arthur was a big man. Isaac wanted Mr Giles to marry Miss Polly. Arthur always said, that he was a mighty fine man: he was very rich: used to come to Monticello in a monstrous fine gig: mighty few gigs in dem days with plated mountins & harness.

* Thomas Mann Randolph's sons were Thomas Jefferson, James Madison, Benjamin Franklin, Merriwether Lewis & George Wythe (Secy. of War of C. S.) daughters Anne, Ellen, Virginia, Cornelia & Septimia.

** Wilson Cary Nicholas, sometime Governor of Virginia.

† Wm C [actually Branch] Giles, M. C. a celebrated debater. Sometime Governor of Virginia. He acquired the sobriquet of "Farmer Giles."

CHAP. 15

Elk Hill: old master had a small brick house there where he used to stay, about a mile from Elk Island on the North Side of the James river. The river forks there: one half runs one side of the island, tother the other side. When Mr Jefferson was Governor he used to stay thar a month or sich a matter & when he was at the mountain he would come & stay a month or so & then go back again. Blenheim was a low large wooden house two storeys high, eight miles from Monticello. Old Col. Carter lived thar: had a light red head like Mr Jefferson. Isaac know'd him & every son he had:—didn't know his daughters

Mr Jefferson used to hunt squirrels & partridges; kept five or six guns; oftentimes carred Isaac wid him: old master would'nt shoot partridges settin: said "he would'nt take advantage of em"—would give 'em a chance for thar life: would'nt shoot a hare settin, nuther; skeer him up fust. "My old master was as neat a hand as ever you see to make keys & locks & small chains, iron & brass"; he kept all kind of blacksmith and carpenter tools in a great case with shelves to it in his library—an upstairs room. Isaac went up thar constant: been up thar a thousand times; used to car coal up thar: old master had a couple of small bellowses up thar.

The likeness of Mr Jefferson (in Linn's Life of him) according to Isaac, is not much like him. "Old master never dat handsome in dis world: dat likeness right between old master & Ginral Washington: old master was squar-shouldered." For amusement he would work sometimes in the garden for half an hour at a time in right good earnest in the cool of the evening: never know'd him to go out anywhar before breakfast.

CHAP. 16

The school at Monticello was in the out-chamber fifty yards off from the great house, on the same level. But the scholars went into the house to old master to git lessons—in the South eend of the house called the South Octagon. Mrs Skipper (Skipwith) had two daughters thar: Mrs Eppes, one.

Mr Jefferson's sister Polly married old Ned Bolling* of Chesterfield about ten miles from Petersburg. Isaac has been thar since his death: saw the old man's grave. Mr John Bradley owns the place now. Isaac slept in the out-chamber where the scholars was: slept on the floor in a blanket: in the winter season git up in the mornin & make fire for them. From Monticello you can see mountains all round as far as the eye can reach: sometimes see it rainin down this course & the sun shining over the tops of the clouds. Willis' mountain sometimes looked in the cloud like a great house with two chimnies to it: fifty miles from Monticello.

* John Bolling of Cobbs in Chesterfield married a sister of Thomas Jefferson.

CHAP. 17

Thar was a sight of pictures at Monticello: pictures of Ginral Washington & the Marcus Lafayette. Isaac saw him fust in the old war in the mountain with old master; saw him agin the last time he was in Vaginny. He gave Isaac a guinea: Isaac saw him in the Capitol at Richmond & talked with him & made him sensible when he fust saw him in the old war. Thar was a large marble at Monticello with twelve angels cut on it that came from Heaven: all cut in marble.

About the time when "my old master" begun to wear spectacles—he was took with a swellin in his legs: used to bathe 'em & bandage 'em: said it was settin too much: when he'd git up & walk it would'nt hurt him. Isaac & John Hemings nursed him two months: had to car him about on a han-barrow. John Hemings* went to the carpenter's trade same year Isaac went to the blacksmiths. Miss Lucy old master's daughter died quite a small child; died down the country at Mrs Eppes' or Mrs Bollings one of her young aunts. Old master was embassador to France at that time. He brought a great many clothes from France with him: a coat of blue cloth trimmed with gold lace; cloak trimmed so too: dar say it weighed fifty pounds: large buttons on the coat as big as half a dollar; cloth set in the button: edge shine like gold: in summer he war silk coat, pearl buttons.

Col. Jack Harvie** owned Belmont, jinin Monticello. Four as big men as any in Petersburg could git in his waistcoat: he owned Belvidere near Richmond: the Colonel died thar: monstrous big man. The washerwoman once buttons his waistcoat on Isaac & three others. Mrs Harvie was a little woman.

* Capt Bacon in his reminiscenses of Mr Jefferson at Monticello says, "John Hemings was a carpenter. He was a first-rate workman, a very extra workman: he could make anything that was wanting in woodwork. He learned his trade with Dinsmore. John Hemings made most of the woodwork of Mr Jefferson's fine carriage.["]

** He had command of the troops of Convention for a time.

CHAP. 18

Mr Jefferson never had nothing to do with horse-racing or cock-fighting: bought two race-horses once, but not in their racing day: bought em arter done runnin. One was Brimmer,* a pretty horse with two white feet: when he bought him he was in Philadelphia: kept him thar. One day Joseph Rattiff the Frenchman was ridin him in the streets of Philadelphia: Brimmer got skeered: run agin shaft of a dray & got killed. Tother horse was Tarkill: (Tarquin?) in his race-day they called him the Roane colt: only race-horse of a roane Isaac ever see: old master used him for a ridin-horse. Davy Watson & Billy were German soldiers: both workmen, both smoked pipes & both drinkers: drank whiskey; git drunk & sing: take a week at a time drinkin & singin. Col. Goode of Chesterfield was a great racer: used to visit Mr Jefferson; had a trainer named Pompey.

Old master had a great many rabbits: made chains for the old buck-rabbits to keep them from killin the young ones: had a rabbit-house (a warren)—a long rock house: some of em white, some blue: they used to burrow under ground. Isaac expects thar is plenty of em bout dar yit: used to eat em at Monticello. Mr Jefferson never danced nor played cards. He had dogs named Ceres, Bull, Armandy, & Claremont: most of em French dogs: he brought em over with him from France. Bull & Ceres were bull-dogs: he brought over Buzzy with him too: she pupped at sea: Armandy & Claremont, stump-tails—both black.

*According to Capt. Bacon, "Brimmer was a son of imported Knowlsby. He was a bay, but a shade darker than any of the others. He was a horse of fair size, full, but not quite as tall as Eagle. He was a good riding-horse & excellent for the harness. Mr Jefferson broke all his horses to both ride & work. I bought Brimmer of General John H Cocke of Fluvanna County."

CHAP. 19

John Brock the overseer that lived next to the great-house had gray hounds to hunt deer. Mr Jefferson had a large park at Monticello: built in a sort of a flat on the side of the mountain. When the hunters run the deer down thar, they'd jump into the park & couldn't git out. When old master heard hunters in the park he used to go down thar wid his gun & order em out. The park was two or three miles round & fenced in with a high fence, twelve rails double-staked & ridered: kept up four or five years arter old master was gone. Isaac & his father (George) fed the deer at sun-up & sun-down: called em up & fed em wid corn: had holes all along the fence at the feedin-place: gave em salt, got right gentle: come up & eat out of your hand.

No wild-cats at Monticello: some lower down at Buck Island: bears sometimes came on the plantation at Monticello: wolves so plenty that they had to build pens round black peoples' quarters & pen sheep in em to keep the wolves from catching them. But they killed five or six of a night in the winter season: come & steal in the pens in the night. When the snow was on the groun you could see the wolves in gangs runnin & howlin, same as drove of hogs: made the deer run up to the feedin-place many a night. The feedin-place was right by the house whar Isaac stayed. They raised many sheep & goats at Monticello.

The woods & mountains was often on fire: Isaac has gone out to help to put out the fire: everybody would turn out from Charlottesville & everywhere: git in the woods & sometimes work all night fightin the fire.

CHAP. 20

Col. Cary of Chesterfield schooled old master: he went to school to old Mr Wayles. Old master had six sisters: Polly married a Bolling; Patsy married old Dabney Carr in the low-grounds: one married Wm Skipwith: Nancy married old Hastings Marks. Old master's brother, mass Randall, (Randolph) was a mighty simple man: used to come out among black people, play the fiddle & dance half the night: had'nt much more sense than Isaac. Jack Eppes (John W Eppes M. C) that married Miss Polly (Jefferson) lived at Mount Black (Mt. Blanc?) on James river & then at Edge Hill, then in Cumberland at Millbrooks. Isaac left Monticello four years before Mr Jefferson died. Tom Mann Randolph that married Mr Jefferson's daughter, wanted Isaac to build a threshing machine at Varina. Old Henrico Court House was thar: pulled down now. Coxendale Island (Dutch Gap) jinin Varina was an Indian Situation: when fresh come, it washed up more Indian bones than ever you see. When Isaac was a boy there want more than ten houses at Jamestown. Charlottesville then not as big as Pocahontas (a village on the Appomattox, opposite Petersburg) is now. Mr DeWitt kept tavern thar.

Isaac knowed Ginral Redhazel (Riedesel commander of the German troops of Convention.): he stayed at Colle, Mr Mazzei's place, two miles & a quarter from Monticello—a long wood house built by Mazzei's servants. The servants' house built of little saplins of oak & hickory instead of lathes: then plastered up: it seemed as if de folks in dem days had'nt sense enough to make lathes. The Italian people raised plenty of vegetables: cooked the most victuals of any people Isaac ever see.

Mr Jefferson bowed to everybody he meet: talked wid his arms folded. Gave the boys in the nail-factory a pound of meat a week, a dozen herrings, a quart of molasses & peck of meal. Give them that wukked the best a suit of red or blue: encouraged them mightily.

Isaac calls him a mighty good master. There would be a great many carriages at Monticello at a time, in particular when people was passing to the Springs.

Isaac is now (1847) at Petersburg, Va. seventy large odd years old: bears his years well: is a blacksmith by trade & has his shop not far from Pocahontas bridge.

He is quite pleased at the idea of having his life written & protests that every word of it is true—that is of course according to the best of his knowledge & belief. Isaac is rather tall of strong frame, stoops a little, in color ebony:—sensible, intelligent pleasant: wears large circular iron-bound spectacles & a leather apron. A capital daguerrotype of him was taken by a Mr Shew. Isaac was so much pleased with it that he had one taken of his wife, a large fat round-faced good-humoured looking black woman. My attention was first drawn to Isaac by Mr Dandridge of Spotswood who had often heard him talk about Mr Jefferson & Monticello.

C. C.

P. S. Isaac died a few years after these his recollections were taken down. He bore a good character.

From the Encyclopedia Virginia, https://encyclopediavirginia.org/primary-documents/life-of-isaac-jefferson-of-petersburg-virginia-blacksmith-by-isaac-jefferson-1847/, as dictated to the Reverend Charles Campbell in 1847.

"Life among the Lowly, no. 1," by Madison Hemings, March 13, 1873

I never knew of but one white man who bore the name of Hemings; he was an Englishman and my greatgrandfather. He was captain of an English trading vessel which sailed between England and Williamsburg, Va., then quite a port. My [great] grandmother was a fullblooded African, and possibly a native of that country. She was the property of John Wales, a Welchman. Capt. Hemings happened to be in the port of Williamsburg at the time my grandmother was born, and acknowledging her fatherhood he tried to purchase her of Mr. Wales, who would not part with the child, though he was offered an extraordinarily large price for her. She was named Elizabeth Hemings. Being thwarted in the purchase, and determining to own his flesh and blood he resolved to take the child by force or stealth, but the knowledge of his intention coming to John Wales' ears, through leaky fellow servants of the mother, she and the child were taken into the "great house" under their master's immediate care. I have been informed that it was not the extra value of that child over other slave children that induced Mr. Wales to refuse to sell it, for slave masters then, as in later days, had no compunctions of conscience which restrained them from parting mother and child of however tender age, but he was restrained by the fact that just about that time amalgamation began, and the child was so great a curiosity that its owner desired to raise it himself that he might see its outcome. Capt. Hemings soon afterwards sailed from Williamsburg, never to return. Such is the story that comes down to me.

Elizabeth Hemings grew to womanhood in the family of John Wales, whose wife dying she (Elizabeth) was taken by the widower Wales as his concubine, by whom she had six children—three sons and three daughters, viz: Robert, James, Peter, Critty, Sally and Thena. These children went by the name of Hemings.

Williamsburg was the capital of Virginia, and of course it was an aristocratic place, where the "bloods" of the Colony and the new State most did congregate. Thomas Jefferson, the author of the Declaration of Independence, was educated at William and Mary

College, which had its seat at Williamsburg. He afterwards studied law with Geo. Wythe, and practiced law at the bar of the general court of the Colony. He was afterwards elected a member of the provincial legislature from Albemarle County. Thos. Jefferson was a visitor at the "great house" of John Wales, who had children about his own age. He formed the acquaintance of his daughter Martha (I believe that was her name, though I am not positively sure,) and an intimacy sprang up between them which ripened into love, and they were married. They afterwards went to live at his country seat, Monticello, and in course of time had born to them a daughter whom they named Martha. About that time she was born my mother, the second daughter of John Wales and Elizabeth Hemings was born. On the death of John Wales, my grandmother, his concubine, and her children by him fell to Martha, Thomas Jefferson's wife, and consequently became the property of Thomas Jefferson, who in the course of time became famous, and was appointed minister to France during our revolutionary troubles, or soon after independence was gained. About the time of the appointment and before he was ready to leave the country his wife died, and as soon after her interment as he could attend to and arrange his domestic affairs in accordance with the changed circumstances of his family in consequence of this misfortune (I think not more than three weeks thereafter) he left for France, taking his eldest daughter with him. He had had sons born to him but they died in early infancy, so he then had but two children—Martha and Maria. The latter was left at home, but was afterwards ordered to follow him to France. She was three years or so younger than Martha. My mother accompanied her as her body servant. When Mr. Jefferson went to France Martha was a young woman grown, my mother was about her age, and Maria was just budding into womanhood. Their stay (my mother and Maria's) was about eighteen months. But during that time my mother became Mr. Jefferson's concubine, and when he was called back home she was *enciente* by him. He desired to bring my mother back to Virginia with him but she demurred. She was just beginning to understand the French language well, and in France she was free, while if she returned to Virginia she would be re-enslaved. So she refused to return with him. To induce her to do so he promised her extraordinary privileges, and made a solemn pledge that her children should be freed at the age of twenty-one years. In consequence of his promises, on which she implicitly relied, she returned with him to Virginia. Soon after their arrival, she gave birth to a child, of whom Thomas Jefferson was the father. It lived but a short time. She gave birth to four others, and Jefferson was the father of all of them. Their names were Beverly, Harriet, Madison (myself), and Eston—three sons and one daughter. We all became free agreeably to the treaty entered into by our parents before we were born. We all married and have raised families.

Beverly left Monticello and went to Washington as a white man. He married a white woman in Maryland, and their only child, a daughter, was not known by the white folks to have any colored blood coursing in her veins. Beverly's wife's family were people in good circumstances.

Harriet married a white man in good standing in Washington City, whose name I could give, but will not, for prudential reasons. She raised a family of children, and so far as I know they were never suspected of being tainted with African blood in the community where she lived or lives. I have not heard from her for ten years, and do not know whether she is dead or alive. She thought it to her interest, on going to Washington, to assume the role of a white woman, and by her dress and conduct as such I am not aware that her identity as Harriet Hemings of Monticello has ever been discovered.

Eston married a colored woman in Virginia, and moved from there to Ohio, and lived in Chillicothe several years. In the fall of 1852 he removed to Wisconsin, where he died a year or two afterwards. He left three children.

As to myself, I was named Madison by the wife of James Madison, who was afterwards President of the United States. Mrs. Madison happened to be at Monticello at the time of my birth, and begged the privilege of naming me, promising my mother a fine present for the honor. She consented, and Mrs. Madison dubbed me by the name I now acknowledge, but like many promises of white folks to the slaves she never gave my mother anything. I was born at my father's seat of Monticello, in Albemarle county, Va., near Charlottesville, on the 19th day of January, 1805. My very earliest recollections are of my grandmother Elizabeth Hemings. That was when I was about three years old. She was sick and upon her death bed. I was eating a piece of bread and asked if she would have some. She replied: "No; granny don't want bread any more." She shortly afterwards breathed her last. I have only a faint recollection of her.

Of my father, Thomas Jefferson, I knew more of his domestic than his public life, during his life time. It is only since his death that I have learned much of the latter, except that he was considered as a foremost man in the land, and held many important trusts, including that of President. I learned to read by inducing the white children to teach me the letters and something more; what else I know of books I have picked up here and there till now I can read and write. I was almost 21½ years of age when my father died, on the 4th of July, 1826. About his own home he was the quietest of men. He was hardly ever known to get angry, though sometimes he was irritated when matters went wrong, but even then he hardly ever allowed himself to be made unhappy any great length of time. Unlike Washington he had but little taste or care for agricultural pursuits. He left matters pertaining to his plantations mostly with his stewards and overseers. He always had mechanics at work for him, such as carpenters, blacksmiths, shoemakers, coopers, &c. It was his mechanics he seemed mostly to direct, and in their operations he took great interest. Almost every day of his latter years he might have been seen among them. He occupied much of the time in his office engaged in correspondence and reading and writing. His general temperament was smooth and even; he was very undemonstrative. He was uniformly kind to all about him. He was not in the habit of showing partiality or fatherly affection to us children. We were the only children of his by a slave woman. He was affectionate toward his white grandchildren, of whom he had fourteen, twelve of whom lived to manhood and womanhood. His daughter Martha married Thomas Mann Randolph by whom she had thirteen children. Two died in infancy. The names of the living were Ann, Thomas Jefferson, Ellen, Cornelia, Virginia, Mary, James, Benj. Franklin, Lewis Madison, Septimia and Geo. Wythe. Thos. Jefferson Randolph was Chairman of the Democratic National Convention in Baltimore last spring which nominated Horace Greeley for the Presidency, and Geo. Wythe Randolph was Jeff. Davis' first Secretary of War in the late "unpleasantness."

Maria married John Epps, and raised one son—Francis.

My father generally enjoyed excellent health. I never knew him to have but one spell of sickness, and that was caused by a visit to the Warm Springs in 1818. Till within three weeks of his death he was hale and hearty, and at the age of 83 years he walked erect and with stately tread. I am now 68, and I well remember that he was a much smarter man physically, even at that age, than I am.

When I was fourteen years old I was put to the carpenter trade under the charge of John Hemings, the youngest son of my grandmother. His father's name was Nelson, who was an Englishman. She had seven children by white men and seven by colored men—fourteen in all. My brothers, sister Harriet and myself were used alike. They were put to some mechanical trade at the age of fourteen. Till then we were permitted to stay about the "great house," and only required to do such light work as going on errands. Harriet learned to spin and to weave in a little factory on the home plantation. We were free from the dread of having to be slaves all our lives long, and were measurably happy. We were always permitted to be with our mother, who was well used. It was her duty, all her life which I can remember, up to the time of father's death, to take care of his chamber and wardrobe, look after us children and do such light work as sewing, &c. Provision was made in the will of our father that we should be freed when we arrived at the age of 21 years. We had all passed that period when he died but Eston, and he was given the remainder of his time shortly after. He and I rented a house and took mother to live with us, till her death, which event occurred in 1835.

In 1831 I married Mary McCoy. Her grandmother was a slave, and lived with her master, Stephen Hughes, near Charlottesville, as his wife. She was manumitted by him, which made their children free born. Mary McCoy's mother was his daughter. I was about 23 and she 22 years of age when we married. We lived and labored together in Virginia till 1836, when we voluntarily left and came to Ohio. We settled in Pebble township, Pike county. We lived there four or five years, and during my stay in that county I worked at my trade on and off for about four years. Joseph Sewell was my first employer. I built for him what is now known as Bizzleport No. 2, in Waverly. I afterwards worked for George Wolfe, Senior, and did the carpenter work of the brick building now owned by John J. Kellison, in which the Pike County Republican is printed. I worked for and with Micajah Hinson. I found him to be a very clever man. I also reconstructed the building on the corner of Market and Water streets from a store to a hotel for the late Judge Jacob Row.

When we came from Virginia we brought one daughter (Sarah) with us, leaving the dust of a son in the soil near Monticello. We have had born to us in this State nine children. Two are dead. The names of the living, besides Sarah, are Harriet, Mary Ann, Catharine, Jane, William Beverly, James Madison and Ellen Wales. Thomas Eston died in the Andersonville prison pen, and Julia died at home. William, James and Ellen are unmarried and live at home, in Huntington township, Ross county. All the others are married and raising families. My post-office address is Pee Pee, Pike county, Ohio.

From the Encyclopedia Virginia, https://encyclopediavirginia.org/primary-documents/life-among-the-lowly-no-1-by-madison-hemings-march-13-1873/; originally published in the *Pike County Republican*, March 13, 1873.

"Life among the Lowly, no. 3," by Israel (Gillette) Jefferson, December 25, 1873

I was born at Monticello, the seat of Thos. Jefferson, third President of the United States, December 25—Christmas day in the morning. The year, I suppose, was 1797. My earliest recollections are the exciting events attending the preparations of Mr. Jefferson and other members of his family on their removal to Washington, D. C., where he was to take upon himself the responsibilities of the Executive of the United States for four years.

My mother's name was Jane. She was a slave of Thomas Jefferson's, and was born and always resided at Monticello till about five years after the death of Mr. Jefferson. She was sold, after his death, by the administrator, to a Mr. Joel Brown, and was taken to Charlottesville, where she died in 1837. She was the mother of thirteen children, all by one father, whose name was Edward Gillett. The children's names were Barnaby, Edward, Priscilla, Agnes, Richard, James, Fanny, Lucy, Gilly, Israel, Moses, Susan and Jane—seven sons and six daughters. All these children, except myself, bore the surname of Gillett. The reason for my name being called Jefferson will appear in the proper place.

After Mr. Jefferson had left his home to assume the duties of the office of President, all became quiet again in Monticello. But as he was esteemed by both whites and blacks as a very great man, his return home, for a brief period, was a great event. His visits were frequent, and attended with considerable ceremony. It was a time looked forward to with great interest by his servants, for when he came home many of them, especially the leading ones, were sure to receive presents from his hands. He was re-elected President in 1804, and took his seat for the second term in 1805. Of course, his final term closed in March, 1809, when he was succeeded by James Madison. At that time I was upwards of twelve years of age.

About the time Mr. Jefferson took his seat as President for the second term, I began the labors of life as a waiter at the family table, and till Mr. J. died was retained in Monticello and very near his person. When about ten years of age, I was employed as postillion. Mr. Jefferson rode in a splendid carriage drawn by four horses.

He called the carriage the landau. It was a sort of double chaise. When the weather was pleasant the occupants could enjoy the open air; when it was rainy, they were protected from it by the closing of the covering, which fell back from the middle. It was splendidly ornamented with silver trimmings, and, taken altogether, was the nicest affair in those aristocratic regions. The harness was made in Paris, France, silver mounted, and quite in keeping with the elegant carriage. The horses were well matched, and of a bay color. I am now speaking of the years of my boyhood and early manhood. My brother Gilly, being older than I was, rode the near wheel horse, while I was mounted on the near leader. In course of time Mr. Jefferson rode less ostentatiously, and the leaders were left off. Then but one rider was needed. Sometimes brother Gilly acted as postillion; at other times I was employed. We were both retained about the person of our master as long as he lived. Mr. Jefferson died on the 4th day of July, 1826, when I was upwards of 29 years of age. His death was an affair of great moment and uncertainty to us slaves, for Mr. Jefferson provided for the freedom of 7 servants only: Sally, his chambermaid, who took the name of Hemmings, her four children—Beverly, Harriet, Madison and Eston—John Hemmings, brother to Sally, and Burrell Colburn, an old and faithful body servant. Madison Hemmings is now a resident of Ross county, Ohio, whose history you gave in the Republican of March 13, 1873. All the rest of us were sold from the auction block, by order of Jefferson Randolph, his grandson and administrator. The sale took place in 1829, three years after Mr. Jefferson's death.

I was purchased by Thomas Walker Gilmer, afterwards Governor of Virginia, and later, member of Congress from the district in which Monticello was situated. He was an attorney-at-law, and a most excellent gentleman.

During the interval of Mr. Jefferson's death and the sale to Mr. Gilmer, I married Mary Ann Colter, a slave, by whom I had four children—Taliola (a daughter) Banobo, (a son) Susan and John. As they were born slaves they took the usual course of most others in the same condition of life. I do not know where they now are, if living; but the last I heard of them they were in Florida and Virginia. My wife died, and while a servant of Mr. Gilmer, I married my present wife, widow Elizabeth Randolph, who was then mother to ten children. Her maiden name was Elizabeth Farrow. Her mother was a white woman named Martha Thackey. Consequently, Elizabeth, (my present wife) was free-born. She supposes that she was born about 1793 or '94. Of her ten children, only two are living—Julia, her first born, and wife of Charles Barnett, who live on an adjoining farm, and Elizabeth, wife of Henry Lewis, who reside within one mile of us.

My wife and I have lived together about thirty-five years. We came to Cincinnati, Ohio, where we were again married in conformity to the laws of this State. At the time we were first married I was in bondage; my wife was free. When my first wife died I made up my mind I would never live with another slave woman. When Governor Gilmer was elected a representative to Congress, he desired to have me go on to Washington with him. But I demurred. I did not refuse, of course, but I laid before him my objections with such earnestness that he looked me in the face with his piercing eye, as if balancing in his mind whether to be soft or severe, and said:

"Israel, you have served me well; you are a faithful servant; now what will you give me for your freedom?"

"I reckon I will give you what you paid years ago—$500," I replied.

"How much will you give to bind the bargain?" he asked.

"Three hundred dollars," was my ready answer.

"When will you pay the remainder?"

"In one and two years."

And on these terms the bargain was concluded, and I was, for the first time, my own man, and almost free, but not quite, for it was against the laws of Virginia for a freed slave to remain in the State beyond a year and a day. Nor were the colored people not in slavery free; they were nominally so. When I came to Ohio I considered myself wholly free, and not till then.

And here let me say, that my good master, Governor Gilmer, was killed by the explosion of the gun Peacemaker, on board the Princeton, in 1842 or 1843, and had I gone to Washington with him it would have been my duty to keep very close to his person, and probably I would have been killed also, as others were.

I was bought in the name of my wife. We remained in Virginia for several years on sufferance. At last we made up our minds to leave the confines of slavery and emigrate to a free State. We went to Charlottesville Court House, in Albemarle county, for my free papers. When there, the clerk, Mr. Garrett, asked me what surname I would take. I hesitated, and he suggested that it should be Jefferson, because I was born at Monticello and had been a good and faithful servant to Thomas Jefferson. Besides, he said, it would give me more dignity to be called after so eminent a man. So I consented to adopt the surname Jefferson, and have been known by it ever since.

When I came to Cincinnati, I was employed as a waiter in a private house, at ten dollars a month for the first month. From that time on I received $20, till I went on board a steamboat, where I got higher wages still. In time, I found myself in receipt of $50 per month, regularly, and sometimes even more. I resided in Cincinnati about fourteen years, and from thence came on to the farm I am now on, in Pebble township, on Brusby Fork of Pee Pee creek. Have been here about sixteen years.

Since my residence in Ohio I have several times visited Monticello. My last visit was in the fall of 1866. Near there I found the same Jefferson Randolph, whose service as administrator I left more than forty years ago, at Monticello. He had grown old, and was outwardly surrounded by the evidences of former ease and opulence gone to decay. He was in poverty. He had lost, he told me, $80,000 in money by joining the South in rebellion against the government. Except his real estate, the rebellion stripped him of everything, save one old, blind mule. He said that had he taken the advice of his sister, Mrs. Cooleridge, gone to New York, and remained there during the war, he could have saved the bulk of his property. But he was a rebel at heart, and chose to go with his people. Consequently, he was served as others had been—he had lost all his servants and nearly all his personal property of every kind. I went back to Virginia to find the proud and haughty Randolph in poverty, at Edge Hill, within four miles of Monticello, where he was bred and born. Indeed, I then realized, more than ever before, the great changes which time brings about in the affairs and circumstances of life.

Since I have been in Ohio I have learned to read and write, but my duties as a laborer would not permit me to acquire much of an education. But such as I possess I am truly thankful for, and consider what education I have as a legitimate fruit of freedom.

The private life of Thomas Jefferson, from my earliest remembrance, in 1804, till the day of his death, was very familiar to me. For fourteen years I made the fire in his bedroom and private chamber, cleaned his office, dusted his books, run of errands, and attended him about home. He used to ride out to his plantations almost every fair day, when at home, but unlike most other Southern gentlemen in similar circumstances, unaccompanied by any servant. Frequently gentlemen would call upon him on business of great importance, whom I used to usher into his presence, and sometimes I would be employed in burnishing or doing some other work in the room where they were. On such occasions I used to remain; otherwise I retired and left the gentlemen to confer together alone. In those times I minded but little concerning the conversations which took place between Mr. Jefferson and his visitors. But I well recollect a conversation he had with the great and good Lafayette, when he visited this country in 1824 or 1825, as it was of personal interest to me and mine. General Lafayette and his son George Washington, remained with Mr. Jefferson six weeks, and almost every day I took them out to a drive.

On the occasion I am now about to speak of, Gen. Lafayette and George were seated in the carriage with him. The conversation turned upon the condition of the colored people—the slaves. Lafayette spoke English indifferently; sometimes I could scarcely understand him. But on this occasion my ears were eagerly taking in every sound that proceeded from the venerable patriot's mouth.

Lafayette remarked that he thought that the slaves ought to be free; that no man could rightfully hold ownership in his brother man; that he gave his best services to and spent his money in behalf of the Americans freely because he felt that they were fighting for a great and noble principle—the freedom of mankind; that instead of all being free a portion were held in bondage, (which seemed to grieve his noble heart); that it would be mutually beneficial to masters and slaves if the latter were educated, and so on. Mr. Jefferson replied that he thought the time would come when the slaves would be free, but did not indicate when or in what manner they would get their freedom. He seemed to think that the time had not then arrived. To the latter proposition of Gen. Lafayette, Mr. Jefferson in part assented. He was in favor of teaching the slaves to learn to read print; that to teach them to write would enable them to forge papers, when they could no longer be kept in subjugation.

This conversation was very gratifying to me, and I treasured it up in my heart.

I know that it was a general statement among the older servants at Monticello, that Mr. Jefferson promised his wife, on her death bed, that he would not again marry. I also know that his servant, Sally Hemmings, (mother to my old friend and former companion at Monticello, Madison Hemmings,) was employed as his chambermaid, and that Mr. Jefferson was on the most intimate terms with her; that, in fact, she was his concubine. This I know from my intimacy with both parties, and when Madison Hemmings declares that he is a natural son of Thomas Jefferson, the author of the Declaration of Independence, and that his brothers Beverly and Eston and sister Harriet are of the same parentage, I can as conscientiously confirm his statement as any other fact which I believe from circumstances but do not positively know.

I think that Mr. Jefferson was 84 years of age when he died. He was hardly ever sick, and till within two weeks of his death he walked erect without a staff or cane. He moved with the seeming alertness and sprightliness of youth.

From the Encyclopedia Virginia, https://encyclopediavirginia.org/primary-documents/life-among-the-lowly-no-3-by-israel-jefferson-december-25-1873/; originally published in the *Pike County Republican*, December 25, 1873.

"Once the Slave of Thomas Jefferson," by the Reverend Peter F. Fossett, January 30, 1898

"I was born," [Mr. Fossett] said, "at Monticello, Jefferson's beautiful Virginia home, on June 6, 1815, just before Waterloo. Jefferson was an ideal master. He was a democrat in practice as well as theory, was opposed to the slave trade, tried to keep it out of the Territories beyond the Ohio river and was in favor of freeing the slaves in Virginia. In 1787 he introduced that famous 'Jefferson proviso' in Congress, prohibiting slavery in all the Northwestern Territory, comprising the States of Ohio, Indiana, Illinois and Missouri. He had made all arrangements to free his slaves at his death by making three prizes of his property, &c.

"I well remember the visit of Gen. Lafayette to Monticello. The whole place was in gala array in his honor. He was met at Red Gate and escorted to Monticello by the Jefferson Guards and the Virginia Militia. The latter consisted of all the school boys in the county, who had been drilled for the occasion, armed with sharp pointed sticks tipped with pikes. The meeting between Jefferson and Lafayette was most affectionate. They fell into each other's arms with these words: 'My dear Lafayette,' 'My dear Jefferson,' and wept. Mrs. Patsy Randolph, who had been Martha Ann Jefferson, received Lafayette with grace and dignity befitting a queen, welcoming him to the hospitality of the home of her father. They all listened to the addresses that followed. Even the slaves wept. A youth of eighteen made the address on behalf of the juvenile soldiers, and, I think, Gen. Chestin Cox, in behalf of the citizens. The next day occurred the visit to the University, which had just been finished except the dome. There was a grand procession that day and the slaves had a holiday. First came the Jefferson Guards, then the carriage bearing Mr. Jefferson, with Gen. Lafayette on his right, with ex-President Monroe and Mr. Madison sitting opposite them. In the second carriage was Gen. Chestin Cox, President of the University Faculty. On his right sat George Washington Lafayette, son of the General, and opposite them were Thomas Jefferson Randolph, the grandson of Mr. Jefferson, and Gen. Lavassor. Surrounding these two carriages were the Virginia Militia. Thomas Jefferson Randolph was orator of the day, and there were addresses by all the great men present. There was never such a time in Virginia as during the visit of Gen. Lafayette. Two years after this Mr. Jefferson died. Then began our troubles. We were scattered all over the country, never to meet each other again until we meet in another world. A peculiar fact about his house servants was that we were all related to one another, and as a matter of fact we did not need to know that we were slaves. As a boy I was not only brought up differently, but dressed unlike the plantation boys. My grandmother was free, and I remember the first suit she gave me. It was of blue nankeen cloth, red morocco hat and red morocco shoes. To complete this unique costume, my father added a silver watch. At Monticello we always had the house full of company. Not only did Jefferson's own countrymen visit him, but people from all parts of Europe came to see his wonderful home. On the first floor was Mr. Jefferson's study, called the 'green room.' Here such men as Madison, Monroe and others were wont to discuss the problems of the day. I was too young to know much about these great men, but I remember [seeing?] them and being in the same house with them. Mr. Madison used to come and stay for days with Mr. Jefferson. He was a very learned man, as was also Mr. Jefferson. He was a kindly looking old gentleman, and his coming looked for with pleasure by the older servants for he never left without leaving each of them a substantial reminder of his visit. Mr. Monroe did not live as far from our home as Mr. Madison, and his visits were more frequent. While he was a wise and great man, and a friend of Mr. Jefferson, their companionship was not as close as that existing between Mr. Jefferson and Madison. He was more of a statesman than a scientist, while Madison and Jefferson were both. On the north terrace of Monticello was the telescope, and it was here that Madison and Jefferson spent a great deal of their time. One day while Mr. Jefferson was looking through his telescope to see how the work was progressing over at Pan Top, one of his plantations, he saw 500 soldiers, headed by Col. Tarleton, and led by a traitor whose name I have forgotten, coming up the north side of the mountain to capture him along with the Congress which was being held at Charlottesville. He hastily called up his servants, told them to collect and hide the silver, and gathered his valuable papers. My mother's uncle saddled his horse and took him up to Carter's Mountain, where Mr. Jefferson hid in the hollow of an old tree. He had told his butler to hoist the flag over the dome of his home while the soldiers were there and to take it down when they were gone. This he did. My father's aunt hid the silver in the potato cellar. When the soldiers came up she was standing over the keyhole. The house was searched and nothing could be found. They came to her and with arms drawn demanded that she should tell them where the silver was. Then they turned their attention to the wine cellar, broke all the casks, and with their swords cut all the tops off the bottles of wine that stood on the shelves. The rare old wine that he sent to France for covered the floor to the depth of three steps. They caroused around the place for about three hours, and one of the soldiers rode up into the house on his horse, and the beautiful floor of the music room, inlaid with gothic fret-work, still bore the prints of the horse's shoes when I left Monticello. His summer residence, Poplar Forest, where he spent three months in each year, was a Mecca for all the great men of the world, and the Indians also. In those days they ran the wisest and best men for office, and not the most unscrupulous, as now. At 10 o'clock every day he went to the University and returned at 2 for dinner. Many times have I ordered his horse, a large chestnut bay, which bore the name of Eagle. As for the social enjoyment of the men of those days the people of this time do not begin to come up to it. Weddings, parties, barbecues and the like, even the slaves participated in. As a master Jefferson was kind and indulgent. Under his management his slaves were seldom punished, except for stealing and fighting. They were tried for any offense as at court and allowed to make their own defense. The slave children were nursed until they were three years old, and left with their parents until thirteen. They were then sent to the overseers' wives to learn trades. Every male child's father received $5 at its birth. Jefferson was a man of sober habits, although his cellars were stocked with wines. No one ever saw him under the influence of liquor. His servants about the house were tasked. If you did your task well you were rewarded; if not, punished. Mrs. Randolph would not let any of the young ladies go anywhere with gentlemen with the exception of their brothers, unless a colored servant accompanied them. On

July 4, 1826, exactly fifty years after the signing of the Declaration of Independence, Jefferson and Adams died. I was eleven years old.

"Sorrow came not only to the homes of two great men who had been such fast friends in life as Jefferson and Adams, but to the slaves of Thomas Jefferson. The story of my own life is like a fairy tale, and you would not believe me if I told to you the scenes enacted during my life of slavery. It passes through my mind like a dream. Born and reared as free, not knowing that I was a slave, then suddenly, at the death of Jefferson, put upon an auction block and sold to strangers. I then commenced an eventful life.

"I was sold to Col. John R. Jones. My father was freed by the Legislature of Virginia. At the request of Mr. Jefferson, my father made an agreement with Mr. Jones that when he was able to raise the amount that Col. Jones paid for me he would give me back to my father, and he also promised to let me learn the blacksmith trade with my father as soon as I was old enough. My father then made a bargain with two sons of Col. Jones—William Jones and James Lawrence Jones—to teach me. They attended the University of Virginia.

"Mr. Jefferson allowed his grandson to teach any of his slaves who desired to learn, and Lewis Randolph first taught me how to read. When I was sold to Col. Jones I took my books along with me. One day I was kneeling before the fireplace spelling the word 'baker,' when Col. Jones opened the door, and I shall never forget the scene as long as I live.

"'What have you got there, sir?' were his words.

"I told him.

"'If I ever catch you with a book in your hands, thirty-and-nine lashes on your bare back.' He took the book and threw it into the fire, then called up his sons and told them that if they ever taught me they would receive the same punishment. But they helped me all they could, as did his daughter Ariadne.

"Among my things was a copy-book that my father gave me, and which I kept hid in the bottom of my trunk. I used to get permission to take a bath, and by the dying embers I learned to write. The first copy was this sentence, 'Art improves nature.'

"Col. Jones, when he bought me, promised my father to let him have me when he could raise the money, but in 1833 he refused to let him have me on any conditions. Mrs. Jones declared that she would sooner part with one of her own children. They had become very attached to me, and then I was a very valuable servant, notwithstanding that all the time I was teaching all the people around me to read and write, and even venturing to write free passes and sending slaves away from their masters. Of course they did not know this, or they would not have thought me so valuable.

"Amid these scenes it was during my stay with Col. Jones that I first saw my state as a sinner. The white Baptists where I lived had no church. They held services in the Court-House and sometimes in the Episcopal Church. The Baptist churches were all in the country near some creek convenient for baptizing. It was in these churches during the summer that they held three-day and ten-day meetings, at which many were converted, and here their greatest revivals took place.

"It was during one of these meetings that I was convicted of my sins from a sermon preached by Cumberland George. I was converted at a two weeks' meeting at Piney Grove. Mrs. Jones, my mistress, was called the mother of the Baptist church, and our house was the stopping place for all the preachers. It was here when they were holding these meetings that my eyes were opened.

"I well remember the struggle they had in the great controversy with Alexander Campbell. Two eloquent young preachers—Lindsay Coleman and James G[]—the pride and hope of the Baptist denomination, took Campbell's side, and tried to take the church from them. The people belonging to the church had a church meeting which lasted for a week, day and night. Every time a vote was taken it was a tie. If it had not been for that young hero, Robert Ryland, who was chaplain at the University of Virginia, they would have succeeded. At last Col. Nimrod Branham, the moderator, who was on the fence, gave the casting vote, and the regular Baptists retained possession of the church.

"Col. Jones had by this time become very fond of me, and would not arrange any terms by which I could gain my freedom. He respected me, and would not let me see him take his 'bitters.' He was surprised and pleased to find that I did not touch liquor. Being with and coming from such a family as Mr. Jefferson's, I knew more than they did about many things. This also raised me in their esteem. My sister Isabel was also left a slave in Virginia. I wrote her a free pass, sent her to Boston, and made [an?] attempt to gain my own freedom. The first time [I fai?]led and had to return. My parents were here in Ohio and I wanted to be with them and be free, so I resolved to get free or die in the attempt. I started the second time, was caught, handcuffed, and taken back and carried to Richmond and put in jail. For the second time I was put up on the auction block and sold like a horse. But friends from among my master's best friends bought me in and sent me to my father in Cincinnati, and I am here to-day."

Concerning the taking of a life mask of Jefferson at Monticello, in 1825, Mr. Fossett said: "I never saw the bust made from this life mask, but I remember when the mask was taken. I was then ten years old. The man who took the mask covered Mr. Jefferson's head, shoulders, arms and body down to the waist with clay or plaster of some kind. He left holes for the nose and eyes. Somehow or other he left the plaster on too long and it got too hard. He had to take a chisel [] knock it off and when he got it off Mr. Jefferson [] greatly exhausted.

"The report got around that Mr. Jefferson had been killed, and there was the greatest excitement until we all saw Mr. Jefferson again alive and well. I see a magazine writer says there was no trouble about taking the life mask, but I know better, for I was there and remember well the excitement it caused everywhere."

From *Frontline*, PBS, https://www.pbs.org/wgbh/pages/frontline/shows/jefferson/slaves/memoir.html; originally published in the *New York World*, January 30, 1898.

INDEX

A NOTE ON THE TYPE

THIS BOOK has been composed in Miller, a Scotch Roman typeface designed by Matthew Carter and first released by Font Bureau in 1997. It resembles Monticello, the typeface developed for The Papers of Thomas Jefferson in the 1940s by C. H. Griffith and P. J. Conkwright and reinterpreted in digital form by Carter in 2003.

Pleasant Jefferson ("P. J.") Conkwright (1905–1986) was Typographer at Princeton University Press from 1939 to 1970. He was an acclaimed book designer and AIGA Medalist.

The ornament used throughout this book was designed by Pierre Simon Fournier (1712–1768) and was a favorite of Conkwright's, used in his design of the *Princeton University Library Chronicle.*